The publisher gratefully acknowledges the generous support of the Lisa See Endowment Fund in Southern California History and Culture of the University of California Press Foundation.

Go West, Young Women!

Go West, Young Women!

The Rise of Early Hollywood

Hilary A. Hallett

UNIVERSITY OF CALIFORNIA PRESS
Berkeley · Los Angeles · London

University of California Press, one of the most
distinguished university presses in the United States,
enriches lives around the world by advancing
scholarship in the humanities, social sciences, and
natural sciences. Its activities are supported by the UC
Press Foundation and by philanthropic contributions
from individuals and institutions. For more information, visit www.ucpress.edu.

University of California Press
Berkeley and Los Angeles, California

University of California Press, Ltd.
London, England

Library of Congress Cataloging-in-Publication Data

Hallett, Hilary A.
  Go west, young women! : the rise of early Hollywood /
Hilary A. Hallett.
     p. cm.
  Includes bibliographical references and index.
  Includes filmography.
  ISBN 978-0-520-27408-2 (cloth : alk. paper) —
  ISBN 978-0-520-27409-9 (pbk. : alk. paper)
   1. Women in the motion picture industry—
California—Los Angeles—History—20th century.
2. Motion picture actors and actresses—California—
Los Angeles.   3. Motion pictures and women—United
States.   4. Hollywood (Los Angeles, Calif.)—
History—20th century.   I. Title.
  PN1995.9.W6H23 2013
  791.43'6522—dc23

                                    2012027596

Manufactured in the United States of America

21   20   19   18   17   16   15   14   13
10   9   8   7   6   5   4   3   2   1

In keeping with a commitment to support environmen-
tally responsible and sustainable printing practices, UC
Press has printed this book on Rolland Enviro100, a
100% postconsumer fiber paper that is FSC certified,
deinked, processed chlorine-free, and manufactured
with renewable biogas energy. It is acid-free and
EcoLogo certified.

For my boys—Miles, Jackson, and Christopher

Contents

Illustrations

PART ONE

Along the Road to Hollywood

Landscapes

I

By 1920, city and country were all mixed up. Between the "War to Liberate Cuba" and the "War to Make the World Safe for Democracy," migrants made their way from rural homes in record numbers. The process was a familiar one, dating back to before the Civil War. What was different about these migrations was the velocity of the movement, the volume of those on the move, and the destinations to which their ambitions drove them. Generally westward migrants continued as before, but few now went in search of a homestead on some sketchily mapped piece of the country. Hopes for a different life lay, for most, along city sidewalks, great and small. Thus the 1920 census made official what many already knew: for the first time, the majority of the U.S. population lived in cities. Imagining the migrants who headed for cities in the new century conjures images of wayfarers in unfamiliar dress disembarking from steamships at Ellis Island, or from trains with the musical rhythms of the race-riven South. Such snapshots abound, documenting the generation between what we now call the Spanish-Cuban-American War and World War I. In this period the movement of the "new immigrants" from Southern and Eastern Europe peaked and the first Great Migration of black Americans streamed north. Both groups mostly settled in midwestern and northern cities, against whose brick, concrete, and steel they hurled their ambitions. The same 1920 census revealed the altered landscape wrought by their resolve: in no major city east of the Mississippi or north of the Ohio did white, native-born citizens remain in the majority.[1]

This book concerns the implications of reimagining another rural exodus of the era, one that explains how the bucolic backwater of Hollywood, California, became HOLLYWOOD, an industry and a place that specialized in shaping people's fantasies and fears about modern times. Although it brings few images to mind today, the dimensions of this crossing were no less immense. Indeed, the movement of native-born, white migrants out of the Midwest—"white" here doubling for the ethnic heritage then commonly called Anglo-Saxon—was enormous enough to leave the proportion of native-born to foreign-born in all American cities unchanged despite the massive waves of Europeans settling in the East. Less absolute need, but as much imagination, sent these erstwhile farmers and shopkeepers across prairies, plains, and mountains in a migration similarly premised on mobility's promise to provide emancipation from the limitations of the known. Southern California was the favored destination of these migrants who helped to create the era's so-called rural problem. "The rural problem" was the term Progressive reformers coined to capture their belief that social deficiencies, as much as economic deprivation, explained the mounting flight of white Americans from the land during a period of unprecedented agricultural prosperity. Those who aimed to address these deficiencies—called "Country Lifers" for the Country Life Commission Theodore Roosevelt created in 1908—viewed the rural problem from a distinctively masculine, nativist perspective. Assistant Secretary of Agriculture William Hays focused on addressing the needs of those he called "the best crop on the farm," native-born, Protestant men from the Midwest and Northeast.[2]

As scholars have well explained, what drew many of those who fit this description to Southern California was the vision that popular writers and savvy commercial developers concocted to advertise the region's special charms, including its natural beauty, temperate climate, romantic "Spanish" history, new work ideals, and singular ethnic composition. Best-selling novels like Helen Hunt Jackson's *Ramona* (1884) helped to explain the different heritages said to distinguish rugged, raucous Northern California from the state's more gently rustic southern half. Here one found the gentleman dons and wine-drenched Spanish missions the novelists used to endow the region with a colorful exoticism. Here the health-giving aspects of the landscape and light promised that, at last, labor might become synonymous with pleasure. Historian Hubert Howe Bancroft's *California Pastoral* (1888) was another early exemplar. "And so they lived," wrote Bancroft, a midwestern transplant, publisher, and bibliophile whose collection of books, maps, and manuscripts formed the basis for the West's first great library, "opening their eyes in the morning when they saw the sun; they breathed the fresh air, and listened to the song of birds; mounting their steeds they rode forth in the enjoyment of healthful exercise; they tended their flocks, held intercourse with each other, and ran up a fair credit in heaven."

The developers of modern Los Angeles used this image of California Pastoral to fashion perhaps the most shining example in the nation's long line of astonishingly successful booster campaigns. Curiosity about such descriptions sent the first waves of tourists to the area, tourists who were the bedrock of the region's economy by 1910. By 1915, just as moviemakers began to venture there in earnest, *Collier's* called Los Angeles "The City Advertising Built," writing, "Here is one dusty little city . . . in the Western desert" made "great by intelligent, consistent, scientific advertising" whose picture of the good life became one of the most tantalizing promotions of the times.[3]

In this way, the Los Angeles of story, history, and, above all else, booster campaign offered a picture of life that attracted the remarkable number of migrants-with-means needed to launch its speculative, service-heavy projects aloft. Here, publicized railroad officials, real estate agencies, agricultural associations, and finally the Los Angeles Chamber of Commerce to the prosperous of the Midwest, lay the country's own Mediterranean garden, greened by the latest technological wonders and filled with freestanding bungalows decorated in a freshly minted Spanish past. Los Angeles beckoned not just as the "farm perfected, saved from loneliness and back breaking labor," but also as a refuge from farming itself and from the new immigrants inundating cities east of the Mississippi. Here, proclaimed booster Charles Lummis, lay a new "Eden for Anglo-Saxon home-seekers" as eager to luxuriate in the sunshine as to escape "the ignorant, hopelessly un-American type of foreigner" who "infests and largely controls Eastern cities." A piece of the heartland responded and moved to Los Angeles, the city that both "benefited from and helped to cause a major internal mass migration in the United States," according to historian Kevin Starr. During the decade after 1910, the city grew faster than all others on the Pacific Coast combined, passing the million-soul mark and San Francisco as the West's largest city just after 1920. Many of these youthful strangers from someplace else shared not only their midwestern Anglo-Saxon Protestant origins but also a willingness to use their economic and imaginative resources to chase new desires in the City of Dreams. In this first great metropolis of the twentieth century, country and city were, indeed, all mixed up.[4]

Yet few have considered the part that Hollywood, that unrivaled generator of good dreams and bad, played in drawing migrants west and subsequently shaping the growth and reputation of modern Los Angeles.[5] The avoidance stems from the long-standing penchant among the city's educated, Anglo elite to discount the influence of the "flickers" and their "movies," as many called the infant industry's workers and product. The idea that Los Angeles was too controlled by uptight, conservative Anglo midwesterners to nurture anything but artless conformity became a shibboleth of the city's image as early as 1915, when Willard Huntington Wright published his infamous essay "Los Angeles—The Chemically Pure" in the *Smart Set*.[6] The tendency supported casting Los Angeles as colorful, cosmopolitan San Francisco's censorious, pale-faced sister and thus eased the erasure of the movie industry's dynamism from most histories about the city's development. By 1920, a leading progressive journal could poke fun at many respectable residents' denial of the city's most obvious attraction: "The Angelo rises and paws the air, when told the present booming prosperity of the city is due to motion pictures and tourists," but "everyone knows that the factories are trivial, that the fruit-growing lands are miles removed from the city, and that the money pouring into Los Angeles is from movies and tourists."[7]

At first Los Angeles was just one faraway destination among many for early filmmakers. "How far will a modern motion picture company go to get the 'atmosphere' for a film drama?" the *Mirror* wondered in 1910. The answer was far indeed. As the nickelodeon business boomed between 1905 and 1914, the thirst for fresh incidents and locations initially sent film companies along many different roads. To avoid "Jersey scenery," a term the *New York Dramatic Mirror* coined to describe the attempt to foist fake locations on eyes grown adept at discerning the real thing, early film studios traveled from northern New York to Florida. Keeping up with the competition in Chicago and New York required a daily program adjustment to satisfy the "nickel madness" that was sweeping the land. The omnivorous demand from thousands of exhibitors left the flickers scrambling for new material. In a pinch for new product, many realized that story pictures, or narrative films, best satisfied the diverse tastes of fans. Story pictures were also easier to make since their dramatic events could be staged, unlike earlier actuality films that displayed brief glimpses of significant places and people, new inventions, and civic events. Film production companies sprang up in response to the demand for story pictures and hit the road in search of gasp-producing vistas to help sustain interest in these longer films.[8]

Los Angeles earned the loyalty of early motion picture makers for several tangible reasons, some as evanescent as the light. First there was the land, which offered to the camera's eye not just unparalleled variety but each thing in a seemingly ideal form. Within a day's drive of Los Angeles, a film crew might access mountains that tumbled down to the Pacific; forests of redwoods, the tallest and oldest trees on Earth; hundreds of miles of beach; uninhabited islands, canyons, and desert. Next came the light, whose color and constancy lived up to the best advertisements, the most lyrical description penned by Bancroft or his like. The sun shone, as *Moving Picture World* reported in 1910, an average of 320 days a year. This surfeit of sunshine and splendid scenery was a critical natural resource for the industry's growth. Selig Polyscope, the first picture studio known to have shot in Los Angeles, left Chicago in the midst of a typically brutal winter in 1907. As Colonel Selig trumpeted, "nowhere, but in the real West could the proper atmosphere and wide vistas have been found."[9]

Southern California also sported several man-made advantages. The Southern Pacific Railroad and the city's electric trolley system offered transportation services with both a national and a neighborhood reach. Ever expanding streets provided access to cheap sprawling spaces on which to build the first enormous production studios, like the new ranch-cum-zoo-cum–technological wonder Universal City that opened its gates in 1915. And finally, the implacable hostility of business leaders toward unions, coupled with many rural Midwesterners' distrust of organized labor, gave the city a well-deserved reputation as a defender of the open shop.[10]

The sum of these natural and commercial charms prompted American film production to relocate to Los Angles in short order as the "Come to California" campaign that attracted Midwesterners and tourists also drew would-be moving picture directors, actors, writers, producers, and technicians when short days and cold settled upon the original film centers of New York, New Jersey, and Chicago. Few in motion pictures had ventured to Los Angeles in 1910. By 1922, industry trade papers estimated that the city produced 84 percent of the pictures made in America and nearly two-thirds of those shown around the world. The modern motion picture industry and Los Angeles, the "Film Capital of the World," sprang up together, and virtually overnight.[11]

Thus *Go West, Young Women!* opens with an insight that was as obvious as Southern Californian sunshine to the era's contemporaries: the Los Angeles that emerged after the city's explosive transformation during the 1910s was largely built around its identity as the "Capital of Movie-Land." A chorus of commentators marveled at how motion pictures had become not just the largest business on the Pacific Coast but the fourth-largest industry in the nation immediately after the conclusion of the Great War, as contemporaries called World War I. By the mid-twenties some 35,000 of the city's residents earned $1.25 million a year working in the picture industry—not including extras paid to wait on call. The publicity surrounding the city's rise as a movie-made metropolis drew many different types of people tempted by its promotions that promised liberation from the Protestant work ethic's mistrust of pleasure and new freedom to reinvent the self. Put differently, as the industry settled in the West, motion pictures embellished the image of California Pastoral in ways that intensified its appeal for many. In advertising this "Picture Eldorado" as the "Chameleon City of the Cinema," this publicity described a shape-shifting, cosmopolitan city within a city, a place "as changeable as a woman," "the biggest city of make-believe in the universe," where "the occident and the Orient" met. Wherever they hailed from, those who created and consumed such promotions imagined Los Angeles as a new kind of city-by-the sea where residents appeared to make something new from once irreconcilable parts.[12]

II

Beginning with the film industry's invention of Los Angeles also recasts the explanation of how the formerly marginal, WASP-controlled and run-amok business of making movies in America became the dominant, highly centralized, cosmopolitan industry of early Hollywood. Indeed, the burden of this book's opening chapters is to reconceive this process by describing the central role that women and the era's sexual politics played in the metamorphosis. Accounts of the transition from the nickelodeon era to the age of the silent feature production in Los Angeles during the 1910s have long focused on how the industry abandoned its working-class, immigrant orientation to become a classless form of respectable entertainment. From this view, the move west helped producers to shed the nickelodeon's identity as a disreputable, working-class form of entertainment "made by and for men." This version of how Hollywood became Hollywood has an aesthetic corollary as well, one that roots American cinema's development as an art form in the innovations of a few heroes out west. "By the end of the silent era [in 1929] the major dramatis personae of the tale were well known," writes film scholar David Bordwell about the invention of what he calls the "Basic Story" about the origins of the look and feel of American-made movies: "American film is the creation of [D.W.] Griffith, Thomas Ince, [Cecil B.] DeMille, Mack Sennett, and Charlie Chaplin." Iris Barry, the English film critic who became the world's first film curator at the Museum of Modern Art in New York in 1933, helped to create this canon by preserving and publicizing these filmmakers' work. Their films display the black-and-white moral certainties of Griffith's traditional melodramas, the sweeping vistas of Ince's many Westerns, and the slapstick antics and pathos of Sennett and Chaplin, the early industry's two favorite clowns. Down to the present-day, retrospectives on American silent film still focus mostly on Griffith, whom Barry called "the ruling planet of the birth of motion picture production" and eulogized in her *D.W. Griffith: American Film Master* (1940).[13]

But even a cursory inspection of the era's fan culture reveals the same assumption at every turn: American silent film was mostly made for women with very different tastes. "Now one thing never to be lost sight of in considering the cinema is that it exists for the purpose of pleasing women," Barry warned in an unhappy acknowledgment of this reality in *The Public's Pleasure* (1926). In their initial heyday, the Western and slapstick films of Ince, Chaplin, and Sennett, were understood to appeal to an increasingly marginalized audience of children and young men. Moreover, many of the most powerful leading ladies of the day deserted Griffith because of his insistence on casting them in what they considered old-fashioned melodramas. Indeed, it is possible to read Barry's elevation of these directors' status in part as a project of replacing early Hollywood's feminine cast with a more manly sheen. For as Barry knew so well, in the years around the Great War, the years in which Hollywood rose, the industry's reputation worldwide increasingly depended upon its mastery at producing the kinds of lavish, thrilling dramas and romances preferred by most of the female trade. The era's contentious sexual politics ensured that women's prominent roles in creating and consuming this distinctive visual landscape would make them into some of the most arresting figures out west. Thus an origin story about how Hollywood became Hollywood that marginalizes women cannot hope to explain why its first "social imaginary" lit up imaginations around the world.[14]

Those who composed the first movie fan culture often framed their tales about the women who made Hollywood as part symbol of the particular desires female fans invested in the picture business, and part realistic picture of what a wage-earning woman who landed in Los Angeles might expect. Margaret Turnbull, the author of the first novel advertised "to lift the veil" on motion picture production in Los Angeles, offered what quickly became the conventional wisdom about these heroines' motivations. Turnbull wrote *The Close-Up* (1918) three years after leaving New York City to help her friend William de Mille organize the new scenario department at Lasky's Feature Play Company in Hollywood. She was a successful playwright, a published novelist, single, and just entering early middle age when she arrived at the Los Angeles Santa Fe depot in 1915 and headed for her new job at an old barn down a dirt road lined with pepper trees. The novel begins with its twenty-seven-year-old protagonist, Kate Lawford, suffocating under the "factory-like" conditions of her secretarial job in New York. When her boss asks her to help him organize a new studio in Los Angeles, Kate assents, thinking, "Here was a vision of the West. The West which spelled adventure, and that fantastic world of make believe, a picture studio, adventure, and strange people hers for the taking, and if God were good, the power to dream again." Life inside the "little [movie] colony" provides a perfect antidote to the dead-end drudgery of life back east. Kate begins as the studio's office manager and ends as its biggest star. At the novel's end, she lovingly bids her friends and fellow workers adieu before retiring to marry a childhood sweetheart and run a California ranch. Here, then, was a place where a working girl "with lots of 'nerve'" could find interesting work and professional mobility, dance till morning with friends of "delightful" warmth, and experiment romantically with several men before selecting the one of her dreams. Like most of the first stories about the "Romance of Making the Movies" in Los Angeles, the tale presented an optimistic picture of what an ambitious working girl with "brains and beauty" (in the parlance of the day) and some luck might find in this New West.[15]

This presentation offered a sharp contrast with the parts played by women in the Old West. For much of the nineteenth century, the great newspaperman Horace Greeley's charge "Go West, young man!" signaled a broad commitment to colonize the continent by sending the discontented men from all manner of Easts west. In the process, the West became not just a region populated mostly by single men but a space that symbolized their hope for seizing the main chance. "To the rightly constituted Man, there always is, there always must be, opportunity," Greeley assured in 1850, exhorting men to "turn . . . to the Great West, and there build up a home and fortune." But by 1900 female migrants outpaced male ones, effecting a "stunning" reversal in western migration patterns. Yet even as the feminization of western migration became entrenched, cultural elites and popular entertainers alike looked west to revitalize and rework masculine ideals that many white men feared under assault as women's entrance into public life, the immigration of non-Anglos, and the corporatization of the workplace threatened their entrenched privileges. In this way, the long shadow cast by the West's relationship to new masculine ideals and the tendency for studies on womanhood to look east have continued to obscure how the modern West's possession of Hollywood created perhaps the most powerful generator and lure for a New Western Woman in full flight from feminine norms.[16]

A cultural concept, social reality, and frustratingly slippery term, the "New Woman" arose with modern urbanity in 1895 and was inconsistently applied to several generations of women who challenged different aspects of Victorian ladyhood. Many of the changes associated with the type emerged from women's soaring participation in work outside the home, as the number of adult wage-earning women shot from 2.6 to 10.8 million between 1890 and 1920. Indeed, the term New Woman gained currency in relationship to the first generation of middle-class women who challenged assumptions about women's intellectual and physical abilities by eschewing marriage in record numbers in favor of work in "male" professions, political activism, and social reform. By the 1910s the expression conjured images of women and "girls" who emerged from the working-class milieu associated with the leisure habits and labor conventions of female bohemians, entertainers, and ordinary wageworkers. As they took jobs in department stores, offices, and social services, for the first time the majority of women, usually those who were white and native-born, experienced work as an endeavor that sent them outside the confines of factories or other women's homes. Exiting their jobs each evening, many of these recently rural transplants treated the city itself as a precious metal to be mined, extracting new pleasures from its burgeoning world of commercial amusements.[17]

Women associated with this less respectable scene did the most to embody, create, and consume the New Western Women associated with Hollywood's original social imaginary, women like the "peerless fearless girl," serial queen Pearl White. "You know my adventurous spirit and desire to live and realize the greatest things," White reminds her crestfallen suitor in the first episode of *The Perils of Pauline* (1914) after rejecting his marriage proposal so she can gather material for the novel she wants to write. The first movie stars like White and actress-writer-producer Mary Pickford invited their female fans to identify with a protagonist liberated from many of the customary restraints that economic dependence and the cult of domesticity placed on their bodies and hearts. As was still customary, White received no credit on celluloid for her portrayal of a heroine whose popularity reached across the Atlantic and beyond the Pacific. Yet as far away as China, publicity trumpeted the western American–styled athleticism displayed by serial queens like White, "riding on a furious horse, climbing the cliff as if walking on flat land." Indeed, the journalistic discourse that ran alongside the print versions of serials in newspapers and magazines made their protagonists into the first American film stars, explaining why the serial craze that began after 1912 coincided with the development of the star system. Like many of the first movie stars, White's supposed real-life persona presented an even more extreme vision of a New Western Woman. Reports detailed her life history as an Ozark-raised former circus performer turned globetrotting single cosmopolitan who sought European "pleasure jaunts" and "beefsteak [or automobiling] and aviation" for fun. Artfully blending social reality with desire, such publicity displayed how even the most ordinary women workers gained access to the movies' bohemian social settings and exciting work environments out west. After opening in 1915, studios like Universal City became major tourist attractions whose novelty and appeal involved their display of women's unrivaled opportunities for physical mobility, romantic exploration, and professional satisfaction. A workplace whose corporate mythology promised an environment "Where Work Is Play and Play Is Work" supported other inversions such as becoming the first city where "'Movie' Actresses Control Its Politics." Such promotions help to explain why so many young women and their elders around the world came to view what happened inside the little movie colony as having consequences for their own lives.[18]

The appeal of these mass-produced narratives and personalities encouraged many women to seek work in some aspect of the picture business, making them a particularly visible eddy in the massive current that washed up in Southern California in the early twentieth century. "There are more women in Los Angeles than any other city in the world and it's the movies that bring them," one shopkeeper bluntly asserted in

1918. The city census supported the claim. In 1920, Los Angeles became the only western city where women outnumbered men, a development sharply at odds with traditional boomtowns that had long been dominated virtually "everywhere and always" by single young men. The city's female residents were unusual in other ways as well. Nearly one in five was divorced or widowed. Since single women tended to work outside the home more than their married counterparts, this helps to explain what one demographer called the most noteworthy characteristic of the Los Angeles labor force: the high number of women who worked after the age of twenty-five.

These gender dynamics were at odds with older western boomtowns. In the decades after gold was discovered in 1848, young single men swarmed the northern reaches of the Pacific Coast in search of riches in sex-restricted occupations like railroad construction, mining, and lumber. Consequently, Portland, Seattle, and San Francisco all initially sported an urban version of the virile, ethnically polyglot masculine culture associated with the Wild West. But Los Angeles's economic base of real estate, tourism, and motion pictures created the service and clerical jobs that attracted women. Women in these sectors of employment in Los Angeles also benefited from California's early passage of woman suffrage and jury service in 1911, as well as legislation establishing the eight-hour day (1911) and a minimum wage (1917) for women. Gender stratification and racial discrimination remained widespread, but white women experienced less social stratification and greater legislative protections than in most cities. In all these ways, Los Angeles better reflected the direction of twentieth-century urban development than San Francisco, Chicago or New York. This urban frontier attracted the modern pink-collar worker out for economic opportunity and excitement as much as it did Midwesterners. Indeed, the two were often one and the same. "At night in bed I would lay [sic] awake and day dream about the big hit I would make if I were to go to California," recalled one young women in the motion picture autobiography she wrote in Chicago in the 1920s, adding parenthetically, "I know better now."[19]

Much to the later consternation of those like Iris Barry, such women were at the center of the film industry's expanding fan base in the years surrounding the Great War, the years in which the movies became Hollywood. The reorientation of fan culture toward women during the 1910s was sped by the creeping conviction among many industry insiders that their good fortune demanded catering to the female trade. Focusing on the ladies in the audience was one of several strategies the flickers adopted from the stage. All types of theatrical impresarios had learned decades earlier that attracting the ladies with new kinds of plays and heroines enlarged their audience and increased the respectability of the entertainment offered. In hopes of effecting the same changes, movie fan culture mostly addressed an idealized, "fanatic" female film spectator with increasing savvy during the 1910s. This book builds upon the explosion of work on women in film's silent era. By examining the motivations and tactics behind attracting more female fans, Shelley Stamp, Janet Staiger, Miriam Hansen, and others have explored how the movies became a space to contest gender norms. By 1914 *Motion Picture News,* a trade paper aimed at exhibitors, was reporting that "women and girls" were the principal readers of "moving picture news," a remarkable shift of opinion given the emphasis on men a few years earlier. By the early twenties, some estimated that women occupied 75 percent of seats. As a result, the movies' ideal spectator became a young white woman. Women's identity as the most fanatic moviegoers led to the feminization of movie fan culture just as the industry's most prestigious fare became a feature-length story picture centered on a female star. Such developments were behind an English actor's lament that Hollywood was "a land where the worship is not of the hero but of the heroine."[20]

Like all good mythmakers, movie fan writers shaped their tales about the industry's female personalities as much to answer the perceived needs of this ideal fan as to fit the facts. As with western myths more generally, these stories were not simple fictions, but a blend of wish fulfillment and social reflection. Stories that aimed to appeal to these movie-struck girls linked their heroine worship of the first movie stars to supporting their ambitions as a sex. As with the tales of an earlier era aimed at boys, these stories romanticized and sensationalized their protagonists' quests for individual success.[21] Yet women's remarkable record of influence inside the movie colony of this era was no fantasy. The increasingly female audience for the movies selected many deserving of their allegiance, but a disproportionate number of those who earned their most enduring fealty were other women. In a trajectory that followed those of other women professionals, their record of influence as actresses, directors, writers, producers, and publicists through the early 1920s would not be equaled until more than half a century later. Involved in all aspects of the business, these women offered some of the most visible models of professional advancement and personal freedom available at the time. Women like Mary Pickford, Alla Nazimova, Norma Talmadge, Gloria Swanson, Anita Loos, Frances Marion, June Mathis, Clara Kimball Young, Elinor Glyn, and Lois Weber were all key players in shaping the infant industry and the new images of femininity and masculinity that it sold. Journalists like Adela Rogers St. Johns and Louella Parsons churned out the publicity that explained who mattered in the industry and why. Such women spun stories about heroines whose fearless navigation of the West's preeminent modern city foretold their ability to win once inconceivable renown.[22]

Future star-producer Gloria Swanson got ideas about the type after meeting Clara Kimball Young, one of the first stars to establish her own production studio. Swanson met Young shortly after moving from Chicago to Los Angeles, recalling how "the world of 1916" was "a man's world" and a "business run entirely by men." But Young's success suggested otherwise. In what other business," Swanson wondered, "could this delightful elegant creature be completely independent," "turning out her own pictures, dealing with men as her equals, being able to use her brains as well as her beauty, having total say as to what stories she played in, who designed her clothes, and who her director and leading man would be."[23] Again, theatrical practices cleared a path for women like Young. By 1900, the field of commercial entertainment had already promised so-called stage-struck girls a unique avenue to individual success. On all types of stages, female performers from "extras" to stars often earned greater recognition and more money than men, making commercial entertainment one of the largest, best-paying fields open to women without much formal education. As the theater's fortunes fell, stories about women's prospects in the movies played to a fresh generation of female wage earners with much more than survival on their minds.[24]

Indeed, one of the few attempts to determine why women migrants dominated the exodus that created the rural problem that had so worried progressives since Teddy Roosevelt suggested why studio work would have appeared to satisfy the impulse that drove so many to cities like Los Angeles. The editors of a massive survey conducted by the United States Department of Agriculture (USDA) in 1912 regarding the opinions of "farm housewives" about why so many rural women left home called the theme of the responses they received the "feeling that the attractiveness of one's surroundings is of more importance than the practical farmer" recognized. Women's letters to the USDA repeatedly recorded how the search for sociable work, more attention to aesthetic pleasures, and "the entertainments and amusements that the towns and cities offer" sent them down country roads to town. One Arkansan succinctly summed up the difference between rural women's and men's needs: "We would rather have free telephones and moving pictures than free seed." Taken together, the letters present the countryside's landscape as so bereft of feminine influence that a woman with a taste for aesthetic pleasures and the society of others was left with few choices but to escape. "Do you wonder we get lonely and discouraged and are ignorant and uncultured and long to get away for good?" The comedic actress Louise Fazenda testified to how many felt they had nothing to lose. "At my home in Utah they impressed on me how utterly useless I was until I could bare [sic] it no longer," Fazenda recalled. "So like the old darky song, 'I packed up my grip and took a trip,' coming to Los Angeles to do or die. And I pretty nearly died." Publicity that depicted studios as the "most perfect democracy the world has ever known," promised migrants a social equality that was still the stuff of dreams. Thus the story about how the déclassé "movie" business became the glamorous industry of Hollywood depended upon its publicists' finesse at advertising "Motion-Picture Land" as located inside a new urban frontier that catered to women pioneers.[25]

For these reasons, the most widely circulated tales about Hollywood's birth often linked the industry to the excitement and alarm prompted by the so-called revolution of manners and morals of modern young girls after the Great War, as this book's second part explores. Strategies first developed in the original film centers of Chicago and New York laid the foundation for associating the movie colony's residents with the era's increasingly voluble, and volatile, debates about the terms under which women's emancipation should advance after winning the fight for suffrage in 1919. In describing the movies as a great new frontier, as a "democratic art" that offered common cultural ground for all, industry publicists wrapped a business still feared by much of the respectable middle class as immoral and un-American in cherished stories about the nation's frontier heritage. But journalists like Louella Parsons did much more than this when they retooled the frontier thesis that then commanded the country's view of its past to describe motion pictures as a gold rush business for ambitious, single, young white women on the make. Most radically, the sexual politics of this booster literature promoted the movie colony as that quintessential metropolitan neighborhood of lusty self-invention, a bohemia—a Hollywood Bohemia to be exact. A novel character best personified the liberation that this bohemian scene promised: the extra girl who went west in search of unparalleled opportunities for self-invention, artistic exploration, professional advancement, romantic adventures, and just plain fun. For some, this Hollywood Bohemia intensified anxieties about the manners and morals of the rising generation of modern girls. For others, it offered a place to bring her to life. In this way, the flickers' mass-produced narratives and personalities became another essential element in the era's broader conversation about the "grounding of modern feminism."[26]

III

Thus the women and men who went to Los Angeles with an interest in making and breaking into pictures entered a contest, often unwittingly, for cultural power that played out along the frontier of mass culture and inside Los Angeles's new urban West. Arriving by train, taxicab, and automobile, the flickers moved into new bungalows and old barns where they quickly attracted both critics and fans. Like many artistic scenes, the so-called movie colony sported a cosmopolitan crew whose often sexually unconventional mien encouraged a kind of social insularity despite the highly public nature of their work. In addition to many prominent New Woman types, the colony also contained a number of powerful immigrant Jews who mostly hailed from the working-class, urban milieus of the business's early fans. In short, the flickers were just the sorts that some already settled in Los Angeles wanted to avoid. Frances Marion, whom many consider the silent era's most successful screenwriter, recalled the tensions that resulted after moving from her native San Francisco to Los Angeles in 1913. After working part-time as a commercial illustrator, the unhappily married Marion found a full-time job as an assistant for Lois Weber, then the most famous director on Universal Studio's new lot. The new paycheck and the close friends she made, including writer Adela Rogers St. Johns and Mary Pickford, gave Marion the courage to divorce her husband. Marion's life as a New Woman was possible only after trading her elite upbringing in more established San Francisco for the bohemian movie colony in Los Angeles. But she still seethed over the bigotry exhibited by some of her new neighbors, fuming over landlords who baldly declared, "No Jews, actors, or

FIGURE 1. Inceville, Thomas Ince's studio by the sea along the Santa Monica coast, c. 1915. Courtesy of Margaret Herrick Library, Academy of Motion Picture Arts and Sciences, Beverly Hills.

dogs allowed." The neighborhood associations that sprung up at this moment also displayed the determination of some local Angelenos to keep the flickers out of their backyards.[27]

Director King Vidor thought that the social insularity and artistic license that the movie colony's residents displayed would have engendered a similar reaction in many other American towns. Hoping to become a director, Vidor left Texas for Los Angeles in 1915, not long after the newsreel cameraman made his directorial debut with the short story picture *Hurricane of Galveston* (1913). According to Vidor, the colony's residents cultivated the experience of living in "a magic bubble," a sense as much nurtured as imposed. Residents of the movie colony "spoke a silent language, a different language from the orange growers who surrounded them," Vidor recalled. Yet they "felt camaraderie with all the other members of their clan" who congregated together inside ever more elaborate production lots like the "Studio by the Sea" that Thomas Ince built in 1912 on several thousand acres of land encompassing a stretch of Pacific coastline and the surrounding hills and plateaus of Santa Ynez Canyon at present-day Pacific Palisades and Malibu (figure 1). These environment's camera-thin walls magnified their workers' goings-on from multiple angles, acting as both blessing and curse for a business that needed viewers' curiosity to survive. Like many early residents, Vidor remembered how the community's isolation encouraged a release from customary restraints, leading inhabitants to believe "they could establish their own habits and behavior," which could appear outlandish, immoral, or glamorously modern depending on the point of view.[28]

The firestorm of local, state, and federal actions to control the movies that swept the country during the 1910s supported Vidor's judgment that the movies and their makers provoked anxiety not just among some Los Angeles landlords and orange growers but across the land. The Supreme Court decision *Mutual Film Corporation v. Ohio Industrial Commission* (1915) displayed the intensification of concern about protecting moviegoers from the influence of films. The *Mutual* case made motion pictures the only medium of communication in the United States ever subject to prior restraint censorship, which allowed for the prescreening, cutting, and licensing of films before the public ever saw a foot of celluloid. Chicago pointed the way toward this type of regulation when it passed the first municipal censorship law in 1907. The law required a police permit for every moving picture shown in the city. During the nickelodeon era many other cities and towns had used their police powers to rectify the dangers presented by firetrap theaters. But police licensing proved a blunt instrument, helpful primarily for ensuring that early movie theaters conformed to fire safety codes and for excising scenes that contained obviously criminal behavior, like murder, arson, and robbery. Since most film censorship activists through the early 1910s believed that immigrant, working-class men dominated movie audiences, the approach indicated their intention to prevent films from inspiring anti-social behavior in this group. Two of the very few story pictures that were entirely suppressed, *The James Boys in Missouri* and *Night Riders* (both 1908), illustrated this concern.[29]

The revised censorship law that Chicago passed in 1914 displayed the shift in regulatory efforts that mirrored the larger change in attitudes about the movies' cultural identity and location by the late 1910s. *Go West! Young Women* enters the history of censorship efforts here, when concerns over the impact of America's newly feminized film audience first peaked. The reorientation of the business toward primarily female consumers caused film reformers to focus more on how film content and stars incited criminal behavior among young women. Chicago's decision in 1915 to replace its police board with a ten-person commission of salaried civilians composed equally of men and women offered the more delicate touch needed to address problems associated with women's immorality. The Supreme Court's *Mutual* decision that same year also assumed that the movies tended to provoke immoral conduct among viewers. Most legal scholars agree that *Mutual*'s reasoning that film's unique capacity to do "evil"—in this case, its special ability to incite sexual immorality—was what justified the Court's protection of the state's right to wield singular controls over the medium. Writing for a unanimous court, Justice McKenna suffused his opinion with fears about how the whole atmosphere of story pictures incited erotic havoc among the "promiscuous" crowd that attended movies. In the dark, throngs "not of women alone, nor of men alone, but together" watched "things which should not have pictorial representation in public places," because of the "prurient interest" they "appealed to and excited," McKenna declared.[30]

Increasingly, reformers argued that the movies' cultural ascendancy had unleashed a flood of "indecent," "sexually immoral" images that had made the number of "problem girls" soar. "Problem girl" was a catchall label given by social workers to young, wage-earning women whose appearance and independent participation in consumer culture created novel difficulties with policing their sexuality. Historians Joanne Meyerowitz, Kathy Peiss, Regina Kunzel, and others have skillfully evoked how such women's new purchase on public spaces generated anxieties as many recently rural women poured into cities to work and play nationwide. These young women's bold attempts to refashion themselves according to their own design also led them to experiment with cosmetics, products previously reserved for actresses and prostitutes. Thus, like many of the first movie stars, their behavior disrupted visual conventions that had long allowed observers to separate the good girls from the bad. "The way the women dress today they all look like prostitutes," a waiter reported to one of the many Progressive reformers who cruised dance halls looking for the prostitutes such environments were thought to breed. What these young women may have experienced as "vistas of autonomy, romance, and pleasure," according to Kunzel, many others judged to be "promiscuous sexuality and inappropriate delinquent behavior." The result: for the first time, state authorities deemed sizable numbers of women criminals who required rehabilitation in the new juvenile courts and homes that went up in cities across the country.[31]

The popularity of, and outrage provoked by, a series of so-called white slave pictures in the early 1910s was an early indication of the trend that made "immorality" and "obscenity" the "keywords" that captured the concerns of censorship boards by 1920. Although judged a moral panic by most historians today, concern about white slavery—the belief that large numbers of young white women, often fresh from the countryside, were being forced into sexual slavery—tracked women's movement into the workplace and onto the city streets after 1900. Muckraker George Kibbe Turner's "The City of Chicago: A Study of the Great Immoralities" first galvanized Progressive reformers into action on the subject. Turner's exposé described a chain that connected the liquor trade to immigrants, and the latter to a white slave market run mostly by Jewish immigrants from Russia. The racial identities of the villain and victim in these tales also revealed how the white slavery scare reflected the era's heightened fears about the racial degeneration of Anglo-Saxons in cities through racial "mongrelization," in the language of the day. Films like *Inside the White Slave Traffic* (1913) became some of the first feature-length blockbusters. At six reels long, white slave films played for over an hour, cost patrons twenty-five cents to view at the first motion pictures palaces in New York, and attracted audiences notably composed of young women. Critics from the *New York Times* and the *Atlantic Monthly* accused the films of inciting the era's "Repeal of Reticence" about sex, of teaching white slaving techniques to men of "the impressionable classes," and of generally pouring "oil upon the flames of vice" before "the promiscuous audiences of the motion picture theaters." They also lamented that so many female fans watched scenes of their imperilment with delight, laughing at the generic conventions and gendered stereotypes employed by these traditional melodramas about the danger the city posed to women's virtue.[32]

In the volatile postwar climate, the fact that so many movie publicists had turned such traditional dark tales about young women's experience of urban modernity—of countrified naïfs brought to ruin in the city—on their head now counted as evidence of the danger presented by the industry's growth in Los Angeles. Having breezily described the City of Angels as an urban El Dorado for intrepid female migrants, these brighter stories' success in drawing women into movie theaters and to Los Angeles reflected the hunger many felt about exploring where their gathering freedoms might lead. But the industry's efforts may have succeeded too well by the early 1920s. Reports announcing that more than ten thousand girls went to Los Angeles each year to work in the movies generated mounting anxiety about the dangers that awaited them in an industry controlled by "morally degenerate," "un-American" Jews.[33] After the Great War, with anti-Semitism and nativism on the rise, fears about Hollywood's impact spread along multiple fronts. A wave of more risqué films, featuring daring, decidedly non-Anglo stars like Pola Negri, Gloria Swanson, and Rudolph Valentino, made headlines. Growing numbers came to believe that protecting the nation from what one activist called, "The Movie Menace" demanded controlling the movie industry itself.

The event that produced the industry's first so-called canonical scandal illustrated these tensions. "S.F. BOOZE PARTY KILLS YOUNG ACTRESS; GIRL STRICKEN AFTER AFFAIR AT S.F. HOTEL; Virginia Rappe Dies after Being Guest at Party Given Here by 'Fatty' Arbuckle; Film Comedian," wailed the headlines that framed the event. The scandal erupted following a party hosted by Roscoe "Fatty" Arbuckle, a slapstick star second only to Charlie Chaplin in popularity. Arbuckle held the party at the St. Francis Hotel on Labor Day, 1921. An actress named Virginia Rappe and two other Angelenos, Maude Delmont and Al Semnacher, were among the first to arrive, around noon. Still wearing pajamas, Arbuckle greeted the trio with a pitcher of bootleg gin and orange juice. Within the hour, the comedian requested a phonograph be brought in to entertain the dozen or so guests who crowded the suite's reception room. Happy revelers later recalled in court a "royal good time, dancing and kidding and drinking," with Arbuckle "at the center" of the "clowning." Rappe and Arbuckle ended up alone in one of the suite's bedrooms for an undetermined length of time. Late in the afternoon, guests discovered the actress there in great pain, tearing at her clothes. Thinking her drunk, some female guests tried to revive her with a cold bath; Arbuckle placed a piece of ice between her legs for the same reason. Around 5 P.M., Arbuckle called the management to have Rappe moved to a separate room, and the party ended. Dr. Beardslee, the hotel staff physician at the St. Francis, administered morphine to relieve Rappe's pain, later testifying at Arbuckle's first trial that "any evidence of alcoholism" "was very slight" and "overshadowed" by her "intense pain." Arbuckle returned to Los Angeles on Tuesday for the premiere of his latest film, *Gasoline Gus* (1921). That same day the hotel's doctor diagnosed Rappe as suffering from a ruptured bladder, recommended Delmont take her to a hospital, and left on a hunting trip. Rappe languished for three days at the St. Francis, mostly unconscious and in pain so severe that only continuous injections of morphine, supplied by a new doctor Delmont hired, provided relief. Late on Thursday Delmont moved Rappe to a private sanitarium where she died the next morning of peritonitis resulting from a ruptured bladder. Delmont immediately told the police that Rappe blamed Arbuckle for her death. The San Francisco district attorney accused the comedian of murder. A media frenzy erupted in which even typically staid papers like the *New York Times* ran headlines based on hearsay that shrieked, "ARBUCKLE DRAGGED RAPPE GIRL TO ROOM, WOMAN TESTIFIES."[34]

That much, and little more, can be said with certainty about the circumstances from which the "'Fatty' Arbuckle Scandal" arose. What happened *after* Rappe's death has interested many for decades, creating a powerful origins text about Hollywood that journalists, novelists, television writers, and popular historians alike return to again and again to convey how the movie colony's licentious spirit combined with the venality of its producers to create its unrivaled moral hypocrisy. After the first jury deadlocked, the largest picture producers banded together in a new industry group, the Motion Picture Producers and Distributors Association (MPPDA, or Hays Office) and hired William Hays as president. Will Hays was everything that the mostly immigrant, Jewish producers in the MPPDA were not: a native Midwesterner, a Presbyterian elder, and a leading Republican and Washington insider who became postmaster general after orchestrating Warren Harding's successful 1920 presidential bid.[35] Arbuckle's second jury also deadlocked. The third jury acquitted the star, issuing an apology to Arbuckle in the press. Nonetheless, in his first public act, Hays shelved all of Arbuckle's films and banned him from the screen. Scholars have mostly located the scandal's significance in the way Hays's act symbolized the rise of an internal system of regulation that controlled the images made by and about Hollywood. This emphasis follows Robert Sklar's pioneering cultural history, *Movie-Made America* (1975). Others have looked to Richard deCordova's work on the emergence of the star system, which emphasizes the scandal's precipitation of a shift in the discourse about Hollywood. Before the scandal, deCordova argues, publicity about the spotless domesticity and fabulous consumptive patterns of stars established the respectability of the movies and their personalities. After the Arbuckle trials, attention focused on exposing the private lives of residents to public view, making the topic of Hollywood's moral impact on fans a subject of social controversy. Yet such accounts fail to explain what made the scandal so scandalous in its day.[36]

The Arbuckle-Rappe scandal of 1921 did not invent Hollywood, but as the final chapter of *Go West, Young Women!* explores, the images and words, stereotypes and censorship drives, "morality clauses" and jury verdicts that produced the scandal did as much to shape ideas about early Hollywood as any other single event. Most simply, the scandal circulated "Hollywood" among a broad audience—as a term indicating a place, product, industry, and approach to life. Used this way, "Hollywood" came into wide usage only in the scandal's wake. As "Hollywood" quickly became a metaphor for the industry's influence on American culture, its meaning, like the scandal itself, was not singular, transparent, or stable but was instead shifting and associational. Tethered to the fears and ambitions of different publics, contests over narrating the scandal continued for decades. Still, in the scandal's immediate aftermath some interpretations clearly dominated others, leaving an impress of Hollywood's social imaginary that stamped all others to come.[37]

Put differently, the scandal reveals much more about Hollywood's origins if we spotlight its other principal character, Virginia Rappe. A former model turned actress of minor success, Rappe initially played a starring role in the scandal that reflected the prominence of unconventional New Western Women in the movie industry's rise in Los Angeles. Yet fickle history has largely forgotten the important part she played in its production. Both scholars and popular writers alike have long reduced her significance to one or the other of two bit parts: an irrelevant, silly starlet, or a two-bit prostitute whose venereal disease caused her death.[38] Like most historical erasures, her casting has served particular purposes, including a wish by some to clear Arbuckle's name. Yet such characterizations have more broadly obscured young women's agency and significance inside the landscape of early Hollywood, in part by trivializing the desires that sent young women like Rappe out west to work. Indeed, Rappe's erasure raises questions about how the sexual double standard and the sociology of knowledge influence which version of an origin story takes hold. For even before the scandal's eruption in 1921, many respectable Americans who could concur on little else agreed that Hollywood and its girls best symbolized the changes in gender roles and sexual feeling threatening to sweep the land. This shared assumption offered a piece of hard-to-come-by common ground in the contentious cultural climate of the postwar era.

Here, then, was the Hollywood born around Los Angeles during the era of the Great War: in a city that mirrored the larger cultural contests among Anglo-Saxon cultural custodians, new immigrants, and problem girls; in the explosion of print that surrounded and produced the first new women stars and their fans; in movie theaters filled with young working- and middle-class women; in the stories whose new western heroines shaped the fantasies and fears of a seemingly ever widening audience. Early Hollywood resulted from the collision of these parts. The rise of the movies in Los Angeles offered both a distillation and a dramatic magnification of tensions played out nationwide, as a multitude of migrants from many different countries crammed cities across the land. In the process, Hollywood provoked both loving devotion and shrill, sustained assault. *Go West, Young Women!* explores the implications of the motion picture industry's development out west and then measures how the emotions generated by Hollywood's birth influenced the sexual revolution to come.

CHAPTER I

"Oh for a girl who could ride a horse like Pearl White"

The Actress Democratizes Fame

Mary Pickford, the silent film era's single greatest star, published her autobiography, *Sunshine and Shadow* (1954), decades after the motion picture industry made her face "better known than the President of the United States."[1] Black-and-white images layer the book, and, with the skillful shorthand so necessary to celebrity, Pickford used the first photo-essay to sketch how her childhood foretold future renown. After opening with a full-page portrait of her pretty, resolute-looking mother, Charlotte Hennessy, the next photographs suggest what tested that resolve. A small cameo of her faraway-eyed, dandified father, John Smith, floats above a snapshot of the simple brick row house in Toronto that he deserted just shy of Mary's fifth birthday, in 1897. The sorrow-faced women in the next grainy snapshot communicate their determination to shelter the three Smith children arrayed beside them on a modest apartment stoop. And here, following this picture of grim resignation and apparent innocence lost, Pickford first spotlights her preschool-aged self, Gladys Smith, a tyke whose manicured ringlets and lacy white ensemble hint at the hopes dashed by her father's desertion. At first glance the portrait appears as conventional as little Gladys's packaging. Closer inspection reveals a child whose furious gaze demolished the era's portraiture conventions for her age and sex. Pickford captioned the image to emphasize both her intelligence and anger: "The cameraman thought me idiotic enough to believe there was 'a little birdie in the black box,'" she explained with still simmering resentment. Thus Pickford used her coming-of-age to tell the story her publicity and films repeatedly retold: a girl needed the courage to ignore men's prescriptions and recommendations in order to triumph over adversity and seize a man-sized share of the world's regard.

In 1917, precisely two decades after her father's signal act of paternal incompetence, poet Vachel Lindsay anointed Pickford "The Queen of the Movies," and her royal highness permanently relocated to Los Angeles, where she reined over the star system that powered Hollywood's rise around the world. By 1920, journalist Louella Parsons could, with unexpected credibility, declare the actress, writer, producer, and cofounder of United Artists—the sole independent film studio to endure in the studio era—the "greatest woman of her age." "To repudiate this girl in haste is a high treason to the national heart," Lindsay wrote, using Pickford's talent to plead the artistic case of the "photoplay," his more elevated term for moving pictures, before the *New Republic*'s high-brow readers. His argument displayed the tendency to equate the famous with the national spirit. For fifteen out of the magazine's first twenty years, readers of *Photoplay,* which began publishing in Chicago in 1912 and quickly became the largest, wittiest, and most literate fan magazine in America, ranked Pickford the most popular star. "There has never been anything just like the public adulation showered on Mary"; she "could have risen to the top of United States Steel, if she had decided to be a Carnegie instead of a movie star," recalled Adolph Zukor, who perfected the vertical integration of the American film industry. As another silent-era filmmaker described the awe her fame produced, Pickford was so "peculiarly pre-eminent that her position at the very top was subject to little question or jealousy."[2]

Pickford's preeminence was not quite so peculiar when placed within the broader sweep of how the actress came to embody the "democratization" of fame as elite men, and then men altogether, lost their monopoly over incarnating the combination of personal achievement, distinction, and freedom at the heart of modern renown. In this way, Pickford modified an already established role in a genre in which the actress performed a female self who grappled with what it meant for a woman to embody these ideals in ways that made her stand out from the crowd. Yet most historians' unease with contemporary celebrity culture has complicated historicizing and assessing what the fame of actresses has to teach about modern gender roles. Without question, contemporary culture creaks under the weight of individuals talented mostly for their self-seeking display. The seemingly inexorable drift of public discourse since the Cold War toward fixating on the antics of those merely "well-known for [their] well-knowness [*sic*]" helped to make Daniel Boorstin's *The Image: A Guide to Pseudo-Events in America* (1961) a classic. Written as the power of television first became evident, Boorstin sketched the kind of declension narrative now so familiar in cultural history: once, somewhere in the past, fame signaled society's recognition of the authentically great deeds and thoughts of a few truly eminent men, whereas modern society's worship of ersatz celebrities reflects our descent into mindless consumerism. A few have strayed from this interpretative path, exploring how famous personalities in modern times continue to reflect the public's interest in changing views of the self and individual achievement. But such works either fail to gender their analysis or reduce the personas of female stars to agents or victims of consumption. Thus women's role in the development of our celebrity-saturated culture remains poorly explained, even as feminist scholarship on how mass culture and female entertainers expressed and cultivated new ideas about sex piles up in the libraries.[3]

Yet one can trace the seeds of a new interpretation of modern fame to another midcentury text, much more infamous than Pickford's or Boorstin's: Simone de Beauvoir's *The Second Sex* (1949). In her ex post facto feminist manifesto, Beauvoir argued that only the actress materialized a worldly, ineffable feminine authority that contradicted the equation of public renown with masculine identity. For this reason, the book's concluding chapter, "The Independent Woman," declared the actress to be the "one category" of woman who pointed the way "toward liberation" of the sex. Born in movie-crazed France in 1908, the year before Pickford made her teenage transition from stage to screen, Beauvoir was a child during the time the "divine" Sarah Bernhardt shone indisputably as the era's brightest star.[4] Several factors accounted for the singular role of actresses, according to Beauvoir, including religious censure, relative financial independence, "a taste for adventure" that equaled men's, and a unique status derived from working with men on equal footing while still attracting recognition for their attractiveness as women. Together these forces explained the actress's identity as "the virile woman," a protagonist liberated from many of the conventions that tethered the Victorians' ideal "true woman" to the home. Above all, the actress's freedom lay in how her work in the wider world, like that of men, produced an independence that supported other pleasures. "Their professional success—like those of men—contribute to their sexual valuation." But by "making their own living and finding the meaning of their lives in their work, [actresses] escape the yoke of men," allowing them "to transcend their given characteristics" as the unessential second sex.[5]

As Beauvoir suggested, the ability of actresses to perform new representations of women's individuality originated in the nineteenth century, as industrialization, the explosion of print media, and the democratic revolutions made room for a few women, and many more men, to make their way, and to make themselves known, beyond the limitations imposed by traditional social hierarchies. In short, the "Pickford Revolution"—as one producer called the transformation from an industry with no stars to one defined by them—was a century in the making. Many of the early American film industry's most notable actresses translated, with the distinct accent of their age, the customs and conventions handed down by their theatrical foremothers on the antebellum stage. To stress the importance of theatrical aesthetics and practices on the democratization of fame, this chapter begins by historicizing and gendering the celebrity of Pickford's most important foremother: Charlotte Cushman, the first American female star. Cushman's fame developed in the 1840s—precisely the moment when both the words "celebrity" and "personality" appeared to denote individuals often of ordinary birth whose idiosyncrasies, accomplishments, and glamour made them such a topic of speculation and appeal that the public sought the kind of knowledge, provided through modern media, that made such people into "intimate strangers." For Cushman to achieve this status, it was necessary to reinvent the actress as a figure of professional influence, artistic triumph, and personal virtue rather than of moral corruption, the latter a particularly acute association in Anglo-American culture.[6]

Charlotte Cushman's embodiment of "Success and her sister Fortune" in the 1850s revealed how the celebrity culture that supported her rise restaged gender as performance rather than essence, thereby aiding the breakdown of the belief that a woman's moral character was immutably encoded in her appearance and distance from the tumult of public life. Put differently, celebrity culture's development reveals how advertising an actress as a model worthy of emulation demanded different strategies of representation than those used to publicize great men. As used by film scholars, the term "persona," which views the star as a text whose complications create ambiguities that can appeal to diverse fans, provides insight into the different dynamics that publicized famous women.[7] Promoting female stars like Cushman required modern publicity to convey information about their private lives that could confound the flouting of respectability that their public performances entailed. New rituals of celebrity, like autobiographical writing in women's magazines, explained this hidden self, offering access to truths that complicated how the actress appeared on stage. Such descriptions stressed how often women's natures might accommodate qualities and characteristics of both sexes. Indeed, Cushman cut such an original figure in her milieu that her 1876 obituary still attributed her acclaim to her merging of seemingly irreconcilable traits. Her persona "manifested to the last the two leading peculiarities of her nature, the tenderness of a woman and the firmness of a Spartan man." In this way, the fame of actresses was not a seamless expression of inner virtues—as had long been the case with men—but a multilayered performance that signaled the crumbling of sexual difference's ability to define individual achievement and desire.[8]

Picturing the actress this way begins to explain what made Hollywood's social imaginary so provocative when it first emerged after the Great War. Like no other industry of its day, the early American film industry publicized the accomplishments of its many successful women workers, including actresses, screenwriters, directors, producers, journalists, and publicists. But without question, the most celebrated of these figures were the first movie stars, women like Pickford, Florence Lawrence, and Pearl White. As with Cushman in the century before, these women's fame dramatized their ability to exercise qualities long reserved for heroic men. But unlike Cushman, these "girls," to use the parlance of the day, also displayed qualities that marketed them as romantic, desiring young women who were emblematic of the new sexual freedoms their sex sought to explore. The fame such actresses incarnated explains why so many girls, as well as their elders, came to consider the actress a personage of serious consequence around the world.

I

When viewed through the lens of gender, the nineteenth-century stage appears as a kind of bellwether for women's entrance into territories that once spelled ruin for the respectable. With the sexual integration of leisure spaces that began with women's participation as audience members of the so-called legitimate stage, women began to stake out new public spaces for socialization. At this theater, women tested old limits as to what they might show and tell in public, including how much the female star could project the type of authority and appetites long reserved for men. By midcentury, Charlotte Cushman's fame displayed how a celebrity culture once sharply segmented by sex and respectability had become mostly ordered by gender and class. This development made room for the celebration of an actress who could act like both a respectable lady and a heroic man.[9]

Before Charlotte Cushman's rise in the 1840s signaled the reconfiguration of the theater, women's appearance "in the play or at the playhouse" took place "under a moral cloud." Through the 1820s the theater was a part social, part political event controlled by elite white men. Men occupied the vast majority of seats in the nation's few stock company theaters, and social class explained where they sat in the typical theater's tripartite seating arrangement: the ground-floor pit for the "middling" sorts, the boxes above for the elite, and the third tier for those with the fewest financial resources, including the prostitutes who paraded their wares along its balcony. Local gentry enjoyed the same repertoire time and again: versions of Shakespeare that made the tragedies less tragic and "fairy tale" melodramas predominated. These plays often turned on the threat posed to a helpless heroine's virtue and her eventual restoration "to the bosom of her home, her father, and her God," offering women little to do but hope for rescue from their travails. All players in this era, male and female, were a morally suspect caste with no social standing. Forsaking womanly modesty and a home to earn a living strutting before strange men, the era's few actresses attracted special censure. The conflation of actresses with prostitutes, the era's other "public women," in the language of the day, was well founded by the standards of the respectable. The more elastic sexual norms of the working-class milieu from which most actresses emerged, their initially low wages, and the desire to accrue the publicity that might follow from attracting well-placed paramours all discouraged a moralistic view of sex. Moreover, the presence of alcohol and prostitutes, as well as the celebration of sensuous display and illusion, made the theater virtually synonymous with corrupt aristocratic tastes, earning it a reputation as the enemy of the middle-class family as that class's "cult of domesticity" took hold. A flat prohibition by the Protestant church followed. Legal scholars consider the special regulation of theatrical exhibitions an anomaly of English law reflecting the conviction of this rising middle class that the playhouse debased audiences, particularly vulnerable female ones. White men could ignore the church and partake of the playhouse's pleasures with little consequence, but women who wished to remain ladies could not. Thus, through performance and space, this theater communicated the same message about women's place in public:

left alone without male protection women moved outside the moral order, inviting the surveillance of strangers that led to sexual exchanges and ruin.[10]

As the nation's capitalist expansion sent ever more people scuttling toward markets in cities and towns, leisure assumed more industrialized forms in which the star system and its celebrity culture played an increasingly central role. A theater manager in Philadelphia bemoaned how "a spirit of locomotiveness hitherto unexampled" erupted during "a commercial season of great excess," making "the system of stars the order of 1835."[11] A set of emerging business practices tied to consumer capitalism's growth, the star system offered the best means to fill the era's larger and more numerous playhouses. The theatrical entrepreneurs who sped the star system's development jettisoned the elite man as the theater's most important protagonist and patron. Instead, they publicized a more diverse set of players in different kinds of melodramatic plays that aimed to attract larger and more specific segments of the public.[12] In this way, the star system encouraged the theater's splintering along lines of class and gender.

Inside and outside these more plentiful theaters, a commercial culture of print and performance resounding with melodramatic expression offered an aesthetic register to express the democratization of fame. Faith in the principle of poetic justice and the possibility of self-transformation for those long excluded from the heroic role distinguished melodrama's form from the start. For this reason, some critics contend that melodrama's roots share the same soil that produced fairy tales and ballads. Wherever its origins, the melodramatic form dominated the commercialized popular culture of the nineteenth century created by the spread of literacy, cheaper reproduction methods, and theatrical exchanges. Varying widely in setting and action, most melodramas relied on a plot structured around the protagonist's triumph over villainy, dished out with strong emotion and leavened with comedic touches. By displacing the elite man as central patron and protagonist, according to writer Robertson Davies, melodrama appealed to the "poor working man and his female counterpart, or bourgeois citizen toiling to keep his place in a hurrying world," encouraging their identification "with the Hero, the Heroine, or the Villain."[13] The variety of terms used to modify the melodramatic plays produced on the era's soaring number of stages—including "apocalyptic," "heroic," "problem," "nautical," "sensational," "immoral," "domestic," and "horse"—signaled not just the form's ubiquity but the desire of producers to target and attract specific slices of an ever widening circle of fans. All variations enticed with skillful spectacles and shared an impassioned register that elevated the apparently average speaker and furthered his or her cause. Much like what the star system aimed to do with its production of intimate strangers, this heart-stopping aesthetic used strong emotions to bridge the chasm separating character from audience. Paradoxically, then, melodrama celebrated the individualism that mass society advanced and acted as an antidote to its isolating effects, making it peculiarly suited to popular culture fashioned in the American grain.[14]

Stars who excelled in heroic or apocalyptic melodramas commanded the country's expanding and increasingly democratic theatrical scene. Producers in cities like New York filled new theaters like the Bowery and the Chatham by encouraging young working-class men to shift the customary site of their all-male socializing, excluding prostitutes, from saloons. Cheaper tickets attracted these urban rowdies, but entrepreneurs discovered that magnetic actors performing in these melodramas drew them back. Privileging the roles and tastes of the city's growing number of proletarian men, this mobile network of male stars disrupted the traditional balance of power between managers and players, and among men of different classes in the audience. Here arose the first American audience, lovingly chronicled by historian Lawrence Levine. The opinionated, passionate, and participatory style of this audience displayed how white men's expanding political rights gave them the confidence to attempt sovereignty over performers and elites alike. Yet, rather than offering a truly democratic space, this theater presented a contained performance of the masculine conflicts and style animating the rise of the Democratic Party of Andrew Jackson.[15]

The celebrity of Edwin Forrest, the first great American star, crystallized the type of man idealized by this political culture. Inside now largely class-segmented theaters, Forrest played the common man's champion, a fearless destroyer of tyrants in plays like *Metamora, or the Last of the Wampanoags* (1829), the tale of a doomed "noble savage" who refuses to submit to the white man's rule. To his legion of male fans, the public performer and the private man were indivisible. "It is no painted shadow you see in Mr. Forrest, no piece of costume," boasted one reviewer, "but a man, there to do his four hours of work brawnily [*sic*], it may be, and sturdily, and with great outlay of muscular power but there's a big heart thrown in."[16] Forrest was no effete English fop, but a vigorous American democrat and Democrat who actively supported the party of Jackson. On stage and off, he displayed what his friend and official biographer

called the "one essential ideal" that distinguished him in this homosocial arena: his "fearless faithful manhood."[17] Thus Forrest's fame grew
from his performance of the qualities that his fans believed he possessed
in private. However ersatz the display, Forrest inspired a devotion based
on his seemingly authentic personification of the new social order's
dominant political culture in ways that drew on established modes of
fame.[18]

Women found little room in this theater as long as it aimed primarily
to satisfy the "mechanics" whose wild and, at times, riotous behavior
became part of the show. Such displays climaxed with the Astor Place
Riots of 1849, a conflagration that pitted supporters of the aristocratic
English star William Macready against Forrest's "native" American fans
and left twenty-two dead. By quickening the drive to segment theaters
along class lines and to tame this audience's participatory style, the
event sped what cultural historians call the feminization of American
culture and its resulting sacralization as Shakespeare moved out of the
mechanics' houses. The drive to clean up theaters—to make them spaces
fit for the ladies of any class—dramatically diminished workingmen's
power in the pit by limiting their ability to use the theater as a space to
strengthen solidarities of gender, class, and party.[19]

Yet, from the perspective of the opposite sex, the move to reconfigure
the gendered moral taxonomy of the theater opened up as much as it
shut down. Not only did a theatrical culture aimed at men figure all
women who joined its public as immoral, but its celebration of a fighting-
style of masculinity also disadvantaged women performers. Shortly before she turned to film acting, Pickford recalled "the great difficulty"
of performing before the remnants of this audience in the "ten-twenty-
thirty" theaters, so called for their popularly priced tickets. Tellingly,
Pickford played a small boy in a play in which the few parts for women
continued to mirror the ideal of true womanhood that had pervaded
popular conventions during the Victorian era. Originating among white
middle-class urbanites, the ideal held that Woman should embody
everything that Man—ever more consumed by the hurrying, competitive outside world of commerce—did not. Leading a pious, passive, and
asexual existence, the true woman was a well-kept "angel in the home"
who exercised spiritual power over loved ones from inside its walls. A
rumor that a lady was not as pure as she appeared could foul her reputation, rendering the bawdy theater off-limits for respectable women
regardless of class. Such attitudes explained why the actress's economic
independence and distance from patriarchal protection, as much her

sexual conduct, made her commensurate with the prostitutes working the third tier.[20]

Ironically, the popular image associated with the entrenched domesticity of the middle class—of the lady of the house with less and less to do—helped to produce its destruction by creating a lucrative target for theatrical entrepreneurs. Managers of the legitimate stage first moved to tap the rising purchasing power of middle-class women during a particularly steep financial free fall between 1837 and 1842. They brought the ladies out to the playhouse in droves by barring prostitutes, turning the third tier into a "family circle," eliminating the sale of alcohol, discouraging the frequent outbursts that led to riotous behavior, and instituting matinees. At midcentury, women's patronage of what became known as the legitimate theater produced the sexual integration of "the first public den of male sociability," according to historian Mary Ryan.[21] In 1856, the first public space conceived especially for the ladies opened: A.T. Stewart, a marble palace department store located in New York City's financial district. 1856 also marked the year in which the forty-year-old Cushman brought her London triumph home. Both events indicated how consumer culture could aid the ladies' conquest of heretofore suspect territories, while creating new jobs for those who struggled to afford the fun. These developments also supported the celebrity culture that allowed Charlotte Cushman to achieve renown.

"I was born a tomboy," began the memoir Charlotte Cushman dictated to her longtime companion, Emma Stebbins, months before her death in 1876. "Tomboy" was "an ugly little phrase," an "epithet in those days," Stebbins later explained, that referred "to pioneers of women's advancement." "Applied to all little girls who showed the least tendency toward thinking and acting for themselves," it kept "the dangerous feminine element within what was considered to be the due bounds of propriety and decorum."[22] The daughter of a schoolteacher, and the granddaughter of a single mother, Cushman credited her maternal line "for one element in my nature—ambition!"[23] Born in 1816, Cushman was the eldest of four children and viewed the stage as a means to provide her family with the upward mobility blocked by her much older father's business failures and desertion. After making her professional debut as a singer in Mozart's The Marriage of Figaro in 1835, Cushman gradually reoriented her interest toward acting. By 1842, the young actress had made a small but considered reputation as Lady Macbeth, and she set about renovating Philadelphia's Walnut Street Theatre to attract the city's "settled and domestic citizens." There she acted as leading lady, publicist, and theater manager. The decision displayed her awareness that she needed a more ordered, if at times no less boisterous, space defined above all by the presence of women themselves. Moreover, the multiple roles she assumed at the Walnut, including her place at its helm, demonstrated how a theatrical work practice called "doubling in the brass" benefited actresses who sought unconventional types of public authority.[24] A phrase that emerged from the contemporary all-male minstrel shows aimed at working-class men, "doubling in the brass" signaled the expectation that all members of a stock company perform roles that crossed conventional gender boundaries, including playing both sexes on-stage and performing tasks typically reserved for the opposite sex off of it. The practice helped to explain why the most successful thespians often excelled at more than just acting. But Cushman's timing was unlucky. The Walnut Street Theatre was opened in the midst of a serious economic downturn, and financial problems forced her to resign in 1846. That same year, after performing alongside the great English tragedian William Macready, the twenty-eight-year-old Cushman set sail for London, touting the older actor's advice (probably invented) that only in England would her "talents be appreciated for their true value."[25] The decision displayed Cushman's belief in the still broadly shared assumption that the English possessed superior aesthetic sensibilities and powers.

Cushman triumphed in her first London season, performing opposite her great American rival, Edwin Forrest, whose fame she eclipsed after midcentury. Like Forrest, Cushman played the same kind of roles, time and again, with a physical power and expressive emotionality that British critics considered characteristically American. But unlike Forrest, her theatrical type celebrated her ability to act like figures she was not and never could be: a powerful queen, whether Scottish, English, or gypsy, and Shakespeare's most romantic male lead, Romeo, in the "breeches roles" that helped so much to earn her fame. The parts Cushman played to audiences' greatest delight reveled in her manifestation of public virtues that confounded traditional femininity. "Her true forte is the character of a woman whose softer traits of womanhood are wanting . . . roused by passion or incited by some earnest and long cherished determination the woman, for the time being, assumes all the power and energy of manhood," declared a review of Sir Walter Scott's *Guy Mannering*.[26] *Guy Mannering* featured her most famous role, next to her power-drunk Lady Macbeth: Meg Merriles, a gypsy queen who saves the hero and whom Cushman played as frightful-looking old crone, to Queen Victoria's

FIGURE 2. Charlotte and Susan Cushman in *Romeo and Juliet,* mid–nineteenth century. Courtesy of the Folger Shakespeare Library.

dismay. Credited with bringing breeches parts into vogue in America, her success as Romeo emphasized the role that acting a "manly" man played in her success.[27] The tall, powerfully built, husky-voiced actress accentuated Romeo's aggressive charms, depicting him as "a militant gallant, a pugnacious lover, who might resort to force should Juliet refuse to marry him."[28]

Cushman's roles also demonstrated how melodrama's splintering licensed women's access, as both performers and fans, to its democratizing, individualistic excesses. "Her style was strong, definite bold and free: for that reason observers described it as 'melodramatic,'" recalled a theater historian in the *Saturday Evening Post* decades after her death. "She neither employed nor made pretense of employing, the soft allurements of her sex. She was incarnate power: she dominated by intrinsic authority."[29] Contemporaries marveled at the passion with which she fought duels and made love to other women on stage, notably with her sister Susan, who often starred opposite her as Juliet.[30] In the end, theatrical lore stressed that her renown emerged from her exhibition of manly heroism. "When a fellow in the audience interrupted the performance" of Romeo and Juliet one night, "Miss Cushman in hose and doublet strode to the footlights and declared: 'Someone must put this person out or I shall be obliged to do it myself'"; thereafter "all honors that a player might win were hers."[31]

Still, Cushman's publicity also ensured that audiences understood how her private virtues justified her breaching feminine decorum. As with most early attempts to justify women's display of privileges and opportunities reserved for men, the protection of loved ones initially posed the best defense. Much as with Pickford a half-century later, stories about Cushman's personal life emphasized her role as family provider, explaining her Puritan pedigree, the collapse of her father's business, her turn to the stage to support her family. Ever her own best publicist, Cushman initiated this presentation in a lightly fictionalized story she sent to *Godey's Lady's Book* in 1836, just weeks after landing her first real job on stage. Entitled "Excerpts from My Journal: The Actress," the story prodded readers to recognize that acting offered many worthy women their best financial alternative when forced to fend for themselves. Cushman also publicized her tender feminine side by making much ado of a decision to forgo marriage after the end of a "tragic love-affair" with a never identified "young gentleman of a Presbyterian family." Warned by his family of the "looseness of the lives of actresses," the gentleman reportedly broke their engagement after finding her "being entertained by some of her theatrical friends and mates at a rather lively supper party."[32] Thereafter she reportedly devoted herself to "work, work, work! study, study, study!" her family, and philanthropy.[33]

In this way, Cushman prefigured the path later taken by the first generation of highly educated, middle-class New Women. After 1900, such women's success in the public sphere challenged assumptions about the female sex's intellectual and physical incapacities while accepting that such pursuits often required forgoing marriage and traditional domesticity.[34] Like many of the New Women to follow her, Cushman instead cultivated a circle of women for domestic partnership and intimacy. Indeed, one biographer speculates that her preference for intimate relationships with women made it easier for her to present an image of ladylike decorum in her private life by removing the threat of sexual scandals with men.[35]

Cushman's bright particular star thus sent multiple, seemingly contradictory impressions about the model of individual achievement she offered to her increasingly female fans. Some critics marveled at how the "manly"-appearing Cushman managed to perform love scenes "of so erotic a character that no man would have dared indulge in them." Yet "the most respectable female audiences" watched actresses in breeches roles fight duels and make love to other women "with much apparent satisfaction."[36] Indeed, female patrons made Cushman into a self-made woman of unrivaled wealth and public stature. "I feel much better about womankind," confided playwright Julia Ward Howe after Cushman's conquest of New York in 1857.[37] In 1874 an "unmarried lady" sent Cushman a letter shortly before her death that conveyed the meager opportunities for self-support, let alone self-definition, available to women of any class. The lady was "proud to direct other ladies who were struggling for their bread, to take example from your noble career, and work out for themselves an independent and individual life." She added: "As a working woman I am under obligation to you for the footprints you leave on the sands of time."[38]

Although poor health finally forced Cushman to retire in 1874, women's importance as theatrical stars and patrons only increased apace with the industrial engine that sped the growth of commercial entertainment after the Civil War. Between 1880 and 1900, the number of shows touring the country jumped from fifty to more than five hundred. By 1900 the number of popular-priced theater seats in cities like Chicago, Denver, Philadelphia, and New York outdistanced population growth by four to one.[39] Women's prospects for employment in the melodramas performed in many of the new, inexpensive (at ten or fifteen cents), family-friendly segments of the theater business like vaudeville soared along with the proliferation of playhouses and touring companies that aimed to attract lower-middle-class workers of both sexes. After employing almost entirely men in 1800, performing became one of the largest professions for women a century later.[40] Many more women worked in nursing and teaching, but both occupations demanded an education, forbade marriage, and paid barely subsistence wages.[41] The stage offered the best chance for both self-support and social mobility for women with the fewest resources—women who otherwise would likely have worked from sunup to sundown in filthy factories, stood six and half days at a department store counter selling products they could not afford, or served at the beck and call of a mistress nearly every hour of each day.[42] Only as performers and writers did women earn the same, or greater, wages as men for equal work. In the celebrity culture that blossomed around the stage, theater directors were distinctly less important than the divas and handsome matinee idols who preened to spark the interest of "matinee girls." And as lionized actresses outnumbered their male counterparts and often visibly doubled in the brass by taking their shows on the road, the stage offered a singular arena for exhibiting a woman's ability to openly compete and best a man.[43]

The mounting centrality of women as consumers and producers of American popular culture continued to create variations in the melodramatic aesthetic that subsequently shaped the development of motion pictures during the 1910s. Variously labeled immoral, problem, and of the emotional hydraulic school, female characters frequently drove the action of these plays, many of which were written, adapted, or commissioned by women.[44] Displaying innovations in stock characters and plot devices, these plays often featured active, independent heroines in stories in which chance and responsibility factored into judgments about women's character.[45] As the publicity about Cushman's private life prefigured, threats to a loved one often justified the exercise of these protagonists' wills. A heroine, not a hero, executed the first hair's-breadth rescue of a victim strapped to railroad tracks. As she batters through a train station door with an axe, her helpless beloved shouts "Courage!" and "That's a true woman!"[46]

Other players in so-called immoral melodramas tackled the sexual double standard that judged chastity as central to a woman's worth and meaningless to a man's.[47] This was the subject of *La dame aux camellias* (1852), an adaptation of the popular novel by Alexandre Dumas fils. After its 1854 American debut, *Camille; or, The Fate of a Coquette,* as it was often called, became not just one of the two most popular plays performed in the United States but also the signature part of the late nineteenth century's greatest international star, the French actress Sarah Bernhardt.[48] Repeated revivals never wanted for an audience, since, following Bernhardt's example, every great actress demanded to assail *Camille*'s lead, Marguerite, the courtesan whose self-sacrifice for her lover demonstrated that even a "fallen woman" could be more than she appeared. After seeing Bernhardt in the role, the great Italian actress Eleanora Duse called the older star's performance "an emancipation." As Duse recalled, "She played, she triumphed, she took possession of us all, she went away . . . and for a long time the atmosphere she brought with her remained in the old theater. A woman had achieved all that!"[49] Like Cushman, Bernhardt displayed qualities associated with both sexes. But in contrast to the Anglo-American context, in Bernhardt's day the French accepted, indeed expected, overt displays of actresses' sexuality, including motherhood without marriage.[50] Yet even the more tepid version of *Camille* performed in the Anglophone world prompted alarm among early critics who called it a "deification of prostitution."[51] Indeed, the play's popularity with women audiences and actresses spawned a host of imitators exploring the erring woman's relationship to society.[52] The trend prompted escalating concern over how the "morbid fictions" of a "herd" of female playwrights threatened to force Shakespeare, Scott, and Dickens to the margins of the American theater.[53] Such views indicated why *Camille* sounded an early note in the swelling cacophony over how women's entrance into masculine preserves threatened to disrupt the nation's fragile cultural standards and social stability.

Indeed, by 1900 many cultural custodians linked the nation's advanced state of democratization and industrialization to its production of an emancipated type of modern woman whose influence had debased American culture. Considered a "quintessentially American" type, the modern woman was one of the first national exports that presaged the reversal in the direction of cultural influence across the Atlantic that Hollywood later intensified.[54] Hugo Munsterberg was one of many leading public intellectuals who predicted that cultural deterioration would follow women having come to "dominate the entire life of America," in the words of his German compatriot Albert Einstein. A specialist in visual perception who taught at Harvard from 1892 until his death in 1916, Munsterberg developed a keen interest in film late in life, creating one of the first theories of film spectatorship.[55] In his guise as a successful popular writer, Munsterberg set about explaining how his foreign perspective offered particular insight into American culture, in writing that often displayed "the strikingly misogynist" tone that characterized much of this commentary. According to Munsterberg, American women's influence spun "a web of triviality and misconception over the whole culture."[56] In 1901 Munsterberg worried that the theater's female audience had placed it under the control of patrons who could not "discriminate between the superficial and the profound." "The whole situation militates against the home and the masculine control of high culture," he lamented, warning, "if the whole national civilization should receive the feminine stamp, it would become powerless and without decisive influence on the world's progress." Munsterberg's estimates were supported by a 1910 survey of theatrical producers and critics that claimed women composed between two-thirds and three-quarters of the audience for performances even at night.[57] The next year Clayton Hamilton, a drama critic at Columbia University, summed up the results of this reality: "Every student of the contemporary theater knows that the destiny of our drama has lain for a long time in the hands of women. Shakespeare wrote for an audience made up mainly of men and boys," but "Ibsen and Pinero have written for an audience made up mainly of women," making the theater "the one great public institution in which 'votes for women' is the rule, and men are overwhelmingly outvoted."[58] And given that Ibsen and Pinero were renowned for controversial female protagonists who blew up the constraints of true womanhood, the fame of these playwrights suggested that women wanted to see actresses who refused to remain trapped in "a doll's house" (the title of Ibsen's 1879 play).[59]

II

By 1900 actresses in vaudeville and on the legitimate stage displayed how a girl might act "the Daddy of the Family," as Mary Pickford's early publicity described her, while still exhibiting a specifically feminine allure. This meant that actresses like Pickford made the ambition to achieve renown compatible with femininity itself. As the first film stars made the transition from stage to screen during the 1910s, many of the most successful occupied a terrain in which the exhibition of feminine charm and public authority coexisted. Not long after her theatrical debut in 1900, Pickford and her now avowedly "stage-minded" mother, Charlotte, met one successful example of the type: the thirteen-year-old vaudeville sensation Elsie Janis. Pickford recalled how Janis

FIGURE 3. The two parts of Pickford's persona: motion picture magnate Mary Pickford keeping track of "Little Mary," c. 1920. Courtesy of Margaret Herrick Library, Academy of Motion Picture Arts and Sciences, Beverly Hills.

earned the "unbelievable salary of seventy-five dollars a week" for her "magnificent imitation" of the Ziegfeld showgirl Anna Held and renditions of songs like "Oh, I Just Can't Make My Eyes Behave!" Pickford and Charlotte asked Janis and her mother how little Gladys might emulate the older girl's "brilliant career."[60] "'Take her to see the finest plays and artists,'" Mrs. Janis advised, but "first, and above all . . . let her be herself." Evoking the modern artist's edict to explore and express the self, the advice registered how the theater nurtured a type of individuality in girls that encouraged them to seek out some kind of happiness for themselves. Pickford made the counsel an axiom, and the four became lifelong friends, the first in a series of mother-daughter teams whose success they first imitated and then supported. "Hollywood was a matriarchy," observed Adela Rogers St. Johns, the journalist who became "Mother Confessor" to the first movie stars. "No more wise, wonderful and remarkable women than Charlotte Pickford, Mrs. Gish, Peg Talmadge, Phyllis Daniels ever lived."[61] Indeed, the prevalence of female-headed households among those who became the greatest actresses of their day suggests that the stereotype of the stage mother who prostitutes her tender charge might be better viewed as a family survival strategy that required tossing norms of feminine decorum into the breach. Not just Cushman, Bernhardt, and Pickford but also Florence Lawrence, Lillian and Dorothy Gish, Norma and Constance Talmadge, Pearl White, Ruth Roland, Pola Negri, and Gloria Swanson were all reared without fathers. Beyond the powerful economic impetus such circumstances engendered, the absence of intimate patriarchal control in childhood may have improved their chances of reinventing how to act like a girl.

For indeed, the personas of the first film stars often involved elaborating the means by which a seemingly conventional girl could incarnate a type of fame that arose from meeting the challenges and opportunities confronting the progress of her sex. By the time she incorporated United Artists in 1919, Mary Pickford's persona was composed of equal parts "America's Sweetheart"—a romantic, spirited ingénue who politely called for women's rights—and "Bank of America's Sweetheart," as her competitor and colleague, Charlie Chaplin called her—a skilled businesswoman who became the highest-paid woman in the world.[62] These two images—one a perennial youth involved in a perpetual process of self-definition, and the other a trailblazing professional engaged with achieving a stature still mostly reserved for daddies—were entwined in the projection of her star image. As with Cushman, her publicity conveyed information that complicated and contradicted her performing type. Press stories, interviews, and the syndicated column "Daily Talks," which Pickford wrote (in name if not in fact) between 1915 and 1917, focused on her salary and work, and made no secret of her real age or the existence of her husband, actor Owen Moore. Both working- and middle-class magazines described her as a woman whose accomplishments placed her alongside the industrial titans who had loomed so large in the imagination of Americans since the dawning of what Mark Twain called the Gilded Age. A piece signed by Pickford in the *Ladies' Home Journal,* the largest-circulation women's monthly and one aimed mostly at the middle class, reported that next to her age ("twenty four, but someday I may not want to tell it"), the question most frequently asked in the five hundred letters she received daily was, "How much do I make?"[63] "I enjoy my work immensely," she reported; "there is a wonderful fascination in the ever changing scenes and the varied excitement." When the workingwomen's monthly *Ladies' World* announced her the winner of a reader's popularity contest

FIGURE 4. Mary Pickford as idol of the "Working Girl" readers of the *Ladies' World* in 1915. Courtesy of Margaret Herrick Library, Academy of Motion Picture Arts and Sciences, Beverly Hills.

months later, "her hundred thousand dollar a year salary" was again central.[64] Her "photo-play supremacy . . . justified" her salary, the piece explained, stressing the breadth of Pickford's achievements. "Her versatility of talent is marvelous, and is evidenced by the fact that she writes as well as she acts." Since only one-quarter of wage-earning women earned the $8 a week that constituted a living wage in 1914, it is easy to imagine why Pickford's annual salary of $50,000 for exciting work led "thousands of American girls to ask about motion picture acting as a profession."[65]

Indeed, Pickford always credited the paternal power her salary made possible with inspiring her devotion to her work. The modest means she earned with her theatrical debut in 1900 had created a "determination nothing could crush . . . to take my father's place in some mysterious way." Her earliest publicity would later use her breadwinner anxieties to justify her decision in 1908 to trade Broadway for the less reputable choice of acting at Biograph film studio in New York. There Pickford used her artistic status to demand twice the rate paid to beginning film players: $10 a day, or $60 a week, a salary she credited with allowing her family to finally "beg[i]n to live."[66] She also recollected her debut in *The Silver King* in terms that presaged the type that brought her such acclaim. Although she claimed to prefer the "villainous little girl" she played in the popular melodrama's first act, she reported that a comic bit of stage business she improvised as the hero's dying son drew the "biggest laugh of the evening" and won the manager's attention. Whatever its accuracy, her description deftly captured her later screen type: a feminine, feisty tomboy, orphaned in spirit if not always in fact, whose fiery emotions jumped from harmless misbehavior to wild humor to tender pathos.

The motivation to win her way in the world brought Pickford's family to New York in 1907, where she resolved to meet "the Wizard of the Modern Stage," David Belasco. A former actor from San Francisco, Belasco's celebrity as a director-producer stemmed from his artful performance as the so-called "Maestro" of the theater's feminization.[67] Belasco built his unrivaled following among women on the "immoral" melodramatic plays that intellectuals like Hugo Munsterberg decried for corrupting the nation's artistic and moral tenor. Noteworthy modern immoral melodramas like *Madame Butterfly* (1900) and *Du Barry* (1901) descended from *Camille*. Unsurprisingly, Belasco's notoriety also derived from his relationships to their female stars. "BELASCO'S LATEST STAR A SUCCESS" was how a Philadelphia paper announced Charlotte Walker's triumph in *The Warrens of Virginia* (1907). "How I do like to develop an actor or an actress. Then is when I am most happy," Belasco explained in one press release. "I like to thrust in my hand, grasp his or her heartstrings and drag them out and play upon them like a musician upon the strings of his instrument," he continued, expertly suggesting his talent for conducting both erotic and gender play.[68] Pickford displayed a similar knack when she auditioned for a small role in *The Warrens*, introducing herself to Belasco as the "father of the family" in a manner that made the Maestro laugh.[69] Her publicity seized on this title when she won a starring role in a 1913 Belasco production of *A Good Little Devil*. Calling herself a daddy emphasized her status as an adult artist who laid claim to the rights and responsibilities of the patriarch, however much she appeared like a spirited, angelic girl. *The Warrens* also featured two other flickers of future importance, playwright (later screenwriter and director) William de Mille and his younger brother, actor (later director) Cecil. The press called its female star simply the latest in a line of actresses who were "FAILURES TILL 'SVENGALI' ARRIVED."[70]

In likening Belasco to Svengali, the newspaper summoned the specter of George du Maurier's *Trilby* (1894), a popular novel that displayed the broader shift in popular culture's depiction of men and women's relationship to the production of art. The best-selling novel modernized the Pygmalion and Galatea myth, long the master print for viewing the male as the agent of the heavenly creative impulse, the female as his aesthetic stimulant. When mortal women fail to meet his moral standards, Pygmalion carves his perfect woman from ivory, worships his creation, and consummates his desire after the goddess Aphrodite gives her life. The fate of Trilby O'Farrell partially reproduced her classical predecessor's. An artist's model whose beauty and availability inspire a group of budding painters in the Latin Quarter, Trilby falls under the spell of Svengali, an evil mesmerist who hypnotizes the "tone-deaf" young grisette into becoming the voice of his musical ambitions. Svengali's control over Trilby indicates why those who emphasize the manager's role as that of proprietor of an actress's talent in this era speak of a "Svengali paradigm." And, no doubt, the Trilby-inspired crazes, from shoes to hats, that swept both sides of the Atlantic near the century's end offered precocious examples of mass culture's ability to turn symbols of women's sexuality into fetishistic, salable parts. Yet Trilby also revised the moral interpretation of the novel's female protagonist and described the male artists in the story as frauds or fallible. The bohemian Trilby "could be naked and unashamed" and was "without any kind of fear." Those who judge Trilby come to grief as well. Still, Pickford's fame displayed the American public's uneasy relationship to female eroticism by celebrating a female artist who sought new professional, rather than sexual, freedoms.

Given her ambition to make herself known, Pickford's landing at Biograph in 1908 was equal parts fortuitous and frustrating. After 1908, the shift to story pictures, or what scholars now call narrative film, threw the work of film acting into relief, focusing audience's attention on gelatine Juliets (a celluloid version of Shakespeare's most famous ingénue). Plot development in story pictures revolved around the action of fictional characters that new camera techniques like close-ups brought within intimate reach. Biograph's leading director, D.W. Griffith, pioneered the close-up's effective use. The technical mastery of both Griffith and early cameramen at the studio probably explains why two of the industry's earliest, if still nameless, stars emerged from Biograph's ranks: Pickford and Florence Lawrence. Since movie players appeared without billing in the earliest years, curious fans dubbed Lawrence the "Biograph Girl" and Pickford "Little Mary," a character name she often used. By 1910, *Motion Picture World*'s new section, "Picture Personalities," answered fans' questions about the identities of performers like Lawrence and Pickford.[71] But, while many production companies began to release the names of leading actors, Biograph continued to refuse to promote its popular players.

Carl Laemmle, a German-born immigrant working in the industry's western hub of Chicago, viewed the mounting popularity of female film players like Lawrence and Pickford as an opportunity to distinguish his new company.[72] In 1909 Laemmle left the first film industry trust, a patents pool engineered by Thomas Edison called the Motion Picture Patents Company (MPPC). Shut out from the MPPC's screens and facing litigation for patent infringement, the Independent Motion Picture Company (IMP, which became Universal in 1912) could survive only by quick success. Laemmle hastily added producing to the studio's functions and lured Lawrence, whom Biograph had fired for seeking better terms, to join its ranks. Laemmle promoted her move by sandwiching a large photograph of her familiar face between her name and a headline proclaiming, "She's an Imp!" Laemmle then orchestrated a stunt to stoke the ardor of audiences. In March 1910 he bought ads that declared "WE NAIL A LIE" above a close-up of Lawrence. The "enemies of the Imp" had "foisted on the public of St. Louis" a horrible story "that Miss Lawrence (the 'Imp' girl, formerly known as the 'Biograph' girl) had been killed by a street car." In good melodramatic fashion, the ad created a stir by casting Lawrence and IMP as scrappy survivors fighting against nefarious rivals. Shortly after the stunt a new motion picture editor in the *Toledo News Bee* declared: "Her name is Florence Lawrence. There. After two years exercise of sway over the admiration and curiosity of the public the most popular moving picture star is known" despite "the so-called moving picture trust" having "fought every effort to learn her identity."[73] "The rumor caused considerable depression among our pa-

FIGURE 5. Florence Lawrence on a postcard for fans, c. 1912.
Courtesy of Margaret Herrick Library, Academy of Motion
Picture Arts and Sciences, Beverly Hills.

trons," a theater owner wrote Lawrence, until the manager promoted
her location "in the land of the living" and promised "the ladies . . .
souvenir photographs" of the actress. "I have taken the greatest interest
in your pictures," wrote sixteen-year-old Betty Melnick from St. Louis
after Lawrence appeared there. "Why you make me cry, laugh, and oh
you make me see things different"; she concluded, "My one great wish
is to pose with you."[74]

Lawrence's persona as a western American–styled New Woman bent on hair-raising demonstrations of women's social and physical mobility likely accounted for the different perspective Betty Melnick took from the star.[75] A cowgirl in an era in which frontier mythology influenced how so many Americans' viewed their past, Lawrence's exceptional equestrian skills made her the female counterpart of an already prized American hero and won the actress her first substantial role in the Edison short *Daniel Boone, or Pioneer Days in America* (1907).[76] Playing a Boone daughter captured by Indians, Lawrence executes a daring escape, riding bareback at breakneck speed, long blonde curls flying behind her. After joining Vitagraph the next month, her first leading role demanded similar skills. Producer J. Stuart Blackton called Lawrence "a splendid rider," extolling her aplomb after she narrowly escaped an accident while playing a Union spy who gets chased on horseback through the woods in *The Dispatch Bearer* (1907).[77] The same qualities also reportedly caught Griffith's eye. "Can you ride horses?" demanded the director at their first meeting. "I would rather ride than eat" was Lawrence's cool reply. Dressed "like a cowgirl in the wild and wooly West" for *The Girl and the Outlaw* (1908), she went on to make over a dozen "Wild West Pictures" there.[78] Yet Lawrence's roles cohered less around a particular filmic type than around the display of a dramatic range that swung from knockabout romantic comedies like the "Jonesy" film series to dramatic love stories like *Resurrection* (1909).[79]

"Florence Lawrence is a tomboy. She told me so herself," began an early publicity piece that used her real-life western background to explain her self-reliance, derring-do, and political progressivism. "I have always been an actress. When I was a child I roamed all over the West leading a gypsy-like life," she explained.[80] The claim was no mere puffery. Lawrence was born Florence Bridgwood in 1886 in Hamilton, Ontario. Her father, George, was a carriage maker; her mother, Lotta, an actress thirty-six years younger than her husband. When Lotta permanently separated from George in 1890, she became "versatile as a leading lady of her own company which produced all sorts of plays," taking "Baby Flo" along while she toured "the West with the Lawrence Dramatic Players."[81] This persona would have prepared readers for her support of woman suffrage, because western women's movements had already won women the vote in most of the American and Canadian West. In 1913 Lawrence attended an eastern suffrage march in Washington, D.C.[82] Parading on horseback, she proclaimed her "politics as a suffragette," a term associated with British women who used violent tactics to demand the vote. This "short and light and slight and sensitive" girl was "a lady of spirit withal. My Yes! An ardent suffragist. A Banner-Bearing, Street-Parading Suffragist!" marveled another report in *Motion Picture Magazine*.[83]

The repeated references in the press to Lawrence's theatrical past and present resemblance to stage star Maude Adams again betrayed how stage conventions framed the emergence of the first movie stars. As Lawrence quickly developed a reputation as one of the screen's greatest actresses, newspapers touted her as "the richest girl in the world" and "The Maude Adams of the Moving Picture Show," the actress whose boyish charms led J.M. Barrie to write *Peter Pan* (1905).[84] By continually likening Lawrence to Adams, the press elevated the status of still-déclassé film acting and placed her first in a line of future female film stars capable of innocently pursuing boyish adventures.[85]

Moreover, her success indicated how the explosive demand for story pictures after 1908 encouraged film producers to absorb both stage actors and their customs, such as doubling in the brass.[86] Experienced at managing all aspects of staging a show, thespians became the cheapest, best-trained labor supply available to make story pictures at the new film studios. The expectation that all workers perform multiple tasks reduced the sex segregation of labor and was supported by a work culture that responded to performative rather than ascriptive modes of authority based on the "natural" hierarchies of race, class, and sex.

Lawrence displayed how the custom licensed women's ability to run the show after joining Lubin Studio in 1911. At Lubin she received more money and control over her work, including the hire of her personal director, husband Harry Solter. One of their first productions, *The Little Rebel* (1911), featured her as a furiously horseback riding, rifle-toting daughter of the Confederacy who falls for a Union solider she fails to kill.[87] Letters to her mother at this point convey a woman who imagined herself a free agent no matter her contractual obligations.[88] Indeed, a multipart interview Lawrence gave entitled "Growing Up with the Movies" has her mother, Lotta Lawrence, reporting, "When Flo was a tiny girl . . . she told the well known actor manager Daniel White that she was going to become a famous actress when she grew up," adding that her "indomitable ambition" meant that "she would become a really famous actress." By year's end, Lawrence traded Lubin for IMP/Universal, where she hired Owen Moore, Pickford's husband, as her leading man to work at Victor Film Company, an independent production unit that likely made her the first film actor to produce her own films.[89] Having attained almost total control of her work, she increasingly played actresses and other professional women such as the comically exacting headmistress of a boys' school in *Flo's Discipline* (1912).[90] Little wonder that "motion picture experts" writing in newspapers touted her success as proof that a "girl with talent, energy, and ambition" could "make a splendid income as an actress in the moving picture show." In advising the "legion of 'stage-struck' girls" to train their sights on this "new business for girls," the counsel displayed the transfer of professional aspirations once directed at the stage to the movie industry.[91]

Still searching for a means to make her name known, Pickford followed Lawrence's path from Biograph to IMP/Universal after Lawrence left the studio in 1911. Laemmle paid Pickford more for the opportunity to fan audience interest in the actress by releasing her name to *Moving Picture World* and then distributing a series of films featured simply as "Little Mary Imps." The films opened with the phrase "Mary Pickford, America's Sweetheart, in . . ." but the lavish credits failed to compensate for the poor quality of the movies.[92] Back at Biograph by the year's end, Pickford appeared in two films that, together, crystallized her appeal as a new type of ingénue. *The Female of the Species* (1912) is typical Griffith fare: a finely constructed, grimly sentimental tale about innate human depravity redeemed by mother love. Yet Pickford's pugnacious sprite excels at demonstrating her physical capacity to deal with obstacles. Employing the more restrained style she thought translated best on film, her character appears to inhabit a different film than her female costars, who weep and roll their eyes with jealousy and fear throughout.[93] Her last film at Biograph, *The New York Hat* (1912), displayed her gift for leavening tales of romantic pathos with comedic touches that capitalized on and modernized the era's enormously popular sentimental literature about girls' struggles to come of age. Pickford's performance and the script, the first by future star scenarist Anita Loos, convey the genuine, if comical, significance of acquiring "the New York hat." The film deftly reveals this small piece of big-city life as a symbol of a world that valued young women's desires for more autonomy. Settlement house reformer Jane Addams similarly interpreted the significance of working girls' fashion choices, declaring, "Through the huge hat, with its wilderness of bedraggled feathers, the girl announces to the world that she is here, she is ready to live, to take her place in the world."[94]

In 1913 Pickford returned to Broadway to play a lead in Belasco's production of *A Good Little Devil*, using the move to gain greater recognition for both herself and the artistry of her craft. Although Pickford later claimed Griffith's domineering personality and preference for "wishy-washy heroines" drove her from Biograph, she became the "NEW BELASCO STAR" in one such role.[95] Demonstrating the short memory of celebrity culture, the press immediately passed Lawrence's nicknames on to Pickford, hailing her as the "BIOGRAPH GIRL" and the "Maude Adams of the 'Movies.'"[96] Pickford used her new theatrical legitimacy to make the case for the superiority of film acting.[97] According to Pickford, "film plays" offered greater artistic, financial, and personal rewards, thereby providing the best opportunity for ambitious working girls. "For years the 'movies' have been looked upon as the inevitable finish of the has been actor," noted the *New York American*, "but according to Miss Pickford—no more." "You can't fool the camera," she declared in one of many reports describing why "This 'Maude Adams of the Movies' Says Self-Reproduction on the Films Can Do More Than Any Director."[98] Such statements underscored that no Svengali controlled her talent behind the scenes. "I have had many years of technical training in the best possible schools of experience," Pickford remarked after her Broadway debut; "it wasn't as if I were a novice or a debutante."[99] Her press also emphasized the masculine concerns that motivated this "Daddy of the Family, Not Old Enough to Vote."[100] The "very small salary" she earned during her first stint on Broadway had led her to work at Biograph years earlier, she explained to a noted theater critic. "The larder was empty. What else could I do?" In short, the theater was "so much harder than acting for the movies." Film work also promoted domestic harmony, since "'Little Mary' and Her Husband" now led a settled life with enough money to enjoy their leisure time.[101] Yet Pickford also credited her hardscrabble theatrical start with her current success: "I am certain that I could not today at my age run the picture company that I do without the struggle" of her life on stage.[102]

Pickford's Broadway stardom made her a singular commodity: a proven film attraction who carried the imprimatur of the legitimate stage.[103] Film producer Adolph Zukor liked the combination. Like Laemmle, Zukor was another recent addition to the ranks of independent producers working outside Edison's trust. The handsome, soft-spoken, and impeccably mannered Hungarian came to the United States as a poor youth, made a tidy sum as a cloak manufacturer in New York, and then invested his profits in nickelodeons.[104] Not much taller than the diminutive Pickford, both immigrants wore their competitive drives lightly and concentrated as much on the long-term potential of motion pictures as on immediate gains.

After Zukor moved from exhibition to production in 1912, the name of the company he founded—Famous Players—made plain his intention to feminize films by luring women into the audience with stars. In order to "kill" what he called "the slum tradition in movies," he focused on making longer movies that appropriated the prestige of well-known stage players in adaptations of equally distinguished plays.[105] He encapsulated the aim in the dictum that he would showcase only "Famous Players in Famous Plays." In 1912 Zukor executed the plan, financing and distributing Sarah Bernhardt in film adaptations of her signature plays, *Queen Elizabeth* and *Camille*. But the Bernhardt venture offered a surprising lesson: stature on stage did not guarantee a following on film. "Movie" audiences had a mind of their own, Zukor learned, and the clearest expressions of their tastes ran to ingénues like Lawrence and Pickford and serial queens like Mary Fuller, star of the first action-adventure episodic serial *What Happened to Mary?* (1912). After parlaying the association with Bernhardt into an alliance with the respected Broadway producer Daniel Frohman, Zukor purchased the rights to film *Little Devil* with an eye toward approaching Pickford about joining Famous Players. "The screen public will choose its favorites. There will be a star system rivaling—maybe outshining—that of the stage," he prophesized to Mary and Charlotte over lunch. Pickford needed little pleading, having witnessed how the "young girls [who] rushed up and said 'Isn't this Mary Pickford?'" at the stage door wanted to meet Little Mary of the screen, not Juliet of the boards.[106] And so, "after a much heated negotiation" over terms, the two incipient titans formed a partnership in the summer of 1913 founded on the belief that the industry's future lay in nurturing the relationship between audiences and stars.[107]

From the start, Pickford and Zukor's collaboration sought to capitalize on the interest fans showed in her rapscallion ingénues. After returning to motion picture work, she played three sharp-witted scamps of humble origins in action-adventure stories that tethered her star's advance to that of her sex's. In *The Bishop's Carriage* (1913), *Caprice* (1913), and *Hearts Adrift* (1914), Pickford played, respectively, an orphan who steals to survive before triumphing on the stage, a mountain girl who captures the heart of a wealthy beau after great difficulty, and the survivor of a shipwreck who starts a family with a man only to have his wife's arrival prompt her suicide.[108] Although these films are lost, the traces that remain exhibit the imprint of the classic Pickford screen type: a fearless, funny, lovely guttersnipe whose poundings by fate bind her audience to her in sympathy and love. These films employed a variation of the melodramatic mode that I call romantic melodramas, whose production swelled along with feature films. Taken up by many of the most popular actresses of the day, romantic melodramas tracked the exploits of a strong-willed heroine attempting to make her way in a hostile world. Charting their heroines' risky adventures along the path to maturity, they required the display of physical comedy, emotional pathos, and derring-do and often abruptly concluded with their heroines clasped in the arms of the right man. Yet however conventional their endings, the action of these melodramas typically focused on women's adventures rather than on capturing the heart of a man, the plot long used to narrate women's lives.[109]

The part Pickford played in *Tess of the Storm Country* (1914) crystallized the appeal of heroines in romantic melodramas. Indeed, tomboy Tess proved so popular that Pickford remade the film as an independent producer at United Artists in 1922. A motherless urchin, Tess is the daughter of a fish poacher who gets framed for a murder. While he languishes in jail, Tess fights off the true killer's attempt to force her into marriage, rescues an unwed pregnant girl from drowning herself, delivers her baby, agrees to raise it, and confers grace upon the dying child when a minister refuses. The film's end features Tess reuniting with the wealthy beau she spurned earlier for his doubts about her moral character. The role showcased her ability to combine contrasting moral qualities into an inoffensive whole: hers was a virtuous rascal, a hoyden of preternatural self-control, a young woman whose mane of golden, Pre-Raphaelite curls telegraphed her sensuality and grace.

From its first frame, *Tess* announced its intention to satisfy female fans' expectations for a rousing romantic melodrama in which a young, beautiful girl saves the day—and then gets her guy. The film's opening credits read: "Daniel Frohman Presents America's Foremost Film Actress, Mary Pickford, in the famous tale of woman's heroism, 'Tess of the Storm Country' by Grace Miller White."[110] Reviews confirmed *Tess* was a feminine affair, calling it "a story by a woman, of a woman, and for women," though conceding the movie was "for men too."[111] In highlighting the film's relationship to White's best-selling novel, the movie aimed to draw the large readership for these novels into movie houses. Future films turned the strategy into a near-formula, as Pickford produced popular "growing girl" novels like *Rebecca of Sunnybrook Farm* (1917), based on Kate Douglas Wiggin's 1903 novel, and *Daddy-Long-Legs* (1919), written by Jean Webster in 1912. Often these films were adapted, written, and in some cases even directed by Frances Marion, Pickford's close friend and one of the era's most successful screenwriters.[112] Given the engrained habit of viewing Pickford as playing innocent children, it is crucial to emphasize the independent, spirited, and adult personalities of most of her heroines. Of her fifty-two feature films, Pickford played a child in seven and remained a child in only three.[113] More typically, whether based on literary adaptations or on original screenplays, as with *The Little American* (1917) and *The Love Light* (1921), Pickford's romantic melodramas featured young women struggling to find happiness and to restore order in a chaotic world.

Zukor called Mary Pickford "the first of the great stars," undoubtedly because the success of *Tess of the Storm County* lifted Famous Players "onto the high road," paving the way for the vertically integrated, monopolistic structure that characterized the studio system of Hollywood's so-called classical era.[114] Pickford used *Tess* to negotiate terms in January 1915 that included a salary of $2,000 a week and an equal share of her productions' profits. Unbeknownst to Pickford, film exhibitors absorbed her raise by paying more for her films than others released by Famous Players' distributor, Paramount. "Block-booking" offered a more efficient means to monopolize the business than the Edison Trust's interminable legal wrangling. By forcing exhibitors to purchase less desirable movies to secure a favored star, block-booking made Pickford the "nucleus around which [Zukor] built his whole program," in William de Mille's words.[115] When she caught on to the practice in 1916, she demanded another raise and a host of concessions that afforded her greater artistic control.[116] Zukor's decision to meet her terms reflected his belief that stars—as the most reliable predictor of box office returns—were also the key element in the industry's profit structure.[117] But Paramount's head balked at Pickford's salary, believing that exhibitors and audiences would revolt at the higher prices it entailed. Rather than lose Pickford, Zukor seized control of distribution by merging with a rival company owned by Jesse Lasky.[118] Combined, the Famous Players–Lasky Corporation accounted for nearly three-quarters of Paramount's product, allowing FPL to control the company.[119] Pickford's revised contract at the end of 1916 guaranteed her the greater of either a million-dollar salary or half the profits of her films, the right to select her director and supporting cast, and created Artcraft as a separate "star series" for her work.

The development was widely reported as making Pickford, "The Latest Addition to Our Actor Managers" and the leading exemplar of a broader trend. By the next year, *Photoplay*'s editor James Quirk decried the effect of this "'her own company' epidemic" on the industry's health.[120] Put differently, Pickford's star may have burned the brightest and lasted longest, but many other female celebrities glimmered around her light. Indeed, a disproportionate number of the players who earned the interest of audiences during the era of silent features were other women.[121] "Remember this was the day of *women*," scenarist Lenore Coffee recalled, "Beautiful women in full flower."[122] Clearly, actors like Charlie Chaplin, William Hart, Wallace Reid, and swashbuckler Douglas Fairbanks, who became Pickford's second husband in 1920, were huge stars. But if the stars of lower-prestige Western films and comedies are set aside, the list of those capable of opening either a movie or an independent film company remains heavily skewed toward the leading ladies of the day. Actresses had a near-monopoly over leading roles in adventure serials and the romantic and society melodramas that became the industry's first prestige features, films that coincided with the star system's development.[123]

The persona of the era's greatest serial queen and Pickford's personal heroine—Pearl White—displayed how important women with virile personas were to the star system's development. Pickford called herself "a devoted fan" of White.[124] Although White probably never set foot in California, Pickford claimed to have encountered her on a train bound for Los Angeles in 1914. "In awe I watched her enter the club car, light a cigarette, and in the presence of all these men, raise a highball to her lips," she recalled, relishing her identification with a woman whose persona was a running rebuke to propriety. The publicity surrounding Pickford's Broadway stardom associated her with serial queens like White: "You have seen her rough riding on the western plains. You have watched her during thrilling moments on runaway motorcars and flying machines. And of course you tried to find out her name and failed." White's example also influenced Pickford's answer to a query about how she kept in shape. "I used to ride broncos, drive racing cars, swim dangerous rapids and slide down precipices."[125]

As the first film genre designed to appeal to women, serials featured young women whose western toughness and virility shaped their allure with both sexes. Released in both print and film formats on a weekly or monthly basis, short serial films were held together by an ongoing adventure plot. Actresses went uncredited as was still customary. But the journalistic discourse that ran alongside the print versions of serial films made Mary Fuller, Helen Holmes, and White into the first international

FIGURE 6. A general publicity photograph of Mary Pickford emphasizing her tough serial-queen side, c. 1922. Courtesy of Margaret Herrick Library, Academy of Motion Picture Arts and Sciences, Beverly Hills.

film stars. Beginning with Mary Fuller in the first female-centered serial thriller, *What Happened to Mary* (1912–1913), stories about these actresses celebrated how their real-life heroism inspired their parts; they were said to perform their own stunts after all.[126] Edna Vercoe, a teenage fan in Chicago, filled her "movy album" with stories about all three actresses' remarkable bravery and romantic successes. "Mary Fuller a Real Heroine," declared one article about Fuller's protection of the cast and crew from snakes during a recent shoot.[127] "Miss Fuller finds that her proficiency in riding, shooting, and other outdoor sports" was "most helpful in creating many of her parts," announced another.[128] Such reporting indicates why most film scholars agree that the focus on these women's authentic bravery and athleticism sold fans "a fantasy of female power." But most also concur that this picture was tempered by an "equally vivid exposition of female defenselessness and weakness" that required the intervention of a strong, male hand for eventual success.[129] Such a view captures the ambivalence that these heroines often provoked, but it misses how female fans may have also enjoyed the erotic tension produced by watching these conventionally feminine-looking but manly-acting heroines oscillate between aggression and subservience, pleasure and pain. Moreover, as specifically western heroines, these actresses needed to be able to both cause and tolerate acute physical distress in order to prove their valor and achieve the type of progress equated with the continent's conquest. This ability was a hallmark of the iconic masculinity associated with western heroes from Davy Crockett to William "Buffalo Bill" Cody. Silent western films exaggerated and then spread the association of modern "Americanism" with sensationally mobile men whose violent actions made possible the nation's continental claim.[130]

The longest-running serial, *The Hazards of Helen* (1914–1917), promoted a similar vision of modern American women. A cursory glance at the extant prints of *Hazards* displays the mise-en-scène of a modern Western, as giant locomotives, fleet horses, speedy motorcycles, and rifle-toting good and bad guys track back and forth across the dusty open spaces of California.[131] Like the men with whom she works, Holmes confronts constant tests of her daring, bravery, and endurance as she attempts to tame her harsh environment. A telegraph operator charged with protecting a railroad station under continual assault, Helen is the film's lone female, a woman who rides, shoots, rescues, and is rescued by her fellows in a landscape in which outlaws abound. The publicity about *Hazards*' first lead, Helen Holmes, emphasized her identity as a genuine westerner, born in "her father's private car somewhere between Chicago and Salt Lake" and raised "in the railroad yards."[132] An excellent horsewoman reputed to perform her own stunts, Holmes insisted that doing so was just "one of the demands upon a leading woman that must be met" without "losing sympathy or that air of femininity of which we are all so proud."

FIGURE 7. Helen Holmes on a postcard for fans, c. 1912.
Courtesy of Margaret Herrick Library, Academy of Motion
Picture Arts and Sciences, Beverly Hills.

By that, she explained, "I mean the heroic side, deeds of valor, based on the
highest ideals."[133] Their identification with the West—a region that valued toughness and endurance in either sex—smoothed serial queens'
display of a type of overtly sexy American girl rarely seen on screens at
the time. "This slim, seductively rounded young woman with the luring
lips and the 'come-hither' eyes, looked to be a most dangerous person,"
one piece about Holmes tempted. Others described her in more conven-

FIGURE 8. Helen Holmes and J.P. MacGowan shooting an episode of *The Hazards of Helen* (1913). Courtesy of Margaret Herrick Library, Academy of Motion Picture Arts and Sciences, Beverly Hills.˙

tionally romantic terms, detailing her marriage to the serial's director, J.P. MacGowan, and decision to adopt a baby girl.[134] Yet marriage and motherhood produced not fewer public responsibilities but more. When MacGowan fell ill in 1915, Holmes took charge of directing, writing, and managing *Hazards;* in 1917 the two started their own film company.

Actress Ruth Roland was another western daredevil whose international popularity displayed the appeal of this model of American womanhood to audiences worldwide. By most accounts, Roland's popularity was second only to Pearl White's. Both women were actress-writer-producers. Between 1911 and 1915, both were also the only women credited with earning spots alongside male Western film stars in popularity contests in a budding film genre that mostly targeted boys.[135] Both also gained fame as serial queens working with the French film company Pathé. "The man sits in his office from nine to five dictating letters, invariably pines to be riding a spirited horse out West in the sixties or seventies and dodging redskins on the warpath," *Photoplay* explained. "That's why Pearl White, Ruth Roland, and Maire Walcamp have a following

FIGURE 9. Ruth Roland riding her horse Joker in a publicity photograph sent to fans, c. 1912. Courtesy of Margaret Herrick Library, Academy of Motion Picture Arts and Sciences, Beverly Hills.

from Oshkosh to Timbuctoo [*sic*]. . . . In India Pearl White is the most popular of all the film stars and serials are about the only form of cinema that the natives will flock to see."[136] Born into a theatrical family in San Francisco, Roland took to the boards at age five, moving to Los Angeles to live with an aunt after her actress-mother died. Eight of her eleven serials were Westerns that showcased her equestrian skills on her horse Joker.[137] Chinese advertisements trumpeted Roland's western American athleticism: "Riding on a furious horse climbing the cliff as if walking on flat land, her talents are unsurpassable." Other publicity emphasized her talent as "a business woman of the first water." Roland also created her own production company, writing, producing, and starring in serials like *The Timber Queen* (1922). Later she put her fortune to work in real estate, buying "a tract of land between Universal City and Hollywood" that she subdivided and sold to "her fellow workers in the movie industry."[138] After largely retiring from the screen in the late 1920s, Roland became a prominent entrepreneur who promoted women's business opportunities until her early death in 1937.

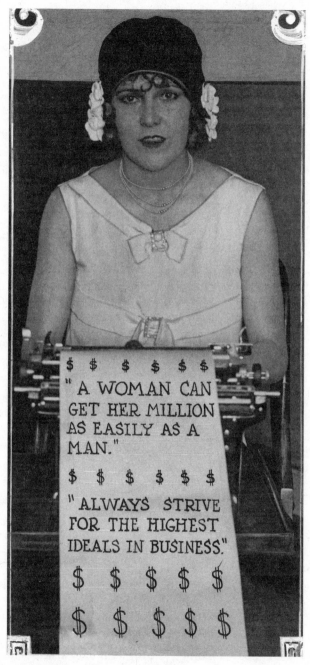

FIGURE 10. Ruth Roland, real estate entrepreneur, promoting women's business opportunities by writing "how to get rich maxims" for women in Los Angles, c. 1928. Courtesy of Margaret Herrick Library, Academy of Motion Picture Arts and Sciences, Beverly Hills.

Pearl White's emergence as a star in *The Perils of Pauline* (1914) has obscured her image as a heroine whose fame also depended on her incarnation of a western persona capable of enduring intense distress.[139] The serial best recalled today, *Perils* ensconced White among the East Coast elite, playing an orphaned heiress whose guardian plots her assassination in order to claim her fortune. Yet White's persona was composed of equal parts western toughness and cosmopolitan glamour, ensuring her fans knew that "Pearl White . . . is quite another person" than Pauline.[140] Publicity about White and her loyal, love-struck costar, Crane Wilbur, dominated Edna Vercoe's scrapbooks. Indeed, White reported that her fan mail was "mostly from women," including more than a "few mash notes."[141] These stories, as well as White's autobiography, *Just Me* (1919), focused on her western upbringing and stressed her rural, hardscrabble start in a "lonely log cabin" in the "Ozark Mountains of Missouri."[142] They also explained how White cultivated her remarkable athleticism during an adolescent tenure as "a bareback rider" in the circus where she perfected the equestrian skills that led to her first film breaks in shorts like *The Horse Shoer's Girl* (1910). "Oh for a girl that could ride a horse like Pearl White," swooned one young man, indicating her appeal to both sexes. After viewing a serial, one woman recalled that White "had done things the like of which I had never dreamed. She became my idol." Her love of White sparked filial rebellion, as her father had prohibited watching serials at "the 'houses of iniquity'," as he called movie houses.[143]

Just such reactions explained why some accused serial queens of encouraging immoral behavior among their female fans.[144] "I have always liked pretty women," explained a woman in a "motion picture autobiography" that sociologist Herbert Blumer collected from Chicago youths for the Payne Film Study (PFS) in 1929. "When I'd see them in the movies I positively would try to act like them. . . . I think the movies have a great deal to do with the present day so-called 'wildness.'"[145] The first large-scale effort to document the effect of movies on youth, the PFS responded to mounting alarm among cultural custodians about movie stars' displacement of traditional models of authority among the young. In the accounts offered by one hundred moviegoers about their habits and preferences from 1915 to 1929, women struck with what *Moving Picture World* called "serialitis" described an experience that supports film critic Elizabeth Cowie's thesis that the process of identification stems from fans sharing "a structural relation of desire" with characters—in this case, with their independent pursuit of sex and adventure.[146] The

Les Vedettes de Cinema
55 _ PEARL WHITE

FIGURE 11. Pearl White on a postcard for French fans, c. 1918.
Courtesy of Margaret Herrick Library, Academy of Motion
Picture Arts and Sciences, Beverly Hills.

account of one self-described "naturally reserved" woman displayed the
intense empathy produced by "following up some serial . . . three or
four nights a week." "I started, I believe, to suffer as much as the girl of
the story did," she admitted, adding, "I admired Miss White for her daring and courage. . . . I can recall distinctly saying to myself, 'Oh, what a
Lucky Girl to have enough money to take a trip like that—a trip across
the wild desert. . . . Oh, how daring! If only it were I!'"[147] Another,

Chicago girl recalled how her "idols" "gave me an inkling of what I could do with that sense of adventure of mine." "All summer this long legged girl in her teens, who should have been learning to bake and sew for her future husband, ran wild," becoming a "bold, brazen hussy" who pursued the men she liked. "When I came away to college instead of getting married . . . I definitely proved that I had no sense."[148]

The personas of vamps, another type that attracted much fanfare before the war, grappled more explicitly with women's sexuality. But the publicity surrounding vamps stressed the adult and distinctly foreign identity of the actresses who played them. Their identities as non-Anglos and foreigners linked the vamp to the femme fatale type so prevalent in fin de siècle European culture. "Grab everything you want and never feel sorry for anyone but yourself," was how one vamp, played by Louise Glaum in *Sex* (1920), summed up their general philosophy.[149] Like the femme fatale, the vamp was an amoral predator who used her sexual power to triumph over weak-willed men. Many films about vamps featured their destruction of a man who exercised the day's sexual double standard, which permitted men's libertinism with less respectable women. The vamp emerges unscathed after cynically using that double standard to get what she wants. Her forgettable leading men, who represent generic stand-ins for a sort of everyman elite, are left wrecked on the shoals of her sexual power.[150] Actress Theda Bara—initially described as half French, half Arab—became synonymous with the type after the release of *A Fool There Was* (1915).[151] Olga Petrova, whose vamps were nearly as well known as Bara's, was exclusively promoted as "a European star." "Madame Petrova is truly an international character," her press assured fans in 1917, "having been born in Warsaw, educated in Paris, London, and Brussels."[152] Fashioned as dark exotics, Bara, Glaum, and Petrova's location outside the American racial mainstream supported their more sexually graphic representations, suggesting why they openly endorsed not just woman suffrage but also feminism, a new concept associated with women's interest in sexual freedom. A widely publicized statement by Bara called her destruction of men a long overdue vengeance for her sex. "Women are my greatest fans. I am in effect a feministe," she declared.[153]

The vamp and the serial queen's shared expression of sexual virility and physical prowess placed their stars on the most volatile boundary that actresses performed in their redefinition of the public woman. A playful story entitled "Lady Gunman" savored explaining the connection created by their taste for masculine conquest. In real life, both vamp Louise Glaum and serial queen Mary Fuller could "handle a six-gun with all the sincerity of Douglas Fairbanks himself," readers were assured. Ellis Oberholtzer, head of Pennsylvania's powerful state film censorship board, objected to just such promotions. In a tract written to channel the growing dismay about the movies' moral influence, Oberholtzer charged that vamps, "sex photoplays," and serial-queen pictures provided the most damning evidence of the need for federal control. Oberholtzer decried how the typical serial depicted its heroine "in high air; in a sewer without an outlet; under straps on a log while the saw draws nearer and nearer." "If I were to travel the country over I should not know where to find women who conceal revolvers in their blouses, or in the drawers of their dressing-tables" or a woman who grasps "an iron from the fire-set on the hearth or seizes the inevitable paper knife to slay the villain, her lover rising in time to take the blame for the crime."[154]

As movie production settled around Los Angeles after 1915, publicity promoted its new habitat as a western frontier that fostered this kind of fearless femininity. "Out in Culver City the girls are growing militant," was how one fan magazine described the behavior of some dare-devil actresses in this new locale: "quick on the trigger, and not one of them is afraid of the smell of [gun]powder—they're used to various kinds."[155] "The 'feel' of Hollywood at this time was like carnival, or the way one feels when the circus is coming to town, only the circus was always there," Lenore Coffee recollected, echoing a sentiment shared by many who attempted to capture the ambience created when the flickers came to town.[156] One early account tracked a reporter wandering around the "big, bustling Western" ranches-cum-studios in "Motion-Picture Land." Here, "in the dazzling California sunshine" a "bewildering democracy" prevailed among players. Here, playacting and reality fused. "No part of the world" was free from the "invasion" of these players, whose work spilled into the cityscape so often that one looked about for a camera when anything happened "unexpectedly."[157]

Another article in *Photoplay* used the mythic history of the West to depict the sex-specific opportunities of this frontier circus by the sea. "The early years of the twentieth century brought to American women the same vast, almost fabulous chances that came to their grandfathers," a writer interviewing Pearl White intoned.[158] "What the expansion of the West and the great organization of industry opened up to many a young man," the article continued, "the motion picture spread before such young girls as were alert enough, and husky enough, and apt enough to take advantage of it." "With the exception of Mary Pickford,

I can think of no girl who has reaped her field of chance so completely, opulently, securely, as Pearl White." White's good fortune derived from a spirit that made her a "female Alexander" bent on finding "new worlds to conquer." But her achievement was also cast in the more modern terms associated with corporate success: Pearl White possessed "that which is really the quality of few men: the true financial instinct." The actress-heroine of Rupert Hughes's *Souls for Sale* (1921), an early novel about the movie colony, defends her little sister's decision to run away and join her in Los Angeles in a manner straight out of the Pearl White mold. "All over the world was full of runaway girls striking out for freedom and for wealth and renown," the heroine of the novel thinks." "Let love wait! The men have kept us waiting for thousands of years, till they were ready. Now let them wait for us."[159]

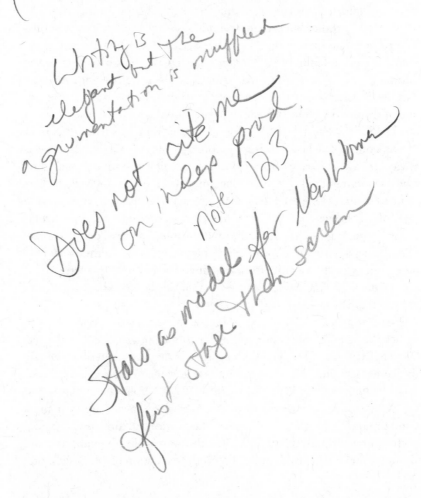

CHAPTER 2

Women-Made Women

Writing the "Movies" before Hollywood

We built the modern movie industry on the star system, but
the public made the stars

—Adolph Zukor

Prominent stories about Mary Pickford and Pearl White in magazines
like the *Ladies' Home Journal* and *Photoplay* augured the rise of the
type of journalism that the star system shaped and spread: celebrity reporting as mainstream news. Advertising "movie" personalities—the
nickname that stuck despite many insiders' preference for the higher-
toned "photoplay" and "motion picture"—quickly became essential to
the industry's profits. Carl Laemmle and Adolph Zukor won the gamble
that audiences would pay more to get closer to favorites, teaching a lesson that became an early axiom of movie production: stars best forecast
box office success. Thus, women's preeminence in the movies' celebrity
culture emerged from the shared assumption that women mostly decided which of the era's exploding number of consumer goods succeeded.
The idea positioned the female consumer at the center of the struggle
between an established ethos of production that prized the industriousness necessary to produce a mountain of things and an emerging ethos
of consumption that celebrated the abandon needed to buy them (possibly even on credit!). As many have shown, the nation's budding advertising industries often addressed this consumer as a paranoid, passive,
irrational conformist who needed the guidance of advertising elites to
navigate this new landscape of desire.[1]

But the movies more often addressed women as experts who understood their importance as figures who acted as the arbiters of what
counted as successful popular culture in modern times. "Three out of

every four of all cinema audiences are women. I suppose all successful novels and plays are also designed to please the female sex too," instructed film curator Iris Barry in *The Public's Pleasure* (1925). The alarm prompted by this idea, after all, generated much of the mounting concern over the feminization of American culture that intellectuals like Hugo Munsterberg expressed. Yet if the task is to explain the broad power of the mass culture consumed by women, rather than to judge its moral implications or aesthetic properties, then what becomes apparent is how it acted as a market domain that tirelessly discussed the problems and promises of managing a new womanhood. Put differently, in becoming a consumer bloc considered to share core interests and desires, movie fans participated in "an intimate public," in Lauren Berlant's influential formulation. Mass-mediated stories about movie personalities addressed fans as holding a common worldview, thereby cultivating a sense that women writers, celebrities, and readers were sharing confidences about their common travails and triumphs. Participation in this fan culture offered lessons not just about how to choose the right things but also about how to help each other survive and thrive in the wider world. Calling herself "a woman's woman" in one interview, Pickford noted in another: "I like to see my own sex achieve. My success has been due to the fact that women like the pictures in which I appear. I think I admire most in the world the girls who earn their own living. I am proud to be one of them."[2]

Women journalists writing in newspapers and fan magazines did the most to help their female readers imagine these movie personalities as women-made women.[3] The "moving picture has opened a great new field for women folk" where her "originality," "perseverance," and "brains are coming to be recognized on the same plane as [a] man's," declared Gertrude Price, one of several prominent female "moving picture experts," in the *Toledo News-Bee*.[4] In *Breaking into the Movies* (1927), publicist Virginia Morris explained how the industry's preoccupation with the female fan turned publicity writing into a field open to both sexes. Since "the large majority of film audiences consisted of women" eager to know about "the feminine star," producers decided "that the woman picture patron could be most easily reached by information written from the feminine angle."[5] The strategy of using women writers to appeal to other women was one of multiple tactics devised to attract more women into movie audiences during the 1910s. By 1914 motion picture editors and publicity departments advised theater owners that "women and girls" were the most avid followers of "motion picture news."[6] By the early 1920s, *Photoplay* claimed that women composed 75 percent of movie fans. One editorial extolled the movies as a "blessed refuge" for "the lonely girl" without "the money for expensive drama" after a hard day's work.[7] As a result, insiders imagined their ideal spectator as a young white woman eager to identify with role models who, however fantastically, reflected the changed condition under which they lived, worked, played, and dreamed.[8]

These writers created new western myths that appealed to these fans' desires, blending wish fulfillment and social reflection.[9] Journalists downplayed some aspects of women's accomplishments, such as their managerial roles, and exaggerated others, such as the frequency with which extras became stars. But, as women experts explained to women readers how ordinary women became extraordinary new women, they created a female-centered leisure space that reinforced two impressions: the movies aimed to help women satisfy their new desires, and fans' support of the industry furthered their ambitions as a sex. The social imaginary that emerged as a consequence mostly described these women-made women as shedding traditional ways of acting female to become "twentieth century," "modern," or "New Women," to use *Photoplay*'s preferred terms.[10] The common use both of contests that promised readers the chance to work alongside their favorite scenario writer, "cutter" (editor), or star in Los Angeles, and of inspirational interviews with female movie personalities allowed fans to imagine experimenting with their own self-transformation.[11]

No single writer in this era did as much as journalist and publicist Louella Parsons to explain to readers who mattered to the movies and why. This chapter uses Parsons's reporting to track the development of the celebrity discourse aimed at female fans. Parsons honed her craft by giving form to the figures inhabiting the movie landscape before the business of making pictures and Hollywood were synonymous.[12] Between 1915 and 1920, Parsons was among the first, and certainly the most successful, reporters to write a nationally syndicated daily column focused not on films, but on the news surrounding the industry and its stars. The industry had provided Parsons with the means to effect the kind of melodramatic, near-magical personal transformation that she later specialized in selling to readers. As a producer of this fan culture, she earned a following by describing the professional and personal activities of the industry's assertive, independent, resourceful, and glamorous female protagonists. And, increasingly, Parsons described the industry's new home in Los Angeles as a novel kind of western frontier that sought women adventurers. In helping to set the tone and content of the movie industry's relationship with women fans, she fashioned an image and role that afforded her a great deal of power. In the process, Parsons became at once agent and symbol, cause and consequence, of the industry's production of new ideas about femininity.

I

Born in 1881 in Dixon, Illinois, Parsons was the granddaughter of a woman's rights activist and the daughter of a "stage-struck girl."[13] Her first heroine was Nellie Bly, the stunt reporter who championed workingwomen and traveled the world, alone, in fewer than eighty days. Part of the first generation of middle-class women who benefited from broader access to higher education, Parsons attended college while working sporadically as a reporter and teacher. Like most of this cohort, she married later, at twenty-four, and then relinquished her ambition to write, moving with husband John Parsons to Burlington, Iowa, where she gave birth to her only child, Harriet. Her choices mirrored those made by most privileged white women in the era, women who skirted the volatile topic of mixing work outside the home with a family inside it by seemingly sacrificing one for the other.[14] Her decision to leave her philandering husband and move to Chicago in 1910 set Parsons on a path closer to the one trod by less privileged urban migrants. Working as a secretary at the *Chicago Tribune,* her $9-a-week salary barely supported her small family. Yet, like many workingwomen, she managed almost nightly trips to the movies, reveling in a fan culture that nurtured her ambition to write.

The few fan magazines that existed in the early 1910s touched lightly on the lives of famous personalities, but lavished attention on scenario writing, offering tips to hopefuls, contests with cash prizes for the best stories, and tales about women who succeeded at the job. Female-authored scenarios poured into film studios, convincing Essanay to hire an editor to evaluate the material.[15] Parsons got the job. Now earning $20 a week, she brought her mother to Chicago to care for Harriet. Parsons loved the work. She read scripts and wrote more than one hundred scenarios. Most important, she turned herself into an authority on the new field, publishing *How to Write for the Movies* in 1915. The book was a hit and Parsons sold the serialization rights to the *Chicago Herald-Record.* With her job at Essanay threatened by an "efficiency man," she flirted her way into a part-time gig at the newspaper, writing the Sunday column "How to Write Photo Plays." After the series' success, she talked her way into a job as a columnist who offered a "behind the scenes look" at the "personalities 'up front'" in motion pictures.[16]

The nationally syndicated daily column that Parsons wrote beginning in 1915 partially presented the movies in ways that prefigured how Hollywood's star system helped to spread the consumer ethos that exploded during the 1920s.[17] Her coffee-klatch tone and "just folks" manner suited the needs of expanding corporate media structures that sought to preserve an intimate feel despite their scale, blurring the lines separating hard (political) from soft (cultural) news, city from country, working from middle class in order to attract the largest possible market audience. As a late-Victorian middle-class woman from the countryside turned single working professional middle-aged mother in the city, Parsons was ideally suited to address the target consumer culture coveted: a cross-class, multigenerational audience of white women with a modicum of disposable cash.[18] All these women led "monotonous and humdrum lives" and craved "glamour and color," according to the advertising trade journal *Printer's Ink*.[19] Parsons's column presented the industry's female celebrities' personal relationships and work lives as designed to fill these needs.

Yet in ways that pointed to the industry's Janus-faced relationship to modern femininity, the mass-mediated fan culture of the movies that Parsons helped to create also treated readers as intimates in a conversation about the pleasures and perils of modern womanhood. A special new series in the *Herald-Record*, "How to Become a Movie Actress," demonstrated the relationship that Parsons cultivated. The paper's announcement of the series assured readers that Parsons's "technical knowledge of the game" and status as "an intimate of all the big movie stars" made her uniquely "qualified to give inside information to girls who are eager to enter the motion picture field." Thus Parsons used the rhetoric of expertise to establish her authority as an instructor in the art of composing a successful personality.[20] But she adopted the stance of a warm, motherly guide rather than the distant scold who later became classic to advertising. Her chatty, tongue-in-cheek style encouraged readers to consider themselves her intimates, thereby nurturing the kind personal connection that fans sought with movie stars.[21] The column's promotion also emphasized that Parsons sold lessons in nothing less than personal transformation. "Others have become rich and famous. Why not you?"[22] The assumptions built into the column testified to the limits of the kind or romantic individualism she preached, while promising women a means to imagine transcending the typical boundaries imposed by gender.

Indeed, the series seemed designed to induce a self-reflective reverie in female readers that encouraged them to take their daydreams to heart. Its opening prelude whispered, "*Dreams—dreams most fascinating to young women all over America are coming true every day. Do you dream of becoming a motion picture actress and actually plan to be one?*"[23] If so, such readers were not to worry, since "*not a day passes but some girl who has shared your fondest fancies is made exquisitely happy.*" The format that followed involved Parsons soliciting tips and advice in short interviews with those already successful in the movies, allowing her to advertise the movies' women personalities as modern celebrities by fleshing out their exploits both on and off screen. Equally important, she then used their personal experiences to create a new genre of success stories for girls whose master plot centered on presenting the movies as a place where those with "brains and beauty," in the parlance of the day, and a little luck could reinvent the terms of feminine success.[24] Parsons, and those she interviewed in "How to Become Movie Actress," treated the ambition to become a star with matter-of-fact aplomb, contradicting the notion that such expectations were at all fabulous. Indeed, in Parsons's hands, the movies' central product was coming-of-age stories for girls that promised happily-ever-after endings. The fact that these stories offered young women the chance to win interesting, lucrative work that celebrated their femininity made them unique. Casting young women in the role of adventurer, Parsons sought "to inspire the ambitious" by making a romance of their quest for individual success.[25]

The column thrived by communicating a host of contradictory messages about the qualities women would need to achieve their ends. This approach in part imitated, in part further twisted the ethics of chance and rational striving that had long coexisted in the coming-of-age tales told to boys.[26] Some of the advice sought to inculcate in young women the so-called masculine values, like aggression and self-promotional skills, which the nation's corporate order prized. Determine "if you genuinely photograph well," Parsons instructed, and ascertain which studio "you think you fit best with, and then send them your picture and a letter saying that you would like a chance to prove your worth as an extra." Here the hopeful's fate depended on possessing an image whose value others recognized. The column also prescribed the traditional path of starting at the bottom, as an "extra girl," in order to reach the top. Yet even as such a course paid tribute to the logic of the Protestant work ethic, chancy factors such as "pictorial beauty" and talent entered into the equation of what determined an aspirant's eventual fate. "Start as an extra in some good studio," Parsons quoted Pearl White's costar Crane Wilbur as having instructed. But Wilbur quickly tempered this statement with one that indicated an awareness that success might lay outside an individual's control. "If you have talent they'll find you quick enough."[27] The column's contradictory messages about how to get ahead—it preached diligent effort in climbing up from the bottom even as it celebrated instant results tied to magical forces outside one's control—were a commonplace of the Protestant work ethic and of the times. Stories by writers like Horatio Alger required that young men exhibit a commitment to the virtues of constant industriousness, thrift, sobriety, and moral rectitude in order to qualify as worthy heroes. Yet, as the plots of these books unfolded, ultimately "luck and patronage" became the architects of the hero's good fortune.[28] Here the relationship between form, as disciplined effort, and content, as talent and a pretty face, grew even more attenuated, as a girl armed only with confidence in her perfect picture went forth to triumph in one of the nation's fasting-growing industries.

These contradictions often intensified when the figure of the male movie director, portrayed as a patron of aspirants, entered the column, causing Parsons to proffer advice that, willy-nilly, wove strategies long considered innately feminine with others long deemed masculine. The advice to "find out the name of the man who holds your destiny in his hands" sounded a conventional note by suggesting that hopefuls locate a Svengali-type master who could orchestrate their path to success. Yet Parsons delivered this pronouncement in the context of teaching aspirants the importance of making their own breaks. Armed with a name, she pragmatically suggested, one had "a much better chance." "Better still," she advised hopefuls to "discover when a big feature is slated for production. To succeed one must be both resourceful and inventive." Parsons solicited tips from D. W. Griffith, the director made famous by the critical praise and social controversy provoked by *The Birth of a Nation* (1915), a traditional melodrama about the era of Reconstruction that glorified the Ku Klux Klan's salvation of the South from Northern carpetbaggers and its white women from the rape of lascivious black men.[29] As described by Parsons, the "new Griffith doctrine," was simply a novel name for the old Pygmalion myth. According to Griffith, the best actresses emerged from "untrained" young women who followed a director's every command. Parsons also reported that directors Cecil B. DeMille and Thomas Ince had a preference for women willing to act as moldable clay. Their talent in shaping such raw material was said to have put "numberless untrained girls on the road to fame and success."[30] Yet even as these men underscored the importance of ladylike behavior on the set, all three also warned that manly "courage" was vital to succeeding in front of the camera.

Indeed, a fan following Parsons's column, or myriad other accounts that circulated about Pickford and the other actresses who worked with Griffith and DeMille, would have encountered many more stories about the control they exercised over men.[31] Certainly, as Parson's column evolved, she devoted far more space to describing women's individual struggles and accomplishments in breaking into the movies than to telling stories about men's role in the process. Written by, for, and about women, these stories predominantly framed the topic of what constituted a successful presentation of femininity in the context of *what other women* wanted to hear in an era in which the New Woman, feminism, and women's influence on popular culture were all topics of social controversy. In fact, when men entered Parsons's column at all, she was more often interested in demonstrating how women managed to get the upper hand. Her description of Clara Kimball Young's relationship with her director husband was one such instance. Parsons presented Young as the "Ideal Film Personality" whose "beauty and brains and wealth" made her the "Ideal of What Every Sixteen-Year-Old Girl Would Like to Possess."[32] "Neither one of us would be willing to submerge his individuality into the thoughts of the other one, no matter how much we love each other," she explained. Indeed, Young declared that although her husband was the director, "he is not always the boss. When I make up my mind I generally get what I want. Sometimes I have to argue with my good friend [producer] Mr. Selznick, my sweet mother, and my dear husband, but if it is for my ultimate good I GET it."[33]

Young's insistence on demanding her way fit neatly into the groove crafted by the stage's prima donnas. Indeed, movie stars like Young magnified this convention on both the silent screen and in the explosion of print that created the first movie stars' personas, making her a visible sign of modernity itself: a glamorous, individualized, and work-defined personality known for breaking and reassembling the codes governing feminine propriety.[34] Griffith, DeMille, and Ince—all former stage actors in the "player-centered institution" that the theater became by 1900—knew exactly what they were up against when confronting the industry's emerging female stars.[35] They also understood as well as any-one in the business the economic basis of these women's power. Virtu-ally everyone in the movies agreed that even the most famous director's name, as Griffith's indubitably was before Cecil B. DeMille's replaced it by 1920, meant little to the average fan and, hence, a movie's bottom line.[36] As Cecil's older brother, William de Mille, put it, since "the names of writers and directors meant nothing to the public, the only thing the customers could count on in advance to give them some de-gree of satisfaction for their money was the name of a favorite player whose work and personality they knew and liked." Only the star's name above the marquee, and the title emblazoned across it, translated into box office.[37] The *Exhibitors' Herald,* the trade paper for theater own-ers, emphasized this reality in a prominently displayed letter from a publicity director. "Take it or leave it," a man from Toledo, Ohio, de-clared, "the star system is what brings the shekels into your box office. This is a rule that might hang in the office of any theatre manager."[38]

For such reasons, Parsons's column emphasized that success in the movies depended on impressing other women as much as men. Par-sons's stories about director Lois Weber demonstrate the point. After visiting the set of her Universal production of *The Dumb Girl of Portici* (1915), starring ballerina Anna Pavlova, Parsons lauded Weber's "ex-ecutive ability," pronouncing her "the most famous woman director and photo playwright." By 1915 Weber was Universal's most famous director, male or female, with a style as distinctive as Griffith's.[39] An-other stage actress turned movie-writer-producer-director, Weber's per-sona stressed her respectability by focusing on her past as a former Salvation Army worker, and on her present as a married middle-class matron. This star image allowed Weber to exploit assumptions about respectable women's inherent moral superiority that smoothed her making films about volatile topics like abortion and birth control. Little wonder that Weber's co-worker at Universal, director Ida May Park, boasted in *Careers for Women,* a well-received 1920 vocational guide aimed at high school and college graduates, that there was "no finer calling for a woman" than directing movies.[40] Another interview de-tailed Weber's career trajectory: her start at Gaumont Film Studio in 1908 with her husband Phillips Smalley; their eventual move to the Rex Company to work with director Edwin Porter, who was said to bequest the production company to their "capable hands" upon his departure. When Rex became a Universal subsidiary in 1912, the couple became co–production heads, but it was Weber who built a national reputation as a filmmaker. "It's all up to Lois Weber," Parsons reported the director confiding; "I am blamed or praised whichever way the picture turns out. Phillips would efface himself entirely and make me director in chief." Parsons left no doubt about who was in charge, noting that Smalley "came to [Weber] for advice upon every question that presented itself." By the time a "distressed masculine voice" from the wardrobe department interrupted the interview, the kinds of gender inversions that flourished on motion picture sets were plain.[41]

Parsons was able to call Weber "the most famous woman director and photo playwright" at Universal, because eleven women directed more than 170 films from the studio's 1912 inception through 1919. The May 1913 opening of Universal City, the company's West Coast headquarters, displayed how publicizing the studio as a tourist attraction involved promoting it as a place that encouraged gender play. "Where Work Is Play and Play Is Work: Universal City, California, the Only Incorporated Moving Picture Town in the World, and Its Unique Features. 'Movie' Actresses Control Its Politics," declared the *Universal Weekly* in December 1913. "Linking work and play," historian Mark Garrett Cooper writes, "the corporate mythos of Universal City valued women who publically played with authoritative parts." A mock election staged by Universal City displayed one outcome when a group of actresses formed what the *Weekly* called "a 'Suffragette' ticket." Reports across the country claimed the suffragette ticket developed because actresses "from the East" were "keenly enthusiastic about exercising their rights of suffrage, recently conferred by the California State Legislature."[42]

Women's political participation in California was one of the many disorienting features that confronted Easterners. One of the first reports about the "big, bustling Western" ranches-cum-studios featured a dazed reporter's catalog of their Kaleidoscopic contents, including "a Japanese pagoda," "a Dutch village with windmills," "the ruins of a Scotch castle," "a New York tenement district," and "the largest private collection" of "jungle animals" "in the world."[43] Universal City's election of actress Laura Oakley as its new police chief and of Lois Weber as its mayor suited a landscape defined by its flair for gender ambiguity. The new Universal City that opened in 1915 supported these performances by including a day-care center and a school for workers' children. Universal City's administrators, called "some of the brainiest as well as the most beautiful women in America," likely understood the necessity of such measures in capitalizing on this self-consciously meritocratic environment's promise to support women's physical and occupational mobility.[44]

Even reporting that purported to temper the enthusiasm of hopefuls about heading to Los Angeles refused to discourage their investment in the success of movie personalities. "HOW ONE 'EXTRA GIRL' CLIMBED TO STARDOM" was the one tale in the "How to Become a Motion Picture Actress" column that sounded a pessimistic note, yet Parsons called it a story to "cheer the heart of every anxious to be photo-player."[45] A more accurate title for the interview with the former Chicago journalist Ruth Stonehouse would have been "HOW ONE 'EXTRA GIRL' *SHOT* TO STARDOM," since Parsons reported that she progressed from an extra girl with no experience to one of "Essanay's brightest stars" in eight short months. Despite her allegedly rapid ascent, Stonehouse confessed that she "felt like telling every girl to stay at home," warning those she called "the movie mad" that "the profession is crowded now . . . it will be survival of the fittest." Yet, Parsons interjected, "haven't you something to say to the poor girls whom you so cruelly condemn to stay at home? 'Tell them that a "pull" does not go in this business,'" she responded, "that unless they have the 'goods to deliver' to stay at home." Thus, even as Stonehouse warned readers that only the most deserving, industrious individuals could hope to triumph, the flavor of the piece encouraged young women to cast themselves into the fray. And indeed, after Stonehouse traded work as a leading lady at Essanay in Chicago for Universal City, she went on to direct herself in many movies, including a successful ten-episode series about a willful orphan named Mary Ann.[46] *Photoplay* later echoed Parsons's strategy, warning that the industry's rapid growth and consolidation meant writers would have "to be increasingly discouraging to the feminine youth of the land." Yet it also called fans' yearnings "to see themselves as they see their favorite stars . . . a very laudable ambition. In passing we might credit the screen with administering a knockout to the old fashioned pre-film days. . . . It is a golden lighted road to fame and fortune that had a dim counterpart yesterday in the way to stage success." The article concluded, "Every one of them has the chance to be a Mary Pickford or a Norma Talmadge."[47] As in all good adventure stories modeled on the dream of social mobility, obstacles met and conquered sweetened eventual success.

Parsons carefully edited her personal history to fit the inspirational lines of her column, crafting a persona that allowed her to stake out new prerogatives for women based on their association with traditional areas of feminine expertise. Published decades after she became a powerhouse in the movie industry, her autobiography sketched an ideal girlhood for one destined to guide young women toward new possibilities in a still-perilous world. This construction of her persona began with a (fictional) fatherless upbringing spent writing stories that, in good Victorian fashion, were "always violently on the side of 'a wronged girl.'" "This prejudice in favor of my sex has followed me along my entire career," she explained. Even as Parsons presented her job as distinctly feminine, she claimed for herself—and for the industry's "other career women"—the same "qualities of loyalty, square shooting, and straight thinking supposedly so exclusive of the masculine sex."[48] They might like to gossip with the girls, in other words, but the industry's female personalities were not frivolous, empty-headed narcissists who fecklessly stumbled their way into success. The title of her memoir, *The Gay Illiterate* (1944), simultaneously mocked and embraced just such stereotypes.

Despite the fact that her Sunday picture page was syndicated in eighteen other cities, Parsons lost her job when newspaper magnate William Randolph Hearst absorbed the *Chicago Herald-Record* into the *Chicago American*, sending the journalist to New York City in 1917. Parsons's country-to-city exodus from her small-town midwestern roots reflected the path taken by many of the women who created the "rural problem." Yet while women composed the majority of these migrants, reformers focused on addressing the problems of men, making a 1913 survey by the U.S. Department of Agriculture of "farm housewives" one of the few attempts to assess what sent them to cities and towns.[49] Women's replies to the USDA repeatedly expressed how the search for sociable work, aesthetic pleasures, and "the entertainments and amusements that the towns and cities offer" prompted their departure.[50] "Why do they come to the city?" sociologist Frances Donovan wondered of these young women that anxious commentators called "women adrift." "Because life is dull in the small town or on the farm and because there is excitement and adventure in the city. . . . The lure of the stage, of the movie, of the shop, and of the office make of it the definite El Dorado of the woman. It is her frontier and in it she is the pioneer." A prairie girl with artistic aspirations, driven to the city by the moral strictures and limited opportunities of small-town life, also became a stock literary protagonist associated with the movement that critic Carl Van Doren memorably called "the revolt from the village" school in 1921.[51] Such women's mobility, real and imagined, reflected the dra-

FIGURE 12. Louella Parson, c. 1924. Courtesy of Margaret Herrick Library, Academy of Motion Picture Arts and Sciences, Beverly Hills.

matic reversal in western migration patterns that had occurred by 1900, when the movement of native-born white girls to western cities first outpaced the boys.[52] But while Parsons increasingly pointed her readers west, at thirty-five, the self-supporting single mother headed east to the center of the publishing industry to find another job.

After working freelance for the fan magazine *Photoplay*, Parsons landed a job at the *New York Morning Telegraph* and was quickly promoted to editor of the motion picture section.[53] In this trade paper that rivaled *Variety*, she continued with her signature tone. Readers must have appreciated her confidences. The paper's Sunday film supplement doubled in size in less than two years. Her quick ascent in New York drew the attention of competitors. As a rival reporter at the city's oldest theatrical magazine, *The Clipper*, recalled, "By 1920 every motion picture columnist who got a break would automatically start gunning for her. Her column meant something. But I'll say this for her, she never pulled the knife first."[54] That same year Parsons accompanied her friend Olga Petrova—the writer, outspoken feminist, and film star best known for the vamp roles she played under the direction of filmmaker Alice Guy Blache—on a trip abroad. In London, Parsons contributed several columns to the British fan magazine *Picture-Goer,* which called her the "Queen of the American publicity writers" and "probably the most prolific writer of fan stuff in the States—which is going some."[55] Receiving the star treatment she dished out for others, Parsons had become a movie personality herself.

II

By the time Parsons got her big break, publishers like Joseph Pulitzer and William Randolph Hearst had reengineered the purpose, look, and tenor of many newspapers in ways that both mimicked and then helped to spread the mass-mediated movie fan culture created by journalists like Parsons. Pulitzer and Hearst published well-made daily papers that appealed to all readers, but especially the city's swelling numbers of blue- and white-collar workers, who as yet had no paper to call their own. Using bold headlines, illustrations, cartoons, and a narrative style that some called melodramatic, and others simply "sensational," the papers with the most spectacular circulation repackaged themselves to entertain as much as to inform or educate. This motivation transformed the newspaper, according to historian David Nasaw, into "an urban institution" that, "like the department store, the vaudeville theater, and the amusement park, transcended traditional categories of class, ethnicity, occupation, and neighborhood."[56] The rise of the city powered the rise of the new style of daily newspapers in other respects. Print offered metropolitan residents the feeling of keeping abreast of local goings-on, a need once satisfied by a trip down Main Street. Between 1850 and 1909, the jump in the number of daily papers almost perfectly mirrored the jump in the number of urban places in the United States. After 1910, the consolidation of papers into chains that cost Parsons her job in Chicago resulted in a steady slide in the total number of mastheads. But the business tactics developed by Hearst and his like continued to attract new readers. The circulation of daily papers outpaced the rate of urbanization after 1900. The use of wire and feature services by chains exploded in the new century, recasting newspapers again, now from an urban institution into a national one. By 1920 the same stories filled the minds of many men and women across the country and, with the advent of movies, around the world. E. W. Scripps, a pioneer in syndication services, summed up his formula for creating reproducible news: "Whatever else it is, our newspaper must be excessively interesting, not to the good, wise men and the pure in spirit, but to the great mass of sordid, squalid humanity. [Humanity] is passionate," he reminded his editors; "therefore the blood that runs in our veins and in our newspapers must be warm."[57]

Scripps's injunction to keep readers' blood near boiling with dramatic stories that spoke to their interests reflected the so-called melodramatic imagination that animated so much of the era's successful mass culture. The mode of expression had only gained momentum during a century of repetition in popular plays aimed at the theater's increasingly female fans, dime store adventure stories for boys, and the penny press.[58] When used in serialized fiction, performance, and news stories, the melodramatic mode attracted huge followings because, unlike classical literature and repertoire, melodrama located drama in the lives of average folks. Current usage associates melodrama strictly with "women's weepies," stories that stick close to hearth and home and register heightened emotionalism and sentimentality, but such tales composed only a small fraction of melodrama's substantial body. And, certainly to audiences in Hearst and Parsons's day, melodramas aimed at women fans displayed extreme emotions in a variety of genres and forms that dramatized the pursuit of something better by ordinary women. Next to production values, Hearst placed the convention of polarization—between good and evil, rich and poor, male and female—at the center of the style he used to increase circulation in his media empire–building years. "Spare no expense," he ordered his staff. "Make a great and continuous noise to attract readers; denounce crooked wealth and promise better conditions for the poor to keep readers."[59] When viewed from the ground, melodrama's popularity also signaled some of the most progressive features of modernism, as the hero's once singular, stentorian tones receded to make room for the clamorous din of many voices.

Certainly by 1912, stories in Hearst's evolving domain of newspapers, national magazines, and movies displayed the importance of women's tastes and female protagonists to their success. As the movies settled around Los Angeles, fictional heroines who hurled themselves into the fray were everywhere. As the coproducer of *The Perils of Pauline* (1914),

Hearst launched one of the best-recalled examples of the type in both his movies and his newspapers. The man who became Parsons's long-term, and beloved, employer in 1924 publicized each film episode's release in an illustrated Sunday feature the week before its filmic release.[60] A review in the *Literary Digest,* a weekly whose circulation and influence among the middle class crested in the twenties, summed up the differences between younger melodramatic heroines and their older sisters. Pauline was "the apotheosis of the old-time melodrama heroine," a girl who would have "perish[ed] ignominiously if faced by half the perils that surround her more advanced sister of the screen."[61] Another reporter noted that while "stars of the first magnitude" like White accounted for the serials' "almost unbelievable financial success," other factors helped as well. "Advertised all over the world in magazines, newspapers, and billboards" until "everybody knows that they exist," serial queens became inescapable symbols that tracked women's physical and professional mobility, as well as the new sexual dangers and freedoms it entailed.[62] Indeed, since discussions of stars' personas in fan culture depended on stories about players' private lives, motion picture sections in newspapers and fan periodicals had ample opportunity to describe their exploits in real life. Thus, by the time Parsons joined the *Morning Telegraph* in New York in 1917, she was well positioned to help fashion what counted as commercially viable news by spinning romantic melodramas about the exploits of these women workers out west.

Parsons new job coincided with America's entry into the Great War. After being ruled a business and not an art by the Supreme Court's *Mutual Film Corporation* decision in 1915, the movies demonstrated how potent their art, and artists, could be at the business of rallying support and raising money for the war effort.[63] Liberty Loan Films "left no doubt," Parsons crowed, "that the moving picture industry had placed a powerful weapon in the hands of the Government with which to spread American propaganda."[64] The government needed all the help it could get, since Woodrow Wilson had been re-elected president a year earlier on the platform "He Kept Us Out of War." "Never before," remembered scenarist William de Mille, "had the services and personalities of our well-known actors been so much in demand." Wilson may have "urged the whole population to 'give until it hurts,'" but de Mille thought it took the "emotional pleading of 'Little Mary' to bring home the bacon." The number of Liberty Loan bonds sold when Pickford, Douglas Fairbanks, and Charlie Chaplin toured the country surpassed even the

FIGURE 13. Mary Pickford entertaining the crowd at the Shaw-Butcher Shipping Works in San Francisco on the fourth Liberty Loan Drive, October 9, 1918. Courtesy of Margaret Herrick Library, Academy of Motion Picture Arts and Sciences, Beverly Hills.

industry's own spectacular standard of success. Thousands in New York gathered "to greet these three film stars but committed murder just to get a glimpse of Mary's golden curls," Parsons cheered.[65] The industry's turn to feature-length story pictures and demonstrations of patriotism, together, improved its standing among the middle class, prompting the first official screening of a movie before the president and Congress. Yet Parsons betrayed how the event signaled the industry's still-precarious reputation, wistfully expressing the hope it might bring the industry closer "to that long wished-for day when the silent drama will be treated with respect and dignified consideration."[66]

Parsons's reporting during the war also documented the industry's rapid relocation to Los Angeles. "Convinced the Coast is the place to make pictures," Metro's president, Richard Rowland, decided to build "a new studio out in Hollywood" in 1918. Since Rowland actually planned to break ground in Culver City, his use of the name "Hollywood" revealed that, among insiders at least, it was increasingly the term of choice for movie-land. Thus Parsons gave readers a scoop on the emergence of a turn of phrase that became commonplace only after the Arbuckle-Rappe scandal of 1921. Rowland's decision to house all of Metro's employees "under one roof with one supervision" also illustrated another trend: giving a central producer the ultimate authority over, and responsibility for, individual films. The central producer system developed alongside the vertically integrated business structure that Zukor perfected. In an innovation designed to reduce the escalating costs of feature films, a central producer was charged with what many might consider to be several unenviable tasks: ensuring enough product to satisfy exhibitors' demands for a complete program change twice a week; deciding which costs on lavish "special" features were necessary; and reigning in the power of movie stars. Although disagreement among producers was rife in the competitive industry, all agreed that stars' demands drove the rapid escalation of production costs, as the price of the average special feature, or "star series," made by those like Pickford and Young jumped 400 percent in 1915.[67]

But stars, however expensive, were the foundation on which Hollywood rose. Zukor's plan to use stars to sell features had perhaps succeeded too well. Now "the people wanted stars, in fact they insisted upon having them." Cutthroat competition for the most popular players resulted. After Pickford's deal with Zukor in 1916, lesser luminaries began to demand and receive enormous raises. Weekly salaries for contract players that averaged $150 to $250 a week in 1915 jumped to $1,000 to $1,500 in 1917.[68] Film stars, typically female ones, also drove the exodus into independent production in this period. The greatest stars like Pickford wielded enormous clout in an industry organized around their appeal, which explains the trend toward actresses, particularly, leaving larger studios for independent production. Exhibitors, unhappy with producers' attempts to dictate the films they showed, and directors, unused to the supervision of central producers, also made choices that favored independent control over streamlined efficiency. Various alliances between performers, producers, exhibitors, and directors regularly resulted in new film companies. Put differently, although the term "Hollywood" may have emerged among insiders during the war years, "Hollywood studio" in no way yet conjured solely a massive factory-like enterprise.[69] Realizing how far they had come in the half-dozen years since they were anonymous figures, many film actors decided to fight rather than relinquish the ground they had won.

The patriotic performances of stars like Pickford during the war only increased their power by graphically demonstrating the pull they exerted over fans across the nation and around the world. On screen and off, Pickford's turn as everyone's favorite "little American" again established the important part that a fearless type of modern American womanhood played in demonstrating the national spirit.[70] *The Little American* (1917) emerged from producer Jesse Lasky's desire to capitalize on the image Pickford so successfully presented during her Liberty Loan propaganda tours. Create "something typically American" for the star, Lasky told Cecil DeMille and scenarist Jeanie MacPherson in Los Angeles. In this case, an American story demanded "a girl in the sort of role that the feminists in the country are now interested in—the kind of girl who jumps in and does a man's work."[71] The film featured Mary helping to route the Huns and nursing French soldiers, targeting the female fans who made Pickford into "the idol of America's young womanhood and girlhood" and FPL/Paramount, consequently, into the nation's most successful movie studio.[72] After the Armistice, a trip Pickford made to London with her new husband, actor Douglas Fairbanks, demonstrated her international stature. The enormity of the crowds and the intensity of their affection frightened many onlookers, including Fairbanks who at one point hoisted his tiny wife onto his shoulders. Parsons crowed over the international attention, reprinting an English editorial that called Pickford "the greatest woman of her age."[73]

Pickford's career after the war also illustrated how the fight to control stars threatened to reshape the film industry again. Seizing the opportunity presented by the business's still-fluid industrial landscape, she decided to resist the imposition of what she considered FPL/Paramount's new "factory methods."[74] With Zukor mostly confined to managing finances in New York, Pickford grew increasingly alienated from Lasky and DeMille and the more corporate atmosphere of the studio.[75] When her contract expired days before the Armistice, she made a change that Parsons announced with the headline, "MARY PICKFORD WILL BE HER OWN FILM DIRECTOR; 'Daddy Longlegs' to Be First of Her Productions."[76] Assuming the role of independent producer, Pickford released her movies through the First National Exhibitors' Circuit, a cooperative distribution company incorporated in 1917.[77] "The First National will have no part in the making of the picture," explained the company's president, J.D. Williams. "Miss Pickford is to select her story, her director, her cast, and, in short, be responsible for the entire production."[78] Begun by exhibitors who controlled some of the nation's most profitable and prestigious theaters, First National created a powerful distribution network that broke Zukor's hold over exhibitors by threatening (ever so delicately since boycotts were illegal) to exclude his pictures from their screens. The threat First National posed to Zukor was complete after it absorbed Pickford's films into its network. Rumors that FPL/Paramount might merge with First National soon pushed Pickford into a more groundbreaking arrangement: the creation of United Artists in 1919, a studio founded to preserve the autonomy of artists within an increasingly centralized system.[79] "'BIG FOUR' NOT 'BIG FIVE' FORM NEW FILM CONCERN," Parsons declared, referring to the fact that Pickford, Fairbanks, Chaplin, and Griffith would run the as yet unnamed company of United Artists.[80]

Pickford's hand in establishing United Artists (UA) would have appeared to Parsons's readers as just one exceptionally dramatic example of the influence that actresses commanded between 1916 and 1921. By the time UA incorporated in 1919, Parsons had featured dozens of stories about actresses running their own shows. As she explained to readers in 1918: "The acme of motion picture fame these days is heading a company of one's very own."[81] After "Mary Pickford started the fashion by making herself the boss, it sounded so good" that every actress "with sufficient backing and bank roll" sought "immediately to possess herself of a motion picture producing company," she continued. Clara Kimball Young was the first to imitate Pickford when she formed the eponymous company with independent producer Lewis Selznick that same year.[82] *Photoplay*'s editor James Quirk disliked the development, exclaiming that the "'her own company' epidemic" indicated the industry's poor health.[83] But Parsons happily hailed the trend, calling Doris Kenyon, "the very latest star to be featured in her own company," a "lucky young lady."[84] In retrospect, Pickford's part in the formation of United Artists was the most enduring example of the clout exercised by a female, or a male, star in this era. Most production companies formed by anyone, actresses included, were short-lived, whether because of mismanagement or because of the mounting difficulty of operating outside a major studio. The extent to which actresses assumed executive roles within these companies also varied widely. But Parsons ignored such pesky details, painting the world in which these women-made women operated with the bold brush of a Matisse rather than the precise strokes of a Vermeer.

Indeed, Parsons justified the star-turned-producer trend by teaching readers about their importance to the industry's profitability. An interview with star Norma Talmadge displayed the lesson. After establishing a following at Fine Arts, Talmadge married independent producer Joseph Schenck, who "created a film company—Select—for her," Parsons explained.[85] Schenck managed the business details, but Parsons left no doubt about who generated the dough. Talmadge more than "justified Mr. Schenck's faith in her," she declared, making "money so fast" that he began "to consider his beautiful wife a financial as well as a love investment." The opening frames of Talmadge movies like *Forbidden City* (1918) graphically illustrated her stature.[86] The film's opening credits displays her name in a type size three times that of Schenck's; the next shot emphasizes her authorship by announcing above an enormous, elegant reproduction of her name: "My latest photoplays, produced in my own studios all bear my signature." Talmadge, a former working-class girl from Brooklyn, offered young women a no-nonsense standard of success: "Being poor may be romantic, but I like being just the way I am, with pleasant work, a devoted husband and a happy home. . . . I can do things for my family and indulge in some pet charities."[87]

Parsons seemed to particularly relish highlighting women who worked in purely executive roles. After lamenting how men still dominated this category, she called Universal's business manager, Eleanor Fried, "one of the 'females of the species' blazing a trail to paths heretofore occupied by men."[88] Emphasizing Fried's leadership and economizing abilities, Parsons announced she had "piloted the entire Henry McRae expedition" through China and Japan, "where her economy had saved Universal thousands of dollars." Her description of Fried's rise through the corporate ranks noted her seven-year tenure as an editor before "her talent for executive management was discovered." "New Film Company Controlled by Woman," proclaimed a headline announcing the appearance of the Catherine Curtis Corporation: "a new company headed, controlled, and planned by a woman."[89] Months later Parsons interviewed Curtis, "who says it's one of life's easiest jobs to raise a million dollars in New York."[90] After remarking that Curtis was "exceedingly easy to gaze upon," she pointed out that the "very big names in the financial and industrial world" who backed Curtis's venture were not the type to "listen to a petticoat for the mere sake of hearing a pretty woman talk." Parsons quizzed Curtis on the secret to her success, observing, "A woman with enough business acumen to raise a million dollars . . . is not a common thing even in the twentieth century world of successful women."

According to Parsons, improving the artistic standing of the movies required more women writers to devise stories that would provide a "higher estimate of the masses." Parsons's more general focus on women writers in her column left the impression that only women, or "girls," as they were called no matter their age, were scriptwriters of note. Since women wrote nearly a majority of screenplays in this era, their frequent appearance was hardly surprising.[91] But the rise of feature-length narrative films, the still-biweekly change of films demanded by exhibitors, and the growing pressure from cultural custodians to produce "cleaner," "higher-class" pictures made the question of exactly what constituted good writing a hot topic of debate. "The burden of every film producer's song these days is 'My Kingdom for a Story,'" Parsons summarized the mood produced by these combined pressures.[92] Parsons sympathetically documented the efforts of movie producers like Samuel Goldwyn to woo "eminent authors" like Rupert Hughes, Gertrude Atherton, and Mary Roberts Rinehart, writers with huge followings in their day. She also approved of forcing exhibitors to accept "fewer and better pictures," since their omnivorous appetites threatened "to exhaust all the literary material in the world."[93] Yet Parsons also faulted producers whose "cheap pictures" "sold old fashioned work" that mapped out an "entirely conventional destiny for the heroine" and "expect[ed] the world to accept a plot as obsolete as the stage coach."[94]

Parsons also celebrated scenario writers as personalities in their own right. Often she accomplished this through a sleight of hand that traded on their associations with more visible players. Anita Loos, "The Girl Who Made Fairbanks Famous," was a good example. Wisecracking Loos later wrote the best-selling novel *Gentlemen Prefer Blondes: The Intimate Diary of a Professional Lady* (1925), about the first so-called dumb blonde, Lorelei Lee, the secretary who marries well and then heads for Hollywood to produce and star in the movies. Her "satire has won her fame and fortune," Parsons declared, before describing Loos as, "the possessor of more originality and honest-to-goodness brains than any six-footer now engaged in plotting for motion pictures." According to Parsons, Loos raised Fairbanks from a "juvenile lead getting about $350 a week" to a star so fast that "he couldn't quite understand himself how it all happened."[95] Similarly, she explained the favorable terms that scenarist Jeanie MacPherson received at FPL/Paramount— "only two scenarios a year" for five years so that she might "spend as much time as she wishes researching works"—through her relationship with director Cecil B. DeMille.[96] Calling MacPherson "one of the best known scenario writers in the business," Parsons presented her as integral to *his* success. Given that MacPherson wrote or adapted virtually every film he made, the claim appears well founded. Pickford lent her glamour to discussions of Frances Marion. Marion "had adapted and written many of the star's best scenarios," Parsons reminded readers before announcing that she would direct the actress at UA. "Personally I think it is a splendid thing," Parsons gushed. "Above everything else," Pickford had "enough brains to recognize ability in another woman."[97]

In the context of her day, Parsons's remarks placed her among the disparate group of individuals who first called themselves feminists. Self-styled "feminist" women and men during the 1910s asked for more than women's formal equality with men, a demand most forcefully symbolized by the mass movement that won a federal amendment for woman suffrage in 1920. The strategy that won the vote attempted to forestall opponents' derailment of woman suffrage by linking it to feminism, a concept signaling a radical reenvisioning of women's place within society. Coined in 1880s France, *feminisme* traveled to fin de siècle England and to the United States during the 1910s. In part because of women's unusual war work, feminism garnered more attention by the late 1910s.[98] Although militant suffragist Alice Paul made the term virtually synonymous with the activities of the National Woman's Party by the late twenties, feminism initially resisted definition. In 1913 *Harper's Weekly* called feminism "of interest to everyone," reflecting "the stir of new life, the palpable awakening of consciousness." Yet one anti-suffrage organization displayed how conflating woman suffrage with a feminist consciousness raised the specter of women's complete rejection of respectable femininity. "Feminism advocates non-motherhood, free love, easy divorce, economic independence for all women, and other demoralizing and destructive theories," explained the Missouri Anti-Suffrage League in 1918.[99] The fact that there was some truth to the argument eased the job of so-called "Antis." For, indeed, suffragists who also considered themselves feminists sought to call into question the whole architecture of customs surrounding sex roles and the meanings attached to sexual difference.[100] The actress's long association with the anarchy of sexual instincts and work in the wider world indicated why she so often acted as a kind of feminist avatar who might teach women how to pursue their ambitions like men while preventing what Simone de Beauvoir called the "mutilation" of their sexuality.[101]

Parsons's description of many female movie personalities placed them among the still-ambiguous collection of individuals who were first called feminists. "I am a feminist," her good friend actress Olga Petrova declared. "By that I do not mean that women should try to do the work of men. They should merely learn to do their own work, live their own lives, be themselves," the producer-actress explained. "They should not be clinging vines, blaming men for all the ills that befall them, and forced to acknowledge men as the source of all their good fortune and happiness." Others had sounded such calls before. Nearly a century earlier lonely voices like Margaret Fuller's had evoked a more complicated vision of human sexuality and ambition; her call to "let [women] be sea captains, if you will," evoked a world where tastes and aptitudes, not abilities assumed to be fixed in the nature of things, set the limits of an individual's horizon.[102] Feminists in the 1910s renewed this appeal, asking that women realize their individual ambitions, admit the importance of their sexuality, and experience—like men, but as women—the pleasures and challenges that went along with both. Women who entered the professions around the turn of the century sidestepped the question of work's impact on the sexual politics and domestic labor of the home. Like Charlotte Cushman half a century earlier, most women still attempting to live within the bounds of respectability carved out new professional territory largely by maintaining exclusively female-centered domestic worlds that, theoretically, erased their sexuality. But the latest generation of so-called New Women began to openly challenge these oppositions by taking on jobs outside the home, frankly exploring their romantic interests, and experimenting with different domestic arrangements that suited both. This interest in women's broader cultural freedoms, rather than specific legal improvements, provided opportunities to attack feminists as "sex radicals" and "free lovers" who sought nothing less than the destruction of the family, the foundation of society. Work after marriage for white middle-class women was viewed as so threatening to society that jobs like teaching, by far the largest occupation for this group, forbade it.[103] Thus Parsons's supportive talk about movie personalities juggling work, marriage, and a new kind of romantic femininity endorsed a practice many viewed as unconventional, if not dangerous. Indeed, movie screens rarely depicted such behavior. On screens, serial queens and the heroines played by Pickford were unfailingly young, single, and childless during their adventures.

Despite the mounting opposition expressed toward the topic of work for wives, Parsons often depicted the movies' new home in Los Angeles as a space that supported gender play within husband-and-wife professional teams. The approach emphasized the collaborative nature of these relationships while simultaneously displaying how a woman's public accomplishments made her a more, rather than less, attractive romantic partner. Parsons called scenarist Ouida Bergere, "the feminine half of the highly successful motion picture team of Bergere and Fitzmaurice; wherein both the lady and her husband figure."[104] The director and writer met while working, married, and had conducted "a neck and neck race for fame and honors" ever since. Describing Bergere as a lady was itself a refashioning of that traditional marker, since ladies, traditionally, did not conduct professional competitions with their husbands. Yet Bergere's behavior, according to Parsons, was not only ladylike but also responsible for her marital success, producing "a happy combination—Ouida Bergere with her brilliant, quick mind; George Fitzmaurice with his scholarly, more restrained intellect." Indeed, Parsons even deftly swept away any hints of society's opposition toward women combining work and motherhood. The announcement of Gloria Swanson's marriage described the actress as having avoided a trip to the altar because of her youthful determination "not to permit matrimony to interfere with her screen career."[105] But Parsons assured readers that Swanson's change of heart was premised on the actress's more hopeful opinion about combining a career and marriage. Indeed, Swanson quickly provided Parsons with a chance to celebrate a working mother. Three months after the actress gave birth to her first child, Parsons approvingly noted that "baby Gloria" was "sufficiently aged to permit her mother to continue her screen career."[106]

One of the earliest stereotypes used to attack the moral reputation of the movie colony in Los Angeles was that the professional interests of its women personalities destroyed their commitment to marital bonds. A journalist in the *Los Angeles Times* complained about how nonmovie residents of Hollywood contended with jokes such as "Are you married?" "No, I live in Hollywood."[107] Alarmist reports about the doubling of the national divorce rate from 4 to 8 percent between 1900 and 1920 fed the controversy.[108] An article on California's "rather appalling statistics" on divorce blamed the problem on the state's unusual number of women in public life. The fact that most men procured divorces on the grounds of desertion demonstrated that "the recent trend of women to enter public life and the lessening ties of the home" was to blame.[109] The argument followed the one first popularized by Theodore Roosevelt a decade earlier in a campaign he waged to stop the so-called "race suicide" of "Anglo Saxons," a development he blamed on a sex role confusion marked equally by the overcivilized effeminacy of white men and the selfishness that led white women to avoid their domestic duties.[110] In a line of thinking that continues to this day, the view held women's new interests outside the home responsible for the rise in divorce, agitation over birth control, and the decline in middle-class birthrates.[111] Yet Parsons initially treated marriage and divorce in the lightest possible terms. An interview with Anita Loos about her start in motion pictures mocked wedlock, conventionally construed. "I always wanted to see New York," Loos told Parsons, so when a man "promised to take me to this wonder city . . . I married him to get my transportation." Since "he only had money enough to get us as far as Omaha, on the third day I went out to get a hair net and I forgot to come back." In response, Parsons merely lauded Loos's "spirit of adventure."[112]

Two of the earliest moral panics over the private lives of movie personalities seemed to teach Parsons a lesson about publicizing a woman's flagrant breach of matrimonial norms. The first involved the uproar over the marital arrangements of Parsons's friend New York writer Fannie Hurst.[113] One of the most notable producers of popular fiction, Hurst was touted as the country's "highest paid short story writer." In an era in which reading short stories and syndicated novels was a virtual obsession, Hurst's work was syndicated weekly in newspapers, was published regularly in prestigious magazines, and was about to appear on the screen. In May 1920 the news that Hurst had secretly wed pianist Jacques Danielson five years earlier splashed across the front pages of newspapers around the country. The timing seems suspicious, given that the story broke the day before the high-profile premiere of the film adaptation of Hurst's short story "Humoresque." But it was the statement that Hurst gave when approached to confirm the marriage that made news. "LIVE APART, THEIR OWN WAY," the *New York Times* declared. After admitting that Mr. Danielson had eroded her "youthful determination that marriage was not for me," Hurst remained steadfast in her belief "that marriage should never lessen my capacity for creative work or pull me down into a state of fat-mindedness." Such a condition, Hurst declared, made "nine out of ten [marriages] . . . merely sordid endurance tests." Hurst and Danielson's marital arrangement included separate apartments, meetings by appointment that resulted in an "average of two breakfasts a week," and the promise to respect the other's privacy when apart. Hurst admitted the plan "was the result of very definite theories concerning wedlock," but emphasized it "was not the result of a fad. . . . We believe in love but not Free Love. Rather we are willing to pay the price in mutual sacrifices toward the preservation of one another's individuality." According to Hurst, the approach improved romance as well: "After a five-year acid test, the dew is still on the rose."[114] Parsons kept silent while Hurst's theories on modern marriage drew attacks from press and pulpit from coast to coast.[115]

This treatment duplicated the response she gave to the news about Mary Pickford's quickie Nevada divorce from Owen Moore later that month. Pickford's remarriage, to Douglas Fairbanks, three weeks later left little doubt that the Catholic star broke more than one commandment. Parsons had hinted at the affair between Pickford and Fairbanks a year earlier, running an interview that featured Fairbanks's first wife declaring her unwillingness to continue to act as "a shield" for her husband's affair with "one of the world's most famous motion picture actresses."[116] Then Parsons dropped the story. When the Fairbankses divorced later that year, she wrote nothing. Indeed, the Fairbanks divorce attracted very little attention from anyone, indicating how the sexual double standard made the subject play very differently for male versus female celebrities. Parsons continued her silence even as editorial commentary raged over Pickford's divorce and the Nevada attorney general's promise to annul it, a pledge that threatened to make the star a bigamist. Parsons also ignored the huge celebratory crowds that sent Pickford and Fairbanks off on their honeymoon, crowds whose enthusiasm indicated that Mary's public did not begrudge America's Sweetheart an affair—as long as it resulted in a marriage to her UA partner and the swashbuckling prince of the new "American aristocracy" (the title of Fairbanks's 1916 film).[117]

But after ignoring Pickford's scandalous divorce and instant remarriage, Parsons covered the pair's return from their honeymoon with a clear intention: publicizing Little Mary's embrace of more conventional ideas about marriage. In response to reporters' repeated questions about "how to be happily married," Pickford "reiterate[d] over and over again that her idea of domestic bliss was not founded on a Fannie Hurst two-breakfasts-a-week cult but upon the very solid and old fashioned basis of seven a week."[118] The *New York Times* made the point more explicit: "Here in New York Fannie Hurst, having consulted her engagement book and found the evening free, mutters madly, 'What is the name of that man I married? I ought to have his telephone somewhere,'" while "out in Hollywood California a little woman with golden hair

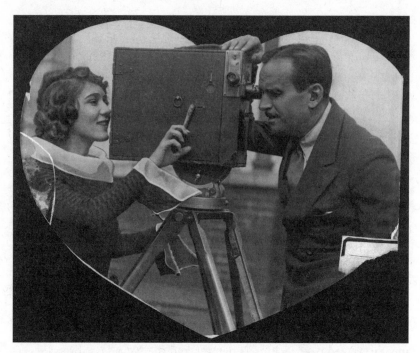

FIGURE 14. Mary Pickford and Douglas Fairbanks after their 1920 marriage. Courtesy of Margaret Herrick Library, Academy of Motion Picture Arts and Sciences, Beverly Hills.

puts the chops on and wonders with a sigh if her adorable fellow will be late."[119] The message was clear. Pickford used unconventional means only to achieve the most conventional marital ends. Subsequent months found Parsons running similar stories that stressed how Hollywood's working wives put their husbands' needs before their careers. An interview with actress Miriam Cooper touted her roots as a convent-bred southerner, before calling her "well qualified to say whether a woman's place is in the home or beside her husband in his work." "Having tried both roles," Cooper concluded that "a woman's place is wherever she is needed most." The verdict was "not at variance with feminist principles," Parsons assured readers. Yet Parsons went on to cast Cooper's work with husband director Raoul Walsh explicitly as work *for* him, noting he had "convinced her that her screen persona was irreplaceable and necessary to his film." "Quick to say that 'he is still the star of the family,'" Cooper also erased any hint of a professional competition. Parsons concluded the interview by noting that her meeting with Cooper "took place before Fannie Hurst startled the world by advocating the personal liberty, separate establishment program." "Despite Miss Cooper's opposite views on how married life should be spent," she gushed, "the dew is still on the roses for the Walshes, after three years of married life."[120]

Considering the engrained association of actresses with unconventionality, if not simple immorality, Parsons's new presentation of actresses' views of marriage was not so surprising. The unusual spaces actresses occupied in the American film business, and thus in the culture at large, made them vulnerable to attacks that used their private lives to undermine their public ones. In effect, Parsons's recasting of actresses as feminists who respected traditional arrangements in the domestic sphere aimed to shore up the increasingly elevated stature of both actresses and the film industry at large. That Parsons continued to write positive stories about Hurst's work even as she glowingly described Pickford and Cooper's anti-Hurst matrimonial philosophy suggests that this was her strategy. The same day she publicized Pickford's rejection of Hurst's private life, Parsons gave an extremely positive review to *Humoresque* (1920), a tale about the power of mother love that won *Photoplay*'s first medal of honor in 1921.[121]

As significantly, she used Hurst as an inspirational symbol for other workingwomen when discussing the professional activities of The Woman Pays Club, a group of feminist creative artists in New York who met to celebrate each other's work. Parson first discussed the club's activities under the headline "THE WOMAN PAYS." The club "was formed because these women never like the men to think they have anything to brag about," Parsons reported. Composed of "forty newspaper women and writers," the club met weekly, honoring guest speakers like Anita Loos and novelist Edna Ferber. The club took its name from the old Victorian saw that referenced how the sexual double standard punished women for the erotic freedoms that men enjoyed with little risk. Since the club was "patterned after the Dutch Treat Club," which encouraged women to pay their own way with men, the name served as a literary reappropriation that signaled members' belief in the economic basis of women's independence, sexual and otherwise. Parsons's article "Earning Her Rights" exhibited the pride members took in the financial independence women earned through their professional success. "Time was when Janet Flanner was a hard working woman. She earned her bread and ham as motion picture editor for the *Indianapolis Star*," Parsons explained. But then Flanner found her prince. "Instead of pursuing the course of many of her married friends and continuing her career Miss Flanner became a typical clinging creature and allowed her husband to provide all the bread and jam." "Janet was content with her lot," Parsons reported, but "her friends found so much fault she knew if she wished to continue as a member of [T]he Woman Pays Club she must bring in some money." Parsons now used Fannie Hurst to illustrate how far Flanner had fallen from grace. "When Fannie Hurst married," Parsons reminded readers, she "proudly proclaimed to the world that she had kept her personal liberty intact by buying her own clothes and paying the grocer." Hurst's example underscored why if Flanner "ever expected to attend another meeting of the Woman Pays Club," she had to "show the Club some money she earned. She wrote fast and furiously." In this case, successfully imitating Hurst put Flanner "back in the Club's good graces. 'We'll make her famous in spite of herself,' said one of her stern judges."[122]

Motion picture production had coalesced on the West Coast by the time Parsons reported on Flanner's skirmish with The Woman Pays Club in 1920. Charting the westward movement of the business left Parsons ideally positioned to teach readers about the significance of the movies settling in the West. Few interested in pictures had ventured to Los Angeles in 1910; by 1920, the city produced 85 percent of American-made movies and two-thirds of those watched around the world.[123] The industry's explosive growth transformed the city's postwar landscape, as the "graceful pepper trees" fell so "tourists could have a better view."[124]

Parsons offered readers a clear view of this new urban frontier in a column that, she declared, "every girl who is determined to become a picture actress should read." After seeing just one movie, Parsons reported, Dorothy Dalton quit her job as a leading player in a stock theater in the Midwest and "took herself to California." "There was Dorothy Dalton, many miles from home," Parsons empathized, "with a good job in the past and nothing in the future. Most girls would have sat down and cried or begged on bended knee for something to keep the wolf from prowling around the door." But not this heroine. After suffering countless refusals for work, Dalton merely "gritted her teeth, clenched her hands and forced herself to smile . . . and said pleasantly, 'Very well, I shall come again tomorrow; perhaps something will unexpectedly develop.'" With Dalton having won a contract in the business, Parsons offered the actress's experience as a parable for what other women with determination, grit, and good grace could expect in this new West.[125]

A piece on the imminent move of scenarist Josephine Quirk from New York to Los Angeles resurrected Horace Greeley's old advice for feminist ends. "When Horace Greeley penned those immortal words, 'Go West, Young Man,' he failed to reckon with the feminine contingent. That of course was before the days of feminism," Parsons excused. "In the good old days when Horace philosophized over the possibilities in the golden west he thought the only interest the fair sex could have in this faraway country was to go as a helpmate to man," she explained. Parsons then spelled out what such a role entailed: "If her husband, her father or her brother set out to explore the vast unknown—she should accompany him as cook, chief sewer of buttons and to make sure that his home was kept clean." Banishing the thought of consigning her readers to such an inglorious fate, Parsons declared, "But that was in the good old days. In the present day, if milady goes west she travels not to sew on buttons or do the family washing, she goeth to make her own fortune." Calling Quirk "one of those up to date young women who is following Greeley's advice," Parsons heralded the better prospects faced by these modern adventurers. No possible calamity faced Quirk. Her "future is assured, since she has accepted a position with the Goldwyn Company."[126]

And so the hopeful responded, traveling westward as before. By the time that Parsons encouraged Quirk's imitators to go west, Los Angeles was known not just as "the Capital of Movie-Land" but as a "picture Eldorado" that particularly attracted ambitious single women.[127] Journalists like Parsons helped to spark women's westward migration by describing the first movie personalities and the social terrain they occupied as fantastically connecting the two most influential environments that young women moved into in this period: the world of mass culture and the world of work. Their stories described some of the most visible freedoms resulting from women's work vis-á-vis the new social conventions that mass cultural forms like the movies and the press engendered and publicized. The place that women occupied within this industry as it settled in the West offered tangible evidence that women could succeed in areas, and on terms, previously reserved for men. And yet, in celebrating the glamorous side of feminine power, women celebrities shaped and sold a fan culture that acted as a bridge from the past, in effect promising young women they could have it all. In the process, the women-made women who helped to midwife the birth of Hollywood demonstrated different ways to act female in public, ways that the movie industry, quite literally, needed to fill its new picture palaces. Out west, women in the motion picture business turned the process of creating Hollywood into an adventure story about just how far women's emancipation could go.

PART TWO

Melodramas of Hollywood's Birth

The Postwar Revolution
in Morals and Manners, Redux

The first part of *Go West, Young Women!* maps the currents that converged in Hollywood, California during the First World War. There, the industry's women-made women helped to power the film industry's explosive growth by attracting the multi-ethnic, cross-class audience of women fans who so buoyed the industry's expectations by the war's end in 1918. The book's second part, "Melodramas of Hollywood's Birth," plunges readers into the tumultuous postwar scene that shaped Hollywood's crystallization as symbol in the City of Angels. To capture what this development meant to different audiences at the time, the next three chapters re-create distinct, if at times overlapping, melodramatic narratives about the significance of Hollywood's birth. "Hollywood Bohemia" and "The Movie Menace" offer two competing stories about how the industry's postwar transformation influenced "the revolution in manners and morals," to use the memorable phrase that Fredrick Lewis Allen coined in his bestselling popular history, *Only Yesterday* (1931), to capture the widely shared belief that traditional gender roles shattered in the conflict's wake.[1] The final chapter, "A Star Is Born," details the multiple melodramas that initially narrated the industry's first sex scandal, and then explains the implications of the one that won out for women, both real and imagined, in early Hollywood.

Historians' use of war as a fulcrum on which to hinge significant cultural fluctuations is a commonplace hard to discard. As engines of social change, wars can generate a momentum like no other, erasing whole sets of possibilities and turning others into dominating realities. Several factors contingent upon the Great War fueled the rapid growth of the American film industry's commercial power, prestige, and visibility, making it the world's leading producer of mass culture after the war's end. The war destroyed the once-dominant French film industry and decimated the flourishing Italian one as well, giving film producers in the United States an advantage they zealously protected over the century to come.[2] The success of stars in selling the war to a doubtful public also graphically demonstrated their powerful appeal from coast to coast, granting newfound legitimacy to the industry.

Indeed, after the war perhaps the only development concerning the motion picture industry that sparked little debate was that American-made movies had become the most popular, and increasingly preeminent, form of cultural entertainment both in the United States and around the industrializing world. By 1920 a chorus of commentators created a stuttering refrain: the picture business was the nation's "fourth or fifth largest industry."[3] This meant the film industry initially offered one of the few economic bright spots on the postwar scene as a recession spurred by demobilization descended. The speed of the industry's growth dumbfounded most. "The evolution of picture production, from a giant weed-like industry, crude and unformed, into an art has been one of the amazing revelations of the past five years," one reporter marveled in 1920.[4] Lavish picture palaces went up along the thoroughfares of cities and towns. Where once the grandest theater held 600 to 1,000 patrons, now movie palaces typically accommodated 1,800 to 3,000— and sometimes triple that number. The conversion of so many stage venues into movie houses also provided tangible evidence of the industry's prosperity and gentrification. "The movie seems to be developing an appetite that will not be content until it has swallowed the whole theater industry," observed the *Literary Digest*. Entitled "Fear of the All-Devouring Movie," the article argued that a cross-class audience of women had driven the film industry's takeover of the stage.[5] "Time was when only lowbrows were supposed to attend the movies," observed another reporter in the *Digest*, "but to-day everybody frankly attends, high and low alike. We are told that the cinema now purveys amusement in America to more than 12,000,000 patrons daily."[6] Indeed, by 1920 an estimated 50 million people—fully half the nation's population— went to the movies every week.[7]

As had happened earlier on the stage, women's decisive influence on this now most popular culture industry prompted worry and wonder among much of the educated elite. Many among this set expressed disgust over how the industry's reorientation toward women had resulted in the production of so many female-centered romantic melodramas. "Let me begin by saying I am not a movie fan," announced Katherine Fullerton Gerould in the *Atlantic Monthly*. "Most of my friends honestly dislike them. But now and then I find one, equally intelligent, equally educated who attends regularly."[8] Despite the admitted lack of firsthand experience, commentators like Gerould remained grimly steadfast about *what* fans watched: romantic, thrill-driven melodramas focused on "the inevitable idealization of the heroine."[9] A *Nation* editor lamented the predictable influence that women's preferences for such heroines had on American culture more broadly. "The popular film 'drama of heart interest' is the lineal descendant of the cheap melodrama of a dozen years ago, and it is the contemporary relative of the fiction of our popular magazine."[10] The *New Republic*'s critic made a similar argument about the effect of women's fondness for "facile romancers" on the "most popular art form" found in "the picture theatre." "The morals of the movies are also the morals of the popular magazine," the piece declared, citing "Fanny Hurst" (and misspelling her name) as the best example of an author who succeeded in both forms.[11] The reporter proved prescient. In 1921 an adaptation of Hurst's story "Humoresque," about which Louella Parsons had raved, won *Photoplay*'s gold Medal of Honor, the equivalent of the first Academy Award for best picture.[12]

Humoresque's selection by *Photoplay*'s mostly female readers highlighted the increasingly widespread recognition of women's role in determining what counted as a success in motion pictures after the war. A 1920 survey of movie exhibitors also made plain that female-centered melodramas did the most to fill the new movie houses. Conducted by First National, the nation's largest distribution company, the survey asked theater owners about audiences' preferences at 10,267 theatres located in "6,511 cities, towns, and villages, ranging from the big cities to lumber camps." On "any single day in the year," the report concluded, "the average" feature film was likely to focus on a "female star" performing in "a light comedy of society life," "an emotional drama," "a drama notable for action," or "a drama of middle class life."[13] In this way, the so-called "flapper fan" became the "representative public" of the movies after the war.[14]

The reorientation of American-made movies toward this audience explained its connection to debates about the postwar revolution in manners and morals. Although purportedly about changes among the entire "younger generation," the debate actually focused on its female half, variously called "modern girls," "problem girls," or "the 'Flapper Problem.'"[15] "The whole revolution in the field of sexual morals turns upon the fact that external control of the chastity of women is becoming impossible." So declared the respected public intellectual, journalist, and founder of the *New Republic*, Walter Lippmann, about the controversy at the end of the 1920s. Scholars now recognize that concern over the breakdown of the Victorian bourgeoisie's code of civilized morality that had idealized respectable women as essentially nonsexual began before the 1920s. The multiple nationwide moral panics that erupted before the war—over "white slavery" (forced prostitution), the birth control movement, and the appearance of a large class of sexually delinquent "problem girls"—all displayed the enormous efforts already unleashed to keep female sexuality under others' control. But the controversy about the subject escalated dramatically after the war, in large measure because of the movies' success at attracting a cross-class audience of female fans by splashing more sexually expressive heroines who specialized in so-called sex conflict across screens and fan magazines. Such heroines often deployed many of the new social habits and sexual customs first popularized by single working girls before the war. But by wrapping them in a glamorous and often exotically foreign aesthetic, early Hollywood spread them more easily among the daughters of the middle class. "Is 'THE OLD FASHIONED GIRL,' with all that she stands for in sweetness, modesty, and innocence, in danger of becoming extinct?" opened the first in a trio of massive surveys on the topic of changes in postwar gender roles published by the *Literary Digest* in 1921. "Girls to-day wear too few clothes and require too much 'petting,'" complained one college boy.[16] Spurred on by the leading ladies of the screen, women's dress changed dramatically after the war, as hemlines went up, ornamentation went down, and the accentuation of breasts and hips disappeared to create a simple silhouette that displayed the body beneath the clothes. As a result, clothes directly articulated the female form, and, for the first time in two centuries, women and men appeared more equal in scale. These easily mass-produced designs showed up not just in fan magazines and films, but on fans across the country. Their use of tactile, mobile fabrics that cut across the back, arms, and calves suggesting "how the female body actually felt to its owner, and how it might feel to the touch of others."[17]

Little wonder, then, that the *Digest*, like so many other cultural custodians, blamed the movies' stars and stories for tempting their once respectable daughters to slip into the skins of glamorous new heroines who displayed a knack for flaunting sexual propriety with impunity. Industry insiders reversed the direction of influence, holding the "flapper's sophistication" responsible for the turn to more passionate melodramas and stars.[18] According to Paramount president Adolph Zukor, "The post war revolution of manners and morals" left the industry "caught in the middle" between young women and their elders. But Zukor also admitted that the American film industry sought to become a glamorous international trendsetter by offering stories and stars that stoked fans' new desires. "Our prime aim was always to keep abreast of audience taste," he asserted.[19]

Thus Hollywood's relationship to the postwar revolution in women's manners and morals provoked as much trouble as success. The revolution's alien origins provided grounds for joining the growing opposition seeking to protect "100 percent" native American morality, in the parlance of the war years, from the corrupting influences of the foreign aesthetic purveyed by the movies' new "Hebrew Trust." Some activists, fresh from their victory enacting the Prohibition amendment in 1919, drew strength and fresh allies by linking their cause to the postwar hysteria over the new immigrants from Southern and Eastern Europe, particularly Jewish ones. By 1920 an unprecedented call for federal regulation of the film industry erupted to stop un-American, sexually perverse "movie morals" from debasing the industry's seemingly ever expanding circle of female fans. Put differently, the unintended consequences of the movies' triumph at selling themselves as a cosmopolitan gender convention–defying new frontier unified reformers around the idea that only respectable American moral regulators could prevent the industry's spread of dangerously foreign ideas among their daughters. Activists' ability to draw on established stereotypes about Jews' penchant for corrupting their "host nations" through racial mixing and sexual perversion helped their case. Moreover, after the war talk about a new "Movie Trust" was well founded in actual material changes to the industry's organizational structure. By the war's end, a new set of mostly immigrant Jewish leaders controlled many of the largest film production studios in Los Angeles. These men were busy building the industry's new trust in a struggle that pitted the largest producers, like Paramount's Adolph Zukor, against independent exhibitors in a battle to control the industry though controlling its screens and stars.

The reference annual most trusted by industry insiders betrayed the unprecedented attempts to control the "giant weed-like industry" that marked the beginning of the 1920s. "Censorship battles in at least 36 states will be fought during the winter of 1921," observed *Wid's Year Book 1920*. Since this was "more legislative battles than have been handled in any one time," *Wid's* predicted that Congress would debate federal regulation in the coming year. Yet an industry symposium entitled "What of the Coming Year?" betrayed almost no evidence of these serious threats.[20] Only one man, Charles Pettijohn, openly contradicted the rosy prognostications offered by most of the film industry executives. Well connected across the political spectrum, the Democratic lawyer had recently helped the Republican National Committee's chairman, William Hays (his hometown friend and political rival in Indiana) marshal thousands of screens to support Warren Harding in the 1920 presidential race. "Watch your step," warned Pettijohn, who had gone to work for producer Lewis Selznick in 1918. "With the prohibition question out of the way, pictures will furnish the most fertile field for salaried reformers," he explained, referring to the long-sought passage of the Eighteenth Amendment, ratified in January 1919.[21] A recent midwestern transplant, Pettijohn well understood how savvy rural activists in the Anti-Saloon League (ASL) had used the war to equate sobriety with 100 percent Americanism. During the war years, the ASL had outmaneuvered new urban majorities with a grassroots strategy that pledged to use a "pure stream of country sentiment and township morals" to "flush out the cesspools of cities." In this way, the nativism stirred by the war and immigration helped to frame alcohol not just as an urban vice but also as "un-American" one. The approach allowed the ASL to cast its "crusade to regulate behavior" as consonant "with the preservation of the American way of life," according to historian John Higham.[22]

Pettijohn argued that reformers who once used the protection of native American morality to control what people drank would now use it to control how they played. "Censorship will be at the high water mark between November 1920 and June 1921," observed the only *Wid's* symposium participant who was connected to political currents that ran outside of the industry and away from seaboard cities. We "will be defeated in several states unless we get busy and equip ourselves to meet the situation. This cannot be done without a mutual understanding

and a working arrangement with a national exhibitors' organization,"
he continued.[23] Like a "prophet," as the contemporary film historian
Terry Ramsaye called him, Pettijohn foretold that the internecine feud
between producers and independent exhibitors had blinded them to the
political storm descending.[24] Put differently, in the war's aftermath the
industry's connection to the revolution in manners and morals threatened to unleash a storm that just might drown them all.

CHAPTER 3

Hollywood Bohemia

One of the first films imported from Germany following the Treaty of Versailles displayed how the "Orientalized" glamour of European artists licensed the startling shift in gender roles that many of early Hollywood's biggest stars and films flaunted after the war.[1] Packing movie houses and drawing critical hosannas throughout the year, *Passion* (1921) starred Pola Negri, a raven-haired Polish actress who rose to fame working with the film's Jewish director, Ernst Lubitsch, in his native Berlin.[2] The fanfare surrounding the film's release in the United States centered on Negri's role as the sexually sophisticated heroine Madame Jeanne du Barry, the infamous milliner-turned–mistress of the king of France. "POLA NEGRI AND A CAST OF 5000 PEOPLE in *Passion*," promised ads. "This is a story of a wonder woman—the world's most daring adventuress."[3] Negri and Lubitsch both exuded the distinctly un-American sensibility that Hollywood offered to postwar audiences. Decades later, when recalling her decision to invite Lubitsch to work at United Artists on what would be his first American-made film, *Rosita* (1923), Pickford still emphasized the difference between her American sensibilities and theirs. "Now of course, [Lubitsch] understood Pola Negri or Gloria Swanson, that type of actress," she said of the man who went on to make the boldest sex comedies of his day, "but he did not understand me because I am of course a purely American type. I'm not European."[4] Yet, however much Pickford later renounced her decision to have Lubitsch direct her as a Spanish street singer, *Rosita* not only succeeded in its day but also indicated her awareness of the growing appeal of a non-Anglo-American allure. Indeed, just this recognition prompted producers like Pickford and Jesse Lasky to absorb the threat that European talent posed after the war by bringing them to Hollywood.[5] After wooing Negri to Los Angeles, Jesse Lasky, FPL/Paramount's (soon to be Paramount's) vice president of production, changed the title of her starring vehicle from *Madame du Barry* to *Passion* to ensure that American audiences understood the romantic nature of the heroine's conquests.[6] As Jeanne du Barry, Negri plays a country girl who heads to Paris to find her fortune. A romantic swashbuckler, Jeanne delights in directing erotic games as she follows "adventure, siren fingered," into the arms of a succession of men. Acting the frightened naïf one minute, the frightening dominatrix the next, she burlesques the prewar era's stereotyped performances of female sexuality for her lovers. Even her plea while waiting to lose her head—"One moment more! Life is so sweet!"—suggests the pleasures taken in her life of sin.[7]

Although Madame Jeanne du Barry pays for her wicked ways in the end, the character's actions drove the film outside the conventions established by Pickford's romantic melodramas. Prewar romantic melodramas made room for assertive women, but typically treated overt demonstrations of female sexuality and desire as what separated good women from the bad, with Theda Bara playing women driven by supernatural forces rather than human needs. But after the war the personas and films of actresses like Swanson and Negri often demolished the conventions that had held the sexuality of heroines hostage for so long. Jeanne offered a different template for understanding women's erotic desires and individuality, since the character's preferences, alone, explained her behavior. Moreover, publicity about the real-life personas of stars like Negri sparked equal alarm. After divorcing a Russian count and moving to Los Angeles, Negri took a series of high-profile lovers, including actors Charlie Chaplin and Rudolph Valentino, and projected a "mysterious aloofness" that became "part of the equipment of every foreign star to follow." Women like Negri and Swanson—who became the first American star to marry into the European aristocracy when she took a French marquis for her third husband in 1925—were sophisticated, globe-trotting cosmopolitans whose personal conduct graphically illustrated their sexual emancipation. The first so-called glamour queen, Swanson was notorious for flaunting her unconventional behavior and opinions, including her demand for more mutually satisfying erotic relationships between the sexes. The ability of stars like Swanson

FIGURE 15. Pola Negri displays the new, decidedly non-Anglo postwar allure on a fan postcard in 1921. Courtesy of Margaret Herrick Library, Academy of Motion Picture Arts and Sciences, Beverly Hills.

to alter what constituted an acceptable, if still contested, performance of femininity involved their success in using strategies that mobilized both artifice and attitude. In this way, actresses like Negri and Swanson used consumer culture's exploding array of aesthetic goods to create themselves as glamorous subjects who stood a better chance of achieving their ends in what was, as Swanson put it, still "a man's world" after all.[8]

This chapter explores the melodramas of passion that publicized early Hollywood's experiments in challenging the boundaries of the sexual order after the war, examining the character of this moment, its icons, and why it flourished in spite of, or perhaps because of, critique. As the nation's first mass cultural form, early Hollywood's birth made it "a great basin" that absorbed artistic practices originating from high and low culture alike and from across national boundaries and then repackaged them into a new whole.[9] The rise of a group of cosmopolitan personalities—including Gloria Swanson, Elinor Glyn, Alla Nazimova, June Mathis, and Rudolph Valentino—offered glamorous instruction in the new gender roles, marital relations, and erotic behavior necessary to embody this style. These women and men helped the industry to stake out a position as an international fashion trendsetter by wedding conventions associated with prewar working girls to continental glamour and Oriental exoticism. These first so-called Hollywoodites were described as inhabiting an ideal environment for facilitating such tendencies and tastes, a Hollywood Bohemia that nurtured all women's personal, professional, and sexual freedoms. Increasingly, cultural commentators from both inside and outside the city fastened on women's unusual prominence within the bohemian movie colony, where even the most ordinary women workers, the so-called extra girls, appeared to live happily like bachelors in boomtowns of yore. In this way, the passionate melodramas surrounding Hollywood's birth challenged the nation's gendered boundaries by celebrating the exploits of these exotic, glamorous workers out west.

I

Initially Hollywood used stars like Norma Talmadge to advance and explain its position as a new, more democratic fashion capital for its "twentieth century," "modern," or "New Woman" fans.[10] Since "the stars of silent drama are not content with following the fashions," but preferred to "introduce them," they "revolutionized fashions as well as a lot of other things," *Photoplay* explained.[11] The revolution that stars like Talmadge led offered all women a realm where they could prove their individual worth, since even fans in "small middle western" towns would know what was "new before Fifth Avenue." The regular fashion column that Talmadge (ostensibly) wrote for *Photoplay* beginning in June 1920 gave lessons in the designers, trends, and jargon associated with haute couture, but it also assured readers the latest custom-fitted Parisian confection was not necessary to look their best. "Good dressing" did not require having "money to burn," Talmadge assured. It was instead, "a matter of line, a matter of studying one's own figure," and then selecting the styles that best suited the wearer. While Talmadge admitted "the services of a great stylist" made things easier, she acknowledged that "most of you girls can't do this—I certainly couldn't during the first years I was in motion picture work." So she advised readers to avoid "the helplessness that leaves you at the mercy of the shopkeeper," and to partake "in the joy of creating something" by making their own clothes instead.[12]

Such comments displayed how Talmadge's persona as the screen's most down-to-earth star created a particularly inviting tone that encouraged women to experiment with their self-fashioning. Founded by one of the many female stars who benefited from the flourishing of independent production in the postwar boom, the Norma Talmadge Film Corporation turned out lavish hit after lavish hit from 1917 until she retired in 1930. Although husband Joseph Schenck ran the company, after the war her movies opened with a credit that emphasized her authorship and control. "I always like to play parts in which modern women have the principal role. I won't play a fast woman and I won't play a stupid one," she explained in *Pictorial Review,* a progressive women's fashion and fiction magazine.[13] She chose parts that appealed "to intelligent women," films in which "a woman is doing something in the world for herself, by herself." Considered by many the greatest dramatic actress of her day, Talmadge played everything from a Chinese aristocrat murdered by the emperor for giving birth to an illegitimate child in *Forbidden City* (1918), to an immigrant girl in *A Daughter of Two Worlds* (1920) who unites high society with working-class ghetto after her father sends her to be educated among the rich.[14] Her persona and films provided a link to prewar modern romantic melodramas that earned her a "heroine worship" that elicited four thousand letters a week, mostly from women between the ages of fourteen and twenty-five.[15]

Talmadge's star persona was thus perfectly positioned to appeal to the cross-class audience of women on whom early Hollywood, and so much of consumer culture, focused after the war. The presentation of her real life consistently emphasized her working-class past and happy present ensconced among the Talmadge clan, depicting her as the screen's most unpretentious star.[16] Though childless, Norma was famously part of a brood that included a devoted mother and Hollywood's most celebrated sister act: younger sisters Constance, a rising comedic star, and Natalie, who married comedian Buster Keaton to great fanfare in 1921. Their press mirrored the formula for success

FIGURE 16. "The Down-Home Girls," (*left to right*) Natalie, Norma, Peg, and Constance Talmadge, setting sail on the *Mauritania* in 1917. Courtesy of Margaret Herrick Library, Academy of Motion Picture Arts and Sciences, Beverly Hills.

that mother Peg described in *The Talmadge Sisters: Norma, Constance, and Natalie* (1924). In need of a job, Norma set her sights on the movies, worked hard, brought her family up through the ranks, enjoyed her career and good fortune, and never let it go to her head.[17] "We love our careers, our successes . . . but more than these we love our Loves—our families and our romance," Norma summarized the sisters' philosophy for fans.[18] In this way, Talmadge's persona projected a model of femininity that combined the extraordinary with the ordinary, the new with the old. Here was an ambitious working girl now at home among the best money could buy, a modern career woman protected by a loving husband and mother, a fantastic professional success who enjoyed nothing better than to dish about fashion with the girls. This explained why F. Scott Fitzgerald memorialized her as a symbol of what made the "cinema" the place "where all American women would be happy." Although *Photoplay*'s mode of address still tipped in favor of addressing working-class women, the magazine increasingly suggested that what all modern young women needed to achieve real happiness was a new kind of leading man, an "ideal hero—so grandly different from all the men you know."[19]

Scenarist Frances Marion was hired to fulfill the demand for heroines who, unlike Talmadge, openly defied respectability to chase after just such handsome heroes. When she returned to Los Angeles after serving as a war correspondent in Europe, Marion recalled, her first assignment was to write a story about the "modern girl who, irked by convention, had joined the erring youth revolt and kicked over the traces. This independence sweeping the country had stamped these girls with the sobriquet flapper." Born Marion Benson Owens in San Francisco in 1888, Marion had married and moved to Los Angeles in 1912. "Grandchild of four pioneers," Marion later recalled that she immediately "sensed a future in this fascinating if cock-eyed business." Lois Weber renamed Marion after giving her a job as an actress-protégé, but Mary Pickford became her most important early mentor. Pickford had secured her a job as a war reporter after the screenwriter had adapted Rupert Hughes's short story "The Mobilizing of Johanna" into the successful Pickford vehicle *Johanna Enlists* (1918). Upon her return to the movie colony, Marion wrote *The Flapper* (1920), which introduced this most fashionable woman as part sophisticate, part ingénue.[20] A slip of a girl with a short skirt and bobbed hair, the flapper smoked, danced to jazz, drank bathtub gin—Prohibition having taken effect that year— and generally pursued a good time along with the boys.[21] Despite her bold behavior, the flapper did little more than "pet," but her eagerness to exhibit her sexuality and skin linked her to the vamp. Trading on this familiarity, *Photoplay* used qualifiers like "Vampette" or "baby vamp" to introduce the type to readers. The flapper was "a youngish little rascal" with "big, innocent" eyes who had "all the experience of her . . . big sister—only she doesn't work at it." The description pointed to why Bara-styled vamps fell out of fashion after the war.[22]

The moral framework that encased the prewar vamp attributed one intention to "the lightning bolt" of women's sexuality: the destruction of foolish men.[23] Prewar fan culture described Bara as a supernatural force, suggesting that only a woman from another world could possess an openly erotic side. But to postwar flapper fans, this formula appeared comically one-dimensional. Articles mocked Bara's style as "bizarre," debunked her persona as "pathetic," "impossible," and "fake," ridiculing her behavior as "hocus pocus," "a ridiculous pose" that "defied any sort of human understanding."[24] Such a climate encouraged the revelation that Bara was really just a nice, middle-class Jewish girl from the Midwest. "Born

Theodosia Goodman, of Cincinnati, Ohio," she got her start performing "in a little Jewish Theatre on the East Side."[25]

No one star in early Hollywood better embodied the shift toward
using continental glamour to present a daringly adult image of who the
modern flapper fan might grow up to become than actress-producer
Gloria Swanson.[26] By 1921 Swanson's success allowed her to demand
star treatment at Paramount, where she replaced Pickford as the reigning "Queen of the Movies." There she also assumed another of Pickford's
former roles, becoming the single star who "bolstered [Paramount's]
whole program" by compelling exhibitors "to take weak features" they
otherwise would have avoided.[27] Swanson rose to stardom in six films,
variously called "marriage and divorce pictures" or "sex pictures," that
Cecil B. DeMille directed between 1919 and 1921. The director said he
spotted her potential after watching the "authority" she radiated "simply leaning against a door."[28] Lasky convinced the initially reluctant
DeMille to make the movies. "What the public demands to-day is modern stuff with plenty of clothes, rich sets, and action" and "full of modern problems and conditions," Lasky wrote to DeMille and scenarist
Jeanie MacPherson before urging the duo to adapt the popular novel
Old Wives for New (1918).

Like so many women filmmakers of the era, MacPherson had begun
working as an actress before directing her own production unit at Universal for two years and then joining DeMille at Lasky's studio in
1914.[29] MacPherson became DeMille's primary collaborator and a top
scenarist of the silent era who offered tips to "amateur continuity and
scenario writers" in motion picture news columns. "The trend in photoplays is toward the romantic," MacPherson advised, before noting the
importance of learning "feminine psychology" for success in the trade.[30]

With the news full of alarmist stories about the country's rising divorce
rates, DeMille's sex picture film cycle—*Old Wives for New* (1918), *Don't
Change Your Husband* (1919), and *Why Change Your Wife?* (1920)—
addressed the question of how to keep the flame burning *after* marriage. The films detailed the exploits of partners who used divorce, infidelity, and fashion makeovers to salvage marriages grown loveless or
simply dull. Awash in lavish costumes and sets, DeMille's films have
been mined for their relationship to the rise of consumer culture because
of the importance they placed on marital partners remaining fashionable and fun. By doing so, according to one prominent historian of
DeMille's work, the films scripted a new woman "entrapped in a process
of self-commodification," making her a "sexual commodity symbolizing

the reification of human relationships, especially marital ones, in a consumer society."[31] But such a view reduces the subjective meanings that motivate and inform conduct to one familiar meaning, the production of passive, narcissistic feminine subjects. The approach ignores stars, and the construction of their personas, to focus on reading a few select films.

Without a doubt, DeMille's films launched Swanson as "a sophisticated clotheshorse," who reveled in wearing the best that money could buy, but this reveals little about why Swanson, as opposed to any other well-dressed actress, emerged as a singular personality: the "screen's first real glamour queen."[32] Understanding what these films meant to fans demands a fuller sense of what made their stars both attractive and controversial. "She looked like she knew what life was all about, and in those days that was a sin for which you could be burned as a witch," one contemporary remembered in describing the effect created by Swanson's performance in *Why Change Your Wife?* (1920). Indeed, Swanson's success as a new kind of sexually sophisticated glamour queen circumvented Lasky's intention to use the films as a cost-cutting measure to subvert the star system. Although Lasky publicized the pictures as "ALL-STAR" productions, he gave no actor above-the-title billing, hoping to attract the public without conceding the privileges such a designation entailed.[33] Yet Swanson quickly emerged as a star. "We do not hesitate to proclaim Gloria Swanson one of the distinct acquisitions of the silent play, not only pictorially, but dramatically," declared *Motion Picture Magazine* after *Don't Change Your Husband* appeared (1919).[34]

Swanson's image set new trends by wrapping her adult sensuality in a cosmopolitan, non-Anglo package. The first to forgo the rage for tiny Cupid's bow lips, she "emphasized the generous outline" of her mouth and wore "her straight dark hair" around "her head, turban fashion, while nary a feminine curl dangled on her forehead to disturb the chiseled contours of her face." As comfortable in Parisian couture as an "Oriental headdress," she made fashion choices that associated her with the famed sensuality of both the French and the "Far East." Her image communicated what the best-selling English writer Elinor Glyn called a "sultry glamour," suggesting "a new kind of woman altogether—daring, provocative, sensuous."[35] Glyn and Marion believed her adult image explained why she became the first star to parade her motherhood, bringing babies "into vogue."[36] Swanson "didn't just represent glamour"; she "invented it," recalled Colleen Moore, poised to become the definitive flapper of the 1920s. In the process, Swanson created what

FIGURE 17. "Not entirely occidental" glamour queen Gloria
Swanson on the cover of the Spanish fan magazine *El Universal*.
Courtesy of the Harry Ransom Center, University of Texas,
Austin.

the journalist Adela Rogers St. Johns called "the all-time prototype image of A Movie Star."[37]

In establishing glamour as essential to the prototype of the postwar
movie star, Swanson deployed a quality that historian Peter Bailey calls
"a distinctively modern visual property." Glamour helped to account
for how consumer capitalism disseminated and normalized new gender
norms regarding sexuality. Glamorous strategies marketed a "middle
ground of sexuality," in Bailey's words. As an "open yet licit" form of
eroticism, glamour was "deployed but contained, carefully channeled
rather than fully discharged."[38] The approach helped to explain why

images of female bodies proliferated so rapidly in the period, becoming an acceptable if contested feature of modern public life. Swanson's star image displayed another important aspect of glamour: its promise that women's sexuality might act as a natural, positive part of her personality. Synonymous with neither beauty nor sex, glamour's provenance lay in poetry, in an allure fashioned from mystery, magic, and contrivance that might transform bearer and beholder alike.[39] Never considered a great beauty in her day, Swanson's famed "ability to wear clothes" indicated glamour's creation through the expert manipulation of externals that changed an ordinary-looking woman into a magnetic force. To this façade, Swanson added a manner characterized as "gracious though cool," "indifferent to the critical glances of women, the flattering attention of men."[40] Distance—in Swanson's case, both the objective absence created by her mechanically reproduced image and the subjective remove fashioned by her aloof persona—was central to the exercise of glamour. Swanson's sexuality did not render her a victim, forced to submit to another's desire. Distance allowed Swanson to enhance the promise of erotic possibility while simultaneously controlling and elevating her status, as not so much an erotic object as a glamorous subject who bestowed value on her beholder. "You walked the entire length of that long room. Looking straight ahead of you, you never once turned to look back or to retrace your steps," a fan who worked briefly with Swanson during the 1910s remembered, suggesting the impression the star's self-confidence left many years later. The poem another fan wrote to her suggests the hope this image gave, "You brought the screen much more than glamour, you brought the dreams a woman dreams! When I read about you / There were holes in my / Stockings / I tried to embroider / And a narrow, gold ring was in hock / But I forgot about it / When I spent my last fifty five cents / Before pay day / To see you on the screen!"[41]

 In the early twentieth century, women pioneered industries built on glamour, including cosmetics, fashion, interior design, and early Hollywood. Stereotypes that designated, and often trivialized, the expertise and interests associated with these businesses as feminine facilitated women's professional roles within them even as they restricted their chances in so-called masculine ones elsewhere. A valuable commodity in consumer culture, glamour sold many of the "expressive goods" that fueled the dramatic expansion of the nation's economy between 1900 and 1930.[42] The amount spent on movies, records, clothes, cosmetics, and home décor accounted for the largest increase in spending: 800

percent in the decade between 1914 and 1924. Such goods shared a connection to considerations of what designer Elsie deWolfe called questions of "aesthetic tastes."[43] A former stage actress turned America's first celebrity interior designer, deWolfe's smash-hit book, *The House in Good Taste* (1915), inspired women to trade the somber clutter of Victorian homes for a "modern house" filled with sunshine and chintz. More important, deWolfe taught women the importance of making their environments reflect the individual "personality of the mistress." Aesthetic or expressive goods mobilized in pursuit of glamour promised to confirm a certain idea of the purchaser to herself: this was a woman capable of creative expression, who valued her fantasies and desires. The women who deployed glamour used it to pursue more financially rewarding, exciting jobs, as well as more independent, free-spirited lives. "While men still shaped the world, it was the women who shaped the style in which we live," deWolfe asserted, suggesting how the glamorous strategies associated with consumer capitalism reflected the possibilities and limitations of the day.[44]

Swanson's rise displayed how glamour offered some women the means to escape the restrictions they faced in a society in which men's dominance was still pervasive. Swanson recalled how "the world of 1916," the year she left her hometown of Chicago for Los Angeles, was not just "a man's world" but also a "business run entirely by men." After signing on as a featured player with Mack Sennett, the king of slapstick comedy, she quickly feared "succeeding too well." According to Swanson, an actress at Sennett's Keystone studio could do little but play a "dumb little cutie serving as a foil to the broadest slapstick comedians in the world," by "having her skirts lifted and dodging flying bricks."[45] So Swanson quit Keystone, shortly after quitting her first, miserable marriage in 1917. Sad and unemployed, she later claimed that she put "every cent" in her purse and set off for "the new Los Angeles department stores" where she purchased a "bottle-green suit with a squirrel collar" and a "perfect fit." The suit seemed in a minute to wipe out the last six months of my life." Indeed, she credited the bottle-green suit with another magical act: landing her a part in the society melodrama *You Can't Believe Everything* (1917), which garnered the actress her first featured piece in *Photoplay*, "Gloria Glorified."[46] "Swanson graduated from light comedy to drama," the article proclaimed, displaying her accurate evaluation of how dramas offered women more stature than comedies. It is impossible to know whether Swanson's tale is apocryphal, but certainly any good actress knew the difference the right

FIGURE 18. "An Actress . . . what Everywoman would like to be." Courtesy of the Harry Ransom Center, University of Texas, Austin.

costume could make. And taking refuge in a department store, a place designed a century earlier as a paradise for women, became a standard practice in Swanson's films for escaping frustrations associated with living in a "man's world."

The personal power of a glamorous woman that Swanson encountered early in her career suggested how such an image promised fans that a woman made of equal parts style and authority could master any situation. Shortly after the release of *You Can't Believe Everything,* Swanson met Clara Kimball Young, one of the first actresses to create her own production company. Young's authority over every detail of her life amazed Swanson. "In what other business," she wondered, "could this delightful elegant creature be completely independent," not just "turning out her own pictures" but "dealing with men as her equals, being able to use her brains as well as her beauty, having total say as to what stories she played in, who designed her clothes, and who her director and leading man would be."[47] Ultimately, glamour required a quality that fan culture repeatedly emphasized that the real Swanson possessed in spades: courage.[48] Swanson's whole career began with "a dare" that "aroused her fighting blood," an article explained to fans; "I wanted to see if it was possible . . . if these others had something I didn't have." "She has *Courage,*" the writer Elinor Glyn declared; "she knows no fear! Imagine what it meant to go down in that den among the lions," Glyn continued, alluding to Swanson's performance in *Male and Female* (1919). The film featured her character's transformation after a shipwreck from an English lady to a scantily clad, Artemis-like huntress who, quite literally, lies down with the lions, proving her the naturally superior woman among the castaways. Swanson also demonstrated courage by advertising her controversial positions on hot topics of the day. "I not only believe in divorce. I sometimes think I don't believe in marriage at all," she announced in *Motion Picture.*[49] Swanson's star persona emphasized that a glamorous woman needed the confidence to turn heads and a willingness to put up a fight. As one critic put it, "Gloria bobs and rouges and lingeries [*sic*], yet always defeats the villain's ends—even if he supplied her with the rouge and the lingerie."[50] Such qualities explained why "An Actress," could claim, "Woman folk like this actress and say so emphatically. She is what Everywoman would like to be when she abandons herself to moments of wild and secret thought."

II

Jesse Lasky also wooed a cadre of famous writers, including the English author Elinor Glyn, to add new glamour to Paramount after the war.[51] In bringing Glyn over in 1920 to script and supervise Swanson's first starring vehicle, *The Great Moment* (1920), Lasky admitted that Glyn's appeal partially derived from the fifty-six-year-old writer's expertise with publicity. According to Lasky, Glyn was already "as adept as Salvador Dali at drawing attention to herself" when she arrived. By comparing Glyn to the great Spanish painter of the surrealist avant-garde, Lasky referred to her skill at drawing upon the engrained cultural superiority of Europeans in the American mind to justify her creation of unconventional romances. More than any other individual in early Hollywood, Glyn taught industry insiders and fans how the romantic ethic of artists demanded, and excused, their franker explorations of sexual desire.[52] The discussions she initiated about "love" (read: sex) and marriage in celebrity culture also offered a means for the industry's female personalities to express their desire for relationships that satisfied them erotically and supported them professionally. In the process, early Hollywood's fan culture described and discussed many of the practices and ideals later associated with companionate marriage and sexual liberalism. Critics charged that the promotion of new sexual norms and marital bonds by glamorous women were "nastifying [sic]" sex and encouraging women to follow their passions wherever they might lead.[53] In this way, early Hollywood sparked much of the heat that fueled the twentieth century's revolution in sexual behavior and attitudes.

Glyn learned to use the glamour of continental artistry as a shield for sex-talk after the publication of her sixth novel, *Three Weeks* (1907). She later held "the limitations and deprivations of my married life" accountable for her turn to writing the kind of passionately erotic melodramas that Hollywood's female fans later devoured. A notable, red-haired beauty, necessity drove Glyn into a misalliance with a country gentleman at twenty-seven. The older, good-humored husband preferred drink, hunting, and the company of other men; the romantic younger wife liked art, conversation, fashionable city life, and travel along the British Empire's edges. Although the marriage and her fashion flair provided Glyn the social entrée she sought, "her romantic temperament craved for a lover."[54] The lifelong diarist turned to her pen when bankruptcy threatened the spendthrift couple and their two daughters. Published when Glyn was forty-two, *Three Weeks* was a departure from her previous novels of manners. The book expressed what the author called her "fierce rebellion" inside, as "the syren [sic]" within vented "itself in the passionate writings. . . . My imagination was roused not by possession and its joys, but by a longing for them." The book told the tale of an older woman's creation of the perfect male lover. The heroine, an "intensely soignée" and unhappily married Slavic noblewoman

グローリア・スワンソン嬢と
女流作家エリナー・グリン女史
（ユニバーサル社特作品「一瞬間」に出演さるゝ
スワンソン嬢の豪奢な衣裳を御覧下さい）

FIGURE 19. Elinor Glyn with protégé Gloria Swanson, in a Tokyo fan
magazine. Courtesy of the Harry Ransom Center, University of Texas, Austin.

called only "Lady," plays Pygmalion to "a great, big, beautiful baby," an
aristocratic English youth named Paul.[55] With only a three-week vacation to create her ideal lover, Lady gives Paul a crash course in the
senses, teaching him to reject his "English conventionalities" and learn
how to love. "Love is tangible—it means to be close—close—to be

clasped—to be touching—to be One!" Properly performed, love requires full commitment to a partner's delight and fantastic attention to details like tiger-skin rugs for lounging, and elicits a woman's complete surrender. After much teaching of technique, Lady orchestrates "their wedding night" in a setting "fit for the Favorite in a harem." "By foolish laws we are sinning," she reminds her besotted lover afterward, "and you would be more nobly employed yawning with some bony English miss for your wife—and I by the side of a mad drunken husband." Rejecting the custom that "a moral woman" must remain "the faithful beast of burden to one man," Lady proposes another code instead: "to live a life with one's own love."[56]

Although Glyn called herself "the first writer to dare openly to glorify the joys of earthy love," she was actually one of the first *female* writers to suggest that men had much to learn from women about satisfying sex. The idea struck a nerve and the book became an international, scandalous hit that stalled the self-described "social pioneer's" climb in England. The stance of both the author and her heroine violated a century of Anglo-American conventions about sexuality that taught "the girl repression, the boy expression." "These lessons," in the words of a well-known Victorian doctor, were learned "not simply by word and book, but . . . graven into their very being by all the traditions, prejudices, and customs of society."[57] Most of the press pilloried Glyn, blaming her (presumed) female readers for the "Scarlet-crested Elinor Glyn wave" of writers who imitated her success. This "Fleshy School of Fiction" was "naturalizing" continental attitudes toward sexuality, British critics charged.[58] By preferring the "garbage spread out in the sun by imitators of the erotic, absinthe-drenched, nerve-racked decadents who swarm about Paris cafes," "readers—chiefly women—who make the fortune of English fiction" endangered "the splendidly wise and tender-hearted tradition of Scott, Dickens, and Thackeray." "Why is it that when women writers of the modern school deal with passion, they succeed only in 'nastifying it?'" wondered an American literary critic who considered Glyn the most shocking example of the trend. Scandalized by women's interest in this openly sexual material, critics protested that she cynically "glamoured over" women's base desires with the "holiness of love."[59]

But Glyn's status as a best-selling author offered a new means to advance, as she seized the "role of 'Elinor Glyn the famous authoress'" and "pioneer in the cause of feminine emancipation" who sought "to free the souls and bodies of women from the heavy age-old trammels of custom and convention."[60] Thus Glyn perfected the part of a glamorous, cosmopolitan authoress who aimed to teach women how to recognize, and enjoy, sensuality. The approach allowed Glyn to hone the strategies that would sell early Hollywood's more erotically daring melodramas and stars after the war.[61] After *Three Week's* publication, Glyn quickly learned that more than love was necessary to justify women's interest in "love." On the Atlantic crossing, headed for her first publicity tour in the United States, an American "dollar princess" schooled the writer about the image that would best impress her compatriots.[62] The reporters who met Glyn when she disembarked in New York encountered "Madame Glyn"—the "title" she insisted on for the rest of her career. Dressed much like her protagonist in *Three Weeks,* she appeared as part exotic, purple-gowned seductress, part aristocrat of devastating refinement who claimed the status of a continental artist. This performance mediated the reception of her unconventional views and likely increased her sales. "Her main complaint about America is that life here lacks the color and tone that effloresces in 'Three Weeks,'" explained one journalist, agreeing that American life was "emotionally drab and lacking in the esthetic values that are the gift of the continental temperament."[63]

Glyn also liberally laced her persona with Orientalism, in another move widely imitated in postwar Hollywood. By the 1910s, Orientalism already offered a well-established means for imperial nations of the so-called West to depict peoples from the Middle East and Asia as a mysterious, exotic "Eastern" mass with passionate, often excitingly dangerous, feminized natures. In political terms, Orientalist stereotypes justified Western imperialism as a "civilizing," paternalistic mission. It also excused the restriction and even outright exclusion of Chinese and Japanese immigrants to the United States as a necessary protection of native American morality and values. But when employed in consumer culture, Orientalism provided Anglo-American audiences with cover to explore "uncivilized" desires. Promising escape from the sexually repressive aspects of Western civilization, Orientalism came to shape the merchandising of a vast array of goods, as well as cultural performances from high to low.[64] Glyn's use of Orientalism helped to explain why her popularity stretched across the class spectrum, uniting "the Colonel's Lady and Judy O'Grady" precisely as the movie industry hoped.[65]

Orientalist marketing explained the image presented by the author upon her arrival in Los Angeles. Noting her hair dyed "the color of red

FIGURE 20. Elinor Glyn in a pose emphasizing her aristocratic credentials. Courtesy of Margaret Herrick Library, Academy of Motion Picture Arts and Sciences, Beverly Hills.

ink," "slanting eyes," and a "red, red, mouth," *Photoplay* described Glyn as a 'very, very well connected . . . old citizen of the world" who, nonsensically, appeared "like one of her heroines" as "an absolutely fantastic 'houri.'"[66] Only Orientalist fantasy could transform a middle-aged Englishwoman with aristocratic associations into an houri, one of the beautiful, young virgins said to await devout Muslim men in paradise. Thus Glyn's use of Orientalism made her good copy, in studio parlance, and a believable cosmopolitan guide for those looking to find products that promised access to passionate pleasures.

Madame Glyn's Orientalized glamour ideally suited the industry's imperial postwar frame of mind. Jesse Lasky's decision to import Glyn to script and supervise Swanson's first official starring vehicle signaled the industry's determination to stir the desires of audiences around the world and to neutralize the revived threat posed by European filmmakers. Having "cast aside its swaddling clothes," Hollywood embarked on a "period of conquest" to secure "a world existence" that inaugurated the "Golden Age of Pictures" in America, *Photoplay* gushed the year Madame Glyn arrived.[67] Once ensconced at the Hollywood Hotel, Glyn created a setting that telegraphed this motivation to the press, emptying her suite of its contemporary furniture and decorating it with scarlet drapes, velvet divans, silk purple pillows, tarot cards, and crystal balls so that it appeared like a "Persian tent," according to Swanson. The privileged cosmopolitan mobility these exotic surroundings communicated were central to Glyn's star image.[68] "Tiger Skins and Temperament," the article that introduced Glyn to American movie fans, laid her out on a tiger-skin rug she had picked up in India as the perfume of an Egyptian fan wafted through the air. The room also emphasized her aristocratic credentials, featuring portraits of her older sister, "Lucile—Lady Duff Gordon—the most celebrated modiste of two continents," and an assortment of royal friends. Lady Duff Gordon had survived a divorce and the sinking of the *Titanic* before opening a successful branch of her couture shop, Lucile, in New York, which featured her signature invention, lingerie. Other stories described her dual residences in "London and Versailles," ultimately underscoring that her Oriental glamour was no act. "Madame Glyn," *Photoplay* declared, "out-Baras Miss Bara. Because Miss Glyn is really Miss Glyn while Theda is Theodosia Goodman, if you get what I mean."[69]

After establishing her credentials as an authentic continental bearer of Oriental glamour, Glyn announced that her mission was "to set fashion on its ear" by teaching Americans to demand stars and stories that displayed real sex appeal rather than the ersatz version they knew. This description by Swanson would have appalled her mentor. Glyn never used so obvious a term as "sex appeal," an expression devoid of the continental aestheticism she sold. Glyn spoke of "it" instead of sex, of "the strange magnetism that attracts both sexes," the decidedly natural, unself-conscious quality exuded by "tigers and cats—both animals being fascinating and mysterious, and quite unbiddable." Glyn delighted in telling the press how American movie stars lacked it. Conveniently, only Swanson, whose "not altogether occidental eyes" revealed her "old soul," escaped Glyn's complaint that American actresses were mere girls incapable of projecting adult sexuality and chic. Male stars fared even ɔrse in her estimation. With casting approval over the male lead in *ɪhe Great Moment,* Glyn conducted a highly publicized search to find the right actor to play opposite Swanson.[70] Advertised as "the vivid drama of a society girl with a gypsy's heart, and the romantic adventures into which her untamed nature led her," the film was "written especially by Elinor Glyn, and personally supervised by her." The male lead needed enough sexual magnetism to pull off a scene in which he sucks rattlesnake poison out of Swanson's breast in a manner that convinces the wayward heroine to settle down. Glyn judged male star after male star unfit, declaring American men "could simply not make love," since they treated their leading ladies like "aunts or sisters."[71]

The search was a brilliant publicity device, but it also exposed how the personas of the period's male stars helped to explain the lack of adult female sensuality on screens. Up through the postwar era, the most successful leading men were "good natured, big brother types" who exuded the kind of boy-next-door, "Arrow Collar" masculine charm epitomized by stars like Douglas Fairbanks and Wallace Reid.[72] More sexually expressive male characters were typically villains played by "swarthy" new immigrants, or even "genuine Orientals" like the Japanese star Sessue Hayakawa.[73] *The Great Moment*'s success vindicated Glyn's opinion that audiences wanted to see more daring contests of passion between men and women on screens. "The public doesn't seem to be able to get enough of Elinor Glyn's first story for the screen," one reviewer declared. "It's a picture that will cause talk," the *Exhibitors Herald* predicted.[74] Theater owners noted that the film's "several daring situations will certainly please the women" and declared that Swanson's performance as "a temperamental English Girl who breaks the bonds of English conventionality to live her own life, as her Romany ancestors did," justified her elevation to "stardom."[75]

Discussions with Swanson, Glyn, and Hollywood's other working wives explored how their glamorous work affected their opinion about what constituted a satisfying marriage. Playing the role of the outsider-provocateur, Glyn blamed bourgeois Anglo-American conventions that demanded artists commit to monogamous marriages for the artistic limitations of many Hollywood stars. "In my beloved Paris, which is the center of Art, whether right or wrong from a conventional point of view—artists do not think highly of Matrimony," she explained in her *Photoplay* article "In Filmdom's Boudoir." Although conceding that America's looser divorce laws made "frequent change of partners" an alternative, she worried that many "foolish, ordinary" wives and "boring, exacting" husbands stalled their partner's artistic growth.[76] A "roundtable" discussion in *Photoplay* also featured Glyn taking an outlier's point of view. "What They Think about Marriage!" found female and male personalities alike contradicting the assertion by "Madame Elinor Glyn, the world famous English authoress and authority on love and marriage," that "motion picture stars—being artists—should not marry." All but one of the men breezily dismissed the idea that combining marriage and art presented any problem at all. The women, however, contradicted Glyn's view more carefully. "Choose your husband well!" ordered Constance Talmadge, expressing the opinion shared by most women that a happy marriage required a husband who supported the work of his wife. Norma Talmadge also thought it "entirely possible to have a happy home life and a career at the same time" if a woman chose a "sympathetic" husband who tried "sincerely to aid his wife in her profession." Frances Marion went further, redefining "true marriage" as not just "a ritual" but a relationship governed by "love and understanding" that did "away with the deadening effects" of traditional marital obligations that prevented a wife from giving "all that is best in her to her profession." According to Marion, a happy marriage Hollywood-style featured partners who "work together and play together, have a happy home and get along splendidly." Only Swanson sounded a different note, declaring, "If motherhood without marriage were possible," she would "dispense with marriage. Since it is not, marriage is the only alternative."[77]

The comments deepened a debate raging in *Photoplay* over what lessons Hollywood's personalities offered about the sex roles that best supported a modern marriage. Of the dozen articles the magazine ran on the subject between 1920 and 1921, a two-part interview with director Cecil B. DeMille presented such contrary, and contested, advice that it provides an interesting entry point into the discussion. In "What Does Marriage Mean?" DeMille challenged the widespread criticism that his sex pictures encouraged fans to treat divorce and infidelity lightly by instead arguing that they aimed to prevent divorce.[78] According to the director, the films illustrated the biblical injunction, "She that is married, careth how she please her husband," by teaching wives the importance of staying attractive and of allowing husbands to retain their freedom. DeMille claimed his own happy marriage illustrated just this principle: "In eighteen years I have never passed a Saturday night at home. I have never said where I was on a Saturday night. . . . And in eighteen years *I have never been asked*." The idea that the films that produced Swanson's star merely cloaked stereotypical Victorian gender roles in modern clothes prompted such an outcry from readers that the director revisited the subject in, "More about Marriage."[79] To the many readers who demanded to know if his wife enjoyed "the same privileges of personal freedom" as DeMille, he replied, "Of course, of course! It never occurred to me that such a question could arise." Perhaps the director believed his sex films taught female fans the importance of retaining traditional Victorian interiors inside modern exteriors.[80] The fact that Lasky pressured him to make the movies and the terms of his own marriage—he described his wife a model of true womanhood, whose "broad, wise, pure, understanding" nature helped him "to overcome the Adamic inheritance of lust and dust that lead to ruin"—suggest he had little interest in experimenting with gender roles at home. But the "overwhelmingly violent denunciations" the magazine reported receiving from readers indicated that this was not the message many fans heard.[81]

Early Hollywood's fan culture typically depicted a social environment that supported redefining gender roles in marriage along more, not less, egalitarian lines.[82] An interview with actress Florence Vidor, who starred in DeMille's first "sex picture," *Old Wives for New,* reappropriated the film's title to make this point: "Old Lives for New; Florence Vidor demonstrates that the New Woman may do justice to both a home and a career." Despite the "old ideals implanted by her southern ancestresses [sic]," who taught that a wife and mother must stay at home, Vidor believed a woman with "a real, deep undeniable craving for a form of self expression" did "more for her family by answering that call."[83] In this way, Vidor modeled a new woman whose reinforcing passions—for home, husband, child, and work—demanded a new life. Like so many interviews with celebrities, the story established a shared terrain of intimacy by describing Vidor as an ordinary woman who confronted the same problems as any wife. But it also underscored that the premium her job placed on "self-expression" offered Hollywood's working wives unusual means to legitimate their desire for unconventional domestic arrangements. An interview with actress Marjorie Rambeau made the same point. After reminding readers how shared marital complaints made "the Colonel's Lady and Judy O'Grady sisters under the skin," Rambeau asserted that actresses' marriages were "the happiest in the world" because their work required husbands who respected their individuality. While "the rule of the laywoman's life is to repress—

repress—repress. The rule of the actress is to express—express—always express," she explained. According to Rambeau, the artist's ethic fostered true understanding in marriage by creating shared commitments that provided "a never ceasing topic" of interest that "fused" the interest of husband and wife. The result could reverse typical gender roles, as when Rambeau's husband decided to play *her* muse. "I shall devote my life to you. We will do whatever is best for your talent. I shall think of but one career. That is yours," he promised, leaving Rambeau with "what every woman wants, a deep, lasting, selfless love."[84]

Such fan discourse indicated how early Hollywood sold its audience norms that prefigured those that historians equate with the later rise of "sexual liberalism," a term signaling sex's divorce from reproduction and the idea that heterosexual pleasure was a value for both sexes as well as a key ingredient of a happy marriage.[85] The term distills many of the reforms that activists during the late 1920s grouped under the new ideal of "companionate marriage."[86] Those like birth control advocate Margaret Sanger argued that the era's climbing divorce rates, agitation for birth control, and youth revolt indicated the frustration many felt over viewing marriage as a union based on obligation and self-sacrifice. Instead, they recommended redesigning the institution along more democratic lines that emphasized sexual chemistry and shared interests. Touting mutual sexual satisfaction and emotional intimacy as the new hallmarks of a good marriage, the ideal justified practicing birth control and jettisoning the idea that respectable wives should tame their husbands' dangerous libidos. Instead, the companionate ideal asked sexually adroit husbands to cultivate their wives different, but no less powerful sexuality and accepted erotic exploration, or "petting," before marriage. But the democratic reforms the companionate ideal promised women took place only within the context of marriage, since most still shared the belief that careers destroyed women's sex drives and made them unsympathetic to men's needs. Thus, like so much of the advice given to women in the 1920s, matrimony, however modified, remained the means to satisfy all of their needs. Many postwar films duplicated the position. But industry fan culture instead often depicted early Hollywood's female personalities as more omnivorous and demanding, both sexually and professionally. As a mountain of sociological studies revealed the growing influence of Hollywood's stars as role models to youths, these glamorous women and their lovers indeed provided examples that set fashion on its ear, as Elinor Glyn liked to say.[87]

Payne Fund

III

The only person to agree with Glyn's view that Anglo-American sexual conventions prevented early Hollywood's artists from exercising the freedom necessary to their art was Antonio Moreno, an actor who represented a new masculine type, the Latin lover. The troubled reception that stars like Moreno met suggested that fans both embraced and feared the industry's exploration of women's passions. "Elinor Glyn is expressing the European point of view," argued the Spanish-born actor, "which I understand but many Americans will not." But of course personalities like Glyn and Moreno were busy ensuring that Hollywood's postwar audience understood just such differences. In *The Philosophy of Love* (1920), Glyn noted the "glorification of romance" required teaching "American girls . . . a desire to be loved like European women are loved."[88] Ironically, as the debate on immigration restriction raged after the war—a debate that put the pollution of the nation's "Anglo stock" by new immigrant men at the center of the danger they posed— just this ethnic type licensed the new displays of passion on screens. When viewed through the virtual intimacy of a camera, many women considered Latin lovers' "strictly continental" methods of "making love" superior to those of Anglo-American men.[89] Put differently, en masse the Southern and Eastern Europeans largely excluded by postwar immigration restrictions appeared as dark outsiders whose feminized degeneracy threatened the nation's health. But early Hollywood's postwar box office exposed the fact that these same qualities proved irresistible when a talented individual could magnify them on the screen.

No other male type appeared as capable of satisfying the passionate natures of the screen's glamorous heroines as Latin lovers. The *Photoplay* article "The Techniques of Lovers" found actress-producer Clara Kimball Young praising "the foreign—Latin—technique" of "screen lovers." According to Young, American men were "too impatient" and "too egotistical" to understand that "love making" was an art. Temperamentally inclined to act the "carpenter" instead of the "artist," the average American man "fusses and fumes over the least squeak in his automobile," yet was "satisfied with the commonest sort of mediocrity in his lovemaking," she complained. Young called "Latins" superior because they studied women "in all their manifestations." Sounding a note similar to Glyn's, Young blamed gender conventions in "Anglo-Saxon countries" that taught women and men to treat each other as asexual "companions." "American women have demanded equality, and they deserve equality," Young noted, but she argued that equality should not prevent "men from studying them—as women." American men assumed women reacted "to the same impulses and emotions as themselves, and make love as they would want a woman to make love to them." Scenarist Lenore Coffee recalled how Young voiced similar complaints in private, when she despaired of ever finding a man off screen who could satisfy her emotional longings and erotic needs.[90]

Luckily, Hollywood's women filmmakers offered an imaginative escape from the demand of playing the sensual instructor to American men by creating the Latin lover, a glamorous, magical "handsome hero" who could intuit a woman's every wish and mesmerize her into becoming a heroine who acted on her desires. In retrospect, the rise of the Latin lover appears as a kind of bridge between two sexual ethics. Under his imaginative tutelage, American men and women might learn to ignite a woman's sensuality so that, together, they could experience erotic bliss. The career of Rudolph Valentino, the actor who both defined and immortalized the type, indicated that many were not ready to make such fantasies a reality. Everything that made Valentino the ideal fantasy lover of millions accentuated his foreign, dark, exotic beauty, his sensual remove from conventional Anglo-American codes of masculinity. Baptized Rodulphus Petrus Philibertus Raphael in Southern Italy in 1895, Valentino's father was an Italian veterinarian; his French mother was a noblewoman's companion before her marriage. Valentino's mother raised her always-mischievous middle child and pet to share her love of languages, poetry, storytelling, and prayer. In 1913, Rodolfo, as friends called him, crossed the Atlantic from Paris to New York in a first-class cabin with a tuxedo in his steamer trunk and the equivalent of $4,000 in his pocket. There the talented dancer found work as a professional tango partner to middle-class women, displaying the qualities that made him such an appealing threat. "Lounge lizards" and "tango pirates," as the men who performed such jobs were called, were stereotyped as lower-class, new-immigrant Italians and Jews who used "feminine" wiles—beauty, grace, and relentless focus on another's pleasure—to prey on women. Rodolfo moved up quickly to the more respectable position of exhibition dancer and began making the theatrical rounds in New York, trying to break into the legitimate stage or motion pictures. His implication in a scandal involving a dance partner's divorce encouraged Valentino to try his luck in the new movie capital, and so he took a job with a dance company and headed west.[91]

Valentino arrived in Los Angeles in September 1917, shortly after the United States entered the war, and quickly fell into the orbit of some of the industry's most powerful women, who intimately supported his professional advance and personal life. D. W. Griffith judged the Italian actor "too foreign looking" for anything but bit parts as "heavies" in low-budget films. But filmmakers like June Mathis, Clara Kimball Young, and Alla Nazimova who were eager to use cosmopolitan, continental aesthetics to explore more daring romances recognized him as a means to help achieve their ends. Always on the lookout for a man who communicated sexual prowess, Young gave Valentino his first break, casting him in one of her company's "special" features, *The Eyes of Youth* (1919).[92] Playing a "cabaret parasite" hired to entrap Young's character in a compromising situation, the actor demonstrated, in one short scene, an ability to tempt a woman down morally dangerous paths. The performance caught the eye of June Mathis, the most powerful woman executive working for a major studio in 1918. Another filmmaker who began her career as a child on stage, Mathis had gotten her break in the movies five years earlier after winning a scenario-writing contest in a fan magazine. Mathis quickly rose to head Metro's scenario department and then to act as the studio's "artistic supervisor," writing, casting, and overseeing productions from start to finish until her sudden death in 1926.[93] An open devotee of European art, she tackled a challenge most thought impossible by adapting Vicente Blasco Ibanez's internationally best-selling novel about the catastrophic costs of the Great War, *The Four Horsemen of the Apocalypse* (1919).[94] Described as possessing an "indomitable will and dangerous temper," Mathis overrode the director's objection to casting an unknown foreigner with a radically different masculine style as the lead.[95] Her determination to make the movie with Valentino demonstrated the motivation behind so much of her work: to raise the stature of the American film industry by associating it with continental artists who explored modern cultural currents.

Valentino's successes in Mathis's *The Four Horsemen of the Apocalypse* (1921) made him the 1920s symbol of masculine glamour, revealing him to be "the continental hero, the polished foreigner, the modern Don Juan" in Hollywood's "unsuspecting midst." Valentino "tangos, makes love, and fights with equal grace," raved one of the many critics who singled out his performance in the film, displaying how he combined

FIGURE 21. June Mathis, the triumphant adaptor of *The Four Horsemen of the Apocalypse*. Courtesy of Margaret Herrick Library, Academy of Motion Picture Arts and Sciences, Beverly Hills.

previously incompatible masculine attributes into a new whole.[96] Valentino plays Julio, the dissolute heir of an Argentine ranching empire who moves to Paris, where he plays at painting until an adulterous love affair awakens his better side, remaking him into a man driven to sacrifice for his country. Valentino embodied the hero as lover, controlled only by passion, circumstance, and the pulse of his partner. Whether guiding a lower-class woman in a languid, intricate tango in a smoke-filled dive, or oh so delicately seducing a married aristocrat in his Parisian atelier, Valentino adjusted his style and tempo to deliver whatever the woman and the situation required. Hailed as a masterpiece, the *Four Horsemen* became one of the decade's most successful films, launching the formerly unknown actor into a stardom that made plain the transformed landscape of women's sexual fantasies.[97]

Valentino's persona centered on how his Orientalized, continental glamour granted his fans new erotic license. His distinctly non-Anglo appeal explained why so many American men resorted to using the nonhuman terms reserved for nonwhites to describe him, comparing his sexuality to that of a "panther" who projected "more sheer animal magnetism than any actor before or since." Like many women, Glyn thought Valentino the very human incarnation of her ideal lover, possessing a technique that appeared at once "masterful and tender" and a confidence that radiated that "he knew everything about love."[98] His performance in *The Sheik* (1921) crystallized this star image. The film was an adaptation of a then-best-selling novel by E. M. Hull. Like Glyn, Hull was another empire-trotting English author who wrote the book while stationed with her soldier-husband in Algeria. But unlike anything Glyn had written, Hull's story tracked the sexual education of a young English, New Woman–styled heroine, Diana, at the hands of an older "Arab" sheik, played by Valentino. On vacation in the Middle East with her brother, Diana rejects the attention of several passionless Anglo suitors before setting off to explore the desert with only local "Arab" guides. Enter Valentino's sheik, ruled by an uncivilized Eastern code that dictates that "when an Arab sees a woman he wants he takes her," as the film's ads proclaimed. The sheik needs only to spy Diana from a distance to understand their mutual desire. After orchestrating her kidnapping, he sweeps his "white gazelle" off to his sumptuous tent, where he unleashes her dormant sexual desires.[99] The film abounded with racist stereotypes that revealed much about the "West" and little about the "East." Despite the constantly stressed superiority of the West, here tied to Englishwomen's freedoms and their beautiful white skin, only the

FIGURE 22. Rudolph Valentino as the Latin lover. Courtesy of
Margaret Herrick Library, Academy of Motion Picture Arts and
Sciences, Beverly Hills.

dark cover of the East and an Orientalized man can liberate Diana's
passion.

Valentino's triumph as the ideal lover in this passionate melodrama
spoke to the desire of female fans to act the independent sensual adventuress, their fears about the part, and the seeming impossibility of lovers
acting on such desires within the context of Western civilization.[100]
Moreover, this ambivalence duplicated the same erotic tension produced by watching heroines like Diana oscillate between aggression
and subservience, pleasure and pain.[101] "Oh, what a Lucky Girl to have
enough money to take a trip like that—a trip across the wild desert
with only Arab guides in her company. Oh, how daring! If it were only
I!" recalled a Chicago moviegoer. "The more I saw the picture the more
I fell in love with the handsome hero—I resented him for his abrupt and

brutal manners but still I used to care for him," another fan recalled of Valentino's effect on her in *The Sheik*. *Variety* called *The Sheik* "preposterous" but admitted that it "won out" because "it dealt with every caged woman's desire to be caught up in a love clasp by some he-man who would take responsibility and dispose of the consequences." "Seems like an ordinary picture," remarked one exhibitor, "but as a lady patron remarked, 'How that man can love!'"[102]

If women in audiences across America "raved" over Valentino, as exhibitor after exhibitor noted, men were "divided in opinion" about the star. Critical commentary impugned the star's virility, seizing on how the film dramatically toned down the novel's brutality by having the sheik awaken the heroine's sensuality with passionate kisses rather than rape. "He is a soft, sapless sort of Sheik beside the character delineated by Edith M. Hull," scoffed one review.[103] Younger men aped the actor's dress and admitted to studying his lovemaking techniques, but their elders lambasted Valentino's feminized manliness as not just unsuitable but fundamentally "un-American." Unquestionably beautiful and always attired to highlight his sinewy physique, Valentino was a glamorous male subject whose power lay in his ability to trade on women's desires. However forceful his erotic technique appeared at times, his performances displayed a single-minded focus on eliciting the pleasure of heroines who needed an encouraging hand. Indeed, male critics' charges that his technique was too gentle displayed the tendency of both sexes to conflate terror with sex under Victorian conventions. It also suggested that men might need to resort to ever more brutal methods to retain the traditional balance of power between the sexes if women began to pursue their desires more aggressively. Men also complained about the actor's nonwhite, foreign appeal. "All men hate Valentino," declared a male writer in *Photoplay*. "I hate his Oriental optics. I hate his classic nose; I hate his Roman face; I hate his smile; I hate his patent leather hair; I hate his Svengali glare; I hate him because he dances too well," and, finally: "I hate him because he's the great lover of the screen . . . too apt in the art of osculation."[104]

June Mathis introduced Valentino to Alla Nazimova, the artist whom he credited with teaching him to act.[105] When remembered at all, Nazimova appears as the first in a line of more familiar European female stars who followed her, including Pola Negri, Greta Garbo, and Marlene Dietrich. Her first Metro studio biography hailed the Russian actress "as the last of the great stage artistes to heed the call of the screen," but Nazimova was actually the first real stage star to use her "artistic temperament" to justify her unconventional femininity and demands, including lending her support for woman suffrage and the Equal Rights Amendment.[106] The words "genius," "intense," "dominant," "mysterious," "exotic," and, finally, "Russian" consistently modified the name of early Hollywood's original "Madame." This was a "Russian Crimean superwoman" "who *made* New York like [playwright Henrik] Ibsen, who actually startled the American theater into newness of life."[107] Such publicity accurately reflected her theatrical status.[108] A small, lithe figure with a mop of short, black curls and large blue eyes, she was among the first actors exposed to the techniques of the Moscow Art Theatre's famed director, Constantin Stanislavski. Nazimova stayed in New York after a tour with a Russian company in 1905. The next year she commandeered the direction of her triumphant English-speaking debut in *Hedda Gabler*, which resulted in Ibsen's first U.S. success.[109] Her Hedda was a woman turned feral inside the cage of a respectable, middle-class marriage.[110] Over the next three years she solidified her stature by playing Ibsen's other "modern," "soul-harassed" wives who, "hell-bent on independence," refused to remain trapped in a "doll's house" (the title of Ibsen's play).

From the start, her publicity emphasized the qualities that Hollywood seized on in the postwar period. "A hint of the Slav, a hint of the Oriental, a hint of the Parisienne, a hint of the woman of the theater," as one critic summed up her persona. Detractors called her Hedda "a bit of feline and voluptuous Orientalism," but more lauded just these qualities.[111] "Our English-speaking actresses lack often the emphatic and expressive temperament. It is Madame Nazimova's by birthright as a Slav," observed one. Another declared, "Our actresses hesitate to ply the appeal of their sex, except, needless to say, in musical plays," but on "the continental stage . . . the wise actress counts it as a telling resource, a ready tool, and cultivates it accordingly. It is strong in Madame Nazimova."[112] Just as the success of Glyn's *Three Weeks* helped to change assumptions about literary tastes, Nazimova's theatrical triumphs altered the landscape of New York theater by shifting the opinion of the powerful producer Charles Frohman about what women wanted to see. Previously Frohman had declared there was no audience for the "erotic and the decadent." After Nazimova's triumph he announced "sex conflict" the order of the day. Nazimova increasingly played these roles in less high-art, more melodramatic plays like *Bella Donna* (1912), an adaptation of Robert Hichens's best-selling novel, which, like his incendiary *The Garden of Allah* (1904), featured passion-starved Anglo heroines awakened under the cover of Orientalist escape.[113]

Nazimova traveled to Los Angeles in 1916 as the "First Femme Fatale of the American theatre," "a dark enchantress from the East." Her first foray into what she called the "photodrama" was an adaptation of *War Brides* (1916), a hit antiwar play in which she starred.[114] The *New York Times* declared that the actress not only "screen[ed] well" but reached "a tragic height never before attained in a motion picture." Though nearly forty, her success convinced Metro's East Coast head of production that she could offer a better interpretation of a modern vamp than prewar stars like Theda Bara.[115] Nazimova signed a five-year contract with Metro in 1918 that included a starting salary of $13,000 a week and the right to approve her director, costars, and scripts. As with Glyn, the authenticity of her exotic glamour as both a "foreigner from that most foreign of all countries" and an artist certified by both New York and European critics was key to her promotion. *Photoplay* described her estate, "The Garden of Alla," as "a three-and-a-half acre compound on Sunset Boulevard filled with the faint pervasive fragrance of the Orient." This "aristocrat of the arts" was called a "rebel" and a "revolutionary" who was such a consummate performer that one could not tell if she was "always acting—or she never acts."[116]

A year of "superlative" box offices hits landed Nazimova at the center of the industry's celebrity culture in 1919, where her star was held aloft by her "seemingly overwhelming appeal for the feminine sex," according to *Motion Picture Magazine*.[117] The protagonists she played highlighted her exotic glamour, including a cabaret singer in the Latin Quarter, a gypsy, the daughter of an Arab sheik, and a "half-caste Eurasian" caught up in the Boxer Rebellion in *The Red Lantern* (1919), a film June Mathis adapted for the actress.[118] Nazimova and Mathis teamed up for several productions, creating passionate melodramas whose heroines ran "the gamut between Vice and Virtue with dazzling effect."[119] Publicity about her real life depicted her as an androgynous figure who preferred to act the boy among the bevy of talented young protégés she kept around her. Fans offered a peek inside Alla's Garden encountered a figure who "abjures makeup" and preferred the "costume of a Chinese boy." This decidedly epicene character wore her "short hair clipped with boyish brevity" and "slightly touched with grey." Extolling her "boyish" charms, fan magazines reported her claim that "most of my friends are young girls," protégés who called her "Peter and sometimes Mimi."[120] More knowing readers would have recognized such references as cues that indicated her sexual preference for women. Among Hollywood insiders Nazimova's taste for the ladies was

FIGURE 23. The Epicene Girls, Alla Nazimova and Natacha Rambova lounge in pajamas at the Garden of Alla. Courtesy of Margaret Herrick Library, Academy of Motion Picture Arts and Sciences, Beverly Hills.

as well known as the cosmopolitan salon she hosted and the all-girl pool parties she often threw, whose regulars included the Talmadge sisters and June Mathis.[121]

The total control Nazimova demanded on the set made her notorious for alienating male directors, but she worked smoothly with women like Mathis and designer Natacha Rambova. After completing *Four Horsemen,* Mathis sought to associate her protégé Valentino with Nazimova's brand of continental artistry. Nazimova and Mathis cast Valentino as Armand, the male lead in their production *Camille: Paris 1921.*[122] "Why not a Camille of today?" asked Mathis's opening intertitle in this "modernized version" of the melodrama that in important senses helped to make possible these women's performance of modern womanhood.[123] Their highly stylized, decidedly nonnaturalistic *Camille* blatantly aligned itself with the avant-garde expressionist films then transforming Berlin's cinematic scene, becoming perhaps the first domestically produced "art film." The film's futuristic, Art Deco costumes and settings created by Nazimova's protégé designer Rambova overshadowed the production. Although the film was a commercial disaster, Valentino felt new freedom inside these women's circle of influence, and a romance between the actor and Rambova led to marriage. Rambova, whose real name was Winifred Shaughnessy Hudnut, was a former dancer who had learned how to mobilize continental glamour to get ahead from her godmother, Elsie deWolfe, the interior designer who so clearly articulated at the fin de siècle how such strategies offered new means for women to get ahead.[124]

IV

A spotlight landed on the movies' new home after the war, as tactics designed to exploit fans' curiosity about the unconventional private lives and folkways of this first Hollywood became a staple in the repertoire of writers in fan culture. Put differently, Nazimova may have possessed the most sexually challenging persona in early Hollywood, but reporting on the colony increasingly focused on the unusual romantic lives and personal predilections of residents, describing the movie colony as a place of "infinite freedom" "where almost everything goes."[125] "In these days of suffragets [sic] and long-haired poets, bifurcated skirts and lisping ladies, it's hard to know who's who and what's what. It's getting to be quite the rage—this exchange of identities," was how *Motion Picture Magazine* explained the colony's penchant for topsy-turvy sex roles. June Mathis cunningly offered a view of such arrangements in two short scenes in *Four Horsemen*. The first displayed two lesbians nuzzling in a Parisian nightclub, one dapperly dressed in a tuxedo, the other in conventional feminine garb. The second involved a bevy of German officers dressed in women's clothes whose entwined embrace created a single mass staggering down the staircase of a captured French chateau. "To hundreds of people that meant no more than a masquerade party," Mathis admitted, but "to those who had lived and read, and who understood life the scene stood out as one of the most terrific things in the picture." "A personally conducted tour of the Hollywood film colony" that *Photoplay* writer Adela Rogers St. Johns gave readers highlighted the unconventional gender role reversals this environment could produce. "On the left, the home of Madame Nazimova and her husband. I beg pardon lady? No, I don't know his name, but I'm sure he's got one."[126] The daughter of California's crusading defense attorney Earl Rogers, St. Johns attended Hollywood High before starting work at Hearst's *Los Angeles Herald Examiner*. After marrying Ike St. Johns, a fellow copy editor at the newspaper, she decided that work at *Photo-*

play was better suited to raising their two children. James Quirk, the magazine's editor in New York, hired St. Johns to fulfill the demand for on-the-spot interviews filled with local color. St. Johns perfected a style of celebrity reporting that turned personal "anecdotes" into stories that revealed "the secret of Hollywood's personalities and the drama and melodrama that sprang from these." Called "Hollywood's Mother Confessor," St. Johns also socialized with many of her subjects, hosting regular "hen parties" whose guests included the industry's most powerful women with Frances Marion, her fellow writer, Californian, and best friend.[127] The journalist recalled how as "the Movies swept the country," after the war, the "news value" of "Hollywood-ites" skyrocketed. "Fan magazines had sprung up and every day the newspapers devoted columnar miles of space to film subjects," Adolph Zukor agreed, admitting, "We co-operated by furnishing copy, raising the shades so to speak, for the public to look at us. Therefore, we had no right to complain if some people didn't like what they saw."[128] Clearly the attention was good for an industry bent on becoming the entertainment and fashion capital of the world. Yet in retrospect it's easy to see how such advertising spun a bit out of control, as "Hollywood took over where [P.T. Barnum] left off" and suddenly became "The Greatest Show on Earth."[129]

News stories marveled at Los Angeles's development as the "Film Capital of the World" and the first new American metropolis of the twentieth century.[130] A place considered little more than a dusty backwater in 1910 had become the nation's fifth-largest city a decade later. Quickly becoming the most prominent industry in both the city and the state, motion picture production provided both the jobs and the publicity that fueled the explosive growth of Los Angeles.[131] Migration to the city peaked immediately after the war, as 100,000 mostly native-born Anglos moved west each year to begin again in the City of Dreams. The young white women who continually disembarked at the city's new railroad station downtown became a particularly visible eddy in the massive current. The *Atlanta Constitution* declared that, "10,000 girls go to Los Angeles every year 'to become a star in movies.'" "There are more women in Los Angeles than any other city in the world and it's the movies that bring them," as one shopkeeper bluntly described the relationship in 1918.[132] By 1920, Los Angeles became the only western boomtown where women outnumbered men.[133] Such changes meant that descriptions of the flickers' Los Angeles as a place of pastoral, innocent play vanished along with the pepper trees that Frances Marion o loved. Confronted with the opulent lives of the industry's stars, and the growth of hierarchy and defined roles within studios, some likened this first Hollywood to a European court, its residents to kings and queens. Yet the spirit that animated the movie colony was hardly an aristocratic social arrangement that prized outward restraint, fixed orders, and emotional reserve.[134]

Instead, keener observers compared Hollywood's new environment to that quintessential modern metropolitan neighborhood of romantic self-reinvention, a Bohemia—a Hollywood Bohemia, to be exact. The regular references by the midteens to Los Angeles's so-called movie colony anticipated the emergence of Hollywood's identity as a bohemian third space, someplace "on the edge of town," on the "margins," where "clannish" and "outlandish" customs set the trends desired and criticized by others in equal measure. This "Chameleon City of the Cinema [was] as changeable as a woman," "the biggest city of make-believe in the universe," and a place where "the occident and the Orient" converged.[135] The image of a shape-shifting, cosmopolitan city within a city keyed to self-reinvention set the stage for the development of the Hollywood Bohemia social imaginary that appeared. The economic and imaginative materials that supported the expansion of the city and its leading industry aided this process by attracting a native-born, female-heavy migrant stream. Such women were eager not just to become movie stars but to find work in routine pink-collar jobs made more romantic by Hollywood's reflected glow. Valeria Belletti, a secretary at the Goldwyn Company, explained how the artistic airs and social culture at studios could transform even routine sex-segregated jobs. "I like the hustle and bustle of this life," Belletti wrote to a friend back east. "Everybody but my boss is so nice and friendly—so different from a regular business office." "You have no idea how glad I am I left New York," she continued. "There was no place so full of romances as California, especially Hollywood," she explained, before conceding that, at times, "it reeks too much of the flesh."[136] These conditions, in turn, supported the western-inflected bohemian style that Hollywood dramatized along the frontier of mass culture.

Calling the movie colony a Bohemia will sound as strange to many today as it did when the article "Oh, Hollywood! A Ramble in Bohemia" appeared in *Photoplay* in 1921. This "Greenwich Village in the West," it admitted, "was not so much exploited or propagandized, but pack[ed] the same wallop in each hand." The idea that Los Angeles was too controlled by uptight, conservative Anglo Midwesterners to nurture anything but conformity became a cornerstone of the city's image in 1913, when Willard Huntington Wright published his infamous essay "Los Angles—The Chemically Pure," in *The Smart Set*.[137] The city's sprawling, sunny, suburban enclaves of bungalows violated the idea of a proper bohemian space as an urban enclave characterized by dilapidated, art-filled apartments, cafés, and nightclubs. British actor Allen Cambell, in a self-published rejoinder to Wright's essay, argued that such clichés blinded most to Los Angeles's Bohemia. Here artists took their inspiration from nature and often staged their revelries "at home," which for Cambell meant "a little house" shared by four women and four men.[138] *Photoplay* also trumpeted how this Bohemia's "tropical" setting created "a reckless, buoyant, sun-warmed, 'joie de vivre'" that differed from a "'daughter of the pavements' like Greenwich Village or the Latin Quarter." St. Johns hit upon the idea of "*exaggeration*" to explain how the "peaceful country village" of Hollywood suddenly came to resemble "the Left Bank," "Bloomsbury of London," and "Greenwich Village when it was not a phony tourist trap." What all these places shared despite their different appearances was their possession of residents who excelled at dramatizing their "artistic temperament." Those who became stars working without sound on the flat canvas of celluloid relied on a process of exaggeration that distilled and enlarged new desires and fantasies. What the Loveliest Working Girl Made Good, the Glamour Queen, the First Lady of Romance, the Ideal Marriage, the Exotic Aristocrat of the Arts, and the Latin Lover all shared was their promise to offer fans lessons in how to discover a more passionate approach to life. And now Hollywood Bohemia, the ideal romantic environment, arose as a space in which to turn these desires into reality. Consuming Hollywood Bohemia let fans identify with an environment that valued daydreaming, originality, play, and pleasure at the expense of utilitarian rationality.[139]

Hollywood secretary Valeria Belletti displayed the personal transformations wrought by embracing a bohemian spirit envisioned as a healthful, beautifying adventure enjoyed equally by women and men. "The bohemian colony in Los Angeles has it all over Greenwich Village because here they are real artists and not fake ones like you find in the Village," explained Belletti. The daughter of Italian immigrants who attended Catholic schools in New Jersey before going to work at a theatrical agency in New York at sixteen, Belletti traveled west with a friend on a vacation after her mother's death. Responding to the atmosphere, she moved to Los Angeles, alone, at twenty-five. Belletti's letters to her best friend in New York lingered on the parties she threw with her roommates, where male guests "always bring some good stuff to drink and we make cocktails and dance" before heading off "to a number of real wild bohemian cafes in Hollywood." Increasingly, her letters embraced the bohemian commitment to pleasure and self-actualization, confiding a desire "to seek and find happiness if possible." Having realized she "wasn't living her own life" back east, "due to some sense of duty," she explained her new code: "Now I do what I want to do and I'm much happier and I believe I'm really fitting myself to do the thing that I desire most—and that is to write. I don't know if I'll ever amount to anything, but what difference does it make. . . . I want to write because that is the thing which will give me the most pleasure."[140]

The movies' crassly commercialized product also made it easy for many elites to discount the industry's art and artists and, therefore, its image as a Bohemia. Adela Rogers St. Johns and Anita Loos associated the colony with Bohemia to emphasize the industry's artistry. In *Breaking into the Movies* (1921), Loos cautioned newcomers, "The colony's outlandish ideas" were "the same ones . . . always associated with artists—a bohemian spirit which is the same whether in Hollywood or the Latin Quarter of Paris." She further warned that, "no matter how pessimistically they may talk, these people . . . consider the photoplay a form of art and themselves as artists. If you think movies are a lowbrow form of making a living . . . you will be quietly frozen out."[141] Yet Hollywood Bohemia was always also a marketing tactic that conveyed the more sexually sophisticated, European-flavored glamour the industry purveyed after the war.[142] The promotion aimed to sell the movies as much as to challenge the sex roles, work ethic, and social norms of the respectable middle class.

But this tension—between the wish to market goods through their association with a life of exotic, liberated fantasy and the desire to carve out spaces on the margins to enact genuine rebellions against middle-class norms—has always lain in Bohemia's heart. The first notable Bohemia appeared in 1845 when a newspaper editor asked the struggling writer Henri Murger for stories about male students in the Latin Quarter and the "*grissettes*" ("country girls" who moved to Paris in search of work), they loved and lost.[143] Murger used *Bohemian Life* to propel himself out of bohemian penury, writing a musical and a collected edition that catapulted the author and Bohemia to fame. It also demonstrated how much bohemia sold a way of living as much as art. As Murger avowed, bohemians were those whose "everyday existence is a work of genius." The most sensitive chronicler of Bohemia's origins, Jerrold Seigel, argues that it arose as a space to express frustration over modern capitalist democracies' failure to create a society based on fraternity, equality, and individual freedom for men rather than social atomization, egotism, and class divisions. "People were or were not bohemian," Seigel asserts, "to the degree that their lives dramatized these tensions and conflicts for themselves, making them visible, demanding they be faced."[144] Bohemia housed the archetypical modern artist—freed or bereft of patrons, depending on one's view, and forced to the market—whose success represented the triumph of talent over circumstance that bourgeois society valorized. Hollywood Bohemia promoted this image of its residents. But as a social phenomenon, it offered both a place and an imaginary space, where the young (for it was always understood as a stage of life) could challenge the hypocrisies and limitations of middle-class life.

Hollywood's bohemian new West built on American modifications that already incorporated women as artists and lovers, as well as muses and mistresses. Greenwich Village's bohemians first modified its once hypermasculine scene, recasting bourgeois sex roles as women actively pursued creative and erotic parts. The first sociologist to study "Chicago's Latin Quarter" found a similar adaptation.[145] But in both instances, old sex roles often reasserted themselves if marriage and children arrived, since most leading artists remained men and most of its bohemian women, aside from those with independent wealth, failed to find stable means of self-sufficiency. In contrast, the movie colony visibly supported many more women artists. Moreover, the comparatively high wages paid even to extras meant that many others in entry-level jobs earned a living wage in the silent era. "Without realizing it," Loos recalled, "I was in on the ground floor of a sex revolution . . . the transfer of female emotions from the boudoir to the marts of trade" as "female hearts of America" began "to flutter with joy as they flew from homes into office buildings."[146] Frances Marion remembered how many residents used "their new freedom" to pull "down all the barriers. . . . At first we were rather shocked by the behavior of our young," she conceded, but the colony's elders (Marion was in her thirties by this time) eventually "forgave the errant ones or looked the other way." Put differently, women's comparative success at achieving professional and social mobility allowed the industry to develop and sell a sexual culture that blended bourgeois Bohemia's already notorious pleasure-seeking ways with working-class youths' more fluid approach to understanding the relationship between women's sexuality, their professional aspirations, and their moral character. The "casting couch was no fiction," scenarist Lenore Coffee declared, quickly adding that the "sweater girl who gives her 'all'" was the same as the one who "gave the same thing to a foreman to get a better job. I heard one woman say, 'Well after all we're just using a gift nature gave us. What is the difference between using this or using a voice the way opera singers do?' I had no answer for that."[147]

The Los Angeles clubwomen who created the Hollywood Studio Club in 1916 sought to curtail the spread of just such sentiments, by building a "suitable home" for single women who were "constantly coming to Hollywood in the hope or prospect of entering the industry." What mattered most to clubwomen, and increasingly to motion picture producers who aimed to protect the industry's reputation as well, was the chance to regulate, contain, and transform these mostly working-class migrants into "a respectable, middle-class emblem of decorous femininity," according to historian Heidi Kenega. Although the club's financial support derived mainly from residents' fees and gifts from motion pictures insiders, like Mrs. Cecil B. DeMille, it was crucial to the club's public relations mission that the Young Women's Christian Association (YWCA) took charge of its administration. The YWCA ran the club out of a little house on Carlos Street until Mrs. DeMille led a campaign to raise funds for a three-story institution styled as a Mediterranean piazza, completed in 1926. Female mentors assisted club residents in their search for work and offered instruction in dancing and literature while creating opportunities for respectable socializing.

Yet a 1923 report about the club's residents during its first seven years contradicted the notion that these women were naïfs who arrived determined only to act and left disillusioned and despoiled. Of sixty past residents, twenty-four had divorced *before* moving into the club, and more than half were over twenty-three years old. Moreover, excluding the ten women who returned home or married, all but four former residents found gainful employment in a variety of jobs, including journalism, publicity, makeup and hair, real estate, set design, scenario writing, and acting—demonstrating the real opportunities some seized in the new West.[148]

The figure of the "extra-girl" best captured the mounting ambivalence provoked by the colony's single women. Discussions about the character and activities of these workers illustrated how the colony challenged both gender norms for single, young white women and a utilitarian approach to life. Even before Hollywood became iconic, depictions of extra-girls in fan culture assaulted traditional gender roles.[149] But by the summer of 1921, a *Photoplay* article about the movie colony's social scene used "Hollywood" as a term to stand in for the industry and its personalities writ large. The article also claimed that what distinguished Hollywood most was that the sexual equality that characterized its bohemian scene made the girls equal partners in rebellion with the boys. "Oh, Hollywood! A Ramble in Bohemia" called "the 'extra girl' type the most notable and effective of the new classes. Indeed, extras composed "the background" of Hollywood's "Bohemianism." Extra girls shared many characteristics with bohemians of the past, trading steady jobs "for the chance to make a masterpiece on celluloid" and living a "lawless, unpremeditated" "hand-to-mouth existence." Putting their quest for artistic success and individual fulfillment first, they led lives exhibiting the bohemian commitment to passion, play, and self-actualization. Ultimately, the article depicted Hollywood as a place where young single women dominated a cosmopolitan culture that drew inspiration from their total emancipation: "Women can—and do—what they like," for "they work, play, love, and draw their pay checks on exactly the same basis as men." A picture peeked into the abode of one "of the mountain colony extra girls." There a Nazimova look-alike, an epicene, dark-haired woman in "Orientalized" garb, lounged above a caption that beckoned, "The rough board walls, the phonograph, the Chinese housecoat, are absolutely typical of the mountain colony extra girls. How'd you like to live here?"[150]

A retort published in the *Los Angeles Times* displayed how Hollywood Bohemia's extra-girl threatened the industry's economic interests. In "Defends Manners of Hollywood," Jane Fredrickson took "violent exception" on behalf of the "90,000 citizens of Hollywood."[151] Fredrickson called on the president of the Hollywood Board of Trade to dispute this portrait of the extra-girl, but she admitted that the influx of flickers into the suburb had changed perceptions about its manners and morals. Many worried that "the movies had spoiled" the recently bucolic town, and jokes like "'Are you married?' 'No, I live in Hollywood'" showed how assumptions about residents' looser morals already creaked with cliché. A cartoon atop the article emphasized the influence of reformers like Fredrickson. Below a depiction of a movie theater door nailed shut with a sign reading "Blue Laws," the caption announced: "Hollywood As It Might Be." Readers knew the cartoon was no joke. Earlier that year a group of citizens had attempted to pass laws mandating Sunday closings, regulating where studios could build, and enforcing a censorship law on the books but not yet used. One petition to the Los Angeles city council captured the broader charge: motion pictures promoted "licentiousness and crime" and were to blame for the "mysterious disappearance" of "over six hundred young women" in the last year.[152]

Other accounts in the mainstream press emphasized two things about the colony's social scene: Hollywood's "money-mad" character and the risks it encouraged ordinary young women to take with the grave business of life. "Money-mad" meant spending serious amounts of cash on frivolous fancies. Such madness was endemic, visible in the shelling out of "$5000 just to get one scene right" and in stars "simply throwing away their money on motors, clothes, and jewelry." Despite the notorious excesses of corporate elites since the Gilded Age, such critics blamed these habits on the working-class origins of most of the industry's employees. The "ex-bartenders, milk-wagon drivers, telephone girls, manicurists, and stenographers" who had invented the colony simply did not take a "business like" attitude toward work that appreciated the value of "*real* money." The extras "swarming" the studio streets illustrated the second problem. And, again, extra-girls dominated the scene: "girls—tall girls and short girls, curly-haired girls and girls with their hair drawn sleekly back over their brows, girls who suggest mignonettes and girls who suggest tuberoses; girls in aprons and girls in evening gowns—girls by the score, their faces all grease paint, waiting in little chattering groups for their big moment of the day." What disturbed the reporter was how these extras knowingly pursued a course that depended on "luck and opportunity," rather than on "the long and more or less bitter struggle" that most rewarding endeavors required. Yet instead of worrying about their uncertain fates, such folks were out on "Saturday nights" "jazzing" among the stars, so "gay and carefree and careless, as to make the puritanical heart cease in its beat."[153]

Other reporting in mainstream periodicals worried that such promotions encouraged women to follow their romantic daydreams in dangerous directions. "In the old days the small boy" used to decamp in search of adventure, "but fashions change with the changing years and now it is girls who run away to emulate their favorites of the screen."[154] Not only girls, but "wives" who "deserted husbands and babies" "and even gray-haired mothers" frequently made "the long trip west" "in hope of gratifying in their latter years a secret dream." These were not savvy bohemian extra-girls jazzing it up, but "gullible girls," fleeced of their money by fake casting directors and photographers, "who have gone the way of oblivion or worse." On the defensive, some industry insiders argued that the moral character of migrants determined their fate. An article on "do's and don'ts" for screen hopefuls written by independent producer Benjamin Hampton blamed the unjustifiably "bad reputation of movie-players" on the fact that the "nice girl" was "almost invariably discouraged" from heading west.[155] According to Hampton, too many "colorful stories" in newspapers and magazines sent "an army of girls to Los Angeles every year." Hampton warned that those with "'Bohemian' bacillus" in their system "reached the end of their journey" in "a store," "a restaurant," or the "morgue." "*The movies need the nice girl.* They need the girl that comes from a good family with education and tradition in back of her," Hampton implored. But, he concluded, "when you do go, take your mother or auntie with you—and *live with her.*"

Such articles assumed that any girl alone was either in danger or dangerous. They also indicated the growing tendency to hold Hollywood's bohemian appeal responsible not just for the trouble with middle-class flappers but also for the rise in sexual delinquency among working-class young women. A *Photoplay* article entitled "The Girl Problem and the Pictures" rebutted critics who made this charge. The article interviewed Reverend Eva Ludgate, who defended motion pictures for displaying "lovely women, charming men, and beautiful homes to many a child who has worked most of her life in a factory—who has lived, for countless years, in a slum." But the article also admitted that early Hollywood's stars and stories fostered young women's romantic expectations and then sent them off, alone, to follow their hearts down unexpected paths. "It has raised her ideals," Reverend Ludgate asserted, "has set her groping after newer, more wonderful vistas. But—it has stopped there. It has not tried to direct her groping."[156]

CHAPTER 4

The Movie Menace

In February of 1921, independent film producer Benjamin Hampton wrote an article purporting to explain the movie industry's descent into sexual immorality after the war. Hampton's "Too Much Sex-Stuff in the Movies? Whose Fault Is It?" appeared in *Pictorial Review*, a fiction, news, and fashion magazine with a progressive slant aimed at middle-class women. According to the *Los Angeles Times*, the article sparked "a hot war" in the "SEX WAR ON IN FILMS."[1] The man who later voiced concern over the "'Bohemian' bacillus" infecting female migrants in Los Angeles argued that American women were responsible for the industry's postwar turn to more risqué storylines and stars.[2] Since women best understood each other's preferences, they both created and consumed the "present preponderance of sex-plays," Hampton explained. Producers "cannot sell hob-nailed boots to the dancing slipper trade," which "hunger[ed] for sex stuff" and "exotic" stars. Female scenarists composed most of these stories since they best understood other women's tastes. Stories written by men needed a "woman writer . . . to jazz it up. She jazzes it and when the male person reads her revised version he realizes that his effusion was about as naughty as one of Little Rollo's adventures." Such feminine predilections also accounted for ambitious actresses' embrace of "sex-appealing" to get ahead. "Beulah La Belle from Birmingham, Alabama," had once triumphed playing "nothing but sad, tearful parts" in traditional melodramas. But now La Belle was "no longer weeping for a living. She is now sex appealing." Hampton also declared women responsible for fixing the sex problem created by their sex, calling on the General Federation of Women's Clubs to use its "tremendous power" to rally support for good, clean films.[3]

A decade later, Hampton claimed he wrote "Too Much Sex-Stuff" to challenge the perception of "professional reformers and agitators" that movie producers, alone, drove the industry's passionate postwar turn. B.A. MacKinnon, *Pictorial Review*'s editor in New York, pressed his friend to write the "sex and censorship" piece, arguing that outrage building over the industry's moral decline meant that unless producers, who "were too busy with the day's work," took notice of the agitation and cleaned house, there would "not be much house left when reformers finished the job."[4] Calling Hampton "the spokesman for the industry," the press left the impression that a powerful producer had confessed to the movies' sins (even if he argued that women were to blame).[5]

In reality, Hampton was merely a little fish in a big pond. A former tobacco executive in New York who had failed to orchestrate the purchase of Paramount, Hampton quit his job and moved to Los Angeles, where he produced, wrote, and directed fifteen films between 1917 and 1922. To Hampton, the response generated by "Too Much Sex-Stuff?" displayed how "the movies had permeated every section of society." As "thousands of letters and newspaper clippings" poured into his study, "the deep hold" Hollywood had "on the classes as well as the masses" became clear. By April 1921, the *Ladies' Home Journal*, the nation's largest monthly, asserted that women were responsible for "the enormous new industry's . . . choice of themes and their execution."[6] By the year's end, the movies' sex problem was on the mind of anyone worried about the nation's health.

Ironically, awareness of the good accomplished by the movies during the war contributed to fears about the industry's power to do evil after its conclusion. The biggest producers, represented in the National Association of the Motion Picture Industry (NAMPI), worked closely with President Woodrow Wilson's Committee on Public Information (CPI) to manage the propaganda campaign designed to stir the support of the public that had re-elected Wilson in 1916 on the platform "He Kept Us Out of War." Directed by the former scenario writer and adman George Creel, the CPI put stars like Mary Pickford to work selling Liberty Bonds and rousing public support.[7] NAMPI also worked with the CPI to transform movie theaters into patriotic centers with the pre-show performances of "Four Minute Men." The CPI's success raised fears about the relationship between the media and the creation of something that social scientists and public intellectuals started to call public opinion (the title of Walter Lippmann's seminal 1922 book).[8] "It has been discovered by individuals, by associations, and by governments," wrote a political scientist in 1920, "that a certain kind of advertising can be used to mold public opinion and control democratic majorities." That same year the Chicago Motion Picture Commission initiated the first "scientific" study about the effect of movies on the morality of youth.[9]

The spiraling anxieties about movie morality took shape within the context of the broad panic over social regulation after the war, helping to explain why so many held the industry's Oriental Trust (in the ethnic terminology of the day)—rather than ordinary American women—accountable for the corruption of native values. Other inflammatory targets first absorbed and inflamed the public's attention, including a wave of often immigrant-led strikes, the first nationwide race riots outside the South, and the revival of immigration itself. But by 1920, the dramatic rise in both proposed movie censorship legislation and public debate over movie morality displayed the new focus on the threat the movies posed to native virtue.[10] The development of Hollywood's free-spirited, bohemian social imaginary fueled such fears. Reformers with once disparate views now agreed that only respectable American moral regulators could prevent the industry's spread of "immoral, unmoral, unAmerican" social conventions and sexual behavior among the masses.[11] New critics created powerful melodramas of sexual danger about the racial degeneration posed by Jews' influence over the most powerful culture industry ever seen. Funded by Henry Ford, these critics charged that a "Hebrew Trust" enticed white womanhood, the fount of America's racial purity, into degrading themselves. All the stories told by Hollywood's critics entwined panics over sexuality and race into a melodrama in which Hollywood's "un-American," immoral sex pictures, social environment, and leaders threatened the nation's health. These melodramas of sexual danger played the flipside of Hollywood Bohemia, spinning stories about Orientalist movie "moguls" who despoiled a Gentile nation by corrupting its women with poolside tango parties and the passionate tales of "a million and one nights."[12]

I

Much like debates over Hollywood's influence, discussions about the need for new immigration restrictions after the war reflected symbolic fears more than reasoned objections. "MUST STOP ALIEN INFLUX: Ellis Island Commissioner Avers Flow of Immigrant Labor Dangerous," screamed a *Los Angeles Daily Times* headline. The *Brooklyn Daily Eagle* cautioned, "GROWING U.S. MUST CHOOSE JAP, JEW OR ITALIAN CITIZENS."[13] Both headlines conveyed the shrill tenor of a discussion in which metaphors of natural disaster abounded. "The struggle with Germany, called forth the most strenuous nationalism *and* the most pervasive nativism the United States had ever known," argues historian John Higham in explaining the passage of new immigration restrictions based on ethnic quotas in 1921. The crusade for "100 percent Americanism" that continued after the war revealed the conflict over immigration as "a major turning point in American nativism."[14] Faith in so-called Americanization efforts designed "to hasten the assimilative process, to heat and stir the melting pot," collapsed.[15] In 1920 the chairman of the House Committee on Immigration, Albert Johnson, proposed "a genuine 100% American immigration law" that halted immigration entirely for two years and then established ethnic quotas that excluded Asians and all but ended immigration from Southern and Eastern Europe. Only such a dam could prevent the "flood of undesirable aliens" from launching "the toboggan slide" of "the white race" toward destruction.[16]

The postwar furor over the influence of the movies and immigrants on native American culture revealed the new tendency to view Jews as a special threat. One popular editor called anti-Semitism "one of the most curious specimens" of "all the dirty spawn germinated in the refuse left by the Great War."[17] A postwar congressional report justifying the ethnic-origins quota act claimed that Jewish immigrants dominated the stream, characterizing them as "abnormally twisted," "unassimilable," and "filthy, un-American, and often dangerous in their habits."[18] The report grossly inflated the potential number of Jewish immigrants, predicting that "five million Polish Jews would attempt to immigrate to America during the next three years." A bemused *Nation* reporter noted the estimate was "50% above the total number of the Jews in Poland."[19] The Senate defeated Johnson's all-out ban. But just as Hampton's article in *Pictorial Review* hit newsstands, the quota measure created by Congress "to check the flow from southern and eastern Europe without hindering the movement from northern and western Europe" easily won approval.[20] The news coverage of these developments, Higham argues, led many in the United States to conclude that "the chief purpose of the immigration law of 1921 was to keep out the Jews."[21]

Indeed, *Current Opinion* called "the strength and intensity of the new movement of anti-Semitism one of the unexpected results of the war."[22] "The after-the-war imagination plays busily about the Jew," *The Nation* concurred. "Books, magazine articles, newspaper editorials, the talk of the man on the street, figure him as a sort of Mephistopheles of the peoples."[23] Both magazines also registered the novelty of viewing Jewish immigrants as a special threat. During the mid-nineteenth century, the tiny number of German Jewish immigrants who traveled among the larger wave of their compatriots drew little attention, as some managed to earn a share of the clout wielded by the Anglo-Saxon Protestant elite.[24] Some historians argue that German Jews encountered increasing social discrimination as the century wore on, but without a doubt, the massive arrival of new-immigrant Jews after 1890 complicated their reception. New-immigrant Jews fled mounting persecution, rising oppression, and mass murder in all parts of Eastern and Central Europe. Often Yiddish speaking, much poorer than their predecessors, and from orthodox religious backgrounds, their folkways, dress, and concentrated settlement in the poorest urban neighborhoods marked them as outsiders much more visibly. The postwar idea that Jews posed a particular sexual threat twisted engrained European stereotypes—about Jews as permanent foreigners who possessed a taste for despoiling Gentile women and wielding power from behind the scenes—to fit current American circumstances.[25]

The most nightmarish melodrama about the cultural power of the predatory Jew emerged from an attack campaign in the Midwest that both shaped and strengthened perceptions about the danger Hollywood posed to American values. The revelation of a secret Jewish plot to control what people thought and bought the world over was the purpose of an ongoing series published in the *Dearborn Independent*, a general magazine operated and distributed by the "Flivver King," Henry Ford. Indisputably a folk hero by the time he launched an investigation of "The Jewish Question," Ford's newspaper detailed the threat "the international Jew, the world's foremost problem," posed to "all that Anglo-Saxons mean by civilization."[26] A farmer's son with little formal education, Ford derived success from his command of the qualities that many Americans most prized: a bent for mechanical tinkering that produced technological innovation, a genius for efficiency, and a will to conquer space by harnessing speed. Estimated as one of America's richest men by 1920, Ford grew so concerned about the modern world's direction that he entered politics. His first major foray involved funding a 1915 "Peace Ship" to Europe to stop a war he thought "money lenders and munitions makers" had engineered. The endeavor drew ridicule in much of the press, and its abject failure seems to have precipitated Ford's repudiation of any venture that whiffed of cosmopolitanism.[27] After narrowly losing Michigan's 1918 Democratic senatorial race, Ford bought the *Dearborn Independent,* christened it the "Chronicler of Neglected Truth," and set out to educate "plain Americans" about the dangers encroaching on their country.[28] He hired a former *New York World* reporter to improve the *Independent*'s anemic sales. The journalist advised a melodramatic solution to the magazine's poor circulation, instructing Ford to "find an evil to attack, go after it, and stay after it."[29]

Thus America's most famous industrialist came to devise and distribute an investigative series about the threat "the international Jew" posed to American virtue, a campaign that took the form of a melodrama of sexual danger that entwined the postwar sex panic over the revolution in manners and morals with a race panic about the influence and visibility of Jewish movie producers. In doing so, it drew upon and inflamed broader cultural anxieties about miscegenation, in the unlovely language of the day, by offering a version of scientific racism for Americans who lacked the patience to parse popular scholarly accounts like Madison Grant's *Passing of the Great Race* (1916). In *Passing,* Grant vividly pictured America's racial degeneration as "old stock" Americans were "literally driven off the streets" by "swarms" of immigrants aping Anglo-Saxon man's dress, imitating his language, and taking "his women."[30] An illustration of the theory of Anglo-Saxon "race suicide," the book was successful enough to prompt two more printings after the war when Grant helped to give the new immigration restrictions the imprimatur of scientific legitimacy. The magazine's investigation of the "Jewish Question" began with a conclusion: innate racial characteristics compelled Jews toward world dominance. At every point, articles exhibited the same style of argument. The "question" was really an assertion that drew its power from the repetition of "facts" framed as common knowledge. Jews' characteristics as a race—a "gift" for all things "commercial" rather than "productive or technical"—rendered them unable to create, explaining their parasitic positions as administrators of finance capitalism.[31] Race also determined who played the hero and who the villain in these stories that pitted "two forces, Industry and Finance"—Gentile and Jew—against each other. Jewish racial solidarity clarified why all Jews, however different their interests or situation, aimed only to destroy the Gentile world.[32] Race solidarity also justified the series' attack on Jewish individuals whose accomplishments Americans like Ford typically equated with moral fitness. Jewish success was not "won by individual initiative; it was rather the extension of financial control across the sea."[33]

The master plot that the *Independent*'s series revealed involved Jewish leaders' resolve to use the nation's "cultural regions" to penetrate "the very heart of American life."[34] The paper claimed that Jewish immigrants already held sway over most of popular culture—including popular music, sports, and "the very news that people read"—making the United States "the center of Jewish power."[35] But the magazine called the stage and motion pictures the most important lairs from which Jews directed their struggle. These arenas lent themselves to Jews' facility for exerting power from behind the scenes as they orchestrated the performances of others who enacted their "program for the guidance of public taste and the influencing of the public mind." In this way, the "Jewish Theatrical Trust," said to control the stage by 1900, ruined the theater's artistic standards. This move laid the groundwork for an even more ambitious plan, throwing "the empty theaters over to the 'movies'" and thereby improving the industry's prestige as well as giving the Jewish race an inside track to dominance over the new business.[36]

Despite calling the movies "a Jewish enterprise from the start," the *Independent*'s history lesson indicated the reverse. "Motion picture photography," the magazine observed, "like most other useful things in the world, was of non-Jewish origin."[37] The subject of the movies' origin raised the specter of the man commonly credited with its invention in America, the "Wizard of Menlo Park," Thomas Edison. In the book Ford wrote about his lifelong mentor in 1930, he called Edison "the chief hero of my boyhood," a "friend in manhood," and "our greatest American."[38] The magazine's repeated rumblings that "the Jews did not invent the art of motion picture" betrayed the grudge Ford carried on Edison's behalf. Edison's so-called invention of motion pictures mostly consisted of directing a legal wrangle to control the industry through licensing and patenting his camera. After harassing virtually all the major producers into joining his Motion Picture Patents Company (MPPC), Edison formed the industry's original monopoly, ruled an illegal conspiracy in violation of the Sherman Anti-trust Act in 1915.[39]

But a group of innovative producers settling around Los Angeles had already rendered the Court's ruling unnecessary. Carl Laemmle, Adolph Zukor, William Fox, and Marcus Loew amassed enough capital to fight the MPPC in court by servicing thousands of unlicensed nickelodeons outside its interest. Their embrace of the star system and feature films enlarged movie audiences by retaining immigrants and working people while adding many more women and middle-class patrons. In this way, a group of upstart, un-American Jews wrested control of Edison's dominion out from under him. Beginning with Adolph Zukor, "conceded to be the leader of the fifth largest industry in the world," the magazine described those who made "Jewish Supremacy in the Motion Picture World" complete. The *Independent* also stressed how Jewish dominance went far beyond "the official heads," since even a "commonly supposed . . . non-Jewish concern" like United Artists was only a "Gentile Front." The race of the industry's leaders created predictable results. "As soon as the Jew gained control of the 'movies,' we had a movie problem," for it was "the genius of that race to create problems of a moral character in whatever business they achieve a majority."[40]

Employing the race science of the day, the magazine placed Jews among a larger racial group whose "Oriental sensuality" challenged Anglo-Saxon sexual morality.[41] The "Oriental ideal" was "essentially different from the Anglo-Saxon, the American view."[42] "American life is bare and meager to the Eastern mind. It is not sensuous enough. It is devoid of intrigue. Its women of the homes do not play continuously and hysterically on the sex motif."[43] In contrast to the "faith and quietness" of "American domesticity," Orientalism took things "as far as you could go," "gravitate[d] naturally to the flesh," and lived "among the more sensual emotions" where "falsity, artificiality, criminality, and jazz" were the "keynotes." Thus Jewish control resulted in "fleshy spectacles" characterized by "frivolity, sensuality, indecency, appalling illiteracy and endless platitudes." Here lay the root of "the whole secret of 'the movies' moral failure": their producers were "racially unqualified to reproduce the American atmosphere."[44] Thus genuine Americans need no longer "wonder where the ideas of the younger generation come from"; if they were "Oriental in their voluptuous abandonment," they had drunk the poison purveyed by the Jewish-controlled "stage and the movies."[45] Indeed, movie Orientalism's perversion of the nation's "Aryan complexion of mind and conscience" explained both Hollywood's popularity and the failure of a film censorship movement to take hold. The "filthy tide" of

Orientalism that "all but engulf[ed]" "Gentile gullibles [sic]" accounted for why growing numbers of "real," "plain" Anglo-Saxon Americans enjoyed Hollywood's detestable products.[46]

Thus the series attributed a racial origin to the feminization of American culture, describing the movies' audience as a dangerously pliable, feminized crowd controlled by dark forces that threatened American culture's purity.[47] Such fans "crowd[ed] through the doors of the movie house at all hours of the day and night, literally an unending line of human beings," begging to have their minds filled with "ideas generated and directed by the suggestion of the screen."[48] The paper singled out "youths," "working people," and "shallow pated wives" as particularly susceptible to the "movie bug." Without the powers of self-control ascribed to self-sufficient Aryan males, the movies turned these groups into addicts whose "appetites," when "whetted and encouraged," became "a mania" that "craved" "two or more pictures a day." Influential Americans were either compromised in "Gentile fronts" or by the demands of "all sorts of causes," like the war effort, that demanded cooperating with movie producers. Such trends left Jewish movie producers free to carry out the plan detailed in *The Protocols of the Elders of Zion* (1903), the fraudulent text first published in Russia that purported to uncover a Jewish conspiracy to control the world. "We have misled, stupefied and demoralized the youth of the Gentiles by means of education in principles and theories, patently false to us, but which we have inspired." Here lay the goal of the "propaganda of the Jewish movie"—to inspire Anglo-Saxon Protestant youths to replace the faith of their fathers with Orientalism.[49]

Since only Gentile movie stars prevented Jewish producers' total control, the series concluded by focusing on the latest trend within the industry: "the abolition of the 'star' system." Despite the industry's having "reached its present importance because of the exaltation of the 'star,'" producers now recognized that "the way to break the control which the public may exercise" was "to eliminate the stars." Once producers succeeded in destroying the independence of stars, exhibitors and the public would "have no choice because there will be no choice; the business will be a standardized 'industry.'" Then, as had happened with the theater, a "dark, Oriental atmosphere" would obliterate the "American *feel*" of the movies.[50] Thus the *Independent*'s final accusation offered a critique of industrial standardization by no less than its prophet. Ford's success was built on production methods that clocked and regulated every aspect of human labor and choice in order to manufacture the ideal one-size-and-low-price-fits-all product, making the criticisms either a virtuoso exercise of irony, or sheer apostasy.

As might be expected, people took notice when the world's most prominent industrialist added virulently anti-Semitic attacks to his product line. Although "not a single paper or magazine of repute" had backed Ford's campaign, a reporter observed, "the movement still continues to excite nation-wide attention."[51] Frank Crane, the influential editor of *Current Opinion,* decried Ford's attack as spreading to America the kind of "Jew hating" that was of "constant quantity in Europe."[52] An open letter in the *New York Times* signed by "citizens of Gentile birth and Christian faith," including Presidents Wilson and Taft, condemned the appearance "of an organized campaign of anti-Semitism, conducted in close conformity to and cooperation with similar campaigns in Europe."[53] Such reactions displayed how open anti-Semitism remained beyond the pale of polite conversation among most of the American educated elite. Jewish leaders and writers in the United States divided over the best response to Ford's attack and what significance to attribute to the *Independent*'s crusade.[54] Most agreed it displayed a broader trend of "Jew-baiting" fueled by the war.[55] New York congressman Fiorello LaGuardia summarily judged Ford's "wealth and ignorance" as making possible "a nefarious warfare against the Jews."[56]

An editorial in *Photoplay* disputed the notion that Jewish producers controlled what appeared on screens. In a juxtaposition that Ford might have argued proved his point about the industry's Oriental sensibility, *Photoplay*'s editor, James Quirk, ran a piece called "Oh, Henry!" opposite an article exploring "vamps of all times." The "magazine holds no brief for the family of Israel," Quirk avowed. Yet he decried any "form of condemnation which denounces a whole people" as "a menace to civilization." Quirk attributed different implications to similar Jewish stereotypes to upend the attack. "The Jew from time immemorial has been given to trade and barter and finance," he wrote—"the man behind the artist—frequently to his own profit, but sometimes quite the reverse—for more than a hundred years." Finally, Quirk offered the collaborative nature of making movies, and fans' estimation of their own good taste, as the best evidence to dispute Ford's charges. Yet Quirk's assurance that Jews had *absolutely no* role in shaping what appeared on screens subtly supported the idea that such an occurrence would threaten fans.[57]

The second Ku Klux Klan, whose presence exploded after 1920, embraced Ford's ideas about the threat that Jewish-produced movies posed to American sexual morality and Gentile girls.[58] Revering "the genuine Americanism" of the anti-Semitic Flivver King, Ford was one of the few industrialists to escape the KKK's attacks. Revived in Atlanta in 1915, the second Klan's membership languished at a few thousand in January 1920. One year later estimates placed it at over one million. The first Klan was a sectional body that aimed to restore white supremacy throughout the South and accepted any white man willing to terrorize black Americans to achieve this end. The second Klan was an Anglo-Saxon nationalist order that promised to restore influence to those who feared the destruction of American morality by "new immigrants," New Negroes," and New Women. A national social movement, the second Klan accepted only native-born white Protestant men and drew recruits mostly from the lower middle classes in urbanizing regions. Using wartime rhetoric, it preached white supremacy, Christianity, and "pure Americanism" to protect members from the threat posed by encroaching cosmopolitan influences from above and below. The 1920s' Klan promised a moral realignment through vigilante actions that aimed to repair the corrosions associated with metropolitan modernity, including new Negroes, Jews, Catholics, monopolists, labor radicals, erring wives, itinerant husbands, "wild women" in short skirts, divorcées, commercial popular culture, and especially "degrading, depraving, or disgusting" movies.[59]

Yet even as the Klan lambasted the movies and their makers, its leaders masterfully deployed modern media to increase the organization's membership by inflaming anxieties about the industry's danger to the "social structure and racial purity" of America. The Klan hired two publicity agents in 1920 to sound such themes by seizing on the melodramas propagated by both the *Independent* and D.W. Griffith's *The Birth of a Nation*. Rereleased in December 1920, Griffith's film provided a touchstone, and central recruiting device, for the second Klan. Based on Thomas Dixon's best-selling novel, *The Clansman—An Historical Romance of the Ku Klux Klan* (1905), Griffith's adaptation was one of the most powerful melodramas of sexual danger about a race panic ever made. *Birth* recounted how the Klan saved the South and reunited the nation by deposing dastardly mulatto politicians and lynching black male predators driven to rape white women. A technical masterpiece, *Birth* glorified the movement's heroism, strengthened members' solidarity, and inflamed others to don the Klan's white robes.[60]

As members rallied in movie theaters across the country, Klan leaders also used Ford's prestige and the *Independent*'s campaign to support their story about the dangers posed by Jewish control over the culture industries. According to Klan spokesmen, the best example of the "Cosmopolitanism advocated by International Jewry" lay in how the "Jew-produced motion pictures industry and the Jew-monopolized jazz music submerge[d]" Gentile youths "in a sea of sensuality and sewage." Here lay the inspiration for the "amatory and erotic tendencies" of young women. Believing that "all Protestant girls are common property and can be bought for a song," Jewish employers underpaid working girls, seduced them with trinkets, and then discarded them like "an old worn-out coat."

Such a charge carried significant implications about the assumedly Gentile girls streaming into Los Angeles. As *Birth of a Nation* did with black men, the Klan placed Jewish men atop their list of racial enemies because of the danger they posed to white women. According to the Klan, black men's bestial strength, vigor, and carnality excused Klan members' violent restraints. The danger Jewish men presented was harder to address since their cunning allowed them to infiltrate economic structures and then manipulate women into degrading themselves. Thus, as Imperial Wizard Hiram Evans declared in 1921, only "strict censorship" would "keep the Jew controlled stage and movies within even gunshot of decency."[61]

II

Open, virulent anti-Semitism distinguished the calls for film censorship made by the Ku Klux Klan and Ford's *Independent* from other censorship efforts after the war. Yet such extreme talk made subtler expressions of similar views sound reasonable by comparison. In making the case for federal regulation of films, leading activists like Ellis Oberholtzer, Reverend Wilbur Crafts and Canon William Chase expressed their anti-Semitism in more polite code. These reformers argued that only federal oversight could stop the spread of a new type of "Sex Picture" purveyed by the "perverse," "degenerate" "Hebrew" film producers who had seized control of the industry during the war. These more polite melodramas of sexual danger surfaced in the postwar censorship campaigns launched by the General Federation of Women's Clubs (GFWC) and in New York, the film industry's financial hub and its most lucrative market. The GFWC and those who fought for state censorship in New York expressed similar concerns. They argued that the "un-American" morality glorified by postwar films and their stars celebrated the erasure of the sexual double standard, thereby perverting the minds of impressionable women and immigrants. For the GFWC's respectable, reform-minded members, ensuring that films conformed to traditional middle-class conventions offered a means to exert public influence. During the postwar panic over immigration and the future direction of women's rights, debates about regulating a "Hebrew trust selling sex pictures" offered evidence that the freedom of modern young girls had gone too far.

Moral custodians considered women's pursuit of "sex partisan politics"—including more liberal divorce laws, birth control, and the Equal Rights Amendment—the wrong way to exercise their new political rights. "Undoubtedly one of the most important national events that will have its effect on the moral standard of the country is the enfranchising of our women," declared John Sumner in an article about the potential trouble caused by ratification of the Nineteenth Amendment in 1920.[62] Sumner, the secretary of the New York Society for the Suppression of Vice, warned that "two paths" lay before women in 1921. Women could either join "with the men to make better laws for herself and her children," or join together "along lines of sex antagonism" that would "breakdown the moral fiber of the nation." Sumner extolled motion picture regulation as a chance for women to take the right path. Yet he seemed more interested in speculating about the "sex warfare" that would result if women ignored his advice.[63] As the headline of one story in this vein put it, "Will the Next War Be Women against Men?"[64] According to Sumner, the goal of these "women who [were] openly antagonistic to men and 'man made' laws and conventions" duplicated Hollywood's aim to grant "modern woman still greater sex freedom" by promoting "a 'single standard': meaning the standard of moral laxity attributed to men."[65]

The new focus of the nation's most powerful state censorship board also illustrated the broader sex war.[66] Created in 1915, the Pennsylvania State Board of Censors set the pattern followed by the three other state movie censor boards in existence.[67] A provision requiring that a woman serve as its vice-president displayed the importance of using respectable women to reestablish proper moral standards.[68] Indeed, the commission's stated objective was to protect "the family in its present form." Twenty-four "standards" specified violations of this goal. Two-thirds proscribed materials that would be "disapproved" because of sexual impropriety and clustered around three aspects of its expression.[69] The first group censored sexual acts committed by men against

women: women seduced, assaulted, betrayed, or forced into "white slavery" (prostitution). The second cluster censored women whose modern
behavior signaled their moral corruption: drunk women, smoking
women, "sensual kissing and lovemaking," nude or "unduly exposed"
bodies, and "lewd and immodest dancing." The final group involved
conduct resulting from actions between women and men who were
judged to imperil the nation's moral hygiene, including divorce, adultery,
"birth control," abortion, and "race suicide." The commission also censored pictures "showing the modus operandi of criminals." But the con-
centration on moral issues revealed that its primary aim was inculcating
fans with genteel middle-class sexual standards and gender roles. The
Pennsylvania Censorship Commission's chairman, Ellis Oberholtzer,
Ph.D., offered testimony before the Chicago Motion Picture Commission in 1919 that indicated why his critics argued that the process was
hopelessly subjective. "Looking at pictures you judge them instinctively,"
Oberholtzer explained. "You know whether such a thing is permissible
or not; you feel it somehow or other . . . then you look to the standard
and try to find a reason for it afterwards."[70]

Oberholtzer's admission also suggested why he became a lightning
rod for the controversy surrounding censorship. A historian, Oberholtzer claimed to have reluctantly relinquished the quiet of a library
and his work on the multivolume *History of the United States since the
Civil War* to answer Pennsylvania governor William Cameron Sproul's
call to serve as the commission's first chairman.[71] The commission's decision in 1918 to condemn outright *Old Wives for New*—the first of the
"salacious divorce and sex plays" directed by Cecil B. DeMille—
prompted heated debate over the anti-democratic implications of let-
ting five people determine what hundreds of thousands could watch.[72]
The next year Oberholtzer declared the fight a matter of "us versus
them" and took to the lecture circuit to propagandize the growing necessity of film censorship.[73] After mounting controversy surrounding
his activities caused the Pennsylvania governor to remove him from office, Oberholtzer became a full-time activist for film censorship. Between 1920 and 1921, he traveled continually to speak about the need
for federal regulation, wrote pamphlets and articles in reform periodicals, and published *The Morals of the Movie* (1922).[74] "Sex," the chapter
"Sex Pictures" began, was the "one potently dominant idea in the minds
of the men who are gambling in the public taste." Written to convince
readers that this new emphasis had made the "morals of the movie" dramatically decline, the book explained why only federal oversight could

neutralize "the magnitude of the evil" represented by films. While Oberholtzer conceded that the industry's "physical sense" had improved with "truly astonishing rapidity," he argued that the "'dramatic' in the movies" had "gone back." This deterioration required regulators of his "class" and "moral opinions" to protect ordinary fans from the displays of murder, incest, and seduction that once only a select few had watched on stage. "We shall have a care for what costs three dollars on Broadway," he admitted, "but infinitely more concern for what is simultaneously shown for a few cents in a thousand places, in hamlet and crossway in all parts of the land." Oberholtzer also emphasized the international nature of the crisis, declaring, "The standards of production established by the manufacturers of the United States" were now "the standards of the world."[75]

Like the *Independent* and the Klan, Oberholtzer held film producers entirely responsible for the escalation of what he called "sex rot" and "motion pictures infected with diseases of the erotic imagination." Their new movie "trust" replaced the "liquor business" as "the most corrupt of the forces now active in the debauchery of the public conscience." Movie producers pretended to "revile 'politics' and yet enter it with their riches to pollute and corrupt [its] sources" and to exploit their "wares without holiness or grace." Although Oberholtzer stopped short of outright naming the Jewishness of producers as creating the sex problem, his mingling of moral pollution, economic power, and godlessness indicated that such was the case. Oberholtzer also accused producers of fooling the public by "disseminat[ing] the impression" that the "so-called National Board" in New York already censored film content. Working in cooperation with producers and funded by them, the National Board of Review (NBR) aired "the dirty linen of New York City" before the country, tempting fans with "wickedness that they have heard about but have never seen." According to Oberholtzer, the NBR was "a mere blind, a ruse to beguile film reformers, particularly organizations of women, who have so real and steadfast an interest in the character of picture exhibitions for the sake of their children." Like Hampton, Oberholtzer emphasized clubwomen's critical role in reforming the "morals of the movie." Detailing their efforts throughout the book, he declared them natural allies to stem the social chaos he associated with the "Bolshevia" created by "producers" who "cover[ed] the country with immoral pictures" to fill "their money sacks." Oberholtzer dedicated his book to the Pennsylvania commission's vice-president, "Katherine A. Niver, my comrade in arms in the thin red line."[76] Women like Niver mobilized conventions about respectable womanhood—which linked middle-class white women's place within the domestic sphere to their innate spiritual and moral superiority—to distinguish their class from those above and below. The tact helped to legitimize their efforts at what reformer Jane Addams called "city housekeeping."[77] Women's ability to transform domestic prerogatives into public authority proved most successful in matters that involved using their maternal authority to lobby the state to protect their so-called dependents, including children, youths, single mothers, and the poor.[78]

The General Federation of Women's Clubs was the largest women's organization to benefit from mobilizing such conventions. Created in 1890 as a national association for society women's literary clubs, the GFWC reoriented its mission from "an old-fashioned culture club" to a clearinghouse that directed the reform activities of nearly two million women in myriad local organizations. "We prefer Doing to Dante," declared one member in 1906; "today nothing but an orgy of philanthropy will satisfy us." By the 1920s, the membership of the GFWC remained largely unchanged despite its new orientation, admitting mostly upper- and middle-class women from "the Anglo-Saxon race."[79] Gender, class, and ethnic conventions all positioned the GFWC's members as the ideal regulators of an entertainment that appealed to children, immigrants, youths, and, increasingly, their own daughters. A contemporary historian of legislation affecting motion pictures expressed the class and racial biases behind the clubwomen's authority. "Since the membership in the clubs is representative of the middle and upper strata of our population," the historian noted, it "must be considered as having social standards which are largely in accord with those of the general public."[80]

As late as 1918, the GFWC viewed the movie industry as no threat to public morals. An opponent of legal censorship, the organization had been an important ally of the NBR.[81] The Women's Municipal League in New York had helped to create the NBR in 1909 after conducting a survey of films that judged them "wholesome" entertainment.[82] The NBR provided a forum for producers, exhibitors, and the general public to reach a consensus about what constituted acceptable motion picture content. Clubwomen were the NBR's unpaid reviewers, screening the vast majority of films, recommending changes to producers, and distributing a weekly bulletin listing approved films. Mary Grey Peck, of the GFWC's Motion Picture Committee, toured the country with the

NBR to criticize the rise of local censorship boards. Peck lectured about the superiority of voluntary efforts to improve movies and praised the movies as wholesome, cheap entertainment that made the industry a "more serious foe" of vice "than the W.C.T.U. [Woman's Christian Temperance Union] or any anti-saloon or anti-cigarette league."[83]

But later that same year, the GFWC broke with the NBR and endorsed legal motion picture censorship on the state level, triggering a permanent reversal in perceptions about the NBR's effectiveness.[84] The GFWC's decision followed two years of study and debate after a 1916 report judged the majority of films approved by the NBR as "bad" or "not worthwhile."[85] The results, gathered by the Chicago Political Equality League, prompted the national federation to ask state branches to carry out similar studies. All the reports indicated a serious decline in the moral content of films. The results were presented at the GFWC's national convention in May 1918, along with a pro-censorship talk by Oberholtzer that included a reel of film scenes he had censored while working in Pennsylvania. After three days of heated debate, the GFWC passed a resolution that condemned voluntary efforts like the NBR, pledged to work for state censorship, and appointed Florence Butler Blanchard to direct the effort. A 1919 pamphlet on the need for "censorship of motion pictures," which Blanchard edited, shot a damning accusation at its former ally. Blanchard charged that any "person of average intelligence" could see that the NBR acted as "camouflage" for the industry by furnishing "well-intentioned, reform-bent ladies with 'harmless busy work'" that "befogged the thinking, befuddled, delayed, diverted, emasculated and perverted the activities of many club women honestly interested in a crusade for better motion pictures."[86] In short, these ladies would no longer act the patsy for corrupt men.

Despite the GFWC's putative call for "a single moral standard" for women and men, the sexual double standard explained why many assumed that the movies produced more female delinquents than male.[87] Like many postwar critics, the GFWC held sex films responsible for the perceived jump in delinquency among both male and female "youths," the age stretching from adolescence through the early twenties. But both critical commentary and the cuts made to film content revealed that censors focused more on protecting girls from scenes of sexual immorality than boys from crime.[88] "Two thirds of girls who appear before the court, charged with immorality," claimed one Ohioan, "owe their misfortune to influences derived directly from the movie, either from the pictures themselves or in the 'picking up' of male acquaintances at the theater."[89] The gendering of sexual misbehavior testified to how the sexual double standard rendered moral vice a girl problem: "Who has ever heard of a 'fallen boy'?" asked one social worker.[90] Thus clubwomen set their virtuous womanhood against the libertine men running the salacious picture business.

A "campaign against unclean movies" launched by the *Brooklyn Daily Eagle* also relied on clubwomen to create a state censorship board in New York.[91] The creation of a state board in the industry's financial hub would send a powerful message about the business's declining morality. One of Brooklyn's most respected papers, the *Eagle* typically offered its native-born, middle-class readers progressive editorial stances. "We have organized to fight disease germs that kill the body. Why not organize to fight the disease germs that eat into the very heart of public morals?" demanded the series' investigative reporter.[92] So-called campaign updates ran weekly in the Sunday section "Music, Art, Theaters and Women"—the part of the paper that functioned as the women's pages by reporting news and reviews of cultural performances, society events, and clubwomen's activities. The section's organization indicated the broader presumption about women's authority over cultural and reform matters and revealed the *Eagle*'s desire to enlist clubwomen, warning those who wanted "to rear red-blooded and clean-cut Americans" to "get into action." Indeed, these women led the charge. Catherine Waterman, head of the City Federation of Women's Clubs' Committee on Moving Pictures, convinced New York's governor, Nathan Miller, that "the sex interest is being made more and more paramount by producers until it is a menace to the youth."[93] Others swayed New York's mayor to join the "fight to bar exhibition of indecent movies."[94]

The campaign reflected clubwomen's concerns by declaring that the NBR's "un-American" moral standards made its protection of womanhood "a farce."[95] The opinions of clubwoman Mrs. O'Grady, whom the *Eagle* cited more than any person, offered a powerful reminder that the campaign shared the front page with debates over immigration restriction. After having worked for twenty years as a probation officer with delinquent youths, O'Grady achieved local notoriety when the police department refused to endorse a 1919 letter she released to the press accusing producers of feeding "immoral and suggestive pictures" to immigrant fans. In protest, she quit her job and turned full-time film censorship activist. O'Grady slightly modified her message by 1921, blaming movies shown on the immigrant East Side "for the horrible increase in juvenile delinquency," particularly among immigrant girls. Hoping to act "like American girls," they imitated the behavior of stars and went "astray," making the movies an Americanization project gone terribly awry. Her clarion cry summoned women to use their new political rights: "Women, we've got big work to do . . . if men in office don't enforce our laws, let's put women in office who will enforce them."[96]

To flesh out what constituted un-American sexuality, the *Eagle* described the "lascivious and suggestive situations" in two high profile "immoral, unmoral, unAmerican" films passed by the NBR: *The Penalty* and *Passion*. *Passion,* of course, showcased the Polish film star Pola Negri's startlingly direct expression of a playful female sexuality. The NBR called *Passion* "a masterpiece," "a work of true photodramatic art."[97] *The Penalty's* heroine, Rose, also challenged acceptable middle-class sexual codes. The film introduces Rose, a New Woman–styled protagonist, as the "most daring operative" on the police force.[98] To trap Blizzard, the film's antihero, Rose goes undercover among the "dance hall girls" employed in his "sweatshops." When warned that "a woman who enters [Blizzard's] den risks worse than death," Rose coolly replies on an exhalation of cigarette smoke, "That's all in a day's work." After scoffing at threats to her virtue, Rose proceeds to chain-smoke her way through a dangerous job that involves making love to, then falling in love with, a villain who transforms into a hero only at the very end. In a metaphor that suggested how such films perpetrated the public's rape, the *Eagle* called the two movies representative of the "conglomerations of vulgarity and filth" that the NBR "continually thrust before the eyes of the public without let or hindrance" and then protected under the "Temple of Art."[99]

The discussion in the *Eagle* also displayed how those determined to resolve the censorship debate—Brooklyn's and, presumably, the nation's storied middle class—disagreed over what constituted suitably American sexual expressions. A group of religious leaders agreed that watching slapstick comedian Fatty Arbuckle get "smacked in the face with a custard pie" was good clean fun. But the "salacious divorce and sex plays" in which Gloria Swanson starred were called dangerously "un-American."[100] The Council of Men's Clubs elaborated on the "ideas of Americanism" these films promoted: "All American men are money chasers by day and cabaret chasers at night, and that marriage is a temporary arrangement."[101] Yet the NBR's explanation of its decision to pass *Passion* indicated that some in the middle class had different ideas. The "crowded houses" in which *Passion* played, "day after day and night after night," gave "a fair indication that public opinion is on the side of The National Board," its secretary declared.[102] A letter pointed to how one person's sexual satire was another's smut. An "aghast" "Brooklyn Woman" reported that a "large and seemingly refined audience at one of our best moving picture theaters . . . expressed amusement only" at a film she thought "indecent in the extreme." The interrogations of several proper, middle-class reviewers who passed the "sensuous kissing scenes" in *Passion* and *The Penalty* also exposed the variety of attitudes toward the display of female desire. When the reviewers denied that the scenes were immoral, the *Eagle*'s reporter demanded: "Have you a daughter?" and "Would you care to have your daughter see this picture?" Their replies—"Oh, I've seen worse kissing than that in the movies" and "If I possessed the same type of mind as you, I would not"—emerged from a different worldview.[103]

The one "representative daughter" whose voice entered the debate described how young women might view these heroines in a distinctive light. "Surely," a letter signed "G. Y. Janes" opened, her age of twenty "entitles me to class myself under the heading of 'our young people.'" Regarding *The Penalty,* Janes claimed to have "forgotten the lasciviousness upon which so much stress was made. But this is what I do recollect: There was a woman in the play who possessed a fine mind, enough so to be considered one of the most valuable assets of the detective force," she began. "I saw the mind of that woman realizing and almost worshipping the powerful mental force of the unfortunate incarnate fiend," she continued. "I saw a most wonderful and uncommon bond drawing them together—their intense love of music." The passionate expression of "that love to me was not lascivious," she asserted. Janes also defended *Passion,* declaring the "New York critic" who believed "nothing has been produced in this country to equal" the movie got it right, and adding, "the immoral side—how delicately it was handled." Janes argued that these heroines' unsanctified sensuality had to be placed in the context of the whole film. That a newspaper known "first and foremost" for "broadmindedness" offered such "one-sided criticisms . . . in the present pursuit of the 'censorship question of the movies'" caused her "bitter disappointment."[104]

Yet the *Eagle*'s campaign revealed that many of Janes's elders believed that such female protagonists also threatened the moral fiber of men. In this melodrama, the villains were movie-made female libertines who endangered the nation's innocent men. Mrs. Maude Canfield lectured in Brooklyn on this view. The "commissioner of the Brooklyn Girl

Scouts" and member of the "New York Federation" of clubs, Canfield had gained her expertise on movie immorality by escorting "more than 42,000 sailors" to the movies for recruiting purposes during the war. "Most pictures dragged out to unlimited lengths the exploits of some immoral, young woman and would then end up having her marry a virtuous young man," she charged. Such movies offered a "representation of life that [was] absolutely a false one." "An immoral woman always pays," she reminded listeners; teaching otherwise schooled "the untutored mind that immorality is almost a virtue."[105] A story entitled "Brooklyn Club Women Disapprove 'Woman Pays Club' Doctrine" suggested that many of her listeners shared the view.[106] Brooklyn clubwomen opposed the ideas behind the "Woman Pays Club," a "feminist organization" that included Louella Parsons and "artists, musicians, motion picture writers, authors, newspaper women and other professional members of the fair sex who" not only believed "in their independence" but also proved it by "earning their living" and keeping their "maiden" names regardless of marital status.[107] An *Eagle* editorial congratulated clubwomen on their critique of the Woman Pays Club, declaring, "The sooner women get back to some of the old-fashioned ideas the happier we will be."[108] The campaign for the presidency of the New York City Federation of Women's Clubs pitted a "home woman" against one such "professional woman." The victory of the "home woman" demonstrated that most clubwomen thought American ideals justified their leaving the home mostly to protect it, indicating why film censorship campaigns fit their needs.[109]

By March, Hollywood's much-reviled producers were making a tone-deaf response to these attacks.[110] William Brady, president of the National Association of the Motion Picture Industry (NAMPI), the trade association representing the largest producers, offered a plan for reform called the "Thirteen Points." Brady then called for a meeting with leaders of the censorship movement, including Ella Boole, president of the WCTU in New York; Catherine Waterman, the clubwoman credited with swaying New York governor Miller to support censorship; and Reverend Wilbur F. Crafts, head of the International Reform Bureau in Washington, D.C.[111] The Thirteen Points enumerated thirteen types of "salacious, obscene, and degrading" situations that producers pledged to exclude from films.[112] Before the meeting on March 15, 1921, Brady assured the *New York Times* that NAMPI could easily implement the Thirteen Points since its members controlled "about 90 percent of the output of films."[113] Acting as the group's spokesman, Crafts told the reporter that it had agreed to allow producers the chance "to clean their own house." Three days later, Wilbur Crafts announced plans to submit to Congress a revised bill for federal censorship. The new bill called for a set of "Exclusive Standards" that duplicated the Thirteen Points. It also created a staff of six commissioners, including at least two women, to enforce them. "Dr. Crafts virtually got the motion picture men to plead guilty by holding out a light sentence," the *New York Times* editorialized, "and now he appeals to the full rigor of the law—with their confession as justification for his severity. The morality of this is no doubt apparent to reformers; among the worldly it excites wonder."[114] What the *Times* failed to note, however, was that Brady's boast about controlling 90 percent of films was also an admission that NAMPI's members acted as a cartel.

One of the industry's longest-standing critics, Reverend Wilbur Crafts, seized on the controversy created by Hampton's article to propagandize his cause.[115] "A Methodist preacher, of Puritan stock," Crafts founded the International Reform Bureau in 1895 and turned full-time reformer.[116] Housed next to the Library of Congress, the bureau was "a permanent 'Christian lobby'" that claimed the distinction of being "the first incorporated agency for promoting moral legislation." Believing that too many had renounced the Protestant ethics that had made America great, Crafts sought to restore "the Puritanism of purity" through law. A book he wrote about his bureau's legislative efforts displayed how intertwined the enforcement of racial, religious, and sexual purity was to his vision of national defense. Crafts lobbied Congress to pass bills that prohibited gambling and divorce, enforced the Sunday Sabbath and temperance, and censored "impure literature and art."[117] The bureau also claimed a major share in the work of securing "'bone dry' prohibition." Its magazine, *20th Century Quarterly,* called the Sims Act—"the act that shut prize fight films out of the country"—the bureau's most "distinctive work." Prizefight films had attracted little attention until Edison's MPPC released the *Johnson-Jeffries Fight* (1910), which displayed black heavyweight world champion Jack Johnson's easy win over the "Great White Hope," Jim Jeffries. Most southern states and several northern cities banned the *Johnson-Jeffries Fight,* arguing that it implanted dangerous ideas of racial equality in children and the "childlike race" of "negroes."[118] In 1912, Congress passed the Sims Act to ensure that the federal government could prevent films showing the triumph of "an African biped beast" over "the old Saxon race." The act defined fight films, and seemingly all movies, as commerce subject to federal regulation under the Constitution's interstate commerce clause.[119]

His success in using the government to preserve proper images of the racial order suggested to Crafts an even grander goal: a federal Motion Picture Commission that could purify all movies. Crafts first proposed the bill in 1914 amidst the controversy over white slave films. Like the Sims Act, it sought to use the interstate commerce clause to empower a presidential commission that would license all films intended for distribution across state lines. In testimony before the House Committee on Education, Crafts cited the Sims Act as an important legal precedent while using the continued circulation of "black and white" fight films to justify the demand for a stricter law.[120] Craft was back at it in 1916. And, with Jack Johnson's recent conviction on spurious charges of white slavery, he again waved before Congress the threat that movies posed to the nation's racial and sexual order. "If only" he could "save the country from being flooded with pictures of a Negro indicted for white slavery and a white man voluntarily standing on the same brutal level," he would die a happy man.[121] What died that year was the bill. But after Prohibition's ratification in 1919, Crafts put "federal motion picture censorship" at the top of the Reform Bureau's agenda.[122]

Crafts's main ally in the quest for federal regulation was the prominent New York purity reformer William Sheafe Chase. An Episcopalian canon at Brooklyn's Christ Church, the founder of the Interdenominational Committee for the Suppression of Sunday Vaudeville, and the recent president of the New York Civic League, Chase focused his energy on the threat posed by picture producers in the postwar era.[123] NAMPI's William Brady provided Chase with new fodder to support his charges against the movie trust. After telling the *New York Times* that NAMPI controlled "90 percent of the output of films," Brady confided to a New Jersey senate committee considering film regulation, "You can't control this business, but I can. I am the President of the Producers' Association and with two or three other men I control every foot of film shown in the United States. What we say goes." Brady further declared that NAMPI's omnipotence arose from the fact that no exhibitor would "go against us. If they were to, we would withdraw our films from them and break them."[124] Chase put an ethnic spin on Brady's admissions. The "Movie Trust" was composed of "degrading, ignorant, greedy degenerates" who exerted "tyrannical control and influence" over screens. Thus he reasoned it was "no more unAmerican to have a small group of censors choose what picture the public shall see than it is to have a small group of producers do the choosing."[125]

A pamphlet Chase wrote to instruct the faithful on how best to argue the case for federal regulation made the anti-Semitism behind these comments explicit. Indeed, the central argument of Chase's "Catechism on Motion Pictures in Inter-state Commerce" involved the danger presented by the "despotic control" of "degrading, ignorant, greedy degenerate" producers—the "four or five Hebrews, such as Messrs. Lasky, Loew, Fox, Zukor and Laemmle."[126] Chase was rumored to be a member of the Klan, and his "Catechism" displayed anti-Semitism akin to the KKK's and Ford's.[127] Chase even used the *Dearborn Independent* to make his case, quoting it as evidence of the charge that producers "had subtly seized" the industry from "the control of men like Mr. Edison" in order to "desecrate the American Sabbath to capture an extra day of the week for vampire films and prize fights." "No true American," he asserted, could afford to ignore the "race purpose" that motivated "the demoralizing effects of motion pictures." According to Chase, the movies' "evil leaders" used their "tyrannical control and influence" to "compel directors and actors to produce wicked scenes and play indecent parts." These performances then infected stars with "the immoral code of ethics they are compelled to teach." Producers particularly threatened young actresses—even "chaste" ones cast to play "a daughter of Puritan New England"—who "must regularly and as a matter of course part with [their] virtue."[128] Like many males in his cohort, Chase placed female virtue and erotic desire in total opposition, a stance that differed from many women reformers in the period. Called a "virtual reincarnation" of Anthony Comstock by one female activist, Chase also fought sex education and birth control, objecting that sex educators' work was a "glorification of sexual pleasure, particularly women's supposed pleasure in sexual intercourse." Chase called the idea of women's "physical enjoyment" of "the sex act" a dangerous untruth—"as my wife says, it is not to be mentioned on the same day with the joy of nursing one's own baby."[129]

These melodramas of sexual danger about degenerate, Oriental movie moguls fomenting the destruction of the nation by morally corrupting its weak-willed women leaked into national news coverage, helping to explain why, amidst so much postwar unrest, the debate over regulating films became "one of the liveliest controversies that the country has seen in years."[130] Why did "nasty" producers insist on making pictures that "flaunted" "sex information" and "foreign ideas" that promoted worshipping of "continental smartness?" wondered one New Yorker.[131] The industry's glamorous new cosmopolitan stars and "Oriental" products only worsened the country's "racial indigestion." Others used the movie producers' indulgence of passionate excess to explain the "many disastrous experiences, especially among women," in Los Angeles. As the industry's new "moguls" attracted more and more of the blame, the general consensus placed "the responsibility for the 'sex-stuff' on the producers." "It is said, the 'perversity' of the producers" compelled a Prohibition-like solution that explained the efforts of "religious leaders, upheld by lay organizations," "to introduce censorship bills in forty-four State legislatures meeting this year."[132] In May 1921 the article "Nation-Wide Battle over Movie Purification" asserted: "There is no longer any dispute as to whether purification is necessary . . . the question is over how the reform will come."[133] The various individuals consulted included the GFWC's Mrs. O'Grady, Cannon Chase, and Benjamin Hampton. Despite the continued opposition of most newspapers to formal censorship, the *Literary Digest* made clear that all kinds of reformers agreed with Chase's claim that "as to the promise of the producers that if they are let alone they will purify the films, . . . we can only say they have been let alone and they haven't done it." Finally, the president of the Motion Picture Theatre Owners of America declared "exaggerated sex appeal as a sin against the common decency of the American people must be laid at the door of the producer," and approvingly noted New York exhibitors' refusal to cooperate with them.[134]

By the summer of 1921, many industry insiders realized that subduing this fire required serious attention. At the national exhibitors' convention in July, Adolph Zukor and Marcus Loew attempted to convince independent exhibitors of their aligned interests, since most of the film regulation legislation called for Sunday closings and worse. Zukor and Loew proclaimed their intention to defeat such legislation by using movie screens "to enter politics" and wage a battle for public opinion.[135] Much like the remark by NAMPI's president that five producers controlled "every foot of film shown in the United States," these declarations demonstrated Hampton's point that the industry's true big shots failed to fully grasp the implications of the very traditional melodrama in which they starred. Together the claims of Brady, Zukor, and Loew provoked two new attacks on the film industry that August: a resolution by the Senate Judiciary Committee to investigate the industry's "political activities," and a complaint issued by the Federal Trade Commission that Zukor's Famous Players–Lasky/Paramount Corporation represented "a combination and conspiracy to secure control and monopolization of the motion picture industry."[136] That same month, three censors in New York began deliberations over what the nation's largest market could watch on screens.[137]

CHAPTER 5

A Star Is Born

Rereading the "Fatty" Arbuckle Scandal

Years before the press used bohemian extra-girls and perverse movie producers to capture the appealing threat the industry posed, the *Chicago American* seized on another unconventional working girl to advertise the windy city's charms. "CHICAGO BEST CITY FOR GIRLS," announced a headline in 1913, the same year Louella Parsons moved to the city on her own. A piece of shameless civic boosterism, the article interviewed a young model named Virginia Rappe to celebrate the unparalleled opportunities Chicago offered women. A large picture of "The Lonely Girl" sat beside the article. Its caption read "Be Original, Girls, and Grow Rich." "They call Miss Rappe the 'all aloney girl' because she has had to make her way all alone in the world," it explained. Being thrust onto her own devices at the age of sixteen had served Rappe well, by fostering the "courage and initiative" necessary to achieve her dreams. Indeed, just two years later, Rappe commanded a salary of "$4,000 a year" working "as a model in commercial lines." Having traveled "all over the United States and a great part of Europe" before returning home, Rappe could attest to what made the city unique. "Chicago affords greater opportunity than any other town in the universe for the working girl," she pronounced. The *American* ordered "aspiring neophytes" who feared competing with the city's "40,000 working sisters" to "now give heed" and "hearken to the voice of experience" by listening to what the "all aloney girl" had to say.[1]

According to Rappe's "philosophy" about how to get ahead, a work-ing girl's imagination determined her chances in Chicago for success. "Every girl can't be a model, but every girl can be original," she de-clared. Originality demanded rejecting the typical low-paying jobs pre-scribed for women. "Chicago has too many stenographers and office women," she warned. Instead of "standing in lines for $6 a week jobs that are heart-breaking and demoralizing," Rappe advised finding a means to take "part of the money all these business men and salaried workers take home with them and leave with their wives." Such a task involved cultivating a flair for modern "feminine" passions, including shopping, socializing, fashion, and interior decorating—as had one friend who had turned "a dilettante devotion to art" into an $8,000-a-year career as "a flat-fixer" [interior decorator]. "If I were marked by small-pox to-morrow I'd turn 'fixer' for flat wives," she assured readers. The invention of new professions, like personal shopper or party planner, by so many women in the "independent brigade" meant "we girls are in a far better position than the men are if only we could realize it." Rappe justified her optimism by touting how Chicago nurtured "boldness" in working girls, making them "the last word in up-to-date femininity . . . superior in intelligence, adaptability and personal attractiveness."[2]

Rappe's avowals about Chicago echoed a developing orthodoxy about the locus of opportunity for ambitious migrants. By the 1913 in-terview, many placed the best chance for class mobility and self-invention along cities' anonymous, teeming streets. Here, proclaimed writers, civic boosters, and the letters of countless migrants, the least fortunate could deal themselves a better hand. What surprised about "CHICAGO BEST CITY FOR GIRLS" was its unabashed enthusiasm about the ability of this city's "utterly independent" working girls to play this game alone. Scholarship often recounts the darker, more fearful responses provoked by young white women's attempts to win "independence and happi-ness" during this era when their participation in wage labor soared and their migration to western cities outpaced the boys'. Yet the interview with Rappe celebrated the adventures of a single young white woman who beat the odds alone. Indeed, the interview betrayed her already successful steps toward self-reinvention as this working girl changed "Rapp" to the bolder, Frenchified "Rappe," signaling her claim of the kind of cultural capital that could help her get ahead.[3]

Not long after Parsons began writing her 1915 series "How to Be-come a Movie Actress" in Chicago, Rappe went west to break into the

FIGURE 24. Virginia Rappe seduces Harold Lockwood poolside in *Paradise Garden* (1917). Courtesy of Margaret Herrick Library, Academy of Motion Picture Arts and Sciences, Beverly Hills.

movies. Rappe worked mostly as an extra-girl during her first few years on the coast. In 1916 she appeared in her first bit part, as a salesgirl in *The Foolish Virgin,* a Clara Kimball Young production that also featured an unaccredited appearance by Rudolph Valentino. The following year, she won a more substantial role in *Paradise Garden* (1917), playing Marcia Van Wyck, a temptress who almost succeeds in luring the rich and handsome hero, played by actor Harold Lockwood, into succumbing to a life of decadent fun. Bad luck destroyed the chance that a more substantial role in the war picture *Over the Rhine* (1918) offered. Starring the famous female impersonator Julian Eltinge, Rappe and the unknown Valentino were again featured together, this time in bigger parts. But the film was pulled as the box office for war films plummeted after the Great War's end.[4] A badly recut version appeared as *An Adventuress* (1920).[5] By this time, Rappe's prospects seemed to be looking up. Shortly after the New Year of 1919, Parsons featured a picture of the actress, announcing she had "recently joined the Henry Lehrman Company to make Sunshine Comedies." Although she played a few lead-

FIGURE 25. Virginia Rappe takes a ride with Rudolph Valentino in *Over the Rhine* (1918). Courtesy of Margaret Herrick Library, Academy of Motion Picture Arts and Sciences, Beverly Hills.

ing comedic roles, the unpredictable alchemy that makes a star eluded Rappe.[6] Her name became known throughout the world only when she died of a ruptured bladder that resulted in peritonitis, four days after falling ill at a party hosted by slapstick star Roscoe "Fatty" Arbuckle.

The scandal that resulted from Rappe's death made her "A STAR AT LAST," one who symbolized the hazards confronting the "millions of pretty girls" who turned "their faces to the gilded west" and imagined going "after the pot of brass at the end of the Cooper-Hewitt rainbow."[7] The press shaped a succession of melodramatic narratives out of the contradictory and constantly changing testimony of witnesses, story lines that explained the event's significance *before* Arbuckle ever set foot inside a courtroom. The first story offered a modernized romantic melodrama of sexual danger, featuring Rappe as a spirited if virtuous victim and Arbuckle as a ghastly beast. The second made room for imagining the event as a consensual "orgy" and blamed middle-class cultural custodians for allowing dangerous moral changes to proceed unchecked. Ultimately the story that won out reverted to a traditional melodrama of sexual danger that cast Rappe as a degraded fallen woman and Hollywood as the villain. Standing in as modernity's scapegoat, Hollywood represented the most powerful force luring the nation's daughters too far outside the home. By the time the periodical press caught up with newspapers whose daily coverage first shaped the meanings given to the event, the *Literary Digest* could already assert its outcome. "What the demand for censorship has been unable to accomplish . . . the revelations of the Arbuckle case" "most thoroughly accomplished," the *Digest* declared.[8] A cartoon illustrating the article succinctly communicated what the "clean up" of "movie morals" entailed. In the foreground, a matronly "ma" confided, "Oh, pa, Tilly has given up wanting to be a movie star," while her daughter, tucked in the kitchen, lightened a load of dishes by singing a song. Here lay the message of this morality tale: "THE GOOD THAT COMES FROM EVIL," proclaimed before any jury's verdict. No longer would the industry's celebrity culture spin such unabashedly romantic adventure stories about the glories awaiting ambitious female migrants who went west to make their fortunes, and to remake themselves, along Hollywood's streets.[9]

I

"S.F. BOOZE PARTY KILLS YOUNG ACTRESS" wailed a two-inch headline across the *San Francisco Examiner*'s masthead on Saturday, September 10, 1921. "GIRL STRICKEN AFTER AFFAIR AT S.F. HOTEL: Virginia Rappe Dies after Being Guest at Party Given Here by 'Fatty' Arbuckle; Film Comedian, When Told of Girl's Death, Telephoned S.F. Police He Would Be Here Today." These headlines, descending in size, announced the media event that reshaped the picture of young women's place in Hollywood. By the time the Rappe-Arbuckle scandal slipped from the front pages of newspapers, images of young women corrupted and destroyed by the stars in their eyes would blot out those of savvy, self-sufficient bohemians. A large, eye-catching composite photograph that combined publicity portraits of the event's two protagonists sat beside the story, visually linking the "GIRL WHO DIED AND HER HOST." At its center, Rappe cocked her head and threw a sly, sideways glance out from under a large hat. Inserted under her shoulder lay a small, oval picture of Arbuckle dressed as a cowboy, looking straight at readers with a devilish grin.[10]

Since the coroner's inquest had yet to begin, the report said little about Rappe's cause of death—beyond the allegation that a "BOOZE

PARTY KILLED" her.[11] It also barely mentioned Arbuckle, counting on readers' familiarity with the slapstick comedian whose success at offering children good, clean fun was rivaled only by Charlie Chaplin.[12] It ignored the statement Arbuckle had given reporters the night before when they surrounded him after a screening of his latest film, *Gasoline Gus* (1921), at Sid Grauman's new "million dollar theater" in Los Angeles.[13] Only the *Los Angeles Times,* published by William Randolph Hearst's great rival Harry Chandler, printed Arbuckle's account in one of the few stories that broke the news on Saturday.[14]

Instead, the coverage in Hearst's *Examiner* introduced readers to "Virginia Rappe, beautiful young movie actress of Los Angeles," and described "the circumstances surrounding" her "tragic denouement."[15] The paper identified her as "a leading woman" for comedy producer Henry Lehrman and "a woman of financial means because of investments in Texas oil." Although not "engaged professionally of late," Rappe remained a popular figure in Hollywood and "a favorite" at hot spots frequented by "film folk" where she "took costly prizes" in dance contests. "Noted in the film colony" for "the richness of her taste in clothes," Rappe was called by some "the best dressed woman in the movies." She had arrived in San Francisco on Sunday morning with "Al Senneca, her manager, and a friend, Mrs. B.M. Del Monte." She "was apparently in the best of health" when the trio went up to the hotel suite shared by Arbuckle, actor L. Sherman, and director "Fred Fishbeck." Except for Sherman, the paper mangled the other attendees' names. "A number of other women" filled out the "afternoon party" at the St. Francis, San Francisco's finest hotel. After the hotel fulfilled Arbuckle's request for a phonograph, with "the understanding that there was to be no dancing," nothing was heard of the "gay occasion" until a woman called the front desk asking that "someone be sent up" because "a woman had become hysterical and was tearing off her clothing." Assistant Manager H.J. Boyle responded to the call. Entering the suite, he found "Arbuckle in pajamas and a bath robe" in the suite's reception room along with "several women and two men." Rappe was in an adjoining room "lying on the bed in a partially nude state and unconscious." Since "several bottles were in evidence," Boyle judged Rappe's condition "the result of a drinking party" and moved her to a different room. "Arbuckle was asked by the management to leave" and returned "at once to Los Angeles"— one of many assertions later disproved.

"ARBUCKLE CHARGED WITH MURDER OF GIRL; ACTRESS' DYING WORDS CAUSE STAR'S ARREST," screamed the *Examiner*'s headline the next day. The lead article took the scant evidence released the previous day and fashioned several conclusions about the event. Rappe's death from peritonitis was "superinduced [sic] by an internal injury sustained at a wild party in Arbuckle's suite at the St. Francis hotel." The "charge of murder was laid" because "the evidence of the various witnesses clearly indicated that [a criminal assault] had been committed and was the superinducing cause of the injury that ended in the girl's death."[16] Arbuckle "passed through the ordeal of questioning, arrest, and incarceration without uttering a single word" and now sat in a solitary cell, denied bail. As the headline's hook promised, the three pages devoted to the story offered readers the chance to eavesdrop on a séance with "the dead beautiful young motion picture actress," or the "dead girl," as the paper repeatedly referred to Rappe.[17] Like much of the early reporting, the tale seemed designed to evoke a kind of necrophilia that incited readers' desire for posthumous intimacy with Rappe. A large photomontage of Rappe's face surrounded by tiny shots of the actress dressed as the "characters she played in film comedies" sat in the center of the second page. Rappe communicated through multiple mediums, including an omniscient narrator and voices attributed to "Mrs. Jean Jameson, nurse who cared for Virginia Rappe and heard her moanings and accusations of Roscoe Arbuckle"; Alice Blake, identified only by her local address; and "Mrs. Delmont," the woman who "laid the accusation" of murder at "Arbuckle's door." Over the next few weeks the degree of Delmont's closeness to Rappe shrank dramatically—from "bosom friend," to "protectorix" and "chaperon," to an "acquaintance" who met her on the drive up the coast to San Francisco.[18]

Early reporting crafted a romantic melodramatic narrative about a battle between virtuous modern girls and libertine men.[19] The fact that these accounts initially included only the opinions of women partygoers strengthened this impression. "I am used to seeing people die. That is my business. I see them die all the time," began the testimony of Nurse Jameson, which formed the narrative's spine. "Nevertheless," the nurse, "who saw the beautiful girl pass away with the words on her lips—'Get Roscoe—follow this to the finish'—last night betrayed distinct emotion in telling of the death of her latest 'patient.'" Explaining that Delmont was "too exhausted" to speak for herself, the nurse spoke for the complaining witness who had reportedly watched over the stricken actress until her death and then told the police that Arbuckle had "forcibly taken Virginia Rappe into his room" and "abused her. Mrs. Delmont said that Virginia was screaming and yelling and that she, Mrs. Delmont, went to the door and found it was locked," so she "kicked on the door several times" until "Arbuckle opened it," revealing Rappe "pulling at her clothes." Alice Blake's claim that she saw Rappe "lying on the bed," "moaning and crying, 'I am dying! I am dying!'" finished the account. Although Jameson's account was riddled with contradictions, including Rappe's alleged comment that "she took three drinks, and then knew nothing," the nurse made one point clear: Rappe "said she blamed Arbuckle for her injuries and wanted him punished for it. . . . Just before she died," she "placed her hand on her abdomen, and said: 'He broke me inside—with his weight.'"[20]

The last page of the coverage focused on the state of Rappe's corpse and the spirit that animated it before her death. A biographical piece, "MISS RAPPE WAS DESIGNER, FILM ACTRESS," sat at its center. "Well-known as a motion picture actress, artists' model, and designer of women's clothes," Rappe lived in Los Angeles with an "aunt who acted as her chaperone." Rappe "first came to prominence" in her hometown of Chicago in 1913 when, as "a traveling art model earning $4,000 a year," the paper featured her advice that "American girls" should "choose original ways of making their living and not slip into the usual, stereotyped" occupations. "Reputed to have independent wealth," she had recently appeared as a leading woman in two films produced by her fiancé, Henry Lehrman of New York. The description of this bright past contrasted sharply with the details of her brutalized present in stories that lingered upon her lifeless remains rather than assessing the cause of her death. "MANY BRUISES ARE FOUND BY THE CORONER ON GIRL'S BODY," blared the headline.[21] A smaller one beneath it declared "NO EVIDENCE OF ASSAULT: DR. W. OPHULS." Dr. Ophuls, the pathologist who performed Rappe's first, unofficial postmortem, stated that "natural causes" had ruptured her bladder and her body showed "absolutely no evidences of a criminal assault." Another story revealed the illegality of Ophuls's examination, since the law required the coroner's office to conduct all autopsies of suspicious deaths. After her move from the St. Francis to Wakefield Sanitarium, Dr. Rumwell had attended Rappe before Ophuls performed his illegal autopsy. Under Rumwell's care at Wakefield, Rappe reportedly rambled continuously of Arbuckle's attack in a delirium produced by drugs and excruciating pain.[22] One nurse at Wakefield quit the case, complaining that by "any opinion it had been handled negligently."[23] Yet Rumwell, who performed an initial postmortem before requesting the pathologist's services, claimed that he failed to notify the city coroner because he "considered the case one of death from purely natural causes." The *Examiner* let stand Rumwell's bewildering statement about the death of an apparently healthy twenty-six-year-old, a statement that blatantly contradicted the paper's own picture of Rappe's death at Arbuckle's hands. Although District Attorney Brady called Rumwell's behavior "the most suspicious part of the whole case," he never called him to the witness stand in subsequent trials. Moreover, when Dr. Arthur Beardslee, who first treated Rappe at the St. Francis before going out of town, returned two weeks later to testify in court, he stated that it was plain to him by Tuesday that she suffered from a ruptured bladder.[24] Rather than uncovering the truth about her medical treatment, the paper focused instead on creating stories out of the sensational claims of the complaining witness, Maude Delmont.

The focus on the "beautiful dead girl"—minus the medical facts surrounding her death—and a particular construction of her past allowed Hearst's media empire to construct a melodrama of sexual danger in which Rappe played the victimized innocent, Arbuckle the rapacious fiend. The fact that Arbuckle and his attorneys "surrounded themselves with a wall of silence" after his arrest aided the ability of newspapers to retain total control of the first narrative about the event.[25] Here was a rousing melodrama of sexual danger in which a beautiful, refined, upper-class, and defenseless young woman walked into a wild party that resulted in her death at the hands of an enormous "beast" of a man.[26] As in all stirring melodramas of virtue assaulted, the motivation for the star's evildoing was less important than conveying the pathos of the victim who embraced the code of death-before-dishonor. This coverage of the scandal in the Hearst papers composed a kind of virtual play, featuring performances by Rappe, Delmont, and Arbuckle—individuals who could not or would not speak for themselves. Stories overflowed with fictive dialogue and hearsay, offering readers an emotion-rich, visceral experience of "ARBUCKLE'S DEATH PARTY."

The Hearst papers were not alone in reporting the scandal this way. Dailies across the country made and shaped the event into sensational national news. By Sunday, typically the largest circulation day, the story sat on front pages from coast to coast.[27] In the coming week, even more typically staid papers like the *New York Times* ran headlines that shrieked, "ARBUCKLE DRAGGED RAPPE GIRL TO ROOM, WOMAN TESTIFIES." But William Randolph Hearst's newspapers, estimated to reach one in four families that year, outdid all others in length, intensity, and storytelling ability.[28] Located at the epicenter of the event, Hearst's flagship newspaper, the *San Francisco Examiner,* often broke what passed for the latest developments in the case throughout September—the period in which the scandal daily produced pages of copy in the multiple editions published. The *Examiner* set the formula for how to tell the story of the scandal, devising a blueprint followed not just by other Hearst-owned dailies but in news organizations across the country. And after papers like the *Brooklyn Daily Eagle,* the *St. Louis Post-Dispatch,* and the *New York Times* backed off the story or began to employ a more skeptical tone, Hearst papers tempted readers with headlines promising the latest "news." In a telegraph responding to Adolph Zukor's entreaty that he act responsibly so as to prevent unfair publicity from damaging the industry, Hearst declared his intention to make the most of the event. "It is difficult to keep the news out of the newspaper," Hearst replied by telegraph, adding, "The people who get into the courts and coroners offices are responsible[;] the newspapers are no more responsible than the courts are."[29] Hearst's belief that Zukor was ruining the career of his mistress, actress Marion Davies, likely played a role in his eagerness to launch the wholesale assault he had threatened two months earlier against Zukor by attacking his new star Arbuckle.

Hearst reporters favored participants with expertise in employing the melodramatic mode, and no one among them excelled in this art like Rappe's "fiancé," Henry Lehrman. Known to members of the film colony as "Pathe" rather than "Henry," Lehrman had moved to New York from Vienna as a teenager, and then worked as a streetcar conductor until talking his way into his first job at Biograph in 1909. By posing as an experienced Parisian player, Lehrman piqued D.W. Griffith's interest. Here was a "student of the motion picture art" who had "learned all there was to learn from the Pathes," the French brothers who were the era's most successful, innovative pioneers. Though his co-workers quickly recognized his biography was a fake, Lehrman proved himself a "genuine funny man with an instinct for comedy," according to Mack Sennett.[30] Moving from acting to directing and writing, and, eventually, with Sennett to Los Angeles, he became a principal director and gagman at Keystone. Yet his career floundered after he left the studio in 1915—the reverse trajectory experienced by his two former Keystone underlings, Charles Chaplin and Roscoe "Fatty" Arbuckle.

"My prayer is that justice be done. I don't want to go to the coast now; I could not face Arbuckle. I would kill him," opened the first of several interviews Lehrman gave to Hearst's *New York American.*[31] The reporter took pains to emphasize the high-browish setting in which he had found Lehrman: a study surrounded by "Japanese prints" and books like "H.G. Wells' 'Outline of History.'" Lehrman's account read like dialogue printed on intertitle cards in one of the many traditional melodramas favored by Griffith—films Lehrman had expertly mocked as a slapstick director and writer. "Before she knew she was going to die Virginia kept saying: 'Don't tell Henry. Don't tell Henry.'" "That means one thing. She had lost the battle she made to defend herself. She didn't want me to know. She knew what I would do." Arbuckle was "a beast" who "boasted" to him in the past that "he had torn the clothing from an unwilling girl and then outraged her." "That's what comes from taking vulgarians from the gutter . . . and making idols of them," he continued. "Arbuckle was a bar boy in a San Francisco saloon. Not a bartender, a bar boy; one of those who wash glasses and clean cuspidors." Lehrman denounced Arbuckle and his bohemian friends as a "disgrace to the film business. They are the ones who resort to cocaine and the opium needle and who participate in orgies that surpass the orgies of degenerate Rome. They should be swept out of the picture business." "Virginia always had a violent, physical aversion for Arbuckle," and her accusation, through Nurse Jameson, showed her determination to "rise from the dead to defend her person from indignity." "I can see now in my mind's eye how she must have fought him like a tiger, even if she had had a couple of drinks." In short, Lehrman ensured that readers knew she observed the death-before-dishonor code of true womanhood. Shortly before the fateful party, he reported, Rappe had read a story about a sexual assault and had confided: "'Henry, if anyone tried to do a thing like that to me, he'd have to kill me.' Well, she's dead."[32]

The spread of this conventional narrative produced a surprising turn of events. As newspapers embroidered stories from Arbuckle's alleged proclivity for outsized hedonism, the event shifted from a "gay" booze party to an "orgy" presided over by a host likened to Falstaff, one of Shakespeare's most complicated villains.[33] A surrogate for disorder, crime, and license, Falstaff's corpulent form embodies the power that flows from smashing custom and convention. A dazzling Fool, he draws strength from puncturing the platitudes of his surrounding society. The "ORGY" exposed the true character of "Yesterday's Jester," the fat jolly man who had once prompted only "childish chirps or wee anticipatory sighs." Arbuckle stood revealed as a "thorough Bohemian" whose working-class origins and rapid success left him grossly unfit for public renown.[34] "Sated with money," his success provided the means to bathe "his decadent soul in every fountain of viciousness." A former

FIGURE 26. Rappe warns her sex about the dangers of "too much liberty." *Philadelphia Evening Public Ledger,* Sept. 14, 1921, Night Extra. Courtesy of Chronicling America, Historical Newspapers, Library of Congress.

"PLUMBER" and "$3-a-Day-Super [stage extra]," Arbuckle had rejected his parents' pleas to become a minister or a doctor and joined the "travelling circus as a stepping stone to the stage."[35] Once a star, this "beast from the gutter" had used his fame to entice Rappe to his party, where he declared, "I've waited for you five years and now I've got you," before dragging her into his hotel bedroom.[36]

Cast as the "Victim of [the] Orgy," the presentation of Rappe shifted to suggest a modern woman driven by her own dangerous passions. Having fallen prey to "the fascinations of the motion picture 'game,'" Rappe was "lured by stardom" and "motion picture advancement" into taking a gamble that "hundreds of thousands of girls" who "forever

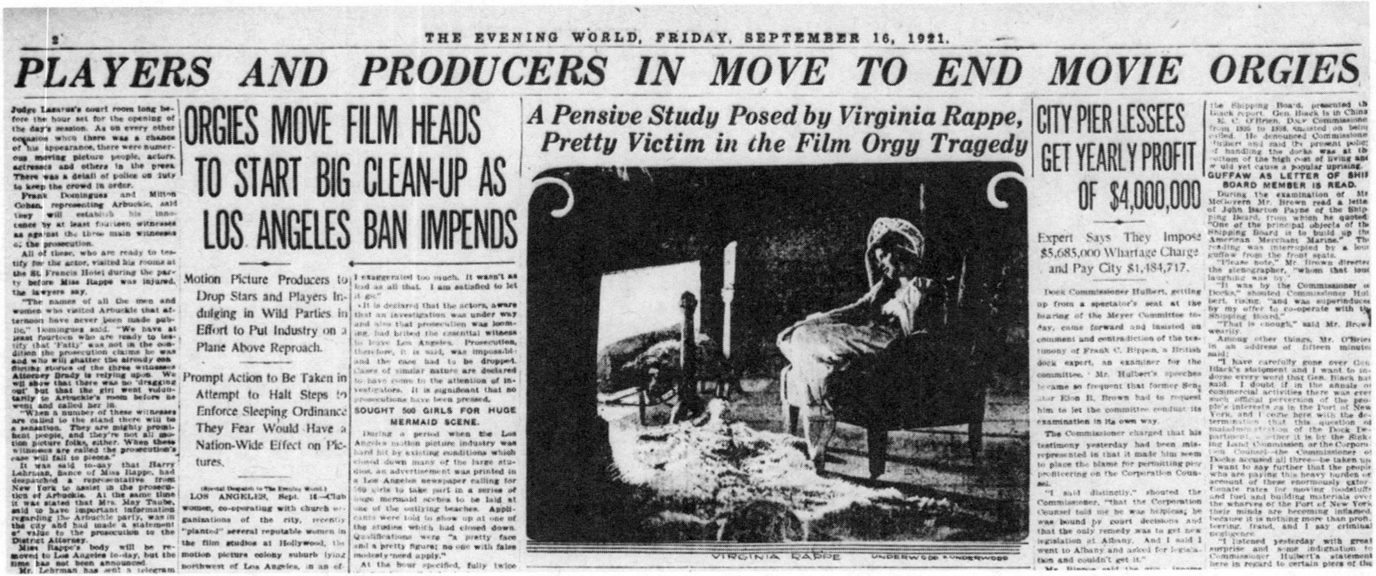

2 THE EVENING WORLD, FRIDAY, SEPTEMBER 16, 1921.

PLAYERS AND PRODUCERS IN MOVE TO END MOVIE ORGIES

Judge Lazarus's court room long before the hour set for the opening of the day's session. As on every other occasion when there was a chance of his appearance, there were numerous moving picture people, actors, actresses and others in the press. There was a detail of police on duty to keep the crowd in order.

Frank Domingues and Milton Cohen, representing Arbuckle, said they will establish his innocence by at least fourteen witnesses as against the three main witnesses of the prosecution.

All of these, who are ready to testify for the actor, visited his rooms at the St. Francis Hotel during the party before Miss Rappe was injured, the lawyers say.

"The names of all the men and women who visited Arbuckle that afternoon have never been made public," Domingues said. "We have at least fourteen who are ready to testify that 'Fatty' was not in the condition the prosecution claims he was and who will shatter the already conflicting stories of the three witnesses Attorney Brady is relying upon. We will show that there was no 'dragging out' but that the girl went voluntarily to Arbuckle's room before he went and called her in.

"When a number of these witnesses are called to the stand there will be a sensation. They are mighty prominent people, and they're not all motion picture folks, either. When these witnesses are called the prosecution's case will fall to pieces."

It was said to-day that Harry Lehrman, fiance of Miss Rappe, had despatched a representative from New York to assist in the prosecution of Arbuckle. At the same time it was stated that Mrs. May Taube, said to have important information regarding the Arbuckle party, was in the city and had made a statement of value to the prosecution to the District Attorney.

Miss Rappe's body will be removed to Los Angeles to-day, but the time has not been announced.

Mr. Lehrman has sent a telegram

ORGIES MOVE FILM HEADS TO START BIG CLEAN-UP AS LOS ANGELES BAN IMPENDS

Motion Picture Producers to Drop Stars and Players Indulging in Wild Parties in Effort to Put Industry on a Plane Above Reproach.

Prompt Action to Be Taken in Attempt to Halt Steps to Enforce Sleeping Ordinance They Fear Would Have a Nation-Wide Effect on Pictures.

(Special Despatch to The Evening World.)

LOS ANGELES, Sept. 16.—Club women, co-operating with church organizations of the city, recently "planted" several reputable women in the film studios at Hollywood, the motion picture colony suburb lying northwest of Los Angeles, in an ef-

I exaggerated too much. It wasn't as bad as all that. I am satisfied to let it go."

It is declared that the actors, aware that an investigation was under way and also that prosecution was looming, had bribed the essential witness to leave Los Angeles. Prosecution, therefore, it is said, was impossible and the case had to be dropped. Cases of similar nature are declared to have come to the attention of investigators. It is significant that no prosecutions have been pressed.

SOUGHT 500 GIRLS FOR HUGE MERMAID SCENE.

During a period when the Los Angeles motion picture industry was hard hit by existing conditions which closed down many of the large studios, an advertisement was printed in a Los Angeles newspaper calling for 500 girls to take part in a series of huge mermaid scenes to be laid at one of the outlying beaches. Applicants were told to show up at one of the studios which had closed down. Qualifications were "a pretty face and a pretty figure; no one with false modesty need apply."

At the hour specified, fully twice

A Pensive Study Posed by Virginia Rappe, Pretty Victim in the Film Orgy Tragedy

VIRGINIA RAPPE UNDERWOOD & UNDERWOOD

CITY PIER LESSEES GET YEARLY PROFIT OF $4,000,000

Expert Says They Impose $5,685,000 Wharfage Charge and Pay City $1,484,717.

Dock Commissioner Hulbert, getting up from a spectator's seat at the hearing of the Meyer Committee to-day, came forward and insisted on comment and contradiction of the testimony of Frank C. Rippen, a British dock expert, an examiner for the committee. Mr. Hulbert's speeches became so frequent that former Senator Elon R. Brown had to request him to let the committee conduct its examination in its own way.

The Commissioner charged that his testimony yesterday had been misrepresented in that it made him seem to place the blame for permitting pier profiteering on the Corporation Counsel.

"I said distinctly," shouted the Commissioner, "that the Corporation Counsel told me he was helpless; he was bound by court decisions and that the only remedy was to get new legislation at Albany. And I said I went to Albany and asked for legislation and couldn't get it."

Mr. Rippen said the gro... income

the Shipping Board, presented the Black report. Gen. Black is in China.

E. C. O'Brien, Dock Commissioner from 1895 to 1898, insisted on being called. He denounced Commissioner Hulbert and said the present policy of handling the docks was at the bottom of the high cost of living and would yet cause a popular uprising.

GUFFAW AS LETTER OF SHIP BOARD MEMBER IS READ.

During the examination of Mr. McGovern Mr. Brown read a letter of John Barton Payne of the Shipping Board, from which he quoted: "One of the principal objects of the Shipping Board is to build up the American Merchant Marine." The reading was interrupted by a loud guffaw from the front seats.

"Please note," Mr. Brown directed the stenographer, "whom that loud laughing was by."

"It was by the Commissioner of Docks," shouted Commissioner Hulbert, rising, "and was superinduced by my offer to co-operate with the Shipping Board."

"That is enough," said Mr. Brown wearily.

Among other things, Mr. O'Brien in an address of fifteen minutes said:

"I have carefully gone over Gen. Black's statement and I want to indorse every word that Gen. Black has said. I doubt if in the annals of commercial activities there was ever such official perversion of the people's interests as in the Port of New York, and I came here with the determination that this question of maladministration of the Dock Department, whether it is by the Sinking Fund Commission or the Corporation Counsel—the Commissioner of Docks accused all three—be taken up. I want to say further that the people who are paying this heavy burden on account of these enormously extortionate rates for moving foodstuffs and fuel and building materials over the wharves of the Port of New York their minds are becoming inflamed, because it is nothing more than profiteering, fraud, and I say criminal negligence.

"I listened yesterday with great surprise and some indignation to Commissioner Hulbert's statement here in regard to certain piers of the

FIGURE 27. Coverage of "movie orgies" consumed newspapers in 1921–1922. *Evening World,* Sept. 16, 1921, Racing Final, p. 2. Courtesy of Chronicling America, Historical Newspapers, Library of Congress.

dream" of the screen would make.[37] In short, "ambition led her to play with fire," though she ultimately "refused to pay [the] price." Before attending the party, she had confessed to Delmont, "He [Arbuckle] says he's got a chance to get me something better in the movies and maybe it's a chance to make a star out of me . . . but I'm afraid. I don't like that man."[38]

Newspapers' eagerness to read the event as an orgy complicated the simpler modernized melodrama of sexual danger with which most began. As the event unfolded, changes in the behavior and testimony of the women witnesses also made the earlier narrative difficult to sustain. The prosecution's "star witness," now referred to as "Maude Bambina Delmont," dramatically changed her description of the party before the coroner's grand jury on September 14. Gone was the tale in which Arbuckle forced Rappe into his bedroom, where she cried for help. Now she told a story in which the two, somehow, ended up in one of the suite's bedrooms, causing her to knock on the door an hour later because it "didn't look 'nice.'" The two "show-girl witnesses" also altered their testimony amidst charges of blackmail and intimidation by District Attorney Brady.[39] The coverage in Hearst papers, which turned to playing up the orgy angle unceasingly, included ever more inventive visual displays, such as one of "show girls" who "WALKED INTO [ARBUCKLE'S] PARLOUR" and got entangled in his "web."[40] The revelry that apparently resulted spilled just outside such pictures' frames.

The more accounts described the party as a sensational sexual orgy, the more space opened up to see it as a bawdy, consensual revelry. "Warm with dancing" and with the ten drinks she admitted to consuming in two hours, Delmont had changed into a pair of actor Lowell Sherman's pajamas. Under oath in court, guests described a "royal good time, dancing and kidding and drinking," with Arbuckle "at the center" of the "clowning"—until Rappe fell ill.[41] The press also circulated a new history for Rappe, presenting her character as more "tragic," "pathetic," and, ultimately, more morally questionable.[42] Her biography now described her as the illegitimate child of an actress and either a "British nobleman" or a "Chicago financier." Her mother, a "queen of the night" who "reaped what she had sown," reportedly died from tuberculosis, leaving the ten-year-old "an orphan cast adrift in the world."[43] After establishing herself as a model, Rappe set off in 1914 on a "pleasure jaunt" to Europe, startling passengers on the ship home with a "Nightie-Tango" performed with a girlfriend. A broken love affair led Rappe to start afresh. "I am going to California" to "'make good' in the 'movies,'" she announced.[44] Although depicting Rappe as a plucky survivor who rebounded after her tragic start, her questionable, exotic origins presented a much less innocent personality than before.

These stories made it difficult to maintain the gendered dichotomies—of passive, pure women ravaged by licentious men—that supported the moral coherency of the initial tale. A chorus of editorial comment quickly declared the evolution of this more complicated ethical landscape to be the real moral of the story. "What's Gone Wrong with [the] World Today?" asked the headline of an article by Annie Laurie, one of Hearst's most popular syndicated columnists.[45] According to Laurie, the world's problems stemmed from girls' rejection of "their right to shelter and protection" and "the old ideals" that buttressed this entitlement. "The spirit of true womanhood—the homemaking, home loving, home protecting spirit that has pulled the race up out of savagery" had become passé. The journalist expounded the point the next day, in "Old Rules for Girls Supplanted by New," a piece one minister called "the ablest article growing out of the whole tragedy."[46] "Ten years ago, any girl who would go to a man's room in a hotel, party or no party, would have thrown away her good name the instant the fact of her visit was known," Laurie lamented. Yet Laurie cautioned readers not to judge Rappe before they judged themselves. "Your daughter or my daughter would probably have jumped at the chance to meet this man," now bent on using "his money and his influence and his 'celebrity' to hush the whole matter up." A front-page story in the New York American offered a similar view. "Orgies in City Ready to Stage a New Tragedy," it declared, warning that "the tragedy of Virginia Rappe just happened to be staged in San Francisco," but could take place in any city. A statement issued by the coroner's jury on September 14 indicated that the jurors had taken the lesson to heart. After recommending an indictment of manslaughter, its members called on both federal Prohibition officers and local law enforcement to "take steps . . . so that San Francisco shall not be made the rendezvous of the debauchee and gangster."[47]

By framing the "orgy" as a quotidian occurrence, not merely an incident involving the exceptional residents of the movie colony, newspapers offered a morality tale on the grandest scale. This story linked a specific example of single young women attending a hotel party without fearing for their good names, to a general assertion about the degeneration of moral standards in cities everywhere, making society the villain for allowing young women freedoms that threatened the "civilized" world.[48] "At last something has shocked the very, very soul of our nation," wrote one reader in Los Angles.[49] According to an English clubwoman, "the scandal at San Francisco" sparked an international moral crusade. By inciting the United States to fight so that "good will overcome evil," the scandal's "moral effect spread around the world," convincing the League of Nations to adopt stricter enforcement laws against white slavery.[50] Here, Hollywood—as a social environment populated by trendsetting stars—represented not a scapegoat for modernity's failures, but a symbol of the country's guilt and need for reformation. "Film characters," an editorialist declared, were "public characters. The Los Angeles colony has been setting the style for the rest of the country.... Keeping up with Mary [Pickford] is as strenuous as 'Keeping up with Lizzie [the Model T Ford].'" Little wonder that girls like Rappe thought it acceptable to go Hollywood, so to speak, and succumb to similar seductions of "wine, women, and song."[51] The fact that Arbuckle's films had been considered morally innocuous strengthened the argument that the industry's threat lay not just with its "sex pictures" but with its celebrity culture more broadly, which glamorized modern attitudes to fans around the world.[52]

Yet this reassertion of a traditional melodrama of sexual danger quickly prepared the way for another one whose villain was better suited to the tastes of many: the idea that Hollywood directly bore responsibility for Rappe's death. The industry's rapidly deteriorating fortunes displayed the effects of viewing Hollywood as the scoundrel that had unleashed the evils associated with modernity. The stock of Paramount, which now handled Arbuckle, dropped from $80 to $40 a share just weeks after the news of Rappe's death hit newsstands. "It is impossible for the people now in control of pictures to borrow money or even carry on with any certainty," a banker reported. *Variety* warned that "society leaders," including Henry Ford, were hatching "schemes designed to take the business of purveying amusement to the masses ... away from those at present in control."[53] "If this keeps up there won't be any motion picture industry," Louis B. Mayer confided to King Vidor.[54]

Industry insiders and Los Angeles's city leaders and residents quickly crafted diverging counternarratives about the event's significance. On one side stood censorship advocates in Los Angeles aligned with the national forces supporting Anglo-Christian Americanism, folks who feared that Hollywood's foreign producers and lower-class celebrities had replaced respectable cultural custodians in deciding what counted

as fashionable and fun.[55] Readers of the *Los Angeles Times* wrote letters protesting how the adulation showered on Arbuckle displayed "the
rewards of an undiluted democracy" conferred on "motion picture
lowbrows" who transformed "liberty into libertinism."[56] Only a censorship board could preserve the influence of the city's ministers, "foster
and develop Christian citizenship," and protect "a thousand years of
Anglo-Saxon development."

Indeed, many ministers in Los Angeles viewed the event as heaven-
sent since only days *before* news of Rappe's death broke, the Ministerial Union had petitioned the Los Angeles City Council (LACC) to acti-
vate a never used ordinance to create a censorship board.[57] Seeking to
use the scandal to propagandize their cause, the union called a meeting
on "the Arbuckle case and motion pictures censorship." There a "row"
broke out when the union's president, Reverend Gustav Briegleb, charged
that "the industry" was "on trial." "The tendency of the producers is to
make immoral pictures," he asserted, adding that "85 per cent" of the
industry was "controlled chiefly by the Jews and that some of the later
care only for the money they make and not the moral effect of their
business." The response of Captain Edmundson, pastor of Hollywood
Methodist Episcopal Church and chaplain for the state's American
Legion, created a ruckus. Refusing to be ruled out of order, Edmundson
protested Briegleb's "aspersions" against the industry's "Jews and actors
and actresses." The meeting then ended abruptly, amidst much hymn
singing. "By innuendo and direct statements [Briegleb] attacked the Jews
and I, who have many friends among the Jews, do not propose to let
such attacks go unchallenged," Edmundson later told the *Times*. Hollywood's pastor would not "let only one side of the censorship and motion
picture industry be presented, even at a ministerial meeting," he said, objecting to "a jury packed against me [that] should Amen and Hallelujah
me down when I had the floor." Briegleb observed that he merely stated
the facts, since "gentlemen of Hebrew extraction" who "consider[ed]
only box office receipts" controlled the business.[58]

Other voices championed the industry's lively cosmopolitan influence on Los Angeles. A letter to the *Los Angeles Times* dismissed the
uproar as a "yowl" caused by "sordid envy" and "jealousy" toward the
industry that "made Los Angeles such an interesting city." The newspapers "reek every day with filthy, sordid divorce cases and crimes . . . in
no way connected with picture folk," another letter admonished, yet
"not a word is said about the class or profession of the people who wal-
low in this mud."[59] Indeed, several letters wondered why the sensa-

tional, violent stories that composed so much of mass-produced popular culture escaped censure. The "righteous" who "berate the movies" loved their "evening paper which in a single issue" contained "more filth, more suggestions of indecency, more stories of illicit love, of rape, of murder, of robbery, than you would see in a picture house in a twelve-month." A letter to the LACC criticized the anti-Semitism that, the writer believed, explained the double standard, decrying the "sanctimonious gentlemen who worship a Jew on Sunday and spend the rest of the week maligning the Jews generally." A petition submitted to the LACC that opposed film censorship lampooned the proposed board, demanding the creation of "a body of Censors of Oratory and Pulpits" since ministers sought "to enforce their religious beliefs, or their ideas of morals, upon all the other residents."[60] Both the Chamber of Commerce and the Merchants and Manufactures Association came out strongly against punishing the industry. In a variety of ways, the business community sought to remind residents over the following weeks that the industry was one of the "main sources of our prosperity."[61]

While remaining silent on a national level, film producers defended the industry's reputation locally by prodding the business community and Chandler's Los Angeles Times for just such support. "The present moment represents a crisis in our business," declared an open letter in the Times from the Motion Picture Producers Association (MPPA).[62] The MPPA called on "the daily press," business associations, and "open minded members of the community" "to come to our aid in crystallizing public opinion" against censorship. Such a measure, the association warned, would "impose a heavy burden" "on possibly the greatest enterprise in California." It would also "give color to the belief in other communities that Los Angeles, known to the world as the 'Capital of Filmdom,' found it necessary to cast a stigma upon the picture business." Such treatment would force the industry to leave town. Seemingly in response to the ultimatum, the coverage in the Los Angeles Times after the open letter shifted from offering readers scoops on the colony's wild ways to striking a more balanced tone than in other newspapers.[63] Little more than one week after the scandal's eruption, the Times blamed the "mob spirit" against Arbuckle on other newspapers "printing every unproven accusation" against the comedian.[64] Yet the paper also recommended Arbuckle's sacrifice as Hollywood's stray "spotted sheep" to preserve the "white sheep" who predominated.[65] In general, the Los Angeles Times presented Arbuckle as outside the pale of respectability while, overall, offering a wholesome picture of the city and its largest industry.[66] The paper conceded that the "Arbuckle Incident" revealed that much more care was necessary to protect "girlish innocence" in Hollywood. But it also came out against censorship, cautioning the public not to confuse all picture folk with the comedian. Ultimately, it suggested the industry needed a chance to solve its own problems "honestly, enthusiastically, patriotically."[67]

In general, the film industry orchestrated a hush on the topic of Arbuckle, "girlish innocence," and all other matters pertaining to the scandal. *Moving Picture World* visualized the approach in "The Arbuckle Case," a full-page notice that declared, "Enclosed in the Following Space Is Our Idea What Should Be Said by Everybody in the Moving Picture Business about the Arbuckle Case from Now Forth until the Entire Matter Is Settled." Below, an empty box filled the entire page.[68]

Only one branch of the industry, the independent exhibitors allied in the Motion Picture Theatre Owners Association (MPTOA), openly discussed how to address the crisis. Martin Quigley, editor of the *Exhibitors Herald,* the MPTOA's trade paper, criticized the decision to hide "ostrich fashion."[69] In several articles, the *Herald* dissected the producers' troubles: the U.S. Senate's call to investigate the "industry's 'political activity'"; the Federal Trade Commission's charge against Zukor's FPL/Paramount; and, finally, how the Arbuckle case was "seized as ammunition by reformers."[70] The paper also noted exhibitors' use of the scandal to challenge producers' control. Just two days after news of the "death party" exploded, "Grauman's 'Million Dollar Theater'" in Los Angeles yanked Arbuckle's *Gasoline Gus.* A cascading series of reports displayed other exhibitors' willingness to do the same.[71] Within weeks, the MPTOA ordered members to pull all of Arbuckle's and Rappe's films, contradicting the wishes of Paramount/FPL, which distributed Arbuckle's movies, and First National, which handled most of those in which Rappe appeared.[72]

Quigley's actions suggested a strategy designed to ensure both exhibitors' independence and the industry's survival. The editor argued that the public's demand for "retribution" should be directed at "persons who have become light-headed in their positions of prominence and popularity." Although probably innocent of the "alleged crime," Arbuckle should be sacrificed for playing "loose and wild" with "the responsibilities of prominence" and getting "plain, every-day American citizens to wonder if they should lend their support to actors and actresses who are so degraded."[73] Next the industry must silence the "brass band" about "going into politics" and use subtler means of "propaganda and solicitation" "to insure a more favorable attitude from legislators." And, finally, members must unite in the *Herald*'s "Public Rights League," which offered exhibitors—free of charge!—twelve slides for "daily screening" to teach the public about the dangers of censorship. In direct imitation of the techniques employed during the war, the Public Rights League would use the screen to convince "millions of patrons to support the industry" by turning them against "enemies of the Film Industry" like "Dr. Wilbur F. Crafts."[74] To fight evangelical fire with fire, Quigley featured the nation's most popular evangelist, Billy Sunday, in one slide declaring that censorship was "un-American and unfair."

II

But Hearst offered readers more exciting enemies that fall than radical Christian reformers like Reverend Crafts. Hearst newspapers ran mutually reinforcing melodramas on front pages during the slower scandal-related news week between the coroner jury's verdict and the opening of Arbuckle's arraignment trial, stories that alternated discussions of Arbuckle's "orgy" with exposés about the new Ku Klux Klan. Both presented a societal siege of apocalyptic proportions. Newspapers tailored some reporting to local audiences. Chicago featured more stories about Rappe, San Francisco more on police efforts to uncover a "S.F.-HOLLYWOOD 'BOOZE RAILROAD.'" Yet mostly the coverage offered the same fodder for discussion, including the scandal-as-orgy, the spectacle of Rappe's burial in Hollywood Cemetery, and the campaign to reveal the "SECRETS OF THE KKK," that "Anti-Jewish, Anti-Catholic and Alien Organization."[75] The mob spirit indeed reigned on the front page of the multiple editions Hearst published, offering readers a virtual experience of its frenzied pleasures. At times the two narratives combined, as with a story about the Klan's advice to the San Francisco district attorney: "Hang Fatty Arbuckle or the KKK will hang him and you." "COWBOYS MOB ARBUCKLE FILM," another headline blared. The story described a celluloid lynching performed by "150 men and boys" (falsely) reported to have shot up a screen in Wyoming and then burned the comedian's film in the street.[76]

Little wonder that Arbuckle was reported to be in "fear of the big throng" anticipated at the arraignment trial's opening on September 22, 1921. Photographs of the day displayed police restraining several hundred women and men pressing for admittance. The crowd prompted the trial judge, Sylvain Lazarus, to bar men without official business from the proceedings.[77] More than concern about possible vigilante violence prompted the ruling. Lazarus sat in Women's Court, a new division within the criminal justice system designed to treat criminal cases by and against women as moral offenses that required special considerations and protections. Many also viewed Women's Court as a means for female jurors, a recent innovation in California, to gain comfort with the judicial system.[78]

California clubwomen drove the creation of Women's Courts, helping to explain why the Woman's Vigilant Committee (WVC) received a level of press attention that initially allowed it to shape the next act of the scandal's drama.[79] An affiliate of the General Federation of Women's Clubs (GFWC), the WVC had a membership composed of socially prominent, middle- and upper-class women from fifty-two local clubs.[80] Unlike those of its parent organization, the WVC's members were of all religious faiths. Its president, Dr. Mariana Bertola, was both a past president of the California Federation of Women's Clubs (CFWC) and a practicing medical surgeon who taught at Mills College. Bertola was the daughter of Italian immigrants who moved to the Bay Area in 1852, made money in mining, and created the region's first large vineyard.[81] After earning a medical degree at Stanford, Bertola became a pioneer in the fields of obstetrics and pediatrics. Her success as a surgeon and philanthropist earned her a place as the only women in *San Francisco: Its Builders Past and Present* (1913), a two-volume local history of more than one hundred notable figures. As the *San Francisco Examiner* lavished attention on the WVC, Bertola assumed the role of spokeswoman to the press.

As other papers followed the *San Francisco Examiner*'s lead, the WVC initially appeared as a moral center in the scandal's storm.[82] Demanding justice for Virginia Rappe, Bertola appointed a committee to monitor the proceedings to prevent the city's infamous political corruption, Arbuckle's wealth, and female witnesses' assumed timidity from influencing the proceedings. In members' own words, the WVC aimed to ensure that sexual assault laws were treated not just as a legal "theory, but a fact."[83] In fact, the WVC sought much more than this, linking these laws' enforcement to the preservation of respectable middle-class gender roles and sexual morality. The case illustrated the need to protect "the sanctity of the home" and "the women within them," Bertola declared, reminding the press, "Remember, it was in one of the most respectable places in San Francisco that this outrage took place." The

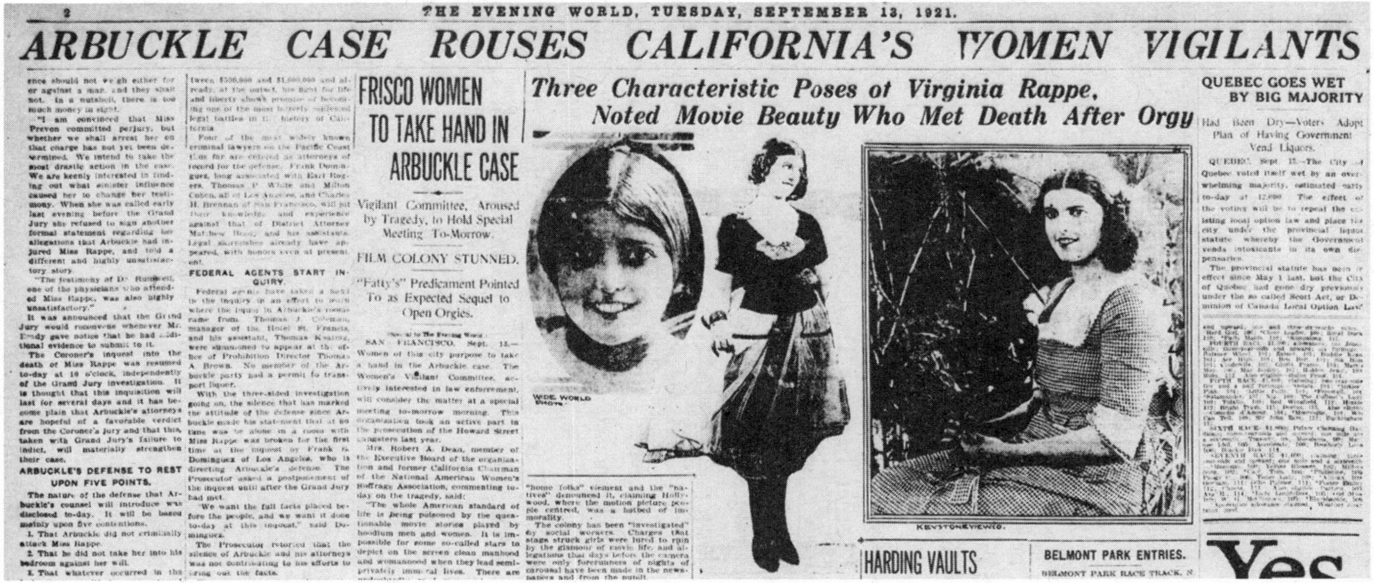

2 THE EVENING WORLD, TUESDAY, SEPTEMBER 13, 1921.

ARBUCKLE CASE ROUSES CALIFORNIA'S WOMEN VIGILANTS

ence should not weigh either for or against a man, and they shall not. In a nutshell, there is too much money in sight.

"I am convinced that Miss Prevon committed perjury, but whether we shall arrest her on that charge has not yet been determined. We intend to take the most drastic action in the case. We are keenly interested in finding out what sinister influence caused her to change her testimony. When she was called early last evening before the Grand Jury she refused to sign another formal statement regarding her allegations that Arbuckle had injured Miss Rappe, and told a different and highly unsatisfactory story.

"The testimony of Dr. Rumwell, one of the physicians who attended Miss Rappe, was also highly unsatisfactory."

It was announced that the Grand Jury would reconvene whenever Mr. Brady gave notice that he had additional evidence to submit to it.

The Coroner's inquest into the death of Miss Rappe was resumed to-day at 10 o'clock, independently of the Grand Jury investigation. It is thought that this inquisition will last for several days and it has become plain that Arbuckle's attorneys are hopeful of a favorable verdict from the Coroner's jury and that this, taken with Grand Jury's failure to indict, will materially strengthen their case.

ARBUCKLE'S DEFENSE TO REST UPON FIVE POINTS.

The nature of the defense that Arbuckle's counsel will introduce was disclosed to-day. It will be based mainly upon five contentions.

1. That Arbuckle did not criminally attack Miss Rappe.

2. That he did not take her into his bedroom against her will.

3. That whatever occurred in the

tween $500,000 and $1,000,000 and already, at the outset, his fight for life and liberty shows promise of becoming one of the most bitterly contested legal battles in the history of California.

Four of the most widely known criminal lawyers on the Pacific Coast thus far are entered as attorneys of record for the defense. Frank Dominguez, long associated with Earl Rogers, Thomas P. White and Milton Cohen, all of Los Angeles, and Charles H. Brennan of San Francisco, will pit their knowledge and experience against that of District Attorney Matthew Brady and his assistants. Legal skirmishes already have appeared, with honors even at present.

FEDERAL AGENTS START INQUIRY.

Federal agents have taken a hand in the inquiry in an effort to learn where the liquor in Arbuckle's rooms came from. Thomas J. Coleman, manager of the Hotel St. Francis, and his assistant, Thomas Keating, were summoned to appear at the office of Prohibition Director Thomas A. Brown. No member of the Arbuckle party had a permit to transport liquor.

With the three-sided investigation going on, the silence that has marked the attitude of the defense since Arbuckle made his statement that at no time was he alone in a room with Miss Rappe was broken for the first time at the inquest by Frank S. Dominguez of Los Angeles, who is directing Arbuckle's defense. The Prosecutor asked a postponement of the inquest until after the Grand Jury had met.

"We want the full facts placed before the people, and we want it done to-day at this inquest," said Dominguez.

The Prosecutor retorted that the silence of Arbuckle and his attorneys was not contributing to his efforts to bring out the facts.

FRISCO WOMEN TO TAKE HAND IN ARBUCKLE CASE

Vigilant Committee, Aroused by Tragedy, to Hold Special Meeting To-Morrow.

FILM COLONY STUNNED.

"Fatty's" Predicament Pointed To as Expected Sequel to Open Orgies.

(Special to The Evening World.)

SAN FRANCISCO, Sept. 13.—Women of this city purpose to take a hand in the Arbuckle case. The Women's Vigilant Committee, actively interested in law enforcement, will consider the matter at a special meeting to-morrow morning. This organization took an active part in the prosecution of the Howard Street gangsters last year.

Mrs. Robert A. Dean, member of the Executive Board of the organization and former California Chairman of the National American Women's Suffrage Association, commenting to-day on the tragedy, said:

"The whole American standard of life is being poisoned by the questionable movie stories played by hoodlum men and women. It is impossible for some so-called stars to depict on the screen clean manhood and womanhood when they lead semi-privately immoral lives. There are [illegible]

"home folks" element and the "natives" denounced it, claiming Hollywood, where the motion picture people centred, was a hotbed of immorality.

The colony has been "investigated" by social workers. Charges that stage struck girls were lured to ruin by the glamour of movie life, and allegations that days before the camera were only forerunners of nights of carousal have been made in the newspapers and from the pulpit.

Three Characteristic Poses of Virginia Rappe, Noted Movie Beauty Who Met Death After Orgy

WIDE WORLD PHOTO

KEYSTONE VIEW CO.

HARDING VAULTS

BELMONT PARK ENTRIES.

BELMONT PARK RACE TRACK, N

QUEBEC GOES WET BY BIG MAJORITY

Had Been Dry—Voters Adopt Plan of Having Government Vend Liquors.

QUEBEC, Sept. 13.—The City of Quebec voted itself wet by an overwhelming majority, estimated early to-day at 12,000. The effect of the voting will be to repeal the existing local option law and place the city under the provincial liquor statute whereby the Government vends intoxicants in its own dispensaries.

The provincial statute has been in effect since May 1 last, but the City of Quebec had gone dry previously under the so called Scott Act, or Dominion of Canada Local Option Law.

Yes

FIGURE 28. "Arbuckle Case Rouses California's Women Vigilants," *Evening World*, Sept. 13, 1921, Racing Final, p. 2. Courtesy of Chronicling America, Historical Newspapers, Library of Congress.

WVC asked Judge Lazarus to limit attendance to "mature," "respectable" women after a disparate crowd of female "sensation seekers" jammed the courthouse steps for admittance.[84] The WVC accused these women of treating the court proceedings like a play. Such behavior illustrated how preventing "a repetition of the awful Arbuckle case" demanded teaching such sensation seekers about the "dangers confronting them" so they might "return to the cultural things of life" and embrace "the so-called 'old-fashioned' ideals."[85]

An article written by Bertola referred to the local history that described the WVC's formation, prominence, and initial influence in framing the trial's presentation. "The Arbuckle party was nothing better than a fashionable gangster case," Bertola asserted.[86] Even though the star had staged his "outrage" in one of the city's "most respectable" and "luxurious" hotels, he was still no better than the "Howard Street gangsters." Bertola alluded to a series of events that had culminated in a lynching a year earlier. Early on Thanksgiving 1920, a young woman named Jean Stanley called the police to report her recent escape from a group of men who were holding a friend captive on Howard Street. When the police raided the "cottage," they found Stanley's friend Jessie Montgomery alone, badly beaten, and "lying nude upon the floor."[87] Seventeen-year-old Jesse Montgomery and twenty-one-year-old Jean Stanley were roommates who worked as telephone operators after having moved to San Francisco in search of jobs months earlier. Before their hospitalization, the friends told "of having been subjected to brutal attacks by eight men." The two had met their assailants the night before at a public dance hall, they explained. After offering the girls a ride home, the men enticed them into a small building on Howard Street with the promise of ice cream. There they were beaten and sexually assaulted. A week after Stanley's call to the police, three police officers were shot and killed in Santa Rosa while attempting to arrest three of the alleged Howard Street "gangsters." Later that day, guards barely repulsed a crowd of two thousand men and women armed with guns and telephone poles who attempted to storm the Santa Rosa jailhouse, chanting "lynch them, lynch them." Four days later "100 masked men" overpowered the sheriff and his deputies during the night and hanged the suspects from a nearby tree.[88] Calling the event "deplorable," the governor promised to deal "adequately with the lynching band." No arrests were ever made and the story sank precipitously from sight.[89]

Instead, the lynching offered a means for leading San Franciscans to demonstrate their commitment to using respectable female virtue to destroy the vestiges of the city's rollicking, Wild West past. In the following weeks, the *Examiner* turned to publicizing, and in crucial respects rousing, an attack on the political corruption and customs held responsible for the events.[90] Emboldened by sympathetic stories in the press, other victims stepped forward to "relate outrages" that displayed the systematic tendency of the criminal justice system to ignore sexual assaults.[91] "Progressive San Francisco" must finally "sweep away traditional barriers of complacency" that many argued explained Los Angeles's meteoric rise as the West Coast's leading metropolis. Showing impeccable timing, clubwomen now announced the creation of their Vigilant Committee.[92] "Like the Vigilant Committee of early days," an account memorializing the group intoned, "these women were assembled with haste to protect young girls of the community" and were "led by the valiant leader, Dr. Mariana Bertola."[93] When reports foretold that defense lawyers planned to put the reputations of the "Gangster victims" on trial, the WVC announced that its members would attend all sexual assault trials to ensure a focus on the men's present criminal actions and not a woman's past.[94] Writing in support of their efforts, Hearst columnist Annie Laurie declared, "I do not believe yet that this girl was a bad girl, but even if she was, that is no excuse for refusing her or any kind of a woman protection against such revolting cruelty." With Laurie as their champion, the WVC articulated what later became the standard feminist analysis of rape as a crime of violence in which a woman's sexual history and reputation bore no part.[95] Such efforts displayed the WVC's determination to use women's new political rights to punish men who violated society's professed moral code.[96] In addition to monitoring trials involving sexual assault, members organized a recall of two more judges and led an investigation of the charge that graft explained the justice system's routine dismissal of sexual assault claims. "There is a new story teller—the woman voter—and she knows just exactly what she wants," Laurie exulted.[97]

The actions of these respectable middle-class ladies displayed how their protection of their less well-off sisters warranted their curtailment of working-class women's independence and economic opportunities. In the name of protecting women through restoring the preeminence of the home's influence, the WVC mobilized a campaign to purify or shutter the city's dance halls.[98] Bertola succinctly described the effort's rationale: places of commercial entertainment threatened to turn young women into "the perverted sex type." The owners of dance halls faced losing their licenses unless they stopped women from attending without chaperones and fired the halls' dance "instructors." The scare quotes indicated the presumption that such women offered more than tango lessons.[99] The city's five hundred dance hall instructors fought back against these attacks on their livelihood and moral character. Seventy-five representatives, ranging from "eighteen to thirty years old," "stormed" the WVC's next weekly meeting. Did the WVC have comparable "work for each of us when you close the dance halls Friday night?" asked their leader, Helen Emick. Emick protested that members "lived clean lives and were dance hall instructors because of the good wages they received."[100] Bertola's tone-deaf response exhibited her class privilege as she advised that, "if this was the case," the women would make "wonderful educators." Both the city's mayor and the police commissioner refused to meet with Emick. But the dancers persevered. The jurors who convened to consider the closings were shocked by the dancers' ordinary appearance when they again "stormed" the grand jury the next day. Declaring that these girls could not be "classed with redlight district habitués," the jurors called for a "thorough investigation" before any more closings took place.[101] Over the following six months, the WVC, reform-minded men, and the *San Francisco Examiner* also used the Howard Street Gangster case to spearhead drives that removed two Police Court judges and several police officers. Sylvain Lazarus—set to preside over Arbuckle's arraignment in Women's Court—replaced one of the recalled judges.[102]

Although the Howard Street case primed the WVC, many civic leaders, and San Francisco's newspapers to view Arbuckle's party as another sex-specific exercise in the abuse of power, the stories that unfolded in Lazarus's courtroom complicated reading Rappe's death this way. At the first of Arbuckle's three trials, the WVC argued successfully for a mixed jury of women and men at a time when women were rarely called as jurors even in states like California, one of the first to allow women to serve.[103] Due to the WVC's efforts, five women and seven men occupied the first jurors' box. After forty-four hours of deliberation, a mistrial resulted when one male juror "chivalrously" joined one of these women—described as "a titan haired Amazon combining the exact knowledge of a housewife and a firm belief in equal rights"—to hang the jury. The confusing testimony offered by the doctors who treated Rappe failed to implicate Arbuckle or to establish why her bladder ruptured. Their jargon-heavy descriptions offered several possible causes, including an external blow, vomiting, laughing, and "spontaneous" rupture.[104] Nonetheless, Hearst papers forced the testimony into a melodrama whose headline read "TWO DOCTORS SAY VIRGINIA RAPPE WAS SLAIN." Most accounts made little of the medical evidence presented, perhaps taking a cue from the "spectators" who reportedly "seemed bored" by that day's proceedings.[105] The three other witnesses who appeared in court—the two "entertainers," Alice Blake and Zey Prevost, and Al Semnacher, the agent who drove Rappe up the coast—drew more interest. They described a party filled with "dancing, talking, drinking," and "plenty of noise." At this gathering participants were "having too good a time to notice the time." By all accounts, a drunken Delmont changed into men's pajamas and then decided independently to demand entrance to the bedroom in which Arbuckle and Rappe had disappeared. When Arbuckle opened the door, still dressed in his pajamas, a fully clothed Rappe began to scream and tear at her clothes. "I'm dying, I'm dying," all agreed she cried. Another female guest added that Rappe later said, "He hurt me." Thinking her drunk, the women undressed Rappe, submerged her in a tub of cold water to revive her, and put her to bed. When Rappe started screaming again, Arbuckle entered the room, warning, "If she don't stop her yelling I will throw her out the window."[106] Rappe stopped screaming and, a short while later, passed out.

The trial revealed the party's atmosphere as bawdy, freewheeling, or offensive, depending on the point of view. Perhaps the most genuinely shocking courtroom revelation proved "too vulgar to be printed"—though over time the decorum that newspapers exercised encouraged even grimmer embellishments, including the rumor that Arbuckle raped Rappe with an ice chipper. Both Blake and Prevost described watching Arbuckle "place a piece of ice on Miss Rappe's body" that, under pressure in the courtroom, they specified as her vagina.[107] "That will make her come to," Arbuckle said before Delmont "shoved his hand away." Semnacher's admission that Arbuckle later joked about the action to the party's male guests attracted much of the publicity because papers refrained from explicitly describing it. "Tell us the exact language the defendant used," the prosecutor demanded, in a quote used in virtually every account.[108] "Pale as a sheet and pleading to the court that he not be forced to repeat in open court the language used by Arbuckle," Semnacher "was made to write out the remarks for the benefit of counsel." The court transcript revealed the note Semnacher passed to the judge read "snatch." "Everyone laughed when Arbuckle made the statement," the witness continued. In retrospect, Semnacher recounted "Arbuckle's prank" with embarrassment. But during the party, it seemed the women considered Arbuckle's behavior a stupid joke, the men a funny one.[109] Arbuckle's "ice bath" confession formed the high point of the trial's coverage. Shortly afterward, the state rested, without ever calling Delmont, the prosecution witness, to the stand.[110] In short, the testimony revealed that the party's participants played by different rules than those who judged them. Semnacher emphasized this point when Arbuckle's attorney tried to force him to admit that Delmont's behavior was unladylike. "Well, everyone has his own ideas of a lady," he replied.[111]

On September 28, less than three weeks after the scandal splashed across front pages, Judge Lazarus ruled that Arbuckle would stand trial for manslaughter—not murder, as the state had requested. After criticizing the district attorney for not putting Delmont on the stand, Lazarus noted that "there is just enough evidence here, I may say barely enough, to justify me in holding the defendant." Judge Lazarus then offered a lengthy disquisition on the scandal's significance. This was "an important case," he contended. "We are not trying Roscoe Arbuckle alone. We are not trying the screen celebrity who has given joy and pleasure to all the world . . . we are trying ourselves," he contended. Lazarus pronounced "the issue" before the court "universal," growing from conditions that "every true lover and protector of our American institutions" should fear. What threatened the American way of life was that at "one of the largest and most pretentious hostelries of the city, in broad daylight,"

> an orgy that continued many hours and resulted in the death of Miss Virginia Rappe, a moving-picture actress, was not repressed by the hotel management. It is of such common occurrence that it was not given attention until something happened, until the climax made it notorious. And the same thing happens in big cities all over the world. In this thing is a public lesson.[112]

The judge's repeated use of "it" and "thing" obscured his placement of the blame on the fashion for orgies, for raucous parties that encouraged consensual sex between men and women. Thus whatever the future determined about Arbuckle's role in Virginia Rappe's death, Lazarus declared that society's present attitudes had sent Rappe to her doom.

Immediately after Lazarus's decision, California's clubwomen indicated their intent to use the scandal to enforce higher moral standards on the nation. But the WVC's view only partially concurred with other reform-minded elites. While agreeing that the evidence failed to warrant an indictment of Arbuckle on capital charges, after his release on bail the WVC argued that "regardless" of whether he was "proved innocent or not of the police charges, his immoral conduct marks him as a person unfit to appear before the American public."[113] That opinion, endorsed by California's 60,000 other clubwomen, restated what was fast becoming the conventional wisdom: Hollywood endorsed sex roles that endangered impressionable young women. But the WVC and columnists like Annie Laurie said more than this. Their insistence on the irrelevance of the sexual histories of Jean Stanley, Jesse Montgomery, and Virginia Rappe reflected a modern feminist analysis of rape. Yet their behavior also demonstrated how they envisioned using women's new rights to empower the "right sort" of women to protect their weaker sisters. Put differently, the WVC, and many of the other clubwomen who sought control over Hollywood in the postwar era, believed in equalizing gender roles for women like themselves so they could regulate women whose age, class, ethnic identities, or behavior made them unable to take advantage of the new rights. Such vulnerable girls needed respectable ladies to perfect a modern type of state chaperonage.

The major picture producers also released a statement that revealed not only their increasing sophistication in shaping the public debate for their own ends, but also their interest in acting the part of moral regulator. Timed to coincide with the arraignment trial's opening, producers announced that "as a direct result of the Arbuckle case" film actors' contracts would contain a "morality clause" that would punish those who did "anything to shock the community or outrage public morals or decency" with immediate termination.[114] Newspapers praised this decision to enforce "a higher standard of morals for stage folks."[115] The morality clause also indicated producers' acceptance of a previously disputed principle: the influence of movie stars had become so great in the postwar era that it warranted special management. Yet the morality clause also cleverly refocused the wider attacks on the industry by reducing the problem of how best to control Hollywood to a question about how to control its stars.

The morality clause held particular implications for female players, though the damning of Arbuckle indicated that males were not exempt. Society's still-widespread endorsement of the sexual double standard, and the interpretation of the scandal as further evidence of Hollywood's role in cracking its edifice, meant the demand that stars behave "with due regard to public conventions" put a heavier burden on the industry's women. The different reactions to the divorces of Douglas Fairbanks and Mary Pickford displayed the disparity. Here lay the roots of the new sexual double standard that celebrity culture developed in the 1920s. In the future, the industry would perfect its ability to trade on women's sexuality while seeking to contain their filmic images inside a moral framework that punished protagonists who transgressed feminine norms, even as the publicity about actresses' lives as "real women" often continued to display just such behavior.

Survival partially precipitated the strategy, as producers absorbed two lessons: the public perceived the industry as particularly endangering young women and took as much interest in "watching stars fall" as "watching them shine."[116] So Jesse Lasky explained to Gloria Swanson in September 1922 when she told him she planned to seek a divorce from her second husband. "Impossible," she recalled Lasky declaring with "almost paternal sincerity" one year after Rappe's death. The producer "predicted there would be a rash of scandals because everyone was looking for them." Lasky warned Swanson how easily her image of "love, passion, glamour," and "the whole sophisticated atmosphere of Cecil B. DeMille and Elinor Glyn" could be turned against her. Then, perhaps she should tone down her image, Swanson proposed. "It's too late to change that," Lasky snapped—a statement Swanson conceded was simply "a fact." The morality clause that gave teeth to Lasky's bite signaled how the scandal sped the creation of constraints that producers exercised over most players in the studio era. The studio system arose as others followed the course that Lasky and Zukor laid down at FPL/Paramount, forming an era in which tighter contracts and the demise of independent production severely curtailed the mobility and power of all the industry's workers.[117] Louella Parsons, who started work for Hearst's *New York American* in 1924, became one of the industry's most effective police dogs, using her bark to make or break reputations in the name of protecting the public.

Indeed, most scholarly discussions of what has been invariably called the "Fatty" Arbuckle scandal tie its importance to the creation of one of the studio system's central institutions, the Motion Picture Producers and Distributors Association (MPPDA, or Hays Office), the trade association of the producers who controlled the industry's new trust.[118] Chronology encourages connecting the two events. Just weeks after Arbuckle's first jury deadlocked in December 1922, producers headed by Zukor announced that William Hays would serve as the new trade association's president.[119] A native midwesterner, a Presbyterian elder, and a leading Republican, the former Assistant Secretary of Agriculture had become postmaster general after helping Warren Harding win the presidency in 1920.[120] With Harding's blessing to take up this "public service," Hays left Washington in 1922 to make "virtue popular."[121] Before Hays assumed the post in March, Arbuckle's second jury deadlocked again. Two more Hollywood scandals also made headlines: the mysterious murder of director William Desmond Taylor and the charge that Pickford's quickie Nevada divorce and immediate remarriage to Fairbanks made her a bigamist.[122] Yet during 1922, Hays stabilized the industry's political and moral capital, defeating a Massachusetts referendum on censorship and directing a savvy exercise in damage control when actor Wallace Reid overdosed on drugs in the spring.[123] By the year's end, the Hays Office also attempted to improve the respectability of what appeared on screens, establishing a Public Relations Committee (PRC) to devise a set of moral standards to guide film production. Better known as the Hays Code, these guidelines aimed to improve the morality of pictures. Clubwomen were among the PRC's most important members. The effects of this moral reckoning were felt later that year when Elinor Glyn scripted *Beyond the Rocks* (1922), a vehicle designed to showcase Gloria Swanson and Rudolph Valentino's passionate exchanges. The director shot two versions of the love scenes: one for the U.S. market and a second for Europe.[124]

Yet the continued emphasis on Hays's hire conceals as much as it reveals by ignoring the sex-specific implications of what made Hollywood's so-called "first canonical" sex scandal so scandalous at the time. It fails to explain why the number of states with censorship drives, and the number of articles on "motion picture morality" through 1930, peaked the year *before* the scandal—*not after it*.[125] It overlooks the fact that Arbuckle's acquittal came about only after his defense reversed its strategy and totally assassinated the moral character and professional aspirations of Virginia Rappe. The picture that Arbuckle's lawyer, Gavin McNab, created of Rappe suggested that she was either a polluted prostitute or a fallen woman degraded by her ambition to become a star. Considered powerful enough to be included in *Classics of the Bar* (1922), McNab's closing statement declared that Rappe, and the other women who attended the party, did "not belong to the wifehood, the sisterhood, the motherhood of the world."[126] According to McNab, they reminded him "of the beautiful line of Ruskin's: 'Wherever a true woman is home is always around her.'"

In other words, the scandal tells us much more about what mattered about Hollywood "in the beginning" if we spotlight its other principal

FIGURE 29. Valentino and Swanson in Elinor Glyn's *Beyond the
Rocks* (1922). Courtesy of Margaret Herrick Library, Academy of
Motion Picture Arts and Sciences, Beverly Hills.

character, Virginia Rappe. Placing Rappe at the center of the scandal's
production, and inside an already polarized social climate, reveals the
event as an explosive round in an ongoing debate about the relationship between motion pictures and the rise of sexual modernism. Concerns about the effect of Hollywood's birth on female morality multi-
plied before Arbuckle and Rappe ever set foot inside the St. Francis
Hotel. Over the course of the scandal any real chance of thinking seriously about Virginia Rappe—who she was, what she wanted, or how
she died—quickly vanished. The dominant narrative of the scandal
that emerged by 1922 shoehorned the event into a traditional early-
nineteenth-century melodrama of sexual danger, casting Rappe as the
pathetic fallen woman who reaped what she had sown. A spate of pop-

ular biographies interested in clearing Arbuckle's name carried this representation into present-day lore. Taking McNab's assertions at the final trial for fact, they cast Rappe as at best a pathetic "starlet," at worst a two-bit prostitute whose venereal disease caused her death. These accounts also caricature the WVC as a hysterical mob of meddling women out for Arbuckle's blood, complete with an apocryphal story about members spitting on the comedian when he arrived in San Francisco for his arraignment. Such narrative tendencies betray how easily women's actions along sex-partisan lines could be ridiculed in the 1920s and beyond. They also reveal a commonplace that continues to parade as analysis today: that a pretty, single, and ambitious woman who was likely far from a sexual innocent was little more than a witless whore.[127]

But the industry was not yet ready to abandon spinning tales to women fans about Hollywood's support of unconventional gender roles. If the new trusts of the picture business were to survive and prosper, a more equivocal register was needed to whisper of Hollywood's bohemian pleasures. After all, despite Jesse Lasky's objections, Gloria Swanson did initiate her second, messy divorce in 1922. When it was finalized, she married into the French aristocracy to great fanfare. Moreover, throughout the 1920s, Swanson continued to write, produce, and star in controversial pictures at United Artists, including *Sadie Thompson* (1928), her adaptation of Somerset Maugham's story about a prostitute. Such presentations became more difficult after 1934, when producers allowed Catholic reformers to administer and enforce a revised Motion Picture Production Code at the Hays Office. Producers finally capitulated to the moral management of outsiders because of the combined pressure created by the outrage that stars like Mae West prompted among the Catholic Church hierarchy, Catholic leaders' threat to launch a nationwide boycott of films, and the unprecedented influence that Wall Street financiers assumed when the Depression followed the industry's expensive conversion to sound. The revised Production Code of 1934 was written by a Catholic priest and enforced by the devout Irish-Catholic layman, and anti-Semitic, Joseph Breen. Speaking to one priest, Breen called Hollywood Jews "lice," explaining they were "a foul bunch, crazed with sex . . . and ignorant in matters having to do with sound morals." Breen was the one man "who could cram decent ethics down the throat of the Jews," he boasted to another priest.[128] Regulating women's independence and enforcing the sexual double standard were the particular "evils" about which Breen obsessed.[129] This development helps to explain why Shirley Temple replaced West as the most popular female star after 1934. Increasingly, stories about adventurous, ambitious single girls in Los Angeles were set in a noir frame that left them dead on the side of the road, reminding us that women's so-called liberation in the twentieth century took a crooked path marked by limitations at every step.

The Girl from Hollywood

Just days before Rappe's death, an interview with Roscoe Arbuckle appeared in *Photoplay* that suggested the mounting ambivalence confronting Hollywood's girls. Adela Rodgers St. Johns, writing in her best "mother confessor" style, solicited Arbuckle's opinion about modern women. "Are you afraid of women?" St. Johns inquired. "You bet I am," he replied. "You just bet I am. So is everybody else that wears pants on the outside in this land of the free and home of the brave. Women are the free and we are the brave. The 19th Amendment is only the hors d'oeuvre to the amendments they will pass now they have found out they can." Arbuckle was in the midst of making a transition from star of slapstick shorts to leading man of feature length comedies. As pre-publicity for three features that Paramount was about to release, the interview sought to broaden his appeal beyond his typical audience of children and men. Strikingly, although the article was written to attract *Photoplay*'s female fans to his films, a current of anxiety and anger about women's demands crackled through the satiric piece. When asked what he thought modern women wanted, Arbuckle allegedly replied:

> Women want to smoke cigarettes, bob their hair, drink wood alcohol, have men friends, spend their own and everybody else's money, cut their skirts off just above the knee, run their own and your business, drive automobiles, go to conventions, elect mayors and presidents and be as independent as the Kaiser thought he was.

Their voracious appetites explained why *Photoplay*'s readers should prefer a "good natured fat man" like Arbuckle. Only such a "kind," "gentle" man could tolerate their many needs, including having husbands who helped to raise the kids since wives were "going to be pretty busy and won't have much time."[1]

Adela Rogers St. Johns's memoir, *The Honeycomb* (1969), suggests that the dialogue attributed to Arbuckle captured her own unease about the consequences produced by Hollywood girls' pursuit of their individual freedoms. To illustrate the central dilemma of her life, her memoir opens with a discussion of "an old Irish proverb" about the impossibility of a woman "driving three mules"—of simultaneously managing wifehood, motherhood, and a career. Expanding on the proverb's significance, St. Johns recalled a 1924 debate on the question "Is Modern Woman a Failure?" that she participated in with Alice Ames Winters, "president of the *all-powerful* General Federation of Women's Clubs." Shortly after St. Johns returned to work as an investigative reporter at William Randolph Hearst's *Los Angeles Evening Herald,* her revered boss "flung me into my famous debate." Hearst staged the public contest because he believed that women's roles had changed too quickly. At his urging, St. Johns joined the debate, arguing the case against the modern woman. "My mother wished to give women every opportunity for bettering themselves and training their talents," Hearst reportedly explained. "I have heard her say that this was the single most drastic move in history, that no one group, no single group had ever entered into so complete a change as the women of the twentieth century." St. Johns bested the older, more experienced GFWC president in the debate by passionately damning her own Hollywood-styled modern life, confessing her failure at "driv[ing] her three mules." Ironically, the woman who defended St. Johns's right to attempt this feat was straight out of Hearst's mother's mold. A respectable matron, Winters lived in Pasadena, wrote under her husband's name, and worked to better the nation, not for wages.[2]

The proverb St. Johns used to frame her memoir illustrated the deepening angst she and many others experienced over embodying a modern woman in the early Hollywood mode. Had she used "careers for women" as an excuse to make herself "a big shot instead of helping [her] husband"? she wondered.[3] Unhappily married to Ike St. Johns at the time of the debate, St. John's later blamed the marriage's demise on her greater professional success. An article her husband wrote for *Photoplay,* where he occasionally worked after several other careers floundered, disputed that women possessed the same artistic abilities as men. It read as an attack not just on his wife, but also on all of early Hollywood's women.[4] Adela Rogers St. Johns's self-critique was one example of a budding genre in the 1920s: confessions of "ex-feminists" who expressed a frustration bordering on despair over the demands that modernity placed on their role as women. Often, many wearily conceded a desire to put the genie of women's emancipation back in the bottle.[5] A backlash regarding the consequences of these experiments spread as the excitement over women's sensational "firsts" wore off. And American society in the twenties offered no practical support to sustain women's public roles in ways that made them compatible with family life: no day care, no takeout, no family leave, no idea that men should share in domestic chores, no acceptance that respectable wives should work at all except in cases of dire need. And this principle—that only calamity justified the wage work of married women, especially those with children— suggests why St. Johns's greater professional success and renown created trouble for her marriage. Many women in early Hollywood said their marriages crumbled under similar pressures. However feminine they looked, these women's individual achievements, their use of glamour to get ahead, and their new demands on their partners threatened the gender roles that traditionally sustained marriage.[6] In "Hollywood: Its Manners and Morals," Theodore Dreiser's bid to explain the scandal, the great naturalistic writer agreed about the conflict these pressures bred between women and men. At nearly fifty, Dreiser had followed his latest lover, the twenty-year-old actress Helen Richardson, to Hollywood in 1919. In the exposé Dreiser wrote purporting to explain the scandal's origin, he declared that most of the colony's women were "by no means innocents," but sophisticates who "relish, I think, the very lively war that is here between the sexes."[7]

But as the term "Hollywood" settled into the nation's vocabulary in the scandal's wake competing interpreters vied to define the picture of women's place there. Edgar Rice Burroughs' novel *The Girl from Hollywood* (1922), described Hollywood as a second sin city whose attractions acted like an addictive drug that endangered women's lives. The best-selling author of *Tarzan of the Apes* (1914), Burroughs wrote *The Girl from Hollywood* at Tarzana, his 540-acre ranch in the San Fernando Valley, an area experiencing a population boom since its greening-by-aqueduct left it a lush retreat walled off by mountains from rapidly urbanizing Los Angeles. The novel offered readers the first noir portrait of Hollywood-cum–Los Angeles. Here was a city whose "unnatural dangers and pressures" were all the more sinister because they took place under a blazing azure sky. Tellingly, the novel's two heroines were not from Los Angeles at all, making the title a sly indication of Hollywood's power to obliterate any girl's true nature. The first young woman, Grace, puts her childhood sweetheart on hold and leaves a ranch in the San Fernando Valley "to make her own way, unassisted, toward her goal." Drug addicted and pregnant by a director-producer within one year, Grace commits suicide. The heroine, Shannon, is the second girl to go Hollywood. A Midwesterner driven west to find work as an actress to support her ailing mother, Shannon ends up dealing drugs in Los Angeles instead, yet manages to protect her chastity. In this way she signals why she can escape to the same ranch Grace deserted, where an infusion of old fashioned California-Pastoral allows her to end up married and drug-free.[8]

Paramount's *Hollywood* (1923), a lost comedy, sent a more gentle warning to female fans by satirizing women's professional ambitions; its poster features Hollywood as a great male maw into which all kinds of girls gaily jump. The film's heroine, Angela, travels to Los Angeles with her grandfather in search of her fortune. At the end, gramps becomes famous, while little Angela succeeds only in finding a man to wed. The film's director, James Cruze, was a notorious partier who had directed Arbuckle in his last five features at Paramount. *Hollywood*'s real draw was the view it offered behind Paramount's walls. As Angela and her grandfather wander the studio's sets, they encounter dozens of kindly, glamorous stars who appear in cameo roles, including Mary Pickford, Pola Negri, Charlie Chaplin, and Roscoe Arbuckle, who plays himself forever waiting at a casting office for a part. Thus *Hollywood* managed simultaneously to tweak the attitudes of moral custodians and young hopefuls, while aiming to incite the curiosity of both.[9]

In contrast to such portraits, Rupert Hughes offered a straightforward feminist defense of Hollywood's unconventional women in *Souls for Sale* (1922). The book indicated that satire and noir—a modernized version of a traditional melodrama of sexual danger—would not be the only ways to tell the story of Hollywood's bohemian girls.[10] Hughes (whose nephew Howard later so enjoyed the Hollywood scene) was one of the most prolific authors of his day, writing plays, histories, novels, and short stories. His enormous commercial appeal derived from his facility for leavening topical issues that attracted the female fiction reading public—divorce, the sexual double standard, and careers for women—with humor, satire, and sentiment. In 1919 producer Samuel

FIGURE 30. Poster from James Cruze's *Hollywood* (1923). Author's collection.

Goldwyn brought Hughes to work as an "eminent author" in Los Angeles, where he quickly outperformed other literary luminaries, including Gertrude Atherton, Anzia Yezierska, and Somerset Maugham. Hughes also embraced life in Los Angeles, permanently relocating and founding the Hollywood Writer's Club (later the Screen Writers Guild), called by one reporter "a place where men and women mingled in disregard of ancient prejudice."[11] Like so many midwestern writers associated with the "revolt from the village" school, Hughes's protagonist was a prairie girl driven west by her home's moral guardians to find redemption in the City of Angels.[12] Thus the book offered a defense of Hollywood in the scandal's aftermath that traded budding cliché for budding cliché.

But Hughes's novel also employed "a feminist philosophy" that one reviewer called "as refreshing as it is provocative."[13] Following fan culture's conventions, Hughes traced his heroine's climb from degraded obscurity to self-respect and fame. The novel opens with Mem's father delivering a sermon on the movies' transformation of Los Angeles into "Los Diablos . . . the central factory of Satan and his minions." After discovering she is pregnant, the unwed preacher's daughter flees to a desert town in the Southwest where she encounters a friendly film crew, suffers a miscarriage, and then moves to Los Angeles after an extra-girl offers her a place to stay and help finding a job. In Hollywood, Remember initially works as a film editor and rooms with four women who lived "with no more thought of chaperonage than a crowd of bachelors." Raised "to believe in duty first—in self-denial, abstention, modesty, demurity, simplicity, meekness, prayer, remorse," she is "aghast at their contempt for conventions." Whether Mem had come to "her ruination or her redemption, she had come to a new world," where "she learned how freely, with what masculine franchise, these women conducted their lives." Embracing these "bohemian standards of behavior," she becomes "mad to act." The decision transforms her into a modern artist, willing "to unleash her soul and body from the shackles of respectability" in order "to build her soul and sell it." The novel's conclusion celebrates this bohemian New Woman's future. Rejecting a director's proposal, she decides to keep house with her sister, another runaway, instead.[14]

Go West, Young Women! offers, in short, neither a declension narrative nor a Whiggish tale of progress about the influence of Hollywood's girls on modern femininity and gender roles. Certainly new risks lurked as more young women worked and socialized without chaperones. It is safe to assume that some Hollywood hopefuls were forced, or felt pressured, into using the casting couch to get ahead. Yet the movie industry held no monopoly on such occurrences. Sensationalizing such dangers mostly justified curtailing women's ability to challenge gender conventions and to instill terror about where their sexual freedom might lead. It is no stretch, I think, to say that the media's penchant for dramatizing instances of young white women's sexual victimization still erases the more typical ways most women are exploited by petty tyrants in average, sex-segregated work-a-day jobs or in their own homes. But as the twentieth century recedes and historians move to chart its contours, returning to the exploits of early Hollywood's women-made women emphasizes one of the most striking aspects of the century's shape: the expansion of women's opportunities in consumer-oriented democratic societies—which is nowhere more visible in the United States than in California, where women exercise unparalleled clout in both politics and culture.[15]

To understand this process, Hollywood's Janus-faced relationship to feminism and modern femininity demands another account.[16] In its heyday the film industry perfected talking to women from at least two directions, providing them with stars and stories that played to their New Woman ambitions, while ridiculing these aspirations and radically constricting their professional opportunities.[17] Even after World War II, during the so-called doldrums of the feminist movement, actresses like Barbara Stanwyck served as rare avatars of the "Independent Woman" that Simone de Beauvoir discussed in *The Second Sex* (1949). Hugo Münsterberg, the Harvard psychologist who offered one of the first theories of film in 1916, worried over how such doublespeak would affect women, writing of the movies' "stirring up of desires" that aimed "to keep the demand and its fulfillment forever awake."[18] Certainly cultural conservatives have never lost sight of Hollywood Bohemia's influence in fomenting the breakdown of traditional sex roles. Such critics have long recognized that it tantalized women not only with the one-in-a-million chance to be a star but, more importantly, with acting the part of bold adventurer that boys had for so long enjoyed, as they experimented with different romantic liaisons and work roles and with self-fashioning free from any but their own control.

The social imaginary of early Hollywood displayed not only women's new professional and physical mobility but also a more general ethos that encouraged female fans to understand their support of the industry as support of their own emancipation. In this way, the movies' women-made women became real and iconic representations of the period's contested sexual politics. Thus fans' heroine worship reflected the desire of many so-called modern young girls to embrace a type of individually oriented, "feminine-friendly" feminism. Compatible both with capitalism and with popular culture, this feminism provides continuity with many of the preoccupations of what some have called third-wave feminism, which is typically thought of as focusing on women's empowerment rather than their victimization and as taking pleasure in fashion, romance, and sex.[19] This approach was more likely to be embraced by working-class secretaries than college graduates; by young, single, or divorced women than middle-aged wives or highly educated, middle-class professionals. It focused on the problem of women's individuality rather than their group identity. It celebrated women's ability to seize prerogatives long enjoyed by single young men—to seek pleasure freely in their professional and personal lives—while cultivating their boy-crazy daydreams and use of a glamorously "femme" façade as a reasonable means to get ahead. In short, it assumed that, more than a political movement, women needed role models like early Hollywood's women-made women who could teach them how to navigate modernity's choppy waters—and come out on top.

Filmography

This filmography includes only the titles discussed in the text of this book or viewed by the author. They are listed alphabetically with information on the original production company, year released, and how viewed by the author, if at all. The following acronyms indicate the archives where the films are held: Library of Congress, Motion Picture and Television Reading Room, Washington, D.C. (LOC); Museum of Modern Art, Film Preservation Center, New York City (MOMA); University of California, Los Angeles, Film and Television Archive (UCLA); George Eastman House, Rochester, New York (Eastman).

The Adventures of Ruth (Pathé, 1919). *Considered lost.*
An Adventuress (Republic, 1920). UCLA.
The Affairs of Anatol (Famous Players–Lasky, 1921). Passport International Entertainment, 2007.
American Aristocracy (Fine Arts Film Corp., 1916). Grapevine Video, 2011.
Beyond the Rocks (Paramount, 1922). Milestone Video, 2006.
Birth of a Nation (Epoch Production Co., 1915). Image Entertainment, 1998.
The Bishop's Carriage (Famous Players, 1913). *Considered lost.*
The Blot (Lois Weber Productions, 1921). Chatsworth Entertainment, 2004.
Camille (Metro, 1921). Warner Home Video, 2005.
Caprice (Famous Players, 1913). *Considered lost.*
The Cheat (Jesse L. Lasky Feature Play Co., 1915). Kino, 1994.
Daddy-Long-Legs (Mary Pickford Co., 1919). Image Entertainment, 1994.
The Danger Girl (Keystone Film Co., 1916). Passport Video.
Daniel Boone; or, Pioneer Days in America (Edison, 1907). MOMA.
Daughter of Two Worlds (Norma Talmadge Film Corp., 1920). LOC.
The Dispatch Bearer (Vitagraph, 1907). MOMA.
Don't Change Your Husband (Famous Players–Lasky, 1919). Passport International Entertainment, 2007.

Dumb Girl of Portia (Universal, 1916). British Film Institute.
Eyes of Youth (Clara Kimball Young Film Corp., 1919). LOC.
The Female of the Species (Biograph, 1912). Image Entertainment, 2002.
The Flapper (Selznick/Select, 1920). Eastman.
Flo's Discipline (Victor, 1912). LOC.
A Foolish Virgin (Clara Kimball Young Film Corp., 1916). *Considered lost.*
A Fool There Was (Fox, 1915). Kino, 2002.
For Better, For Worse (Famous Players–Lasky, 1919). Eastman.
Forbidden City (Norma Talmadge Film Corp./First National, 1918). LOC.
The Four Horsemen of the Apocalypse (Metro, 1921). Nostalgia Family Video,
    1997.
Gasoline Gus (Famous Players–Lasky, 1921). Cinémathèque Royale (Bruxelles).
The Girl and the Outlaw (Biograph, 1908). MOMA.
The Great Moment (Paramount, 1921). *Considered lost.*
The Hazards of Helen (Kalem Company, 1914–1917). Nos. 1–4, Video Yester-
    year, 1983.
Heart o' the Hills (Mary Pickford Co., 1919). Image Entertainment, 2005.
Hearts Adrift (Famous Players, 1914). *Considered lost.*
His Musical Sneeze (Sunshine Comedies, Fox Film Corp., 1919). *Considered
lost.*
His New Job (Essanay Film Manufacturing Co., 1915). Passport Video.
Hollywood (Famous Players–Lasky, 1923). *Considered lost.*
Humoresque (Cosmopolitan Productions, 1920). UCLA.
Hypocrites (Hobart Bosworth Productions, 1914). Kino, 2008.
In Old Madrid (IMP, 1911). Hollywood's Attic, 1996.
The Jew's Christmas (Universal, 1913). *Considered lost.*
Johanna Enlists (Pickford Film Corp., 1918). UCLA.
The Little American (Pickford Film Corp., 1917). Passport International Enter-
    tainment, 2007.
Little Lord Fauntleroy (Mary Pickford Co., 1921). Image Entertainment, 2005.
The Little Rebel (Lubin, 1911). MOMA.
The Love Light (Mary Pickford Co., 1921). LOC.
Male and Female (Famous Players–Lasky, 1919). Passport International Enter-
    tainment, 2007.
M'Liss (Pickford Film Corp., 1918). Image Entertainment, 2005.
The New York Hat (Biograph, 1912). Hollywood's Attic, 1996.
Old Wives for New (Famous Players–Lasky, 1918). Passport International En-
    tertainment, 2007.
Paradise Garden (Metro, 1917). *Considered lost.*
Passion (First National, 1920). LOC.
The Penalty (Goldwyn Pictures Corp., 1920). Kino, 1998.
The Perils of Pauline (Pathé, 1914). Episodes 1–9, Grapevine Video.
The Poor Little Rich Girl (Pickford Film Corp., 1917). St. Clair Entertainment
    Group, 2008.
The Pride of the Clan (Pickford Film Corp., 1917). Classic Video Streams,
    2009.
The Punch of the Irish (First National, 1921). MOMA.

Rebecca of Sunnybrook Farm (Pickford Film Corp., 1917). St. Clair Entertainment Group, 2008.

The Red Lantern (Nazimova Productions, 1919). Women's Film History screening, Museum of Modern Art, New York, 2011.

Resurrection (Biograph, 1909). UCLA

Rosita (Mary Pickford Film Co., 1923). UCLA.

Ruth of the Range (1923). *Considered lost.*

Ruth of the Rockies (Ruth Roland Serial Productions, Inc., 1920). Nos. 14, 15, UCLA.

Sadie Thompson (United Artists, 1928). Kino, 2001.

Salome (Nazimova Productions, 1923). Video Yesteryear, 1986.

Sex (Parker Read Productions, 1920). LOC.

The Sheik (Famous Players–Lasky/Paramount, 1921). Image Entertainment, 2002.

The Sign on the Door (Norma Talmadge Film Co., 1921). LOC.

The Social Secretary (Fine Arts Film Co., 1916). UCLA.

The Son of the Sheik (Paramount, 1926). Image Entertainment, 2002.

Stella Maris (Mary Pickford Film Corp., 1918). Grapevine Video, 1992.

The Sultan's Wife (Keystone Film Co., 1917). Passport Video.

Sweet Memories (IMP, 1911). MOMA.

Teddy at the Throttle (Keystone Film Co., 1917). Passport Video.

Tess of the Storm Country (Famous Players, 1914). UCLA.

Tess of the Storm Country (Mary Pickford Company, 1922). Image Entertainment, 1999.

The Timber Queen (Pathé, 1922). Episodes 1, 4, 8, 9, UCLA.

Too Wise Wives (Famous Players–Lasky, 1921). LOC, 1993.

Traffic in Souls (George Loane Tucker, 1913). Image Entertainment, 1995.

A Twilight Baby (Sunshine Comedies, 1920). MOMA.

What Happened to Mary (Edison, 1912–1913). Episodes, 5–8, 10, 11.

Where Are My Children? (Universal, 1916). Image Entertainment, 2007.

Why Change Your Wife? (Famous Players–Lasky, 1920). Image Entertainment, 2005.

You Can't Believe Everything (Triangle, 1918). *Considered lost.*

Notes

MPOH	Mary Pickford Oral History Transcript, Columbia Center for Oral History, Butler Library, Columbia University, New York
NYA	*New York American*
NYPL-TC	New York Public Library for the Performing Arts, Theater Collection
NYT	*New York Times*
PCC	Mary Pickford Core Clipping File, MHL
Rappe Death Report	Death Report, Coroner's Office, San Francisco Department of Public Health, Bureau of Records and Statistics
RCC	Ruth Roland's Core Clippings, MHL
RLC	Robinson Locke Dramatic Collection, Billy Rose Theater Division, New York Public Library of the Performing Arts, New York City
SFC	*San Francisco Chronicle*
SFX	*San Francisco Examiner*
STL	*St. Louis Post-Dispatch*
Studio Club	Young Women's Christian Association of Los Angeles Collection, Hollywood Studio Club, Urban Archives Center, University Library, California State University, Northridge
VC	Fan scrapbooks compiled by Edna G. Vercoe, MHL

PROLOGUE I. LANDSCAPES

1. In 1920, the U.S. Census revealed that more than half of Americans lived in cities, defined as settlements with more than 2,500 people. It also revealed the nation contained sixty-eight cities of 100,000 persons or more. See Paul Boyer, *Urban Masses and Moral Order in America* (Cambridge, MA: Harvard University Press, 1978), 189. The inflow of "new immigrants" from Southern and Eastern Europe peaked in 1907, then hovered above 650,000 until World War I. John Higham, *Strangers in the Land: Patterns of American Nativism, 1860–1925,* 2nd ed. (New Brunswick, NJ: Rutgers University Press, 1988), 159. See David Ward, *Cities and Immigrants: A Geography of Change in Nineteenth-Century America* (New York: Oxford University Press, 1971), 56. On the migration of black southerners, see James Grossman, *Land of Hope: Chicago, Black Southerners, and the Great Migration* (Chicago: University of Chicago Press, 1989); Ann Douglas, *Terrible Honesty: Mongrel Manhattan in the 1920s* (New York: Farrar, Straus & Giroux, 1995). Cities include the country's largest: New York, Boston, Chicago, Cleveland, Milwaukee, Detroit, Buffalo, Minneapolis, Pittsburgh, Philadelphia, St. Louis, Cincinnati, and Baltimore. See the

federal census tables in Robert Fogelson, *The Fragmented Metropolis: Los Angeles, 1850–1930* (Berkeley: University of California Press, 1967), 75–83.

2. William Hays, "The Organization of Country Life," in *Proceedings of the Thirty-First Annual Session of the Farmers' National Congress* (Washington, DC: Government Printing Office, 1911), 140. On the rural problem, see Katherine Hempstead, "Agricultural Change and the Rural Problem" (Ph.D. diss. University of Pennsylvania, 1992); William L. Bowers, *The Country Life Movement in America, 1900–1920* (Port Washington, NY: Kennikat, 1974). In 1926, the American Country Life president conceded that "agricultural movements have been distinctively masculine"; quoted in Janet Galligani Casey, " 'This Is Your Magazine': Domesticity, Agrarianism, and the Farmer's Wife," *American Periodicals* 14.2 (2004): 179. See also Fogelson, *The Fragmented Metropolis,* 78–79; Higham, *Strangers in the Land,* 158–160. On the constitution of whiteness, see Matthew Frye Jacobson, *Whiteness of a Different Color: European Immigrants and the Alchemy of Race* (Cambridge, MA: Harvard University Press, 1998).

3. Hubert Howe Bancroft, *California Pastoral, 1769–1848* (San Francisco: The History Company, 1888), 360. According to the 1910 census, LA's population of 319,198 was augmented by approximately 150,000 tourists. Cited in Eileen Bowser, *The Transformation of Cinema, 1907–1915* (Berkeley: University of California Press, 1990), 159. On the early myth-making of Southern California, I am especially indebted to Kevin Starr, *Inventing the Dream: California through the Progressive Era* (New York: Oxford University Press, 1985), 54–74, 75–98; Carey McWilliams, *Southern California Country: An Island on the Land* (New York: Sloan and Pierce, 1946), 113–164; David Fine, *Imagining Los Angeles: A City in Fiction* (Albuquerque: University of New Mexico Press, 2000). On boosting, see also Denise McKenna, "The City That Made the Pictures Move: Gender, Labor, and the Film Industry in Los Angeles, 1908–1917" (Ph.D. dissertation, New York University, 2008), ch. 1; William Issel, "Citizens outside of the Government: Business and Urban Policy in San Francisco and Los Angeles, 1890–1932," *Pacific Historical Review* 62.2 (May 1988): 117–139. On *Ramona,* see Dydia DeLyser, *Ramona Memories: Tourism and the Shaping of Southern California* (Minneapolis: University of Minnesota Press, 2005). On the rivalry between Northern and Southern California, see Roger W. Lotchin, *Fortress California, 1910–1961: From Warfare to Welfare* (New York: Oxford University Press, 1992), 1–22. On how LA celebrated a Spanish rather than Mexican history, see William Deverell, *Whitewashed Adobe: The Rise of Los Angeles and the Remaking of Its Mexican Past* (Berkeley: University of California Press, 2005).

4. Lummis quoted in Starr, *Inventing the Dream,* 89, 45. On the creation of the city's racialized imaginary, see also George Sanchez, *Becoming Mexican America; Ethnicity, Culture, and Identity in Chicano Los Angeles, 1910–1945* (New York: Oxford University Press, 1995); Alexander McClung, *Landscapes of Desire: Anglo Mythologies of Los Angeles* (Berkeley: University of California Press, 2000). On single-family homes, see Fogelson, *Fragmented Metropolis,* 142–152; on "Spanish" architecture, see Starr, *Inventing the Dream,* 41–42, 65–68, 78. Between 1900 and 1920, 60% of migrants were between the ages of

25 and 44; by 1920 the largest nativity group in California was native-born migrants of mid-American origin; see Warren S. Thompson, *Growth and Changes in California's Population*, (Los Angeles: Haynes Foundation, 1955), 16–17, 47–51, 53–65; Kevin Starr, *Material Dreams: Southern California through the 1920s* (New York: Oxford University Press, 1990), 69.

5. When addressed, Hollywood's influence is reduced to assessing admittedly important founding fathers, including D.W. Griffith, Cecil B. DeMille, Adolph Zukor, the Warner brothers, and Thomas Ince. See Starr, *Inventing the Dream*, chs. 8–9; Neal Gabler, *An Empire of Their Own: How the Jews Invented Hollywood* (New York: Doubleday, 1988); David Bordwell, *On the History of Film Style* (Cambridge, MA: Harvard University Press, 1997), ch. 1.

6. Willard Huntington Wright, "Los Angeles—The Chemically Pure," in Burton Rascoe and Groff Conklin, eds., *The Smart Set Anthology* (New York: Reynal & Hitchcock, 1934 [1913]), 90–102. Both "movie" and "flicker" were early terms that lost favor during the late teens. See Jesse Lasky, with Don Weldon, "The Flickers Become Respectable," in *I Blow My Own Horn* (Garden City, NY: Doubleday, 1957), 112–120; Terry Ramsaye, *A Million and One Nights: A History of the Motion Picture through 1925* (New York: Simon & Schuster, 1954 [1926]), 550–552; Lillian Gish, *Dorothy and Lillian Gish* (New York: Scribner's, 1973), 60.

7. "A Visit to Movieland, the Film Capital of the World—Los Angeles," *The Forum* 63 (Jan. 1920): 17–29 (available at American Periodical Series Online, via ProQuest [hereinafter, APS]).

8. Bowser, *The Transformation of Cinema*, 18, 22–26, 151–155. Months after beginning publishing in 1907, *Moving Picture World*, the first periodical devoted entirely to the business of pictures, estimated that between 2,500 and 3,000 nickelodeons existed; a year later an Oakland newspaper put the total at 8,000. See, ibid., 4. For one "conservative" estimate of a 26 million weekly in attendance in 1910, see Russell Merritt, "Nickelodeon Theatres, 1905–14," in Tino Balio, ed., *The American Film Industry* (Madison: University of Wisconsin Press, 1976), 86. On the role that audience demand played, see Charles Musser, *Before the Nickelodeon* (Berkeley: University of California Press, 1991). On how the new director-centered mode of production arose in part as a means to rationalize production to satisfy this demand, see David Bordwell, Janet Staiger, and Kristin Thompson, *The Classical Hollywood Cinema: Film Style and Mode of Production to 1960* (New York: Columbia University Press, 1985), 121–122. On the industry's shift to fictional "story" films, see Bowser, *The Transformation of Cinema*, 53–55; and Robert C. Allen, *Vaudeville and Film, 1895–1915* (New York: Arno Press, 1980), 127–128, 212–213. Allen's analysis of copyrighted titles found a dramatic shift to fictional narratives from 1907 to 1908. Copyrighted titles of sport, travel, and documentary shorts along with newsreels comprised 86.9% of production before 1906; by 1908 the production of dramatic story films had risen from 17% to 66%.

9. "A Visit to Movieland," 17–29. Early producers describe the lure of cheap land, weather, and scenery; see Adolph Zukor, with Dale Kramer, *The Public Is Never Wrong* (New York: G.P. Putnam's Sons, 1953), 100–103; Lasky, *I Blow My Own Horn*, 94–96, 122; Cecil B. DeMille, *The Autobiography of Cecil B.*

DeMille, ed. Donald Hayne (Englewood Cliffs, NJ: Prentice-Hall, 1959), 77–81; Mack Sennett, with Cameron Shipp, *King of Comedy* (Garden City, NY: Doubleday, 1954), 63–64. *Moving Picture World* quoted in Bordwell, Staiger, and Thompson, *The Classical Hollywood Cinema,* 122. Selig quoted in Bowser, *The Transformation of Cinema,* 122. On Selig's early trip, see Ramsaye, *A Million and One Nights,* 532–542; Kenneth MacGowan, *Behind the Screen* (New York: Dell, 1965), 138–139; Robert Sklar, *Movie-Made America* (New York: Vintage, 1976), 67.

10. On LA's transportation system, see Fogelson, *Fragmented Metropolis,* 85–94. On the city's reputation as a bastion of the open shop, see Murray Ross, *Stars and Strikes: The Unionization of Hollywood* (New York: AMS Press, 1967 [1942]); Louis B. Perry and Richard S. Perry, *A History of the Los Angeles Labor Movement, 1911–1941* (Berkeley: University of California Press, 1963), 16–21, 23, 30, 37–38, 73–75; Laurie Pintar, "Behind the Scenes," in Tom Sitton and William Deverell, eds., *Metropolis in the Making: Los Angeles in the 1920s* (Berkeley: University of California Press, 2001), 319–324. On the industry's growth, see Richard Koszarski, *An Evening's Entertainment: The Age of the Silent Picture Feature* (Berkeley: University of California Press, 1991), 17–19, 102–104.

11. On the industry's economic relationship to Los Angeles and California, see Starr, *Material Dreams,* 98. To live in "health and decency" in 1923, a family of five had to earn between $1,500 and $1,700. More than half of American families failed to earn this amount in the 1920s; see Winifred Wandersee, *Women's Work and Family Values, 1920–1940* (Cambridge, MA: Harvard University Press, 1981), 10–11. In the 1920s the average annual wage of female clerical workers was less than $1,200, and saleswomen earned between $688 and $1,085; see Lynn Dumenil, *The Modern Temper: American Culture and Society in the 1920s* (New York: Hill & Wang, 1995), 115–116. The claim that the film industry had become the fourth or fifth largest was common by the early twenties. See *Exhibitors Herald* (Oct. 22, 1921): 41; "The 'Movie' as an Industry," *Literary Digest* (Oct. 16, 1917): 55; "The Jazzy, Money-Mad Spot Where Movies Are Made," *Literary Digest* (Mar. 6, 1921): 71–72, 75; "Film-Making Means Millions to Los Angeles," *Los Angeles Times,* Jan. 1, 1916; "Real Estate Conditions in Hollywood," *Los Angeles Times,* Jan. 2, 1921, p. 16; "Cinema Factor in City's Wealth," *Los Angeles Times,* Jan. 17, 1921, pt. II, p. 11. (All *Los Angeles Times* articles cited in this note were accessed through ProQuest Historical Newspapers. Unless otherwise noted, all other newspapers and periodicals were viewed on microfilm or in bound volumes.) Recent work suggests these claims were inflated; see Koszarski, *An Evening's Entertainment,* 91–94. Others argue they are true when capital investment in theaters and the American industry's virtual domination of European markets after the war are included; see Richard Maltby and Ian Craven, *Hollywood Cinema* (Oxford: Blackwell, 1995), 60; Ruth Vasey, *The World According to Hollywood, 1918–1939* (Madison: University of Wisconsin Press, 1997), 14–15.

12. "In the Capital of Movie-Land," *Literary Digest* (Nov. 10, 1917): 82–89. "El Dorado": in "Confessions of a Motion Picture Press Agent," *The Independent,* Aug. 24, 1918 (APS); "Chameleon City of the Cinema," from Strand

230 | Notes to Prologue I

Magazine, *Washington Post,* June 20, 1915 (ProQuest Historical Newspapers).
Rufus Steele, "In the Sun Spot," *Sunset* (April 1915): 699; "The Romance of
Making the 'Movies,'" *Literary Digest* (Oct. 23, 1915): 90–93; "The 'Movie' as
an Industry," *Literary Digest* (Oct. 16, 1917): 55–62; John Bruce Mitchell, "A
'Close-Up' of California," *The Forum* (April–May 1920) 474 (*APS*).

13. "For men," in Charles Musser, *The Emergence of Cinema: The American
Screen to 1907* (New York: Charles Scribner's Sons, 1990), 6. For those who
argue that audiences were primarily working-class men, see Joseph H. North,
The Early Development of the Motion Picture, 1887–1909 (New York: Arno
Press, 1973), 239; Sklar, *Movie-Made America,* 3, 14–20, Roy Rosenzweig,
Eight Hours for What We Will (New York: Cambridge University Press, 1983);
Ben Singer, "Manhattan Nickelodeons: New Data on Audiences and Exhibi-
tors," *Cinema Journal* 35.3 (1996): 3–35; Ben Singer, "Manhattan Melodrama,"
Cinema Journal 36.4 (1997): 107–112; David Nasaw, *Going Out: The Rise and
Fall of Public Amusements* (New York: Basic Books, 1993), 174–178. For revi-
sionists who challenge this class orientation, see Merritt, "Nickelodeon The-
atres," 59–79; Robert C. Allen, "Motion Picture Exhibition in Manhattan,
1906–12," *Cinema Journal* 18.2 (1979): 2–15; Robert C. Allen, "Manhattan
Myopia; or Oh! Iowa!" *Cinema Journal* 35.3 (1996): 75–103; Sumiko Higashi,
"Dialogue: Manhattan Nickelodeons," *Cinema Journal* 35.3 (1996): 72–73;
Judith Thissen, "Oy, Myopia!" *Cinema Journal* 36.4 (1997): 107–117. For the
most recent, and possibly romantic, view of American film as a medium that
betrayed its early working-class orientation, see Steven Ross, *Working-Class
Hollywood: Silent Film and the Shaping of Class in America* (Princeton: Prince-
ton University Press, 1998). An interesting exception that attempts to balance
the impact of ethnic, class, and gender conflicts and social change is Lary May,
*Screening Out the Past: The Birth of Mass Culture and the Motion Picture In-
dustry* (New York: Oxford University Press, 1980). David Bordwell, *On the
History of Film Style* (Cambridge, MA: Harvard University Press, 1997), 21;
Barry quoted at 26.

14. Iris Barry quoted in Antonia Lant, with Ingrid Periz, eds., *Red Velvet
Seat: Women's Writing on the First Fifty Years of Cinema* (London: Verso,
2006), 26. On the audience for westerns, see Andrew Brodie Smith, *Shooting
Cowboys and Indians: Silent Westerns, American Culture, and the Birth of Hollywood* (Denver: University of Colorado Press, 2004). The definitive survey of
the silent era argues that adults deserted the Western en masse after 1915, leading it to become a cheap "B" category of films that were so degraded by the
1920s that they "were the only genre segregated from the balance of studio's
production." See Koszarski, *An Evening's Entertainment,* 182–183, 288–290.
For a contemporary's view, see Randolph Bartlett, "Where Do We Ride from
Here?" *Photoplay* (February 1919): 36–37, 109. On the not fully realized attempts of slapstick to shed its association as vulgar working-class entertainment aimed at children and men, see Rob King, *The Fun Factory: The Keystone
Film Company and the Emergence of Mass Culture* (Berkeley: University of
California Press, 2008), 174–177. On the limitations imposed on women by
Griffith's insistence on traditional melodramas, see for instance Mary Pickford's
view of Griffith in Kevin Brownlow, *Mary Pickford Rediscovered* (New York:

Abrams, 1999), 67. Here I have in mind the idea that "the social imaginary . . . is what enables, through making sense of, the practices of society"; Charles Taylor, "Modern Social Imaginaries," *Public Culture* 14 (Winter 2002): 90.

15. "The Close-up," *New York Times,* Dec. 29, 1918, p. 61. Margaret Turnbull, *The Close-Up* (New York, 1918), 1, 35, 64, 80, 222. On Margaret Turnbull, see "Notes Written on the Screen," *New York Times,* Jan. 24, 1915, p. 8; "The Marriage Problem," *Atlanta Constitution,* March 10, 1927, p. 9; and "Miss M. Turnbull, Author, Scenarist," *New York Times,* June 13, 1942, p. 15. From 1910 through 1930, women wrote between a quarter and half of all screenplays. See Lizzie Francke, *Script Girls: Women Screenwriters in Hollywood* (London: British Film Institute, 1994), ch. 1. On the culture of screenwriting, see Cari Beauchamp, *Without Lying Down: Frances Marion and the Powerful Women of Early Hollywood* (Berkeley: University of California Press, 1997); Wendy Holliday, "Hollywood's Modern Women: Screenwriting, Work Culture, and Feminism, 1910–1940" (Ph.D. dissertation, New York University, 1995). "The Romance of Making the 'Movies,'". On "brains," see for instance the caption under Norma Talmadge's photograph, "In and Out of Focus: Norma Talmadge," Feb. 2, 1919, Louella Parsons Scrapbook no. 3, Margaret Herrick Library, Academy of Motion Picture Arts and Sciences, Beverly Hills (hereinafter Parsons Scrapbook no. 3, MHL). These professionally compiled press books contain the majority of what she wrote; I read those from 1915 to 1922. Novels in which ambitious women flourished in the movie industry were written by some of the most popular authors of the day, including B.M. Bower, *The Quirt* (Boston, 1920); Henry Kitchell Webster, *Real Life: Into Which Miss Leda Swan of Hollywood Makes an Adventurous Excursion* (Indianapolis, 1921); Rupert Hughes, *Souls for Sale* (New York, 1922); Louis Joseph Vance, *Linda Lee Inc.* (New York, 1922); and Harry Leon Wilson, *Merton of the Movies* (New York, 1922). Negative tales include Nina Putnam, *Laughter Limited* (New York, 1923), and Edgar Rice Burroughs, *The Girl from Hollywood* (New York, 1923).

16. Horace Greeley quoted in Thomas Fuller, "'Go West, young man!'—An Elusive Slogan," *Indiana Magazine of History* 100 (2004): 238. Coy F. Cross, *Go West, Young Man! Horace Greeley's Vision for America* (Albuquerque: University of New Mexico Press, 1995); William Deverell, "To Loosen the Safety Valve: Eastern Workers in Western Lands," *Western Historical Quarterly* 19 (1988), 269–285. On population imbalance, see Glenda Riley, *The Female Frontier: A Comparative View of Women on the Prairie and the Plains* (Lawrence: University Press of Kansas, 1988), ch. 2. On the reversal of western migration patterns, see Robert V. Hine and John Mack Faragher, *The American West: A New Interpretive History* (New Haven: Yale University Press, 2000), 418. On the defeminization of the Midwest, see Bengt Ankarloo, "Agriculture and Women's Work: Directions of Change in the West, 1700–1900," *Journal of Family History* 4 (Summer 1979): 111–120; Joanne Meyerowitz, *Women Adrift: Independent Wage Earners in Chicago, 1880–1930* (Chicago: University of Chicago Press, 1988), 8–14; and Joan Jensen, "I'd Rather Be Dancing: Wisconsin Women Moving On," *Frontiers: A Journal of Women Studies* 22.1 (2001): 1–20. On the West's relationship to modern manhood, see G. Edward White, *The Eastern*

Establishment and the Western Experience: The West of Frederic Remington, Theodore Roosevelt, and Owen Wister (New Haven: Yale University Press, 1968); E. Anthony Rotundo, *American Manhood: Transformations in Masculinity from the Revolution to the Modern Era* (New York: Basic Books, 1993), chs. 10–11; Matthew Basso, Laura McCall, and Dee Garceau-Hagen, *Across the Great Divide: Cultures of Manhood in the American West* (New York: Routledge, 2001), 1–24. For a focus on the iconicity of western women, see Renee M. Laegreid, *Riding Pretty: Rodeo Royalty and the American West* (Lincoln: University of Nebraska Press, 2006).

17. On New Women see, Lois Rudnick, "The New Woman," in Adele Heller and Lois Rudnick, eds., *1915, the Cultural Moment: The New Politics, the New Woman, the New Psychology, the New Art, and the New Theatre in America* (New Brunswick, NJ: Rutgers University Press, 1991), 68–91; Estelle Freedman, "The New Woman," *Journal of American History* 61 (1974): 372–393; Rosalind Rosenberg, *Beyond Separate Spheres: Intellectual Roots of Modern Feminism* (New Haven: Yale University Press, 1982). Kathy Peiss, *Cheap Amusements: Working Women and Leisure in Turn of the Century New York* (Philadelphia: Temple University Press, 1986); Nan Enstad, *Ladies of Labor, Girls of Adventure: Working Women, Popular Culture, and Labor Culture at the Turn of the Twentieth Century* (New York: Columbia University Press, 1999); Susan Glenn, *Female Spectacle: The Theatrical Roots of Modern Feminism* (Cambridge, MA: Harvard University Press, 2000); Christine Stansell, *American Moderns: Bohemian New York and the Creation of a New Century* (New York: Metropolitan Books, 2000). Much has been written on Victorian middle-class sexual ideology; here I follow Barbara Welter, "The Cult of True Womanhood, 1820–1860," *American Quarterly* 2 (1966), 151–174; Nancy Cott, "Passionlessness: An Interpretation of Victorian Sexual Ideology," *Signs* 21 (1978), 219–236; Ellen Carol DuBois and Linda Gordon, "Seeking Ecstasy on the Battlefield: Danger and Pleasure in Nineteenth Century Feminist Thought," *Feminist Studies* (Spring 1983): 7–25. On the shift in women's wage-earning in the early twentieth century, see Alice Kessler-Harris, *Out To Work: A History of Wage-Earning Women in the United States* (New York: Oxford, 1982), ch.5; Meyerowitz, *Women Adrift*, ch.1; On how the city's commercial entertainment industries transformed the pleasure-seeking habits of young women at the turn of the century, see Rosenzweig, *Eight Hours for What We Will*, 197–198, 202; Elizabeth Ewen, *Immigrant Women in the Land of Dollars* (New York: Monthly Review Press, 1985), 208–224; Lauren Rabinovitz, *For the Love of Pleasure: Women, Movies, and Culture in Turn-of-the-Century Chicago* (New Brunswick, NJ: Rutgers University Press, 1998), 105–177; Miriam Hansen, *Babel and Babylon: Spectatorship in American Silent Film* (Cambridge, MA: Harvard University Press, 1991), 60–126.

18. Manuel Weltmann, *Pearl White: The Peerless Fearless Girl* (South Brunswick, UK: A.S. Barnes, 1969). Pearl White, "Through Fire and Air," *The Perils of Pauline* (Pathé 1914) (viewed on Kino). As was common, White said her fan mail was "mostly from women," including more than a "few mash notes"; Julian Johnson, "The Girl on the Cover," *Photoplay* (April 1919): 58. Scholarship on how serial queens "abetted feminist propaganda" dates to Wallace Davies,

"The Truth about Pearl White," *Films in Review* (November 1959): 544. For the best recent treatments of serial queens' representation of tensions over normative audience practices and femininity, see Shelley Stamp, *Movie-Struck Girls: Women and Motion Picture Culture after the Nickelodeon* (Princeton: Princeton University Press, 2000); ch. 3; Ben Singer, *Melodrama and Modernity: Early Sensation Cinema and Its Contexts* (New York: Columbia University Press, 2001), ch. 8. Shenbao, May 2, 1921, quoted in Weihong Bao, "From Pearl White to White Rose Woo," *Camera Obscura* 20, no. 3 (2005): 200. *Moving Picture Stories*, Feb. 21, 1919, p. 3, quoted in Stamp, *Movie-Struck Girls*, 143. *Universal Weekly* (1913) quoted in Mark Garrett Cooper, *Universal Women: Filmmaking and Institutional Change in Early Hollywood* (Urbana: University of Illinois Press, 2010), 45. Cooper's chapter "Universal City" explores at length the studio's creation of this image. Few reliable statistics on the industry's audience in this era exist, but most agree that the industry increasingly focused on attracting women after 1910, viewing them as its "ideal," most "fanatic" members between the 1920s and 1940s. My interest is this widespread perception, not a particular statistic. See Benjamin Hampton, *A History of the Movies, from its Beginnings to 1931* (New York: Dover, 1970 [1931]), 224–226; Leo Rosten, *Hollywood: The Movie Colony, the Movie Makers* (New York: Harcourt, Brace & Co., 1941), 12–15, appendix H, "Fan Mail"; Stamp, *Movie-Struck Girls*, 10–40; Gaylyn Studlar, "The Perils of Pleasure? Fan Magazine Discourse as Women's Commodified Culture in the 1920s," *Wide Angle* 13 (Jan. 1991): 6–33; Rabinovitz, *For the Love of Pleasure*; Koszarski, *An Evening's Entertainment*, 29–30; Hansen, *Babel and Babylon*, 245–268; Melvyn Stokes, "The Female Audience of the 1920s and Early 1930s," in Stokes and Richard Maltby, eds., *Identifying Hollywood's Audiences: Cultural Identity and the Movies* (London: British Film Institute, 1999), 42–60; Richard Abel, "Fan Discourse in the Heartland: The Early 1910s," *Film History* 18 (2006): 146.

19. Suzette Booth, "Breaking into the Movies," *Motion Picture Magazine* (June 1917): 76. This was a monthly serial that ran between January and June 1917. In 1920 the city's sex ratio was 97.8:100; see Thompson, *Growth and Change in California's Population*, 48–51, 88–89; Frank L. Beach, "The Effects of Westward Movement on California's Growth and Development, 1900–1920," *International Migration Review* 3 (1969): 25–28. Rebecca J. Mead, "'Let the Women Get Their Wages as Men Do': Trade Union Women and the Legislated Minimum Wage in California," *Pacific Historical Review* 67.3 (1998), 317–347; Rebecca Mead, *How the Vote Was Won: Woman Suffrage in the Western United States, 1868–1914* (New York: New York University Press, 2004). Thompson, *Growth and Change in California's Population*, 89–93, 112–115. On unmarried women's higher work rates, see Joseph Hill, *Women in Gainful Occupations, 1870 to 1920*, Census Monograph IX (Westport, CT: Greenwood Press, 1970, [1929]), 270–276. "The Motion Picture Autobiographies," Case 9, compiled by Herbert Blumer, in Garth Jowett, I.C. Jarvie, and Kathryn Fuller-Seeley, eds., *Children and the Movies: Media Influence and the Payne Fund Controversy* (Cambridge: Cambridge University Press, 1996), 275.

20. *Motion Picture News*, quoted in Richard Abel, "Fan Discourse in the Heartland," *Film History* 19 (2006): 140–153. *Photoplay* (Nov. 1924), quoted

in Studlar, "Perils of Pleasure?" 7. Janet Flanner, "The Male Background," *Photoplay* (Dec. 1920): 33. On the reorientation of fan magazines toward women readers, see Kathryn Fuller, *At the Picture Show: Small-Town Audiences and the Creation of Movie Fan Culture* (Washington, DC: Smithsonian Institution Press, 1996). I distinguish between, on one hand, trade papers aimed at those with a stake in manufacturing and exhibiting films and, on the other, fan periodicals or newspaper movie sections designed only for fans. Trade papers existed from the industry's start, but periodicals for fans and celebrity reporting developed only in the mid-1910s. For a sense of the period's fan culture, I read the Parsons Scrapbooks, MHL, between 1915 and 1922. I also read everything in *Photoplay* during these years. A national publication with a circulation of 2 million, it was the largest of all fan magazines. Finally, I used the periodical database at the Herrick Library to read all the stories published in these same years turned up by keyword searches on *extras, contests, how to become an actress, Hollywood,* and *marriage and divorce.* For "mainstream" reporting I read all relevant articles indexed on motion pictures in *The Readers' Guide to Periodical to Literature,* as well as those yielded by keyword searches on *extras, motion picture actors, motion picture stars,* and *Hollywood* in ProQuest Historical Newspapers and APS. In addition to works already cited, see Janet Staiger, *Bad Women: Regulating Sexuality in Early American Cinema* (Minneapolis: University of Minnesota Press, 1995); Karen Ward Mahar, *Women Filmmakers in Early Hollywood* (Baltimore: Johns Hopkins University Press, 2006); Samantha Barbas, *The First Lady of Hollywood: A Biography of Louella Parsons* (Berkeley: University of California Press, 2006); Jennifer M. Bean and Diane Negra, *A Feminist Reader in Early Cinema* (Durham, NC: Duke University Press, 2002); Alison McMahan, *Alice Guy Blache* (New York: Continuum, 2002); Kay Armatage, *The Girl from God's Country* (Toronto: University of Toronto Press, 2003); Anthony Slide, *The Silent Feminists* (Lanham, MD: Scarecrow Press, 1996; rev. ed. of *Early Women Directors,* 1977); Eileen Whitfield, *Pickford: The Woman Who Made Hollywood* (Lexington: University of Kentucky Press, 1997); Gavin Lambert, *Nazimova* (New York: Knopf, 1997); "Women and the Silent Screen," ed. Shelley Stamp and Amelie Hastie, special issue, *Film History* 18.2 (2006); Women Film Pioneers Project, http://wfpp.cdrs.columbia.edu.

21. Daniel T. Rodgers, *The Work Ethic in Industrial America* (Chicago: University of Chicago Press, 1974), ch. 5.

22. This is a general impression of mine that particularly pertains to performers in high-profile, prestige products and does not mean that men were not popular as well. However, when one subtracts western heroes and comedians from those considered most capable of opening pictures—or worthy of independent producing companies within studios—the list that remains is predominantly the leading ladies of the day. Even with such men, the number of females among the highest-paid performers outranked the number of men. For such a list in 1923, see Koszarski, *An Evening's Entertainment,* 116. In autobiographies and interviews with female stars of the period, women consistently note their belief that young women largely supported their popularity. Similar important contemporary views include those of three of the most important men

involved in pioneering feature fiction films and the studio system: Adolph Zukor, Cecil DeMille, and Jesse Lasky. See letters between Jesse Lasky and Cecil
De Mille, in Paolo Cherchi and Lornzo Codelli, eds., *The DeMille Legacy*
(Pordenone, Italy: Le Giornate del Cinema Muto, 1991), i, 489–491. On the
decline in the number of female college students and professionals from 1920
to 1960, see William O'Neill, *Everyone Was Brave: A History of Feminism in
America* (Chicago: Quadrangle Books, 1969), 304–305. On actresses, screenwriters, and producers, see Ally Acker, *Reel Women: Pioneers of the Cinema
1896 to the Present* (New York: Continuum, 1991), 1–8; Francke, *Script
Girls*, ch. 1.

23. Gloria Swanson, *Swanson on Swanson* (New York: Random House,
1980), 63, 135.

24. On the theatrical roots of such behavior, see chapter 1 herein; Glenn,
Female Spectacle; Faye Dudden, *Women in the American Theater: Actresses
and Audiences, 1790–1870* (New Haven: Yale University Press, 1994); Benjamin McArthur, *Actors and American Culture, 1880–1920* (Philadelphia: Temple
University Press, 1984). On women's formation of independent production
companies in the silent period, see Mahar, *Women Filmmakers*, 62–66, 126,
154–160, 175–176. On workers' dreams of more than economic survival in this
period, see Kessler-Harris, *Out to Work,* ch. 8. On the comparably excellent
wages paid to even the lowest-paid actresses in this period, see Claudia Johnson, *American Actresses: Perspectives on the Nineteenth Century* (Chicago:
Nelson-Hall, 1984), 54–57; Robert C. Allen, "The Movies in Vaudeville," in
Balio, *The American Film Industry,* 42. For instance, the beginning salary of a
"ballet-girl" at mid-century was between $3 and $4 a week, doubling to $8 af-
ter one month; the typical factory wage averaged $1.50 a week in the period.

25. United States Department of Agriculture, *Social and Labor Needs of
Farm Women,* Report No. 103 (Washington, DC: Government Printing Office,
1915), 4, 14, 12. See also United States Department of Agriculture, *Domestic
Needs of Farm Women,* Report No. 104 (Washington, DC: Government Printing Office, 1915), 4. Grace Kingsley, "Extra Girls Who Became Stars: Thousands Annually Storm Fortune's Citadel," *Photoplay* (April 1915): 145. "Movie
'Extras' Whose Lives Rival Screen Romance," *Literary Digest,* Sept. 20, 1920,
p. 69; William Allen Johnston, "In Motion-Picture Land," *Everybody's Magazine* 33.4 (Oct. 1915): 437–448.

26. I follow Nancy Cott in emphasizing the importance to feminism of "sex
rights," sexual equality, difference, and variety; my definition does not emphasize formal political action, since this would exclude most women outside the
educated middle class and was not originally central to feminism; see Nancy F.
Cott, *The Grounding of Modern Feminism* (New Haven: Yale University Press,
1987), 7–9. My reading here can be contrasted with that of Shelley Stamp, who
argues that extras were only portrayed with derision; Stamp, "It's a Long Way
to Filmland," in Charles Keil and Shelley Stamp, eds., *American Cinema's Transitional Era: Audiences, Institutions, and Practices* (Berkeley: University of California Press, 2004), 332–351.

27. Frances Marion, *Off with Their Heads!* (New York: Macmillan, 1972).
On the local efforts of neighborhood associations, see "Evil Influence of Motion

Pictures," Petition 2524, Sept. 6, 1921, in "Motion Picture File to be known as 2723"; File 614, 1916; File 387, 1917; File 2619, 1918; File 1000, 1918. File 387, 1917; File 1000, 1918, City Clerk's Office, Records Management Division, Los Angeles City Archives (hereafter Los Angeles City Archive). On Marion's move, see Beauchamp, *Without Lying Down*, 11–13. On Weber, see Shelley Stamp, "'Exit Flapper, Enter Woman,' or Lois Weber in Jazz Age Hollywood," *Framework* (Fall 2010): 358–387.

28. King Vidor, quoted in A. Scott Berg, *Goldwyn: A Biography* (New York: Knopf, 1989), 105.

29. *Mutual Film Corporation v. Ohio Industrial Commission*, 236 U.S. 230 (1915). For an insightful reading of how *Mutual* reflected the desire to impose a "pure version" of "Protestant Americanism" on screens, though the author ignores the importance of sexual obscenity, see Garth Jowett, "'A Capacity for Evil': The 1915 Supreme Court *Mutual* Decision," *Historical Journal of Film, Television, and Radio* 9.1 (1989): 59–78. For more on the importance of sexual obscenity, see Edward deGrazia and Roger Newman, *Banned Films: Movies, Censors and the First Amendment* (New York: R.R. Bowker, 1982), 7–9; Richard Randall, *Censorship of the Movies* (Madison: University of Wisconsin Press, 1968), 18–24; Kathleen McCarthy, "Nickel Vice and Virtue: Movie Censorship in Chicago, 1907–1915," *Journal of Popular Film* 5.1 (1976): 37–55. My account of the film censorship movement owes the most to DeGrazia, Randall, and Lee Grieveson, *Policing Cinema: Movies and Censorship in Early Twentieth Century America* (Berkeley: University of California Press, 2004). Grieveson describes how regulators of the movie industry sought to reproduce the cultural dominance of white, middle-class social conventions associated with respectability. He argues that the stylistic and industrial norms associated with "classical Hollywood cinema" were determined by legal struggles ending with *Mutual* in 1915. After this, the industry offered "harmless and culturally affirmative entertainment." His careful readings of regulation efforts are compelling, but his functionalist interpretation appears too neatly timed to coincide with the emergence of classical Hollywood cinema and treats entertainment and Hollywood cinema as stable, transparent concepts whose meanings lay outside the shifting pressures of historical context and contingency. This is especially troublesome since "Hollywood cinema" lacked definition in this era. It also ignores the producers' refusal to bow to systematic regulation until the Production Code of 1934, thereby ignoring another commercial imperative: the need to appeal to audiences. *The James Boys in Missouri* (Essanay, 1908); *Night Riders* (Kalem, 1908). The decision to suppress the film was supported by *Block v. City of Chicago*, 87 N.E. 1011 (1909).

30. *Mutual*, 236 U.S. 244, 246–247. The decision was made on three grounds: films were primarily entertainment, were made wholly for profit, and possessed a special capacity for evil. McCarthy, "Nickel Vice and Virtue," 48–53; De Grazia, *Banned Films*, 8–9; Randall, *Censorship of the Movies*, 20–21.

31. Reformer quoted in Peiss, *Cheap Amusements*, 98. Regina Kunzel, *Fallen Women, Problem Girls: Unmarried Mothers and the Professionalization of Social Work, 1890–1945* (New Haven: Yale University Press, 1993), 58. Both

Kunzel and Meyerowitz (in *Women Adrift*) note a shift during the 1910s from considering these women as victims of male sexual predators to assuming they were predators themselves. On the gendered construction of delinquency, see also Ruth Alexander, *The "Girl Problem": Female Sexual Delinquency in New York, 1900–1930* (Ithaca, NY: Cornell University Press, 1995); Mary Odem, *Delinquent Daughters: Protecting and Policing Adolescent Female Sexuality in the United States, 1885–1920* (Chapel Hill: University of North Carolina Press, 1995). On makeup and actresses, see Kathy Peiss, *Hope in a Jar: The Making of America's Beauty Culture* (New York: Henry Holt, 1998), 27–29, 47–50, 53–56.

32. George Kibbe Turner, "The City of Chicago: A Study of the Great Immoralities," *McClure's Magazine* 28.6 (April 1907): 572–592. *Inside the White Slave Traffic* (Social Research Corporation, 1913). On the belief that the white-slave picture *Traffic in Souls* helped to legitimate talk about sex, see Agnes Repplier, "The Repeal of Reticence," *Atlantic Monthly* (March 1914): 297–304. *New York Times* editorial, quoted in Stamp, *Movie-Struck Girls*, 67. On the content and reception of *Inside the White Slave Traffic*, see Staiger, *Bad Women*, 128–146; Stamp, *Movie-Struck Girls*, 69–70, 94–101. On white slave films more generally, see Grieveson, *Policing Cinema*, 151–191; Stamp, *Movie-Struck Girls*, 42–101, Staiger, *Bad Women*, 116–146. In 1911 Pennsylvania passed the first state censorship law, but it did not begin operating until 1915. Between 1916 and 1920, Ohio, Kansas, and Maryland created state boards modeled on Pennsylvania's law. The literature on white slavery is vast. A good place to start is Brian Donovan, *White Slave Crusades: Race, Gender, and Anti-Vice Activism, 1887–1917* (Urbana: University of Illinois Press, 2006). The best case for white slavery as a moral panic is made by Mark Connelly in *The Response to Prostitution in the Progressive Era* (Chapel Hill: University of North Carolina Press, 1980), 114–135.

Treatments of prostitution also abound; one good place to start is Barbara Meil Hobson, *Uneasy Virtue: The Politics of Prostitution and the American Reform Tradition* (New York: Basic Books, 1987).

33. "Girls Crave Stardom," *Atlanta Constitution*, June 26, 1921, p. D5 (ProQuest Historical Newspapers).

34. I base the foregoing account on the least-disputed facts gleaned from reading (on microfilm) the coverage in eight daily newspapers between August 1921 and May 1922: *New York American, Chicago Herald and Examiner, San Francisco Examiner, St. Louis Post-Dispatch, Brooklyn Daily Eagle, Los Angeles Times, New York Times,* and *San Francisco Chronicle.* I also looked at all references to the scandal listed in *The Readers' Guide to Periodical Literature* and the proceedings of Arbuckle's trial in police court in "The People of the State of California vs. Roscoe Arbuckle for murder in The Police Court of the City and County of San Francisco, Department No. 2, Honorable Sylvain J. Lazarus, Judge," 158, Special Collections, San Francisco Public Library (hereinafter, Court Transcript). "Dying Girl Hid Secret," *Chicago Herald and Examiner,* Sept. 14, 1921, p. 3. See also the reference to guests "having too good a time to notice the time," in Zey Prevost, Court Transcript, 310. Arthur Beardslee,

Court Transcript, 195. Death Report, Virginia Rappe, San Francisco Coroner's Office. "Arbuckle Dragged Rappe Girl to Room, Woman Testifies," *New York Times*, Sept. 12, 1921, p. 1.

35. On Hays's role in Harding's election, see Ellis Hawley, *The Great War and the Search for Modern Order* (New York: St. Martin's Press, 1992), 44–49; Michael McGerr, *The Decline of Popular Politics* (New York: Oxford University Press, 1986), 169–171; John Braeman, "American Politics in the Age of Normalcy," 17–18, in John Earl Haynes, ed., *Calvin Coolidge and the Coolidge Era* (Washington, DC: Library of Congress, 1998); Ramsaye, *A Million and One Nights*, 811–813.

36. "New Organization of Distributors and Producers Planned—Will Hays Offered Presidency," *Wid's Daily*, Dec. 9, 1921, pp. 1–2; "Says Hays Accepts," *Wid's Daily*, Dec. 21, 1921, p. 1; "Hays Accepts Offer to Head Producer-Distributor Alliance," *Exhibitors Herald*, Jan. 28, 1922, pp. 43–45. Accounts of the idea for the MPPDA and the precise timing of the approach to Hays vary. See Ramsaye, *A Million and One Nights*, 803–821; Sklar, *Movie-Made America*, 82–88, 132; Garth Jowett, *Film: The Democratic Art* (Boston: Little, Brown, 1976), 152–159. May, *Screening Out the Past*, 179, 204- 205; Richard deCordova, *Picture Personalities: The Emergence of the Star System in America* (Urbana: University of Illinois Press, 1990), 131–132; Gregory Black, *Hollywood Censored: Morality Codes, Catholics, and the Movies* (New York: Cambridge University Press, 1994), 29–33. All agree that the scandal convinced producers to go ahead with Hays's hire and to create the MPPDA. For a broader analysis, see Gary Alan Fine, *Difficult Reputations: Collective Memories of the Evil, Inept, and Controversial* (Chicago: University of Chicago Press, 2001), ch. 4.

37. "Hollywood" first appeared in the *Readers' Guide to Periodical Literature* (Minneapolis: H.W. Wilson Co.) with "In the Capital of Movie-Land," *Literary Digest* (Nov. 10, 1917): 82–89. The term appeared regularly only after 1922. Similarly, in ProQuest Historical Newspapers, "Hollywood" was first used to mean something more than a location in "Hollywood Is Interested," *Atlanta Constitution*, July 3, 1921, p. F3. The usage proliferated during 1922.

38. Scholarly descriptions of Rappe rely on popular accounts. See David Yallop, *The Day the Laughter Stopped* (New York: St. Martin's Press, 1976); Andy Edmonds, *Frame-Up! The Untold Story of Roscoe "Fatty" Arbuckle* (New York: William Morrow, 1991); Stuart Oderman, *Roscoe "Fatty" Arbuckle* (Jefferson, NC: McFarland, 1994); Robert Young, *Roscoe "Fatty" Arbuckle: A Bio-bibliography* (Westport, Conn.: Greenwood Press, 1994).

CHAPTER 1. "OH FOR A GIRL WHO COULD RIDE
A HORSE LIKE PEARL WHITE"

1. Mary Pickford, *Sunshine and Shadow* (Garden City, NY: Doubleday, 1954), 99. "In and Out of Focus: Mary Pickford," Aug. 1, 1920, Parsons Scrapbook no. 4, MHL.

2. Vachel Lindsay, "Queen of My People," *New Republic* (July 17, 1917): 280–281. See also Vachel Lindsay, *The Art of the Moving Picture* (New York: Liveright, 1970 [1915]), 3–4, 16, 54, 64, 127. "Mary Pickford," Aug.1, 1920,

Parsons Scrapbook no. 3, MHL. Zukor, *The Public Is Never Wrong*, 110, 171. Benjamin Hampton, *History of the American Film Industry, from Its Beginnings to 1931* (New York: Dover, 1970 [1931]), 166, 190. On Lindsay, see Myron Lounsbury, "The Origins of American Film Criticism" (Ph.D. dissertation, University of Pennsylvania, 1966), 50–58. The first film histories by participant observers convey Pickford's undisputed importance. See Ramsaye, *A Million and One Nights*, 746; Hampton, *History of the American Film Industry*, ch. 8; DeMille, *Autobiography of DeMille*, 182. Pickford's reappraisal began with popular treatments that built upon the restoration of her films; see Eileen Whitfield, *Pickford: The Woman Who Made Hollywood* (Lexington: University of Kentucky Press, 1997); Kevin Brownlow, *Mary Pickford Rediscovered: Rare Pictures of a Hollywood Legend* (New York: Harry N. Abrams, in association with the Academy of Arts and Sciences, 1999); Jeanine Basinger, *Silent Stars* (Middletown, CT: Wesleyan University Press, 2000 [1999]; distr. by University Press of New England), ch. 1. The first scholar to treat Pickford seriously argued for her marginalization as a child; see Sumiko Higashi, *Virgins, Vamps, and Flappers: The American Silent Movie Heroine* (Montreal: Eden Press, 1978). For a more nuanced approach focused on her marriage's promotion of consumerism, see May, *Screening Out the Past*, ch. 5. For an excellent summation of her career through the founding of United Artists, see Tino Balio, "Stars in Business," in Balio, *The American Film Industry*, 153–172. See also the presented-minded work Gaylyn Studlar, "'Oh Doll Divine': Mary Pickford, Masquerade, and the Pedophilic Gaze," in Jennifer M. Bean and Diane Negra, eds., *A Feminist Reader in Early Cinema* (Durham, NC: Duke University Press, 2002), 349–373. On these heroines' literary provenance, see John C. Tibbetts, "*Mary Pickford* and the American 'Growing Girl,'" *Journal of Popular Film and Television*, 29.2 (Summer 2001): 50–62. On *Photoplay*, see Fuller, *At the Picture Show*, ch. 8.

3. Fame's democratization is magisterially captured by Leo Braudy, who ignores gender; see *The Frenzy of Renown: Fame and its History* (New York: Vintage, 1997 [1986]), 315–598. Daniel Boorstin, *The Image: A Guide to Pseudo-Events in America* (Atheneum: New York, 1987 [1961]), 57. The most influential treatment on personality's reflection of new views of the self is Warren Susman, "'Personality' and the Making of Twentieth-Century Culture," in *Culture as History* (New York: Pantheon Books, 1984), 271–285. Susman argued that the shift from "character" to "personality" addressed the dilemma of standing out in a mass society and the growing importance placed on consumption, noting that motion picture stars most vividly displayed the process, using Pickford's husband, Douglas Fairbanks, to illustrate the shift; here Susman relied on the popular critic Richard Schickel, in *His Picture in the Papers: A Speculation on Celebrity in America Based on the Life of Douglas Fairbanks, Sr.* (New York: Charterhouse, 1973). Schickel ignores women except as victims; see *Intimate Strangers: The Culture of Celebrity in America* (Chicago: Ivan R. Dee, 1985), ch. 2. For a more sustained examination of celebrity's relationship to modernity that emphasizes its relationship to the negative values associated with consumption, see Charles L. Ponce de Leon, *Self-Exposure: Human-Interest Journalism and the Emergence of Celebrity in America, 1890–1940*

(Chapel Hill: University of North Carolina Press, 2002). See also Richard Dyer, *Stars* (London: BFI, 1998); Richard Dyer, *Heavenly Bodies: Film Stars and Celebrity* (New York: Routledge, 1986); Fred Inglis, *A Short History of Celebrity* (Princeton: Princeton University Press, 2010). DeCordova, in *Picture Personalities*, notes that women were singled out for fame first, but he doesn't explore the point; Inglis looks only at Marilyn Monroe. Those who examine celebrity's different implications for American women include Glenn, *Female Spectacle*. The scholarship on American serial queens begins with Wallace Davies, "The Truth about Pearl White," *Films in Review* (Nov. 1959): 544. The best recent treatments include Stamp, *Movie-Struck Girls*, ch. 3; Singer, *Melodramas and Modernity*, ch. 8. Important treatments on the ways commercial leisure spaces supported new gender norms include Peiss, *Cheap Amusements*; Nasaw, *Going Out*; Enstad, *Ladies of Labor, Girls of Adventure;* Rabinovitz, *For the Love of Pleasure: Women*; Hansen, *Babel and Babylon*. On how women entertainers fulfilled this role, see Faye E. Dudden, *Women in the American Theatre: Actresses and Audiences, 1790–1879* (New Haven: Yale University Press, 1995); Robert C. Allen, *Horrible Prettiness: Burlesque and American Culture* (Chapel Hill: University of North Carolina Press, 1991); M. Alison Kibler, *Rank Ladies: Gender and Cultural Hierarchy in American Vaudeville* (Chapel Hill: University of North Carolina Press, 1999); Karen Ward Mahar, *Women Filmmakers in Early Hollywood* (Baltimore: Johns Hopkins University Press, 2006); Mark Garrett Cooper, *Universal Women: Filmmaking and Institutional Change in Early Hollywood* (Urbana: University of Illinois Press, 2010).

4. On Bernhardt, see Robert Gottlieb, *Sarah: The Life of Sarah Bernhardt* (New Haven: Yale University Press, 2010); Ruth Brandon, *Being Divine: A Biography of Sarah Bernhardt* (London: Mandarin, 1991); Mary Louise Roberts, *Disruptive Acts: The New Woman in Fin-de-Siècle France* (Chicago: University of Chicago Press, 2002).

5. Simone de Beauvoir, "The Independent Woman," in *The Second Sex* (New York: Vintage, 1989 [1949]), 702–703. On the book's "scandalous" reception, see Judith G. Coffin, "Sex, Love, and Letters: Writing Simone de Beauvoir, 1949–1963," *American Historical Review* 115.4 (2010): 1061–1088. On Victorian middle-class sexual ideology, I follow Barbara Welter, "The Cult of True Womanhood, 1820–1860," *American Quarterly* 2 (1966): 151–174; and Cott, "Passionlessness." Welter identified the core components of the ideal as piety, purity, submissiveness, and domesticity. Later scholars linked the emergence of the New Woman to mass, rather than female, culture; see the special issue "The Cult of True Womanhood," *Journal of Women's History* 14.1 (2002).

6. Hampton, "The Pickford Revolution," ch. 8 in *History of the American Film Industry. The Oxford English Dictionary,* online edition, records the first use of "celebrity" as by a female author celebrated for her story about a poor boy making good: 1849 D.M. Mulock *Ogilvies* ii, "Did you see any of those 'celebrities,' as you call them?" "Personality," the older term, suggested someone with noteworthy personal characteristics and was used almost interchangeably with "celebrity" during the second half of the nineteenth century. On Cushman, see Joseph Leach, *Bright Particular Star: The Life and Times of Charlotte Cushman* (New Haven: Yale University Press, 1972); Lisa Merrill, *When*

Romeo Was a Woman: Charlotte Cushman and Her Circle of Female Specta-tors (Ann Arbor: University of Michigan Press, 1999). French and English ac-tresses help to make the point; see Lenard Berlanstein, *Daughters of Eve: French Theater Women from the Old Regime to the Fin de Siècle* (Cambridge, MA: Harvard University Press, 2001); Lenard R. Berlanstein, "Historicizing and Gendering Celebrity Culture: Famous Women in Nineteenth-Century France," *Journal of Women's History* 16.4 (2004): 65–91; Gail Marshall, *Ac-tresses on the Victorian Stage: Feminine Performance and the Galatea Myth* (Cambridge: Cambridge University Press, 1998).

7. DeCordova argues that the focus on film stars' "real lives" distinguished their personas from theatrical stars, but my own view is that this began earlier, with stage actresses; deCordova, *Picture Personalities*, 98–117.

8. "Miss Cushman," Feb. 26, 1876, in *The Spirit of the Times: The American Gentleman's Newspaper*, vol. 131, Robinson Locke Collection, Billy Rose The-ater Division, New York Public Library of the Performing Arts, New York City (hereinafter RLC), 25. On Cushman's magazine writing, see Merrill, *When Romeo Was a Woman*, ch. 2. See also Mary Jean Corbett, "Performing Identi-ties; Actresses and Autobiography," *Biographies* 24.1 (Winter 2001): 16.

9. "Legitimate productions" first distinguished plays with spoken dialogue from melodramas with music and accompanying dialogue. By 1900, the term suggested higher-brow content to fans, but in the theatrical circles it merely separated dramatic plays from comedy, slapstick, and acrobatics. Gerald Boardman, *The Oxford Companion to American Theatre* (New York: Oxford University Press, 1992), 66–67, 213, 295.

10. "Playhouse," in Dudden, *Women in the American Theatre*, 21. On wom-en's relationship to the nineteenth-century stage, see Claudia Durst Johnson, *American Actress: Perspective on the Nineteenth Century* (Chicago: Nelson-Hall, 1984), chs. 1, 3. The Revolution created a brief opening for pioneering female playwrights to write more active roles for actresses; see Linda K. Kerber, *Women of the Republic: Intellect and Ideology in Revolutionary America* (Cha-pel Hill: University of North Carolina Press, 1980), 271–273. On melodrama in the early republic, see Bruce McConachie, *Melodramatic Formations: Theater and Society, 1820–1870* (Iowa City: University of Iowa Press, 1992), 38, ch. 1; Lawrence Levine, *Highbrow/Lowbrow: The Emergence of Cultural Hierarchy in America* (Cambridge, MA: Harvard University Press, 1988), 35–44. On the theater's special regulation and association with sinfulness, see "Censorship of the Motion Picture," *Yale Law Journal* 49.1 (1939): 89; Paul Boyer, *Urban Masses and Moral Order in America, 1820–1920* (Cambridge, MA: Harvard University Press, 1978), 52–53; T. J. Jackson Lears, *Something for Nothing: Luck in America* (New York: Viking, 2002), 154–155.

11. William B. Wood, *Personal Recollections of the Stage, Embracing No-tions of Actors, Authors, Auditors, during a Period of Forty Years* (Philadelphia: H. C. Baird, 1855), 391.

12. Celebrity's link to industrialization is usefully discussed in Inglis, *A Short History of Celebrity*, chs. 1, 5. On the growth and segmentation of theaters, see Dudden, *Women in the American Theatre*, 58–60; McConachie, *Melodramatic Formations*, 26–31.

13. Robertson Davies, *The Mirror of Nature* (Toronto: University of Toronto Press, 1983), 22–26.

14. Scholars' use of "melodrama" began with Peter Brooks, *The Melodramatic Imagination* (New Haven: Yale University Press, 1976). Brooks defined melodrama as a "mode of conception and expression, as a certain fictional system for making sense of experience, as a semantic field of force, a sense making system," xiii. For a review of the literature on melodrama, see Rohan McWilliam, "Melodrama and the Historians," *Radical History Review* 78 (2000): 57–84. It seems to me that melodramatic plays and literature shaped the popular press, which then shaped movies. Robert Park suggests as much in "The Natural History of the Newspaper," in Park, Ernest Burgess, and Roderick McKenzie, eds., *The City* (Chicago: University of Press Chicago, 1925), 94–95. But part of the difficulty in discussing melodrama's development is that the histories of the press, theater, and popular fiction are separate, though their developments were intertwined. On printing, see Helmutt Lehmann-Haupt et al., *The Book in America* (New York: Bowker, 1952). On dime novels, see Michael Denning, *Mechanic Accents,* rev. ed. (London: Verso Press, 1998). On domestic novels, see Nina Baym, *Women's Fiction* (Ithaca, NY: Cornell University Press, 1978). On antebellum theater, see Dudden, *Women in the American Theatre,* 6–7, 57, 60–62, 67, 70–74; McConachie, *Melodramatic Formations,* chs. 2, 4, and 5; Richard Butsch, *The Making of American Audiences: From Stage to Television, 1750–1900* (Cambridge: Cambridge University Press, 2000), ch. 9. On the "penny press," see James L. Crouthamel, *Bennett's New York Herald and the Rise of the Popular Press* (Syracuse, NY: Syracuse University Press, 1989), 20–25; George Juergens, *Joseph Pulitzer and the* New York World (Princeton: Princeton University Press, 1960), viii–ix. Juergens does not use the term "melodrama," but the emphasis on personality-driven stories stretched out for suspense and treachery, spectacular stunts, and a crusading editorial stance championing the common man fits. William Randolph Hearst employed a similar strategy; see David Nasaw, *The Chief: The Life of William Randolph Hearst* (New York: Houghton Mifflin, 2000), 95–125. The privileging of possessive individualism, a characteristic of the middle class that views social status as purely a function of the individual, has been noted by many, including Stuart Blumin, *The Emergence of the Middle Class* (Cambridge: Cambridge University Press, 1989).

15. On this theater as a virtually all male, "American" space, see McConachie, *Melodramatic Formations,* 22–28; Butsch, *The Making of American Audiences,* ch. 3; Allen, *Horrible Prettiness,* 81–82. David Grimsted, *Melodrama Unveiled* (Chicago: University of Chicago Press, 1968), 33–36; Dudden, *Women in the American Theatre,* 108–111; Christine Stansell, *City of Women: Sex and Class in New York, 1789–1860* (Urbana: University of Illinois Press, 1987), ch. 5. Stansell notes that women were a demographic majority in New York City by 1830 and argues this made working women a significant presence on the streets and in places of commercial amusement. But she also writes: "Bowery men saw public life—in their case, working-class life—as a place where men were the main show and women the supporting cast" (96).

16. *Democratic Review* (1845), quoted in McConachie, *Melodramatic Formations*, 85.

17. Reverend William Alger, quoted in ibid., 88. On the important role that Forrest's homosocial bonds and appeal played in his celebrity, see Ginger Strand, "My Noble Spartacus," in Robert A. Schanke and Kim Marra, eds., *Passing Performances: Queer Reading of Leading Players in American Theater History* (Ann Arbor: University of Michigan, 1998), 30–31.

18. On Edwin Forrest, see McConachie, *Melodramatic Formations*, 77–109; Strand, "My Noble Spartacus," 19–40. On the importance of authenticity to fame's classical model, see Inglis, *A Short History of Celebrity*, 3–34; Braudy, *Frenzy of Renown*, 450–507.

19. On the Astor Place Riots, see Allen, *Horrible Prettiness*, 58–66; on sacralization, see Levine, *Highbrow/Lowbrow*, 83–168; on feminization, see Ann Douglas, *The Feminization of American Culture* (New York: Knopf, 1977); T. J. Jackson Lears, *No Place of Grace: Antimodernism and the Transformation of American Culture, 1880–1920* (Chicago: University of Chicago Press, 1983), 221–226, 241–260.

20. Mary Pickford Oral History Transcript, Butler Library, Columbia University, New York City (hereinafter MPOH), 2654. Stansell, *City of Women*, 90–127; Ruth Rosen, *The Lost Sisterhood: Prostitution in America, 1900–1918* (Baltimore: Johns Hopkins University Press, 1982), 40–44.

21. Mary Ryan, *Women in Public: Between Banners and Ballots, 1825–1880* (Baltimore: Johns Hopkins University Press, 1990), 76–79. See also Johnson *American Actress*, 39; Dudden, *Women in the American Theatre*, 78–82.

22. Emma Stebbins, ed., *Charlotte Cushman: Her Letters and Memories of Her Life* (Boston: Houghton, Osgood, 1878), 1.

23. Cushman quoted in Merrill, *When Romeo Was a Woman*, 52.

24. On "doubling in the brass," see Mahar, *Women Filmmakers*, 39–43. On minstrelsy, see Eric Lott, *Love and Theft: Blackface Minstrelsy and the American Working Class* (New York: Oxford University Press, 1993), 195–201; Robert Toll, *Blacking Up: The Minstrel Show in Nineteenth Century America* (New York: Oxford University Press, 1974), 3–64.

25. Cushman quoted in Merrill, *When Romeo Was a Woman*, 75.

26. "Charlotte Cushman," unsourced, Nov. 4, 1874, vol. 131, RLC, 20.

27. On Cushman's reputation as "the best breeches figure in America," see Denise A. Wallen, "Such a Romeo as We Had Never Ventured to Hope For," in Schanke and Marra, *Passing Performances*, 41–62; Dudden, *Women in the American Theatre*, 92–99. To me, actresses' popularity in breeches roles with female fans suggests women's enjoyment of their gender-defying conventions. Some argue that breeches roles acted primarily as a means for men to gape at women's legs, but since it was easy elsewhere to see them wearing less, this argument seems less persuasive to me; see Tracy Davis, "Questions for a Feminist Methodology in Theater History," in Thomas Postlewait and Bruce A. McConachie, eds., *Interpreting the Theatrical Past: Essays in the Historiography of Performance* (Iowa City: University of Iowa Press, 1989), 79.

28. Willis J. Abbot, "Famous Women of History," unsourced, Dec. 31, 1912, vol. 131, RLC, 150.

29. William Winter, "Great Actresses and Great Women: Charlotte Cushman," *Saturday Evening Post*, Sept. 29, 1906, vol. 131, RLC, 151.

30. Benjamin Brown French, *Witness to the Young Republic: A Yankees Journal, 1828–1870,* ed. Donald B. Cole and John J. McDonough (Hanover, NH: University Press of New England, 1989), 58.

31. Abbot, "Famous Women of History."

32. "Miss Cushman," *Spirit of the Times: The American Gentleman's Newspaper,* Feb. 26, 1876, vol. 131, RLC, 25.

33. *Reminiscences of the Life of the World-Renowned Charlotte Cushman, Compiled from Various Records by Mrs. Dr. Walker, Her Chosen Medium* (Boston: William P. Tenny, 1876), 49.

34. Carroll Smith-Rosenberg, "The New Woman as Social Androgyne: Social Disorder and Gender Crisis," in *Disorderly Conduct: Visions of Gender in Nineteenth Century America* (New York: Knopf, 1985), 245–296.

35. Merrill, *When Romeo Was a Woman,* 205–242.

36. John Coleman, *Fifty Years of an Actor's Life,* Vol. 1 (New York: Hames, Pott and Co., 1902), 363.

37. Julia Ward Howe to Charlotte Cushman, Sept. 20, 1857, quoted in Leach, *Bright Particular Star,* 278.

38. S.A.E. Walton to Charlotte Cushman, Nov. 2, 1874, quoted in Dudden, *Women in the American Theatre,* 77.

39. Figures cited in Nasaw, *Going Out,* 37. On women's entrance into vaudeville, see Kibler, *Rank Ladies.*

40. Hill, *Women in Gainful Occupations, 1870 to 1920,* 42.

41. Cott, *The Grounding of Modern Feminism,* 190–191.

42. On women's wage work, see Barbara Wertheimer, *We Were There* (New York: Pantheon Books, 1977), 95, 157. On actresses' wages, see Johnson, *American Actress,* 54–57. The beginning salary of a "ballet-girl" at midcentury was $3 to $4 dollars a week, doubling to $8 after one month; the typical factory wage averaged $1.50 a week.

43. According to the *New York Mirror Annual,* by the late nineteenth century, there were more women stars than men; the *Annual* listed 73 women (7.7% of total actresses) and 68 men (4.7 of total actors). Reprinted in McArthur, *Actors and American Culture,* 13–14. On actresses as theater managers, see Johnson, *American Actress,* 63–74; Dudden, *Women in the American Theatre,* 123–148.

44. Most have followed the reductive treatment of women's roles in this period by relying on a book that treated them only slightly: Grimsted's *Melodrama Unveiled.* On the greater variety of theatrical heroines after 1850, see Dudden, *Women in the American Theatre,* 70–78; Rosemarie K. Blank, "The Second Face of the Idol," in Helen Krich Chinoy and Linda Walsh Jenkins, eds., *Women in American Theatre* (New York: Crown Publishers, 1981); Martha Vicinus, "Helpless and Unfriended," in Judith L. Fisher and Stephen Watt, eds., *When They Weren't Doing Shakespeare* (Athens: University of Georgia Press, 1989); Gabrielle Hyslop, "Deviant and Dangerous Behavior," *Journal of Popular Culture* 19 (Winter 1985): 65–78.

45. Stephen Stanton, ed., *Camille and Other Plays* (New York: Hill & Wang, 1957). As Stanton notes, these plays downplayed moral lessons in favor of intense action and suspense.

46. Augustin Daly's *Under the Gaslight* (1867).

47. On the label, see the editorial *New York Herald,* Jan. 20, 1857, p. 4. On *Camille* as the "grand prototype for the whole sensational school of drama and acting," see Lawrence Hutton, *Plays and Players* (New York: Hurd & Houghton, 1875), 158.

48. Boardman, *The Oxford Companion to American Theatre,* 66–67, 213, 295. On the popularity of *Camille,* see Stanton, *Camille and Other Plays,* xxvi; Brandon, *Being Divine,* 236–244.

49. Duse quoted in Henry W. Knepler, *The Gilded Stage: The Lives and Careers of Four Great Actresses: Rachel Félix, Adelaide Ristori, Sarah Bernhardt and Eleanora Duse* (London: Constable, 1968), 183.

50. Roberts, *Disruptive Acts,* 165–219; Berlanstein, *Daughters of Eve,* 115–124.

51. Quoted in Dudden, *Women in the American Theatre,* 228n22.

52. Clayton Hamilton, "The Career of Camille," in *The Theory of the Theater* (New York: Henry Holt, 1910), 369–371.

53. *New York Herald,* April 21, 1857. Other critics delighted in how these "unconventional" heroines offended moralists; see Tice Miller, *Bohemians and Critics: American Theatre Criticism in the Nineteenth Century* (Metuchen, NJ: Scarecrow Press, 1981), 30–31, 60–62.

54. Quote is from Dorothy Schneider and Carl J. Schneider, *American Women in the Progressive Era, 1900–1920* (New York: Anchor, 1994), 16. See also Elizabeth Otto and Vanessa Rocco, eds., *The New Woman International: Representations in Photography and Film from the 1870s through the 1960s* (Ann Arbor: University of Michigan Press, 2011).

55. Einstein quoted in Rena Sanderson, "Gender and Modernity in Transnational Perspective: Hugo Munsterberg and the American Woman," *Prospects* (Jan. 1998): 285. Miriam Hansen, "Early Silent Cinema: Whose Public Sphere?" *New German Critique* 29 (Spring–Summer 1983): 153; Noel Carroll, "Film/Mind Analogies: The Case of Hugo Munsterberg," *Journal of Aesthetics and Art Criticism* 46 (Summer 1988): 489–499.

56. Butsch, *The Making of American Audiences,* 123; Hugo Munsterberg, *The Americans* (New York: McClure, Philips, 1904), 587.

57. Hugo Munsterberg, *American Traits* (Port Washington, NY: Kennikat Press, 1971 [1901]), 138–139, 160; Walter Prichard Eaton, "Women as Theater-Goers," *Woman's Home Companion* 37 (Oct. 1910): 79.

58. Clayton Hamilton, "Organizing the Audience," *Bookman* (Oct. 1911): 34.

59. See also Arthur Wang Pinero's *The Second Miss Tanqueray* (1893); *The Amazons* (1894).

60. On female variety stars, see Linda Mizejewski, *Ziegfeld Girls: Image and Icon in Culture and Cinema* (Durham, NC: Duke University Press, 1999). Janis introduced Pickford to her future husband Douglas Fairbanks; see Elsie Janis, *So Far, So Good!* (New York: E.P. Dutton & Co., 1932), 167, 340. Pickford got

the Gishes their break at Biograph; see Charles Affron, *Lillian Gish: Her Life, Her Legend* (New York: Scribner, 2001), 43–47.

61. Adela Rodgers St. Johns, *The Honeycomb* (Garden City, NY: Doubleday, 1969), 97. See also Louise Brooks and Ruth St. Denis's discussion of mothers, quoted in Barry Paris, *Louise Brooks: A Biography* (New York: Knopf, 1989), 37.

62. Charlie Chaplin, *My Autobiography* (New York: Simon & Schuster, 1964), 222. On the centrality of her salary and business renegotiations to her persona, see Mary Pickford Core Clipping File (hereinafter PCC), MHL; Higashi, "Million Dollar Mary," in *Virgins, Vamps, and Flappers.*

63. Mary Pickford, "The Best Known Girl in America: Mary Pickford Tells What It Is Like to Be a 'Movie' Actress," *Ladies' Home Journal* (Jan. 1915): 9, PCC, MHL. On the *Ladies' Home Journal,* see Roland Marchand, *Advertising the American Dream: Making Way for Modernity, 1920–1940* (Berkeley: University of California Press, 1986), 54, 112.

64. "Mary Pickford Wins! Her Letter to Our Readers," *Ladies' World* (April 1915): n.p., PCC, MHL. Pickford won with 1,147,550 votes out of 2,682,900, and was followed by Alice Joyce, Mary Fuller, Blanche Sweet, Clara Kimball Young, and Norma Phillips.

65. Estimate by economist John Commons, quoted in Alice Kessler-Harris, *Women Have Always Worked* (New York: Feminist Press, 1981), 63. Pickford, "The Best Known Girl in America," 9.

66. "Thanks to a Silly White Goose, Mary Is Back in Belasco Ranks Again," *New York American,* Jan. 1, 1913, r. 12, David Belasco Scrapbooks, Robinson Locke Collection, New York Public Library of the Performing Arts (hereinafter DBSB, RLC).

67. Pickford, *Sunshine and Shadow,* 55–56; Whitfield, *Pickford,* 36–53.

68. "Belasco's Latest Star a Success," *Philadelphia Press,* Dec. 24, 1907, r. 25, DBSB, RLC.

69. MPOH, 2676.

70. *Boston American* (untitled article), Sept. 20, 1908, r. 25, DBSB, RLC.

71. On the shift to naming players, see deCordova, *Picture Personalities,* ch. 1. On branding actors, see Catherine Kerr, "Incorporating the Star: The Intersection of Business and Aesthetic Strategies in Early American Film," *Business History Review* 68.3 (1990): 383–410.

72. Much has been written on Laemmle's promotion. Here I rely on deCordova, *Picture Personalities,* 55–64.

73. "The Maude Adams of the Moving Picture Show," *Toledo News Bee,* Mar. 30, 1910, env. 1125, Florence Lawrence Collection, Robinson Locke Collection, New York Public Library of the Performing Arts (hereinafter FLC, RLC).

74. E. W. Dustin to Florence Lawrence, Mar. 7, 1910; Betty Melnick to Florence Lawrence, April 9, 1910, both in Lawrence Collection, MHL.

75. Hilary A. Hallett, "Based on a True Story: New Western Women and the Birth of Hollywood," *Pacific Historical Review* (May 2011): 176–187.

76. *Daniel Boone; or, Pioneer days in America* (Edison, 1906), Museum of Modern Art, New York City (hereinafter MOMA). Like most films from the

silent era, the vast majority of the shorts in which Lawrence played a leading role between 1908 and 1914 are lost, complicating claims about their content and character. Yet film synopses, critical reaction, and what celluloid remains make some generalizations possible. The filmography of Lawrence's biographer includes 175 films in which she played a leading role; see Kelly Brown, *Florence Lawrence* (Jefferson, NC: McFarland, 1999), 159–180. According to the FIAF's International Index to Film Periodicals, Treasures from Film Archives, Lawrence appears in 103 films still in existence. Of these, all but 10 were made at Biograph, and many of these feature Lawrence in small parts. By "mythology" I mean a metaphorical guide to a society's values that suggests how a culture frames and answers key questions and contradictions. Myths depict an imagined past while structuring an equally imagined present and future. The literature on western mythology is immense; my approach follows Fred Erisman, "The Enduring Myth and the Modern West," in Gerald Nash and Richard Etulain, eds., *Researching Western History: Topics in the Twentieth Century* (Albuquerque: University of New Mexico Press, 1997), 167–186; Robert Hine and John Mack Faragher, *The American West: A New Interpretative History* (New Haven: Yale University Press, 2000), 472–511; William Cronon, "Turner's First Stand," in Richard W. Etulain, ed., *Writing Western History: Essays on Major Western Historians* (Albuquerque: University of New Mexico Press, 1991), 73–102; Ann Fabian, "History for the Masses," in William Cronon, George Miles, and Jay Gitlin, eds., *Under an Open Sky: Rethinking America's Western Past* (New York: W.W. Norton, 1992), 223–238.

77. *The Dispatch Bearer* (Vitagraph, 1907), MOMA. Florence Lawrence, with Monte Katterjohn, "Growing Up with the Movies, Part II," *Photoplay* (Dec. 1914), Florence Lawrence, env. 1125, FLC, RLC.

78. *The Girl and the Outlaw* (Vitagraph, 1908), MOMA. Florence Lawrence, with Monte Katterjohn, "Growing Up with the Movies, Part III," *Photoplay* (Jan. 1915): 99, env. 1125, FLC, RLC.

79. On these films, see Brown, *Florence Lawrence*, 28–29, 154–157, 166–169.

80. "Florence Lawrence," unsourced, n.d., env. 1125; "Miss Florence Lawrence of the Lubin Company" (she was at Lubin in 1911); "A Film Favorite Who Is Also an Inventor," *Green Book Magazine* (May 1914): 841, env. 1125, all in FLC, RLC.

81. Florence Lawrence, with Monte Katterjohn, "Growing Up with the Movies," part 1, *Photoplay* (Nov. 1914): 36–38, env. 1125, FLC, RLC.

82. Mead, "'Let the Women Get Their Wages as Men Do,'"; Mead, *How the Vote Was Won*. On the suffrage movement's use of actresses as glamorous front women, see Albert Auster, *Actresses and Suffragists: Women in the American Theater, 1890–1920* (New York: Praeger, 1984); Ellen Carol DuBois, *Harriet Stanton Blatch and the Winning of Woman Suffrage* (New Haven: Yale University Press, 1997); Margaret Finnegan, *Selling Suffrage: Consumer Culture and Votes for Women* (New York: Columbia University Press, 1999).

83. "Miss Florence Lawrence of the Lubin Company"; Gladys Roosevelt, "Miss Florence Lawrence of the Victor Film Company," *Motion Picture Magazine* (Oct. 1913): n.p., both in env. 1125, FLC, RLC.

84. "Maude Adams," *Toledo News*; "Florence Lawrence," *Cleveland Press*, Feb. 16, 1914, env. 1128, FLC, RLC.

85. Phyllis Robbins, *Maude Adams: An Intimate Biography* (New York: Putnam, 1956).

86. Charles Musser, "Pre-classical American Cinema: Its Changing Modes of Production," in Richard Abel, ed., *Silent Film* (New Brunswick, NJ: Rutgers University Press, 1996), 85–108.

87. *The Little Rebel* (1911, Lubin), MOMA. Lawrence made forty-eight films at Lubin in 1911; three others remain: *The Cook* (George Eastman House, Rochester); *Her Child's Hour* (Filmmuseum, Amsterdam); *The Two Fathers* (British Film Institute, London).

88. Brown, *Florence Lawrence*, 74–75.

89. Lotta Lawrence quoted in Florence Lawrence with Monte Katterjohn, "Growing Up with the Movies," 38, FLC, RLC. On Lawrence's move to Victor, see Brown, *Florence Lawrence*, 77–79, 80–84, 89–90.

90. *Flo's Discipline* (Victor, 1912), one of two Victor films that remains (Library of Congress). More than one-third of her films involved such roles during her Lubin years (8 of 48) and Victor years (8 of 45), including actresses foremost. By contrast, only 3 of the 77 films at Biograph involved such roles; see filmography in Brown, *Florence Lawrence*, 159–180.

91. "Maude Adams," *Toledo News*; "Florence Lawrence," *Cleveland Press*.

92. Balio, "Stars in Business," 156–157. *Sweet Memories* (IMP, 1911); *In Old Madrid* (IMP, 1911); *Mary Pickford Collection of Early Silent Short Subjects* (Hollywood's Attic, 1996).

93. On how the more naturalistic acting techniques common on stage made their way to the screen, see Bowser, *The Transformation of Cinema*, 87–97.

94. Jane Addams, *The Spirit of Youth and the City Streets* (New York: Macmillan Company, 1909), 5.

95. Pickford, *Sunshine and Shadow*, 73. Pickford recalled that "I would not run around like a goose with its head off, crying 'oooooh . . . the little birds! Ooooh . . . look! A little bunny!' That's what he [Griffith] taught all his ingenues, and they all did the same thing"; quoted in Brownlow, *Mary Pickford Rediscovered*, 67. On how Biograph rigorously imposed anonymity on players while using their real names as character names, see Kerr, "Incorporating the Star," 397–399.

96. "The Biograph Girl," *New York Morning Telegram*, Dec. 21, 1912, n.p.; "The Maude Adams of the 'Movies,'" *Theatre Magazine* (June 1913): n.p.; New Belasco Star," *New York Press*, Jan. 5, 1913, r. 12; Stuart Clyde, "Out of a Picture to Fame," *The World Magazine*, Dec. 22, 1912, n.p.; "Belasco Contract Christmas Present to this 'Movies Heroine,'" *Worchester Massachusetts Gazette*, Dec. 12, 1912, r. 12, all, DBSB, RLC.

97. Mary Jean Corbett, *Representing Femininity* (New York: Oxford University Press, 1992); Bernard Shaw, *Pygmalion*, ed. L.W. Conolly (London: Methuen Drama, 2008), introduction.

98. "The Gelatine Juliet," *The North American*, Jan. 12, 1912, r. 12; "This 'Maude Adams of the Movies' Says," *New York American*, Jan. 20, 1913, vol. 386, both in DBSB, RLC.

99. "Miss Pickford Likes Things Baltimorean," Dec 13, 1913, unsourced clipping, r. 12, DBSB, RLC.

100. Gertrude Price, "Daddy of the Family," n.d., unsourced, r. 12; "Maude Adams," *Theatre Magazine,* June 1913, DBSB, RLC. On the strategy of using women writers to appeal to other women, see Virginia Morris, "Women in Publicity," in Charles Reed Jones, ed., *Breaking into the Movies* (New York: Unicorn Press, 1927), 204–205.

101. "Alan Dale Has a Chat with Mary Pickford," *Pittsburgh Leader,* Dec. 27, 1914, 102, vol. 141, RLC. Mary Pickford, "My Own Story," *Ladies' Home Journal* (July 1913): r. 14, DBSB, RLC. Richard C. Wallace, "Little Mary and Her Husband," *Motion Picture Album* 1.10 (March 1913): 5–8, vol. 386, RLC. "Miss Pickford Likes," unsourced clipping; "New Belasco Star Presented Wednesday Night," *New York Press,* Jan. 5, 1913, r. 12, DBSB, RLC.

102. Pickford, "My Own Story."

103. On her continued struggles with Griffith, see Pickford, *Sunshine and Shadow,* 88–91.

104. See William de Mille, *Hollywood Saga* (New York: E. P. Dutton & Co., 1939); Hampton, *History of the American Film Industry,* 153–154.

105. Will Irwin, *The House That Shadows Built* (Garden City, NY: Doubleday, Doran, & Co., 1928), 151. On Zukor's exhibition of the European features through the road show method, in which patrons were charged $.75 to $2.00, see Tino Balio, "Struggles for Control," in Balio, *The American Film Industry,* 109–113. On how more expensive features became standard by 1915, see Bowser, *The Transformation of Cinema,* 192, 212–215.

106. "Miss Pickford Likes Things Baltimorean."

107. Zukor, *The Public Is Never Wrong,* 59, 71, 93–95, 98; Pickford, *Sunshine and Shadow,* 97. See also Daniel Frohman, *Daniel Frohman Presents* (New York: Claude Kendall & Willoughby Sharp, 1935), 248, 249, 275. Frohman credits Pickford's salary, not Bernhardt, with sparking Charles's interest in the movies.

108. On these films, see Whitfield, *Pickford,* 123–143.

109. Carolyn Heilbrun, *Writing a Woman's Life* (New York: W. W. Norton, 1988), 48.

110. *Tess of the Storm Country* (Famous Players, 1914), Library of Congress.

111. *Moving Picture World,* n.d., MPCC, MHL.

112. Tibbetts, "*Mary Pickford* and the American '*Growing Girl,*'" 50–62; Lynne Vallone, *Disciplines of Virtue* (New Haven: Yale University Press, 1995). Readers' responses might reflect the "liberatory" approach discussed in Angela Hubler, "Can Ann Shirley Help 'Revive Ophelia'?" in Sherrie Inness, ed., *Delinquents and Debutantes* (New York: Columbia University Press, 1998), 270–272. On Marion's career, see Beauchamp, *Without Lying Down.*

113. Pickford remained a child or adolescent only in *The Poor Little Rich Girl* (Artcraft, 1917), *Rebecca of Sunnybrook Farm* (Artcraft, 1917), and *The Little Princess* (Artcraft 1917).

114. Zukor, *The Public Is Never Wrong,* 4, 102. Although he downplays how controlling the star system figured in Zukor's calculations, the best summary of

this remains, Sklar, *Movie-Made America,* ch. 9. On the stylistic and industrial norms associated with "Classical Hollywood," see Bordwell, Staiger, and Thompson, *The Classical Hollywood Cinema,* 121–122.

115. Balio, "Stars in Business," 158; De Mille, *Hollywood Saga,* 146.

116. Hampton, *History of the American Film Industry,* 156–159. Hampton sought to sign Pickford for the American Tobacco Company so as to control a merger between First National, VLSE, and Famous Players; see Balio, "Stars in Business," 159–160.

117. For an account that portrays Zukor as the chief stalwart supporting the star system against a rising "anti-star faction," including Griffith, Sennett, and Ince's Triangle Productions, see Alfred A. Cohn, "'Stars or No Stars'—That *Is* the Question," *Photoplay* (Jan. 1918): 95–96. On the point more generally, see Balio, "Struggles for Control," 110–115; Bordwell, Staiger, and Thompson, *The Classical Hollywood Cinema,* 98–99.

118. Hampton, *History of the American Film Industry,* 162, 174. Lasky Feature Play Company was an independent committed to producing feature-length films that used Paramount to distribute. See also Ramsaye, *A Million and One Nights,* 744–750.

119. Correspondence between Lasky and DeMille reveals a slightly different chronology than the one customarily described, indicating that Lasky Features became the partner of Famous on a fifty-fifty basis in the Mary Pickford contract of June 1916, but did not merge with FPL until June 1917. See letters between Jesse Lasky and Cecil DeMille, in Cherchi and Codelli, *The DeMille Legacy,* 366, 383–385, 405–406.

120. See Balio, "Stars in Business," 159–160. Louella Parsons, "How Mary Pickford Makes Good as a Businesswoman," *Columbus Dispatch,* Dec. 10, 1916; "Mary Pickford to Be Independent," *New York Telegraph,* Mar. 26, 1916, vol. 387, RLC; "Mary Pickford Tells Her Own Story," *Toledo News Bee,* Mar. 22, 1915; "Ambitions and Other Vices, by Mary Pickford," *Green Book Magazine,* n.d., all Mary Pickford, vol. 386, RLC.

121. *Photoplay* (May 1917): 121. On the loyalty of Pickford's female fans, see Adela Rogers St. Johns, "Why Does the World Love Mary?" *Photoplay* (Dec. 1921): 108–111. See also the letters between Zukor, DeMille, and Lasky, in Cherchi and Codelli, *The DeMille Legacy,* 489–491.

122. Lenore Coffee, *Storyline: Reflections of a Hollywood Screenwriter* (London: Cassell, 1973), 45 (italics in the original). Actress Clara Kimball Young gave Coffee her break writing in 1919.

123. This is a general impression of mine but is not meant to suggest men were ignored. For a list of leading ladies in 1923, see Koszarski, *An Evening's Entertainment,* 116.

124. Pickford, *Sunshine and Shadow,* 99.

125. "Belasco Contract Christmas Present." Pickford, "Best Known Girl in America," 9. On her athleticism, see also Lindsay, *The Art of the Moving Picture,* 3.

126. *What Happened to Mary* (Edison, 1912). On the focus on danger, see Jennifer Bean, "Technologies of Gender and the Extraordinary Body," in Bean and Negra, *A Feminist Reader in Early Cinema,* 404–443.

127. Edna Vercoe ("EV") to Floss Schreiber, Dec. [?], 1914, file 4, vol. 2, box 1, fan scrapbooks compiled by Edna G. Vercoe (hereafter VC), MHL; "Mary Fuller a Real Heroine," n.p., n.d., file 7, scrapbook 3, box 1, VC, MHL.

128. N.d., p. 89, file 1, scrapbook 1, box 1, VC, MHL.

129. Singer, *Melodramas and Modernity,* 224, 255.

130. Richard Slotkin, *Gunfighter Nation: The Myth of the Frontier in Twentieth Century America* (New York: Atheneum, 1992), 11. Andrew B. Smith, *Shooting Cowboys and Indians: Silent Western Films, American Culture, and the Birth of Hollywood* (Boulder: University Press of Colorado, 2003); Richard Abel, *Americanizing the Movies and "Movie-Mad" Audiences* (Berkeley: University of California Press, 2006), ch. 4.

131. *The Hazards of Helen* (Kalem, 1914–1917). Series titles viewed on Yesteryear Video include No. 82, *Leap from the Water Tower;* No. 62, *Pay Train;* No. 60, *In Danger's Path;* and No. 63, *The Open Track.* Miriam Hansen, "The Mass Production of the Senses," in Linda Williams and Christine Gledhill, eds., *Reinventing Film Studies* (London: Arnold, 2000), 332–350.

132. On Holmes's persona, see file 7, scrapbook 3, box 1, VC, MHL; Holmes Core Clippings, MHL (hereinafter HCC, MHL); Helen Holmes Clippings, Robinson Locke Collection, New York Public Library for the Performing Arts (hereinafter HHC, RLC).

133. "Action Is the Spice of Life," *New York Telegraph,* Nov. 21, 1915, env. 737, vol. 1, HHC, RLC.

134. "A Charming Dare-Devil," *Pictures and the Picture-Goer,* Mar. 13, 1915, env. 737, vol. 1, HHC, RLC; George Craig, "When Helen Rented a Baby," n.p., n.d., file 7, scrapbook 3, box 1, VC, MHL.

135. "Ruth Roland Rides Again," n.d., Roland's Core Clippings (hereinafter RCC), MHL. On Roland's persona, see also Roland's Files, RLC. On western fans, see Smith, *Shooting Cowboys and Indians,* ch. 7.

136. Frank V. Bruner, "The Modern Dime Novel," *Photoplay* (June 1919): 118.

137. *The Red Circle* (Balboa, 1915). Roland's next seven films with Pathé were *Hands Up* (1918), *The Tiger's Trail* (1919), *The Adventures of Ruth* (1919), *Ruth of the Rockies* (1920), *The Avenging Arrow* (1921), *White Eagle* (1922), *The Timber Queen* (1922), and *Ruth of the Range* (1923).

138. *Shenbao,* May 2, 1921, quoted in, Weihong Bao, "From Pearl White to White Rose Woo," *Camera Obscura* 20.3 (2005): 200. "Blue Book of the Screen 1923," RCC, MHL.

139. I viewed the surviving chapters of *The Perils of Pauline* (Pathé, 1914) on Grapevine Video.

140. "A Model of the 'Movies,'" n.d., p. 52, file 1, scrapbook 1, box 1, VC, MHL. White's autobiography also emphasized this composite persona; see Pearl White, *Just Me* (New York: Georg H. Doran Co., 1919).

141. "Great Cast Contest," n.d., n.p., file 1, scrapbook 1, box 1, VC, MHL; Johnson, "The Girl on the Cover," 58.

142. "The Real Perils of Pauline," *Photoplay,* n.p., n.d., file 7, scrapbook 3, box 1, VC, MHL. "Pathe Star's Humble Start," n.d., pp. 6–7; "Pearl White," n.d., p. 10, both in file 13, scrapbook 6, box 2, VC, MHL.

143. "Oh for a girl": "The Motion Picture Autobiographies," Case 6; "my idol": ibid., case 7, both comp. Herbert Blumer, in Jowett, Jarvie, and Fuller-Seeley, *Children and the Movies,* 263, 267.

144. So said the University of Chicago's Payne Film Study (PFS), conducted between 1928 and 1932. For the best-selling version, see Henry James Forman, *Our Movie Made Children* (New York: Macmillan, 1933). On the study's politics, see Jowett, Jarvie, and Fuller-Seeley, *Children and the Movies,* 1–14. See also Robert S. Lynd and Helen Merrell Lynd, *Middletown: A Study in Modern American Culture* (San Diego: Harcourt, Brace, and World, 1929), 242–267; Fred Greenstein, "New Light on Changing Values," *Social Forces* 42 (1964): 441–450.

145. "The Motion Picture Autobiographies," Case 9, comp. Herbert Blumer, in Jowett, Jarvie, and Fuller-Seeley, *Children and the Movies,* 275–276.

146. 'Serialitis,' *Moving Picture World,* Feb. 10, 1917, p. 818. Elizabeth Cowie, *Representing the Woman: Cinema and Psychoanalysis* (Minneapolis: University of Minnesota Press, 1997), 72–121.

147. "The Motion Picture Autobiographies," Case 1, comp. Herbert Blumer, in Jowett, Jarvie, and Fuller-Seeley, *Children and the Movies,* 245, 242–243.

148. "The Motion Picture Autobiographies," Case 7, comp. Herbert Blumer, in ibid., 267–269.

149. *Sex* (Parker Read Productions, 1920), Library of Congress. On Glaum, see Hebert Howe, "Vampire or Ingénue?" *Photoplay* (Aug. 1919): 34–35. *A Fool There Was* (Fox, 1915).

150. "A Fool There Was," *New York Dramatic Mirror,* Jan. 20, 1915, p. 21. The film established Bara's star and set the formula for her performances in all but 6 of her 39 films at Fox. On the type, see Staiger, *Bad Women,* 147–152.

151. On the rigorous typing of Bara's performances at Fox and the end of her career in 1919, see Robert Genini, *Theda Bara: A Biography of the Silent Screen Vamp, with a Filmography* (Jefferson, NC: McFarland, 1996).

152. On the promotion of Bara, see Wallace Franklin, "Purgatory's Ivory Angel," *Photoplay* (Sept. 1915): 69–72; Roberta Courtland, "The Divine Theda," *Motion Picture* (April 1917): 59–62. See also Theda Bara Scrapbook, RLC. Randolph Bartlett, "Petrova—Prophetess," *Photoplay* (Dec. 1917): 27. Petrova is quoted as saying, "I am feminist." See also "We Take Our Hats Off to—Olga Petrova," *Photoplay* (Feb. 1921): 34. *New York Dramatic Mirror,* June 23, 1917, p. 21, box 5, Alfred Smith Collection, Charles Young Library, University of California, Los Angeles.

153. Bara quoted in May, *Screening Out the Past,* 106.

154. "Six-gun": "Lady Gunmen," *Photoplay* (Jan. 1918): 91. Ellis Paxson Oberholtzer, "Melodrama, Serials, and 'Comics,'" in *The Morals of the Movie* (Philadelphia: Penn Publishing Company, 1922), 55, 60. See also ibid., chs. 3 and 5.

155. "Lady Gunmen," 91.

156. Coffee, *Storyline,* 23. See, for instance, Sennett, *King of Comedy,* 45.

157. "The Romance of Making the 'Movies.'"; Johnston, "In Motion-Picture Land." "The Romance," *Literary Digest,* 902; Johnston, "In Motion-Picture Land," 443.

158. Johnson, "The Girl on the Cover," 57–58.

159. Hughes, *Souls for Sale,* 403. For other celebrations of women in the movie colony, see Turnbull, *The Close-Up*; Bower, *The Quirt*; Webster, *Real Life*; Hughes, *Souls for Sale*; Vance, *Linda Lee Inc.*; Wilson, *Merton of the Movies.* Negative tales include Putnam, *Laughter Limited*; Burroughs, *The Girl from Hollywood.*

CHAPTER 2. WOMEN-MADE WOMEN

Epigraph, page 69: Zukor, *The Public Is Never Wrong,* 4.

1. By 1920, the six leading fan magazine cost between 5 and 25 cents and had circulations of almost half a million each. Tino Balio, *Grand Designs: Hollywood as a Modern Business Enterprise, 1930–1939* (Berkeley: University of California Press, 1993), 170. On the cultural shifts associated with the rise of consumer-oriented capitalism, see William Leach, *Land of Desire: Merchants, Power, and the Rise of a New American Culture* (New York: Pantheon, 1993); Marchand, *Advertising the American Dream,* ch. 3; T.J. Jackson Lears, "From Salvation to Self-Realization," in Richard Wightman Fox and Lears, eds., *The Culture of Consumption: Critical Essays in American History, 1880–1980* (New York: Pantheon, 1983); Jennifer Scanlon, *Inarticulate Longings:* The Ladies' Home Journal, *Gender, and the Promise of Consumer Culture* (New York: Routledge, 1995); Ellen Gruber Garvey, *The Adman in the Parlor: Magazines and the Gendering of Consumer Culture* (New York: Oxford University Press, 1996).

2. Iris Barry, *The Public's Pleasure,* quoted in Antonia Lant, ed., with Ingrid Periz, *Red Velvet Seat: Women's Writing on the First Fifty Years of Cinema* (London: Verso, 2006), 128. "Woman's woman," Mary Pickford Scrapbook, RLC. "Sex achieve": Pickford, Mar. 5, 1915, quoted in May, *Screening Out the Past,* 119. "The Romance of Making the 'Movies,'" *Literary Digest* (Oct. 23, 1915): 902–903; Johnston, "In Motion-Picture Land.". Lauren Berlant, *The Female Complaint: The Unfinished Business of American Sentimentality* (Durham, NC: Duke University Press, 2008), 5-13.

3. I distinguish between trade papers aimed at those with a commercial stake in films and press aimed at fans. Trade papers existed from the start, but periodicals for fans focused on celebrities developed only in the mid-1910s. See Marsha Orgeron, "Making It in Hollywood: Clara Bow, Fandom, and Consumer Culture," *Cinema Journal* 42.4 (Summer 2003): 76–97; Richard Abel, "Fan Discourse in the Heartland," *Film History* 19 (2006): 140–153; Studlar, "The Perils of Pleasure?"; Fuller, *At the Picture Show,* ch. 8. Women wrote more than two out of three stories with bylines in *Photoplay* in these years.

I base my arguments about Hollywood's publicity and mainstream reactions on the following sources: Everything between 1915 and 1922 included in Parsons Scrapbook, MHL. The Parsons collection contains professionally compiled press scrapbooks that pasted together the majority of what she wrote. The content of *Photoplay* between 1915 and 1922; a national publication with a circulation of two million, it was the largest of all fan magazines. Finally, I used the periodical database at the MHL to read all the stories indicated by keyword searches on "extras," "contests," "how to become an actress," "Hollywood," and "marriage and divorce" in these same years. For mainstream reporting, I read all relevant articles indexed on "motion pictures" in *The Readers' Guide to Periodical to Literature,* as well as those produced by keyword searches on "extras," "motion picture actors," "motion picture stars," and "Hollywood" in *ProQuest: Historical Newspapers.*

4. *Toledo News-Bee,* Mar. 3, 1914, quoted in Abel, *Americanizing the Movies,* 247. Beginning in 1912, Price was the "moving picture expert" for the Scripps-McRae newspapers that targeted working-class women, see Gerald Baldasty, *E. W. Scripps and the Business of Newspapers* (Urbana: University of Illinois Press, 1999).

5. Virginia Morris, "Women in Publicity," in Jones, *Breaking into the Movies,* 204–205.

6. See Abel, "Fan Discourse in the Heartland," 146–147. Few reliable statistics exist, but most agree that the industry focused on attracting women after 1910. Again, my interest lies with this shared perception, not a particular statistic; see introduction, note 17.

7. *Photoplay,* Nov. 1924, quoted in Studlar, "Perils of Pleasure?" 7. "The Lonely Girl," *Photoplay* (Aug. 1919): 27; "To a Young Girl," *Photoplay* (Feb. 1919): 23.

8. Norman Anthony, "Movie Fanatics," *Photoplay* (June 1921): 40.

9. For my use of the terms "myth" and "mythology," see chapter 1, note 76.

10. Janet Flanner, "The Male Background," *Photoplay* (Dec. 1920): 33. Sydney Valentine, "The Careers of Catherine Calvert," *Photoplay* (May 1921): 62, 90.

11. The periodical index of fan magazines at the MHL lists 120 articles on contests between 1912 and 1922. These virtually disappear after 1930. For the best description of this process, see Stamp, *Movie-Struck Girls,* 10–40.

12. George Eells, *Hedda and Louella* (New York: Warner, 1973). Eells first disputed the idea that Parsons's success was due only to her association with William Randolph Hearst. See also Barbas, *First Lady of Hollywood.*

13. On Parsons's childhood, see Barbas, *First Lady of Hollywood,* ch. 1.

14. On these proscriptions, see Cott, *The Grounding of Modern Feminism,* ch. 6; and Barbara Miller Solomon, *In the Company of Educated Women* (New Haven: Yale University Press, 1985).

15. See Francke, *Script Girls,* ch. 1. On the culture of screenwriting, see Beauchamp, *Without Lying Down;* Holliday, "Hollywood's Modern Women."

16. Louella O. Parsons, *How to Write for the Movies* (Chicago: A. C. McClurg, 1915). The book was successful enough to be revised and reprinted in 1917. Barbas, *First Lady of Hollywood,* 40; Louella Parsons, *The Gay Illiterate* (Garden City, NY: Doubleday, Doran, and Co., 1944), 29.

17. May, *Screening Out the Past,* ch. 8.

18. After 1924, advertisers called this group "the Colonel's lady and Judy O'Grady"; see Marchand, *Advertising the American Dream,* 65. The first example that I found is Dorothy Philips (Mrs. Allen Holubar), "How to Hold Him," *Photoplay* (Nov. 1920): 47.

19. Quoted in Marchand, *Advertising the American Dream*, 67.

20. N.d., Parsons Scrapbook no. 1, MHL. The series ran on Sundays for several months in 1915. On the "expert" strategy, see Marchand, *Advertising the American Dream*, 35–37.

21. My use here of the word "personal" is strategic. Following Janice A. Radway, in *A Feeling for Books: The Book-of-the-Month Club, Literary Taste, and Middle-Class Desire* (Chapel Hill: University of North Carolina Press, 1997), 282–6, 484, I employ the concept of personalism to stress a different aspect of what this literature may have offered female fans. Radway uses "personalism" to emphasize the affective, emotional, and empathetic aspects of individualism, rather than viewing it as a purely economic and highly intellectualized concept.

22. N.d., Parsons Scrapbook 1, MHL.

23. "How to Become a Movie Actress," Sept. 15, 1915, Parsons Scrapbook no. 1, MHL (italics in the original).

24. Caption under Norma Talmadge's photograph, in "In and Out of Focus: Norma Talmadge."

25. "How to Become a Movie Star," Oct. 5, 1915, Parsons Scrapbook no. 1, MHL. Colleen Moore, *Silent Star* (Garden City, NY: Doubleday, 1968), 27, 73. The quintessential flapper, Moore describes studying such interviews in her Florida home. Mary Astor also describes how a "Fame and Fortune" contest whetted her appetite to become an actress in small-town Illinois. Astor recalled: "I was being propagandized and didn't know it." Mary Astor, *Mary Astor: A Life on Film* (New York: Delacorte Press, 1967), 2, 4–6. Parsons mentions boys as possible aspirants only once.

26. On stories for boys, see Rodgers, *The Work Ethic in Industrial America*, ch. 5. On the gendering of traditional cultures of chance, see Lears, *Something for Nothing*.

27. "How to Become a Movie Actress," Sept. 22, 1915; "How to Become a Movie Star," Sept. 29, 1915; "How to Become a Movie Star," Oct. 5, 1915, Parsons Scrapbook 1, MHL.

28. Rodgers, *The Work Ethic in Industrial America*, 141.

29. "How to Become a Movie Actress: How Can You Win Entrance to the Enchanted Palace of Your Dreams—the Motion Picture Studio? There Are Several Paths That You May Follow and in Today's Article You Are Told Which Are Best," n.d., Parsons Scrapbook no. 1, MHL. On *Birth of a Nation*, see Thomas Cripps, *Slow Fade to Black* (New York: Oxford University Press, 1989), 41–59.

30. "How to Become a Movie Star; One of the Best Known Producers Places Little Value upon Stage Training and Contends That the Best Asset for Success Is Inability to Become Discouraged," n.d.; "How to Become a Movie Star," Oct. 31, 1915, both in Parsons Scrapbook no. 1, MHL.

31. N.d., Parsons Scrapbook no. 1, MHL.

32. "In and Out of Focus: Norma Talmadge," Feb. 2, 1919.

33. "Here's the Ideal Film Personality—Clara Kimball Young Is Playful Child and Brainy Woman," n.d., Parsons Scrapbook no. 1, MHL.

34. On modernity, see Marshall Berman, *All That Is Solid Melts into Air* (New York: Penguin, 1982).

35. Cohn, "'Stars or No Star'—That *Is* the Question." It notes that Griffith, Mack Sennett, and Thomas Ince battled against the star system. On DeMille's fight for directorial authority, see De Mille, *Autobiography*, 180–181. "Player centered institution": Glenn, *Female Spectacle*, 217.

36. The two earliest American film historians make the point about directors' lack of box office draw. See Ramsaye, *A Million and One Nights*, 499–507; Hampton, *A History of the American Film Industry*, 86–92, 140–142, 193–195. The auteur theory of cinema shaped how scholars learned to think about film. Concerned with elevating the status of movies, the theory emerged from New Wave cinema movements and the professionalization of film studies. The most recent generation of scholars has emphasized historical reception and production.

37. de Mille, *Hollywood Saga*, 233. See Cohn, "'Stars or No Star'—That *Is* the Question," 95–101; James Quirk, "Star Dust," *Photoplay* (June 1918): 18–20; Frank Woods, "Why Is a Star?" *Photoplay* (Oct. 1919): 70–73, 117–118. Fan magazines' focus on stories about stars also bore this out.

38. Harold Wendt, "A Trifle Long but Worth It," *Exhibitors Herald*, July 9, 1921, p. 70.

39. N.d., Parsons Scrapbook no. 1, MHL. A concert pianist, Weber was from a religious middle-class family and worked for the Church Army Workers before she entered the stage after her father's death. *The Jew's Christmas* (1913), an attack on ethnic and religious intolerance, gained her public attention. Weber later directed two controversial films on birth control, *Where Are My Children* (1916) and *The Hand That Rocks the Cradle* (1917). On Weber's career, see Shelley Stamp, "Presenting the Smalleys," *Film History* 18.2 (2006): 119–128; Mahar, *Women Filmmakers in Early Hollywood*.

40. Catherine Filene, ed., *Careers for Women* (Boston: Houghton Mifflin, 1920); *New York Times*, Dec. 16, 1920. The edition published in 1934 dropped directing.

41. N.d., Parsons Scrapbook no. 1, MHL.

42. Carl Laemmle created Universal in 1912 by merging IMP with several other companies. On Universal's promotion of women, see Slide, *The Silent Feminists*, ch. 4; Mark Garrett Cooper, *Universal Women: Filmmaking and Institutional Change in Early Hollywood* (Urbana: University of Illinois Press, 2010), 1–90. *Universal Weekly*, Dec. 1913, quoted in ibid., 8. On the studio's election, see ibid., 51–52.

43. "Chameleon City of the Cinema," *The Strand Magazine*, quoted in *Washington Post*, June 20, 1915.

44. Johnston, "In Motion-Picture Land," 441, 440.

45. "How One 'Extra Girl' Climbed to Stardom," n.d., Parsons Scrapbook no. 1, MHL.

46. Cooper, *Universal Women*, 113, 166.

47. Alfred A. Cohn, "What Every Girl Wants to Know," *Photoplay* (June 1919): 28–29. This article was the most discouraging piece that I read, through 1922, on hopefuls' chances for success.

48. For her story of a "fatherless" upbringing, see Parsons, *Gay Illiterate*, 10–11. Parsons claimed she was born in 1893, but the real date was August 6, 1881; Eells, *Hedda and Louella*, 28. "This prejudice": Parsons, *Gay Illiterate*, 12.

49. United States Department of Agriculture, *Social and Labor Needs of Farm Women*, 4. See also United States Department of Agriculture, *Domestic Needs of Farm Women*, 4. On the rural problem, see Hempstead, "Agricultural Change and the Rural Problem"; Bowers, *The Country Life Movement in America*.

50. United States Department of Agriculture, *Social and Labor Needs of Farm Women*, 11–12.

51. Frances Donovan, *The Woman Who Waits* (New York: Arno Press, 1974 [1920]), 9. Donovan found that waitresses spent most of their leisure time at the movies, in cabarets, or in restaurants. Carl Van Doren, "The Revolt from the Village: 1920," *The Nation* 113 (1921): 407–412. For a recent critic who notes the prevalence of such female protagonists, see Carl Smith, *Chicago and the Literary Imagination* (Chicago: University of Chicago Press, 1984), 40–56. Major works about such characters include Theodore Dreiser, *Sister Carrie*, ed. Neda M. Westlake et al. (Philadelphia: University of Pennsylvania Press, 1981 [1900]); Edna Ferber, *Dawn O'Hara, the Girl Who Laughed* (Charleston, SC: BiblioBazaar: 2006 [1911]); Mary Austin, *A Woman of Genius* (New York: Feminist Press, 1985 [1912]); Willa Cather, *The Song of the Lark* (Boston: Houghton Mifflin, 1988 [1915]); Zona Gale, *Miss Lulu Bett* (New York: D. Appleton & Co., 1920); Sinclair Lewis, *Main Street* (New York: Bantam, 1996 [1920]).

52. Hine and Faragher, *American West*, 418.

53. See Louella Parsons, "Propaganda!" *Photoplay* (Sept. 1918): 43–45, 115.

54. Eells, *Hedda and Louella*, 44; Jerry Hoffman quoted, 88.

55. *Picture-Goer* quoted in Eells, *Hedda and Louella*, 89. Petrova starred in 26 films between 1914 and 1918, 4 under Blache's direction. Not satisfied with playing just vamps, she formed Petrova Pictures in 1917 "to play strong women.... I am a feminist," she explained to Randolph Bartlett in "Petrova—Prophetess," 27. See also Fredrick Smith, "Petrova and Her Philosophy of Life," *Photoplay* (Oct. 1916): 56–58; Anthony Slide, *Silent Players* (Lexington: University of Kentucky Press, 2002); Olga Petrova, *Butter with My Bread* (Indianapolis: Bobbs-Merrill, 1942).

56. Nasaw, *The Chief*, 53.

57. E. W. Scripps quoted in Alfred M. Lee, *The Daily Newspaper in America* (New York: Macmillan, 1937), 10. Between 1850 and 1880, circulation increased along with the urban population; between 1880 and 1930, it grew faster. The degree of control depended on the chain. See ibid., 64, 70–71.

58. Brooks, *The Melodramatic Imagination*, xiii. See discussion in chapter 1, note 14.

59. Quoted in J. K. Winkler, *W. R. Hearst, An American Phenomenon* (New York: Simon and Schuster, 1928), 22.

60. On Hearst's relationship to the working classes and the production of *Perils*, see Nasaw, *The Chief*, chs. 4, 19; pp. 235–236.

61. Frank Luther Mott, *A History of American Magazines,* Vol. 5 (Cambridge, MA: Harvard University Press, 1968), 296. "The Real Perils of Pearl White," *Literary Digest* (Dec. 4, 1921): 147–149.

62. "Movies of the Future: A Review and a Prophesy," *McClure's Magazine* (Oct. 1915): 87.

63. De Mille, *Hollywood Saga,* 175. *Mutual Film Corporation v. Ohio Industrial Commission,* 236 U.S. 230 (1915).

64. Sept. 20, 1918, Parsons Scrapbook no. 3, MHL. On the Liberty Loan drive, and Pickford's role as its most spectacular seller, see Leslie Midkiff DeBauche, *Reel Patriotism* (Madison: University of Wisconsin Press, 1997), 70–71, 119–120, 155–156; Nell Irving Painter, *Standing at Armageddon* (New York: W.W. Norton, 1987), 332–333. Painter notes that all five series of the Liberty Loans were oversubscribed, raising an estimated $23 billion of the war's $33.5 billion cost. See also George Creel, *How We Advertised America: The First Telling of the Amazing Story of the Committee on Public Information That Carried the Gospel of Americanism to Every Corner of the Globe* (New York: Harper, 1920).

65. De Mille, *Hollywood Saga,* 185. "Film Stars Here to Aid War Loan: Can You 'Guess' Who They Are?" April 5, 1918, Parsons Scrapbook no. 2, MHL.

66. "Official Washington to See Liberty Loan Films," Sept. 21, 1918, Parsons Scrapbook no. 3, MHL.

67. "Metro Plans to Move Studio to Hollywood," Sept. 20, 1918, Parsons Scrapbook no. 3, MHL. I make this claim about Parsons use of the term based on having read the scrapbooks through no. 8, MHL. For the first listing of "Hollywood" in the *Readers' Guide to Periodical Literature* (Minneapolis: H.W. Wilson Co.), see "In the Capital of Movie-Land." "Bankers May Cooperate in Lasky Undertaking," Oct. 15, 1919, Parsons Scrapbook no. 3, MHL. On how Zukor was not the first, but only the most successful, to do this, see Sklar, *Movie-Made America,* ch. 9. On the escalation in the cost of making features, see Hampton, *A History of the Movies,* 167–168; Mae Huettig, *Economic Control of the Motion Picture Industry* (Philadelphia: University of Philadelphia Press, 1944), 26–28; Frank Woods, "The Academy for Motion Picture Arts and Sciences," *Transactions of the Society for Motion Picture Engineers* 12.33 (April 1928): 25–32. Anita Loos and director John Emerson attributed the escalation to the rise in salaries paid to directors, actors, and writers and claimed that the average feature in 1911 cost between $5,000 and $7,000 and by 1921 between $50,000 to $150,000; *Breaking into the Movies* (New York: James A. McCann Co., 1921), 51. This was born out in "A Visit to Movieland the Film Capital of the World—Los Angeles," *The Forum* (Jan. 1920): 17–29. The article reproduced the accounting for a "special": out of a total cost of $119,158.38, approximately $54,000 was spent on director, actors, and writers—with the largest single expense category being extras. *The Forum* also noted that "the average movie" cost between $25,000 and $50,000.

68. De Mille, *Hollywood Saga,* 233; Hampton, *A History of the Movies,* 146–149, 179–192.

69. Independent production was described as the "most important event of the year"; *Wid's Yearbook 1918* (New York: Wid's Films; Hollywood: Film Folks, Inc., 1921), 69.

70. *The Little American* (Famous Players, 1917).

71. Jesse Lasky (JL) to Cecil B. DeMille (CD), Feb. 5, 1917, in Cherchi and Codelli, *The DeMille Legacy,* 62.

72. Rogers St. Johns, "Why Does the World Love Mary? 110.

73. "In and Out of Focus: Mary Pickford," Aug. 1, 1920.

74. Federal Trade Commission brief, Part I, 56–58, in case against FPL Corporation, quoted in *Harvard Business Reports,* 8 (New York: McGraw-Hill, 1930), 16 (hereinafter cited as 8 H.B.R., as requested.)

75. The actress called the merger a shift from "an intimate little family group" to "a huge machine," blaming the low quality of her next two pictures on her "new masters"; Pickford, *Sunshine and Shadow,* 105. See also Irwin, *The House That Shadows Built,* 251; DeMille, *Autobiography,* 180; letters between Jesse Lasky and DeMille, in Cherchi and Codelli, *The DeMille Legacy,* 449, 540–541, 531–533.

76. "Mary Pickford Will Be Her Own Film Director," Nov. 13, 1918, Parsons Scrapbook no. 3, MHL.

77. 8 H.B.R., "First National Exhibitors' Circuit, Incorporated," 13–25; Hampton, *History of the American Film Industry,* ch. 9; William Marston Seabury, *The Public and the Motion Picture Industry* (New York: Macmillan, 1926), 21.

78. "Mary Pickford Will Be Her Own Film Director."

79. Tino Balio, *United Artists* (Madison: University of Wisconsin Press, 1976), 3; Chaplin, *My Autobiography,* 222.

80. "'Big Four' Not 'Big Five' Form New Film Concern," Feb. 8, 1919, Parsons Scrapbook no. 3, MHL. Parsons originally included William Hart. See also "UA to Keep All Their Stock," Feb. 13, 1919, Parsons Scrapbook no. 3, MHL.

81. "Doris Kenyon Latest to Reach Pinnacle of the Film Star's Ambition," March 31, 1918, Parsons Scrapbook no. 2, MHL.

82. With the exclusion of Chaplin and Fairbanks, I found no mention by Parsons of male actors forming independent production companies. Other actresses whom she did not mention here include Olga Petrova, Anita Stewart, Marie Doro, Gail Kane, Alma Ruebens, Madame Mureal, Ethel Clayton, Irene Castle, Justine Johnstone, Vivian Martin, Dorothy Gish, Louise Glaum, and Lillian Walker. See Mahar, *Women Filmmakers,* 303–307.

83. *Photoplay* (May 1917): 121.

84. "Doris Kenyon Latest to Reach Pinnacle of the Film Star's Ambition," March 31, 1918. For 1920, see also "New Film Corporation Formed," April 13, 1920, on Mae Murray; "Enid Bennett to Sever Relations with Ince," May 13, 1920; "Virginia Strikes for Liberty," July 4, 1920, all in Parsons Scrapbooks nos. 2 and 4, MHL.

85. "In and Out of Focus: Norma Talmadge." Schenck arranged to release the films of Norma Talmadge Film Corporation through First National and later UA.

86. *Forbidden City* (Norma Talmadge Film Corp./First National, 1918), Library of Congress.

87. "In and Out of Focus: Norma Talmadge."

88. "In and Out of Focus: Eleanor Fried," May 15, 1920, Parsons Scrapbook no. 4, MHL.

89. "New Film Company Controlled by Woman," Aug. 26, 1919, Parsons Scrapbook no. 3, MHL.

90. "In and Out of Focus: Catherine Curtis," April 4, 1920. Parsons Scrapbook no. 4, MHL.

91. Francke, *Script Girls,* ch. 1.

92. "Film Producers Seek Material for Plays," July 26, 1919, Parsons Scrapbook no. 3, MHL.

93. "Eminent Authors Active," July 23, 1919; "Goldwyn to Make Fewer and Better Pictures," Mar. 5, 1919, both in Parsons Scrapbook no. 3, MHL.

94. "In and Out of Focus: Cheap Pictures to Blame," July 11, 1920, Parsons Scrapbook no. 4, MHL.

95. "The Girl Who Made Fairbanks Famous," Mar. 24, 1918, Parsons Scrapbook no. 2, MHL. Loos wrote the screenplay for Fairbanks's breakout role in *His Picture in the Papers* (1916). She recalled that "Bess Meredith, Frances Marion, and Jeanie McPherson were the foremost scenarists of the day"; Parsons, *Gay Illiterate,* 85.

96. "Jeanine McPherson Signs Contract with DeMille," June 26, 1920, Parsons Scrapbook no. 4, MHL.

97. "Frances Marion to Direct Mary Pickford," July 29, 1920, Parsons Scrapbook no. 4, MHL. The picture was *The Love Light* (UA, 1921), the 11th feature on which the two collaborated.

98. On feminism's relationship to nineteenth-century women's rights, see Cott, *The Grounding of Modern Feminism,* 4–5, 8–10, 213–215, 224–226, 230–239, 276.

99. Missouri Anti-Suffrage League quoted in ibid., 13, 14. On suffrage, see also Eleanor Flexner and Ellen Fitzpatrick, *Century of Struggle* (Cambridge, MA: Harvard University Press, 1996). For a critique for its ideological limitations, see Aileen S. Kraditor, *The Ideas of the Woman Suffrage Movement* (New York: W. W. Norton, 1981 [1965]).

100. Of course, here I refer to what scholars today call gender. See Joan Scott, *Gender and the Politics of History* (New York: Columbia University Press, 1986).

101. De Beauvoir, "The Independent Woman," 683. "Man is a human being with sexuality; woman is a complete individual, equal to the male, only if she too is a human being with sexuality."

102. Randolph Bartlett, "Petrova—Prophetess," *Photoplay* (December 1917): 26–27. The article describes how Petrova was "producing for herself, assuming full charge of every detail of her operations." Margaret Fuller, *Women in the Nineteenth Century* (1845).

103. In the twenties the number of married women working outside the home increased by more than 25 percent; Kessler-Harris, *Out to Work,* 229. Work after marriage became the main topic of debate regarding women's

emancipation in the 1920s. By 1930, less than 4 percent of married working-women held white-collar jobs; see Cott, *The Grounding of Modern Feminism*, ch. 6.

104. "In and Out of Focus: Ouida Bergere," Jan. 18, 1920, Parsons Scrapbook no. 4, MHL.

105. "Gloria Swanson a Bride," Dec.12, 1919, Parsons Scrapbook no. 4, MHL. Swanson married Somborn hoping he would help manage her independent production company. Instead he relied on her for support and they divorced; see Swanson, *Swanson on Swanson*, 131–134, 142–163.

106. "Gloria Swanson in Elinor Glyn Story," Nov. 24, 1920, Parsons Scrapbook no. 4, MHL.

107. Jane Fredrickson, "Defends Manners of Hollywood," *Los Angeles Times*, May 1, 1921. For two other attempts to discredit the promotion of Hollywood as a Bohemia, see "The Real Bohemia," an editorial in the *Los Angeles Times*, Jan. 2, 1921, pt. 2, p. 4; Benjamin Hampton, "Cattar Lattan, USA," *Photoplay* (June 1921): 80–82.

108. Statistic cited in Dorothy Schneider and Carl Schneider, *American Women in the Progressive Era* (New York: Facts on File, 1992), 146.

109. "Steady Growth in California's Divorces Shown," *San Francisco Bulletin*, April, 21, 1920, p. 3.

110. See Gail Bederman, *Manliness and Civilization* (Chicago: University of Chicago Press, 1995), 184–206.

111. John D'Emilio and Estelle Freedman, *Intimate Matters* (New York: Harper& Row, 1988), 173–175. The decline in the birthrate among the native-born urban middle class was particularly pronounced. By 1900, two-thirds had two children and 15 percent remained childless. On the birth control movement, see Ellen Chesler, *Woman of Valor: Margaret Sanger and the Birth Control Movement in America* (New York: Simon & Schuster, 1992).

112. "In and Out of Focus: Anita Loos, Who Looks like a Movie Star and in Reality is the Brainy Young Woman Who Writes for Them," Mar. 16, 1919, Parsons Scrapbook no. 3, MHL.

113. Brooke Kroeger, *Fannie* (New York: Random House, 1999), 49, 28–53. See also Grant Overton, *The Women Who Make Our Novels* (New York: Moffat, Yard, 1922), 180–186; Grant Overton, *Fannie Hurst* (New York: Harper & Brothers, 1928).

114. "Fannie Hurst Wed," *New York Times*, May 4, 1920, pp. 1, 4.

115. See, for instance, "Part Time Marriage," *San Francisco Bulletin*, May 7, 1920, p. 6; "Husband Approves Fannie Hurst's Idea," *New York Times*, May 5, 1920. "Doug Fairbanks and Mary Pickford Here," June 2, 1920, Parsons Scrapbook no. 4, MHL.

116. "Douglas Fairbanks Liberated for Love," April 11, 1918, Parsons Scrapbook no. 3, MHL. The two divorced later that year, and Beth Fairbanks remarried in 1919.

117. *American Aristocracy* (Paramount, 1916).

118. "In and Out of Focus: Mary Pickford," June 6, 1920, Parsons Scrapbook no. 4, MHL.

119. *New York Times*, June 2, 1920, p. 9.

120. "In and Out of Focus: Miriam Cooper," July 25, 1920, Parsons Scrapbook no. 4, MHL. When discussing why actresses married younger, Parsons noted that "actresses, particularly the successful ones, are extraordinarily independent. Many of them manage their own financial affairs as competently as any businessman. It is not easy for an independent woman to bow to anyone other than herself as the head of the house. Younger men are far more tractable than older husbands." Parsons, *The Gay Illiterate*, 184.

121. "Humoresque," June 6, 1920, Parsons Scrapbook no. 4, MHL.

122. "The Woman Pays Club," April 18, 1920, Parsons Scrapbook no. 4, MHL; "Earning Her Rights," May 20, 1920, Parsons Scrapbook no. 4, MHL. "This feminist organization consists of artists, musicians, motion picture writers, authors, newspaper women and other professional members of the fair sex who believe in their independence and prove it by earning their living"; "The Woman Pays Party," Jan. 8, 1921, Parsons Scrapbook no. 6, MHL.

123. Koszarski, *An Evening's Entertainment*, 102–104.

124. Marion, *Off with Their Heads!* 66.

125. "Every Girl Who Is Determined to Become a Picture Actress Should Read This Story of Dorothy Dalton, Who Quit a Good Job, Bought a Ticket to the Coast and Just Stuck Around and Smiled and SMILED till She Got a Contract," Feb. 10, 1918, Parsons Scrapbook no. 2, MHL.

126. "In and Out of Focus: Josephine Quirk; She Is Following Horace Greeley's Advice and Going West," Nov. 21, 1920, Parsons Scrapbook no. 4, MHL.

127. "Confessions of a Motion Picture Press Agent," *The Independent*, Aug. 24, 1918; "In the Capital of Movie-Land," 82–83.

PROLOGUE II. THE REVOLUTION IN MANNERS AND MORALS, REDUX

1. Fredrick Lewis Allen, *Only Yesterday: An Informal History of the 1920s* (New York: Harper & Row, 1931), ch. 5, "The Revolution in Manners and Morals." Scholars largely followed Allen's lead in emphasizing dramatic postwar cultural changes among young middle class women in the 1920s until the critique offered by Estelle Freedman in "The New Woman: Changing Views of Women in the 1920s," *Journal of American History* 61 (1974): 372–393. Freedman argued that too much emphasis had been placed on cultural freedoms among this set at the expense of evaluating women's continued political involvement.

2. On the early dominance of the French industry, see Richard Abel, *The Red Rooster Scare: Making Cinema American, 1900–1910* (Berkeley: University of California Press, 1999). On postwar shifts, see Ruth Vasey, *The World According to Hollywood, 1918–1939*, ch. 1.

3. *Exhibitors Herald* (Oct. 22, 1921): 41; "The 'Movie' as an Industry," *Literary Digest* (Oct. 6, 1917): 55. See also works cited in note 10 of prologue to part I.

4. Dwinelle Benthall, "Movie Influence," *Los Angeles Times Illustrated Magazine*, Jan. 2, 1921, p. 17.

5. Hampton, *A History of the American Film Industry*, 172–173, 204–205. "Fear of the All-Devouring Movie," *Literary Digest* (March, 20, 1920): 40–41. On the *Digest*'s influence, see Frank Luther Mott, *A History of American Magazines*, vol. 5 (Cambridge: Harvard University Press, 1968), 296.

6. "A Movie of the Movie Fan at the Movies," *Literary Digest* (Feb. 26, 1921): 47. See also Bailey Millard, "The Photoplay Has Come to Stay," *San Francisco Chronicle*, March 27, 1921, p. 3.

7. The best source for statistics on the film industry is to be found in the annuals *Wid's Year Book* or, after 1922, *Wid's Film Yearbook* (New York: Jack Alicoate). The figure 50 million is an estimate based on all taxes paid on amusements. See *Wid's Year Book 1921*, 20. For the estimate of 18,000,000 attending daily, see *Current Opinion* (May 1921): 652. See also Joel Finler, *The Hollywood Story* (London: Octopus Books, 1988).

8. Katherine Fullerton Gerould, "Movies," *Atlantic Monthly* (July 1921): 22–30.

9. "Movie Morals," *New Republic* (Aug. 25, 1917): 100–101. See also Carl Van Doren, *Contemporary American Novelists, 1900–1920* (New York: Macmillan, 1922), 13–17.

10. "Morals and the Movies," *The Nation* (April 21, 1921): 581.

11. "Movie Morals," *New Republic*, 100–101.

12. See "Announcing the Photoplay Magazine Medal of Honor," *Photoplay* (June 1921): 29; "'Humoresque' Wins Medal as 1920 Prize Film," *Chicago Herald and Examiner*, Oct. 30, 1921, pt. 5, p. 9. On the reorientation of *Photoplay*'s audience toward women, see Kathryn Fuller, *At the Picture Show*, 135, 145.

13. "First National Completes Interesting Survey," *Wid's Daily*, Oct. 18, 1920, p. 1. Estimates of the total number of theaters showing only movies usually hovered at around 15,000. The "average" feature film combined percentages specifying "female stars" totaled 43.8%; specifying men, 6.01%, specifying "all-star," 19.39%. Other categories that did not mention stars included two-reel short slapstick, 9.9%; rural comedy drama, 7.98%; feature-length slapstick, 6.25%; adaptations of comedy stage successes, 6.01%; feature-length "stunt" comedy, 5.4%.

14. Herbert Howe, "Is Mary Pickford Finished?" *The Preview*, March 25, 1924, pp. 7–11, PCC, MHL. Again, there is no reliable means to precisely judge audience composition, but my interest is more in this perception than in the statistics. In 1920, the *New York Times* reported that women made up 60 percent of movie audiences; by 1924 *Photoplay* put the figure at 75 percent; see Stephen Bush, "Scenarios by the Bushel," *New York Times*, Dec. 5, 1920, quoted in Koszarski, *An Evening's Entertainment*, 30. Fredrick James Smith, "Does Decency Help or Hinder?" *Photoplay* (Nov. 1924): 36.

15. After conducting three massive surveys of colleges, religious institutions, and newspapers, *Literary Digest* published its findings in "Is the Younger Generation in Peril?" (May 14, 1921): 9–12, 58–73; "The Religious Press on Youthful Morals" (May 21, 1921): 27–28, 52–60; "To-Day's Morals and Manners— The Side of 'the Girls'" (July 9, 1921): 34–42. *Pictorial Review*, a woman's

monthly aimed at the middle class, displayed a similar obsession, running more stories on the topic than any other; see particularly Marion Harland, "What Shall We Do with These Young Girls?" *Pictorial Review* (Nov. 1920): 17; Helen Ferris, "Just a Moment Mrs. Grundy!" *Pictorial Review* (Aug. 1921): 23, 26; "Is the Girl of To-day as Bad as She's Painted?" *Pictorial Review* (Jan. 1922): 12–13, 49; Nellie Weathers, "The Modern Girl Speaks for Herself," *Pictorial Review* (March 1922): 22, 106. The indispensable account of the "youth revolt" among the college set remains Paula Fass, *The Damned and the Beautiful: American Youth in the 1920s* (New York: Oxford University Press, 1977).

16. Walter Lippmann, *A Preface to Morals* (New York, Macmillan: 1929), 288. On civilized morality, see D'Emilio and Freedman, *Intimate Matters,* 171–202. "Is the Younger Generation in Peril?" 9, 58.

17. Here I follow Anne Hollander, *Sex and Suits* (New York: Knopf, 1994), 126–138. Hollander argues that changes in modern fashions for women had less to do with comfort—formerly most women found concealment, constriction, and decorative projection "comfortable"—and more with expressing female corporeal pleasure linked to changes in sexual fantasies associated with practices like close dancing and the movies. See also Kevin Yellis, "Prosperity's Child," *American Quarterly* 21.2 (1969): 44–64.

18. Frank Dyer of General Film Co., speaking for producers: "Motion Picture Commission, Hearings before the Education Committee, House of Representatives, Sixty-Third Congress, Second Session; Bills to Establish a Federal Motion Picture Commission" (Washington, D.C.: Government Printing Office, 1914), 23. On how the rate of premarital intercourse jumped to roughly 50% of women coming of age in the 1920s, see D'Emilio and Freedman, *Intimate Matters,* 256. A survey of middle-class females in 1938 found that of those born between 1890 and 1900, 74% remained virgins until marriage; for those born after 1910 the figure dropped to 31.7%; see William Chafe, *The American Woman* (New York: Oxford University Press, 1972), 95. See also Daniel Scott Smith and Michael S. Hindus, "Pre-marital Pregnancy in America," *Journal of Interdisciplinary History* 5.4 (1975): 537–570. The authors found that the percentage of pregnant brides rose steadily after 1900.

19. Zukor, *The Public Is Never Wrong,* 202.

20. *Wid's Year Book 1920* (New York: Wid's Films; Hollywood: Film Folks, Inc.), 333, 217–225. The summary took up only two of the volume's five hundred pages. The *Year Book* noted censorship struggles in New York, Kentucky, Massachusetts, Missouri, Oregon, South Carolina, Virginia, Idaho, Wisconsin, Ohio, and Pennsylvania (333–335). State censorship already existed in Maryland, Pennsylvania, Ohio, and Kansas and in an uncounted number of cities.

21. *Wid's Year Book 1920,* 225, 237. On Pettijohn, see Ramsaye, *A Million and One Nights,* 806–814; Hampton, *History of the American Film Industry,* 247. Pettijohn served as the chairman of the Indiana Democratic Party and as the state boss's aide-de-camp.

22. "Pure stream": Anti-Saloon League in 1915, quoted in Boyer, *Urban Masses and Moral Order,* 212. On prohibition, see Boyer, *Urban Masses and Moral Order,* 181–182, 191–200, 205–221; Jack S. Blocker, *Retreat from Re-*

form (Westport, CT: Greenwood Press, 1976), 11, 156. Higham, *Strangers in the Land,* 267–269.

23. *Wid's Year Book 1920,* 225.

24. Ramsaye, *A Million and One Nights,* 810.

CHAPTER 3. HOLLYWOOD BOHEMIA

1. The film was released in Germany as *Madame du Barry* (UFA, 1919).

2. On box office, see "'Passion' Sets Record," *Exhibitors Herald,* July 23, 1921, p. 56. On *Passion*'s success, see "The Menace of German Films," *Literary Digest* (May 14, 1921): 28–30; Paul Scaramazza, ed., *Ten Years in Paradise* (Arlington, VA: Pleasant Press, 1974), 15. The Berlin film scene took off under the Allied blockade and the German government's decision to invest in cinema as a tool of propaganda. See John Baxter, *The Hollywood Exiles* (New York: Taplinger, 1976), 19–53. On Berlin, see Peter Gay, *Weimar Culture: The Outsider as Insider* (New York: Harper & Row, 1970).

3. So read posters and newspaper ads for the film; quoted in Basinger, *Silent Stars,* 242.

4. MPOH, 2733–2734.

5. The trend is described in "The Foreign Invasion," *Wid's Yearbook 1921* (New York: Wid's Films; Hollywood: Film Folks, Inc., 1921), 207–209. See also "The Menace of German Films." On the importance of the international audience to the industry after 1917, see Vasey, *The World According to Hollywood.*

6. Pola Negri's given name was Apollonia Chalupetz. On her wooing, see Pola Negri, *Memoirs of a Star* (Garden City, NY: Doubleday, 1970), 180–185; Zukor, *The Public Is Never Wrong,* 226–227; Herbert Howe, "The Real Pola Negri," *Photoplay* (November 1922): 38; Joan Jordan, "You Can't Hurry Pola," *Photoplay* (March 1923): 63.

7. Originally released in Germany as *Madame du Barry* (UFA, 1919), the film appeared in the United States as *Passion* (First National, 1920) (viewed at Library of Congress).

8. Negri, *Memoirs of a Star,* 187; Swanson, *Swanson on Swanson,* 63.

9. Gerald Early, *Tuxedo Junction* (Hopewell, NJ: Ecco Press, 1989), ix. Early refers to popular culture. For a synthesis of critical debates over the definition of popular and mass culture in the United States, see Michael Kammen, *American Culture, American Tastes* (New York: Knopf, 1999). I follow Kammen in defining mass culture as commercialized products deliberately designed to appeal to, at least, a national audience with a tendency to commodify what it absorbs. I do not follow his definition of commodification or his periodization, which considers mass culture to have emerged with television in the 1950s. This view ignores the movies. Nor do I agree that mass culture induced only passivity and the privatization of culture. Through the 1920s, moviegoing was a public, interactive experience, and a politically charged activity because of the controversy surrounding it. Moreover, while mass culture's absorption of popular culture often erases the agency of socially marginal groups, its products often

emerges explicitly from the realm of outsiders, helping to give them their fris-
son. For an analysis of moviegoing as an alternative public sphere for women
during the 1910s, see Hansen, *Babel and Babylon,* 90–125.

10. Sydney Valentine, "The Careers of Catherine Calvert," *Photoplay* (May
1921): 62, 90. On Hollywood stars as fashion trendsetters in the 1920s and
their impact on designers, see Kevin Yellis, "Prosperity's Child," *American
Quarterly* 21.2 (1969): 58–61; Anne Hollander, *Sex and Suits* (New York:
Knopf, 1994), 136–137, 148, 159.

11. May Stanley, "Jazzing Up the Fashions," *Photoplay* (May 1920): 57–8.

12. The first article was Norma Talmadge, "What Fashion Really Means,"
Photoplay (June 1920), 64–65, 113. Illustrations accompanying the articles often anticipated trends that turned up later in catalogues like Sears'; see Stella
Blum, ed., *Everyday Fashions of the Twenties* (New York: Dover, 1981), 15–19,
35–38. Talmadge, "What Fashion Really Means," 64, 65, 112.

13. "Most Important Event of the Year," *Wid's Yearbook 1918,* 69; Norma
Talmadge, "What Do You Mean by 'Sex Plays'?" *Pictorial Review* (June 1921): 1.

14. *Forbidden City* (Norma Talmadge Film Corp., 1918); *Daughter of Two
Worlds* (Norma Talmadge Film Corp., 1920), both Library of Congress. On
Talmadge's dramatic reputation, see Adela Rogers St. Johns, "Our ONE and
ONLY Great Actress," *Photoplay* (Feb. 1926): 58, 135–137. For her top ranking
as the era's great dramatic actress, see Koszarski, *An Evening's Entertainment,*
262, 281–283; Slide, *Silent Players,* 372–374. High-brow fans did not share this
opinion, bestowing the honor on Lillian Gish; see Charles Affron, *Lillian Gish*
(New York: Scribner, 2001). See also Basinger, *Silent Stars,* 141–158.

15. "Heroine worship," quoted in *Chicago Herald and Examiner,* Oct. 16,
1921, pt. 5, p. 5. On her fan mail, see Talmadge, "What Do You Mean by 'Sex
Plays'?" 91.

16. "Before They Were Stars: Norma Talmadge," *New York Dramatic Mir-
ror,* April 17, 1920, pp. 744, 765; Marjorie Lachmund, "Our Norma," *Motion
Picture* (Jan. 1917): 110–112; Margaret MacDonald, "Norma Talmadge, a
Modern Female," *Moving Picture World,* July 21, 1917, p. 390; Faith Service,
"The Amazing Interview," *Motion Picture Classic* (Jan. 1920): 22–23, 87.

17. On Natalie's marriage to Keaton, see "Before and After Taking," *Photoplay* (Sept. 1921): 31. Margaret Talmadge, *The Talmadge Sisters: Norma, Constance, and Natalie* (Philadelphia: J.B. Lippincott, 1924). Friends and co-workers
described mother Peg as universally shrewd and beloved and the family as even
more "down-home" than their press; see Anita Loos, *The Talmadge Girls* (New
York: Viking Press, 1978), 4–7; Marion, *Off with Their Heads!* 65; St. Johns,
The Honeycomb, 97.

18. Adele Whitney Fletcher, "Floating on Island on Olympus," *Motion Picture* (March 1921): 22–23, 109.

19. F. Scott Fitzgerald, *Tender Is the Night* (New York: Charles Scribner's
Sons, 1934), 310. "To a Young Girl Going to a Photoplay," *Photoplay* (Feb.
1919): 23.

20. Marion, *Off with Their Heads!* 64–68. On Marion's early career, see
Beauchamp, *Without Lying Down,* 25–104. *Joanna Enlists* (Mary Pickford
Corp./Artcraft, 1918); *The Flapper* (Selznick/Select, 1920).

21. For contrasting readings on the flapper, see Lori Landay, "The Film Flapper: Comedy, Dance, and Jazz Age Kinaesthetics," in Bean and Negra, *A Feminist Reader in Early Cinema,* 221–248; Mary Ryan, "The Projection of New Womanhood: The Movie Moderns in the 1920s," in Jean Friedman and William Shade, eds., *Our American Sisters* (Lexington, MA: D.C. Heath, 1978), 499–518.

22. Kenneth McGaffey, "Introducing the 'Vampette,'" *Photoplay* (Mar. 1919): 47. A sampling of articles on the vamp's decline includes Louise Glaum, "Vampire or Ingenue?" *Photoplay* (Aug. 1919): 334; "A Fan's Prayer," *Photoplay* (May 1920): 45; Harry Carr, "Era of Sanity Commencing," *Los Angeles Times,* Jan. 16, 1921, n.p.; "At Last! The Secret of the Vampire Is Bared," *Chicago Herald and Examiner,* Oct. 2, 1921, pt. 5, p. 9.

23. "A Fool There Was," 21. *A Fool There Was* (Fox, 1915) (print viewed on Kino). On Fox's rigorous typing of Bara, see Genini, *Theda Bara.* Establishing shots cut from Bara to the ocean and a thunderstorm to suggest the supernatural aspect of her sexuality. The asexuality of typical good women and wives is what protects men. Bara only destroys men with her sexuality, acting like a classic fin de siècle femme fatale whose independence makes her revert to a dangerously animalistic natural state. See Bram Dijkstra, *Idols of Perversity* (New York: Oxford University Press, 1986), 33–51.

24. See, for instance, Franklin, "Purgatory's Ivory Angel"; Courtland, "The Divine Theda." Delight Evans, "Does Theda Bara Believe Her Own Press Agent?" *Photoplay* (May 1918): 62; Agnes Smith, "The Confessions of Theda Bara," *Photoplay* (June 1920): 57. See also Bara's attempts to escape and explain the vamp type, in Theda Bara, "How I Became a Film Vampire," *Forum* 62 (June 1919): 715–727; Theda Bara, "The Curse of the Moving-Picture Actress," *Forum* 62 (July 1919): 83–93.

25. Evans, "Does Theda Bara Believe Her Own Press Agent," 63, 107.

26. On Swanson's unsurpassed reputation in the 1920s and her appeal to women, see Ramsaye, *A Million and One Nights,* 824–830. See also Koszarski, *An Evening's Entertainment,* 293-296.

27. See Jesse Lasky to Adolph Zukor, June 29, 1925; Lasky to Zukor, July 3–4, 1925, Adolf Zukor correspondence, file 8, MHL. These telegrams describe the 1925 negotiation to keep Swanson from moving to UA. Lasky offered her a six-picture, two-year contract with a $300,000 advance per picture against 50 percent of its profits. Swanson moved to UA anyway.

28. DeMille, *Autobiography,* 221. Swanson's films with DeMille include *Don't Change Your Husband* (Famous Players–Lasky, 1919); *Male and Female* (Famous Players–Lasky 1919); *For Better, For Worse* (Famous Players–Lasky, 1919); *Why Change Your Wife?* (Famous Players–Lasky, 1920); *Something to Think About* (Famous Players–Lasky, 1920); *The Affairs of Anatol* (Famous Players–Lasky, 1921).

29. Lasky to DeMille, Jan. 6, 1917, quoted in Sumiko Higashi, "The New Woman and Consumer Culture," in Bean and Negra, *A Feminist Reader in Early Cinema,* 301. DeMille also attributed the production of the films to Lasky's repeated urgings; DeMille, *Autobiography,* 212–214. On MacPherson's career, see Lee Shippey, "Lee Side o' LA," *Los Angeles Times,* Mar. 6, 1942, A4;

Franke, *Script Girls,* 13–15; Donna R. Casella, "Feminism and the Female Author," *Quarterly Review of Film and Video* 23 (2206): 217–235.

30. "Movie Facts and Fancies," *Boston Daily Globe,* Feb. 20, 1922, 12. A search in *ProQuest Historical Newspapers* turns up MacPherson appearing in this capacity in several dozen features. "Feminine psychology": Jeanie MacPherson, "Would You Write a Photoplay?" *Atlanta Constitution,* Aug. 7, 1921, D2.

31. Higashi, "The New Woman," 302, 303. See also Sumiko Higashi, *Cecil B. DeMille and American Culture: The Silent Years* (Berkeley: University of California Press, 1994). Higashi's approach dominated feminist film studies after the publication of Laura Mulvey, "Visual Pleasure and Narrative Cinema," *Screen* 16.3 (1975): 6–18. The analysis of marriage as an economic exchange began of course with women's rights activists in the nineteenth century. More nuanced readings include May, *Screening Out the Past,* ch. 8; Orgeron, "Making It in Hollywood"; and Studlar, "The Perils of Pleasure?"

32. See Lasky, *I Blow My Own Horn,* 140.

33. Herbert Howe, "Is Mary Pickford Finished?" *The Preview,* March 25, 1924, pp. 7–11, PCC, MHL. "She Changed Her Coiffure," *Photoplay* (Sept. 1920): 33. On Lasky's intention, see Lasky to DeMille, Jan. 6, 1917, quoted in Higashi, "The New Woman," 301. Actor Antonio Moreno sued Vitagraph for trying to force him to accept this condition when his contract called for starring roles; see Antonio Moreno, Deposition, Box 7, Albert E. Smith Papers, Department of Special Collections, Young Research Library, University of California, Los Angeles. For how the move to "unstarring" became a widely recognized technique, see "Era of Sanity Is Commencing," *Los Angeles Times,* Jan. 16, 1921, pt. III, p. 1.

34. http://www.silentsaregolden.com/dontchangehusbandreview.html.

35. Marion, *Off with Their Heads!* 69; "She Changed Her Coiffure," 33; Glyn quoted in Anthony Glyn, *Elinor Glyn* (London: Hutchinson & Co., 1955), 278. Swanson, *Swanson on Swanson,* 160.

36. Marion, *Off with Their Heads!* 98. For accounts of motherhood, see "Gloria Swanson in Elinor Glyn Story"; Adela Rogers St. Johns, "Sight-Seeing the Movies: A Personally Conducted Tour of the Hollywood Film Colony," *Photoplay* (April 1921): 31; Elinor Glyn, "A Photobiography of Gloria Swanson," *Photoplay* (June 1921): 24.

37. Moore, *Silent Star,* 103. Moore bobbed her hair in 1920, but did not become the definitive flapper until the release of *Flaming Youth* (First National, 1923). "All-time prototype": St. Johns, *Honeycomb,* 103.

38. Peter Bailey, "The Victorian Barmaid as Cultural Prototype," in *Popular Culture and Performance in the Victorian City* (Cambridge: Cambridge University Press, 1998), 156, 151. See also Joanne Meyerowitz, "Women, Cheesecake, and Borderline Material," *Journal of Women's History* 8.3 (Fall 1996): 9–33.

39. *The New Shorter Oxford English Dictionary,* s.v. "glamour."

40. Marshall Neilan, "Acting for the Screen," in *Opportunities in the Motion Picture Industry* (Los Angeles: Photoplay Research Society, 1922), 11; Marion, *Off with Their Heads!* 69.

41. Anonymous undated item; Frances Norton Manning ("Mrs. H.T. Manning") to Gloria Swanson, June 30, 1937, both in "Fan Mail," box 66, file 4,

Gloria Swanson Collection, Harry Ransom Center, University of Texas, Austin (hereinafter HRC).

42. On the cosmetics industry, see Peiss, *Hope in a Jar*. On women fashion designers, see Hollander, *Sex and Suits*, 134–136. On department stores, see William R. Leach, "Transformations in a Culture of Consumption," *Journal of American History* 71.2 (1984): 319–341. The term "expressive goods" is taken from Lorna Weatherill, "The Meaning of Consumer Behavior in Late Seventeenth-Century and Early Eighteenth-Century England," in John Brewer and Roy Porter, eds., *Consumption and the World of Goods* (London: Routledge, 1993), 207–227. The term focuses attention on the demand for, and meanings of, the goods that fueled the consumer revolution.

43. The net national product climbed from $15.8 to $70.3 billion in the United States during this era; see May, *Screening Out the Past*, 201–203. For a discussion of the widespread assumption that women did 85 percent of all shopping, see Marchand, *Advertising the American Dream*, 66–69. Since the mid-1950s, the film industry has made the opposite assumption, targeting teenage boys in what is called the "Peter Pan syndrome"; see Richard Maltby, *Hollywood Cinema* (Oxford: Blackwell, 1995), 10, 221; Elsie deWolfe, *The House in Good Taste* (New York: Century Co., 1915), 3. On deWolfe's career, see Jane S. Smith, *Elsie deWolfe* (New York: Atheneum, 1982); Stanley Abercrombie, *A Century of Interior Design* (New York: Rizzoli, 2003), 22, 31, 41–5.

44. DeWolfe, *The House in Good Taste*, 4–5. DeWolfe declared, "This American home is always the woman's home," in which "men are forever guests." "The style in which we live": de Wolfe quoted in Alfred Lewis, *Ladies and Not-So-Gentle-Women* (New York: Viking, 2000), 283.

45. Swanson, *Swanson on Swanson*, 63. Basinger, *Silent Stars*, 207; Sennett echoed Swanson, writing that "her dramatic talents and beauty were so outstanding" that "comedy merchants" couldn't keep her; see Sennett, *King of Comedy*, 171–173, 194.

46. Swanson, *Swanson on Swanson*, 81. "Gloria Glorified," *Photoplay* (Aug. 1918): 28. *You Can't Believe Everything* (Triangle, 1917).

47. Swanson, *Swanson on Swanson*, 135.

48. See, for instance, Gloria Swanson's studio press biography, "Blue Book of the Screen" for 1924, Gloria Swanson Core Clipping File (hereinafter GS File), MHL.

49. "Gloria Glorified"; Glyn, "A Photobiography," 24; Gloria Swanson, "Gloria Swanson Talks on Divorce," *Motion Picture* (Dec. 1919): n.p., GS File, MHL. See also, "Intolerance Blamed for Divorce," *San Francisco Bulletin*, April 23, 1920, p. 3. Swanson again states her support of divorce in this interview.

50. Howe, "Is Mary Pickford Finished?"

51. Berg, *Goldwyn*, 92.

52. Lasky, *I Blow My Own Horn*, 140. DeMille recalled Glyn "deserved more credit than I for inventing sex-appeal"; DeMille, *Autobiography*, 231. Goldwyn agreed; see Anthony Dawson, *Elinor Glyn* (Garden City, NY: Doubleday, 1955), 279.

53. "Three Weeks," *Current Literature* (Dec. 1907) (APS). On this trend in American fiction, see also Frank Luther Mott, *Golden Multitudes* (New York: R.R. Bowker Co., 1947), ch. 2; Nina Baym, "Melodramas of Beset Manhood," in Lucy Maddox, ed., *Locating American Studies* (Baltimore: Johns Hopkins University Press, 1999), 215–231.

54. Elinor Glyn, *Romantic Adventure: The Autobiography of Elinor Glyn* (New York: E.P. Dutton & Co., 1937), 128–138; Joan Hardwick, *Addicted to Romance* (London: Andre Deutsch Ltd., 1994), 53–78.

55. Elinor Glyn, *Three Weeks* (New York: Duffield Co., 1907), 124, 51. Sales in Great Britain, the British Empire, and the United States reached two million by 1916. In 1917, three separate publishers released cheap editions, causing the total number sold by 1933 to reach five million. The book was also immediately published in every European language. Anthony Glyn, *Elinor Glyn*, 126; Mott, *Golden Multitudes*, 249–251, 312.

56. Glyn, *Three Weeks*, 80, 109–110, 77, 157, 106, 194.

57. Glyn, *Romantic Adventure*, 131. Dr. Alice Stockham, in her sex education manual for women, quoted in D'Emilio and Freedman, *Intimate Matters*, 179.

58. George Jean Nathan, "The Girl-Alone-in-the-City Novels," *The Bookman* (April 1911); "Why Do Women Write More Bad Books Than Men?" *Current Literature* (Jan. 1908) (both APS).

59. "Three Weeks," *Current Literature* (Dec. 1907): 693. See also Mott, *Golden Multitudes*, 248–249.

60. Glyn, *Romantic Adventure*, 131–132, 8.

61. Here I follow Colin Campbell, "Understanding Traditional and Modern Practices of Consumption in Eighteenth Century England: A Character-Action Approach," ch. 3, in Brewer and Porter, *Consumption and the World of Goods*. See also Colin Campbell, *The Romantic Ethic and the Spirit of Modern Consumerism* (Oxford: Basil Blackwell, 1987), pt. 1.

62. Hardwick, *Addicted to Romance*, 128–129, 211.

63. Glyn, *Romantic Adventure*, 139; Hardwick, *Addicted to Romance*, 127–133; "Elizabeth Visits America," *Current Literature* (Aug. 1909).

64. Edward Said, *Orientalism* (New York: Vintage, 1978).On film Orientalism, see Matthew Bernstein and Gaylyn Studlar, eds., *Visions of the East* (New Brunswick, NJ: Rutgers University Press, 1997). On Orientalism in advertising, see M.H. Dunlop, *Gilded City* (New York: Harper Collins, 2000): 59, 96–98, 100–104; Leach, *Land of Desire*, 104–111. For its role in modern dance, see Judith Walkowitz, "The 'Vision of Salome,'" *Journal of American History* 108.2 (April 2003): 337–376; Elizabeth Kendall, *Where She Danced* (New York: Knopf, 1979).

65. Walter S. Trumbull, "Served Her Right," *Lippincott's Monthly Magazine* (May 1908); *Current Opinion*, "Lite Ratu Re An D-Art" (May 1916); M.E. Ravage, "I Laugh as I Think," *Puck* (Jan. 20, 1917); George Jean Nathan, "What the Public Wants," *McClure's Magazine* (Nov. 1917).

66. Delight Evans, "Tiger Skins and Temperament," *Photoplay* (Jan. 1921): 70, 120; Elinor Glyn, "In Filmdom's Boudoir," *Photoplay* (March 1921): 29; Glyn, *Romantic Adventure*, 139.

67. O.R. Geyer, "The Golden Age of Pictures," *Photoplay* (June 1920): 53–54. The article describes the 300 percent increase in foreign trade between 1916 and 1919. See also "American Films Corrupting Britain," *Literary Digest* (Dec. 4, 1920): 34–35.

68. Swanson, *Swanson on Swanson*, 159; Walkowitz, "The 'Vision of Salome,'" 340.

69. Evans, "Tiger Skins," 70; Glyn, "In Filmdom's Boudoir," 29. On Glyn's sister, the clothing designer Lucile, Lady Duff Gordon, see Meredith Etherington-Smith and Jeremy Pilcher, *The "It" Girls* (London: H. Hamilton, 1986); Lady Duff Gordon, *Discretions and Indiscretions* (London: Jarrolds, 1932).

70. Swanson, *Swanson on Swanson*, 160; Anthony Glyn, *Elinor Glyn*, 302; Glyn, "In Filmdom's Boudoir," 29; Glyn, "A Photobiography," 24. On Glyn's casting approval, see Lasky, *I Blow My Own Horn*, 141–143.

71. Ad in the *Exhibitors Herald* (July 9, 1921): 5. Glyn, *Romantic Adventure,* 299; Lasky, *I Blow My Own Horn,* 142.

72. Lasky, *I Blow My Own Horn,* 146. On Reid as heir to the "Arrow Collar" tradition, see Koszarski, *An Evening's Entertainment,* 276–278; Gaylyn Studlar, *This Mad Masquerade: Stardom and Masculinity in the Jazz Age* (New York: Columbia University Press, 1996), 191.

73. See "Sessue Hayakawa," *Films in Review* 27.4 (1976): 193–208. For an early hit that contrasts his sexual power with an American man's asexuality, see *The Cheat* (Jesse L. Lasky Feature Play Co., 1915).

74. "'The Great Moment' Hit at Alhambra," *Los Angeles Daily Times,* Oct. 5, 1921, pt. III, p. 2. *The Great Moment* (Paramount, 1921). *Exhibitors Herald* (Aug. 6, 1921): 46.

75. Review of "The Great Moment," *Exhibitors Herald* (Aug. 6, 1921): 49. Many exhibitors wrote in to "What the Picture Did for Me" section of the *Herald,* praising Swanson and the film's success with the ladies; see, *Exhibitors Herald,* March 11, 1922, p. 75; March 25, 1922, p. 75; April 1, 1922, p. 70; April 15, 1922, p. 80.

76. Glyn, "In Filmdom's Boudoir," 28–30.

77. "What They Think about Marriage!" *Photoplay* (April 1921): 20–22, 110. Those interviewed included DeMille, Swanson, George Fitzmaurice, Will Rogers, Frances Marion, Pearl White, Marshall Neilan, Thomas Meighan, Norma Talmadge, Constance Talmadge, Mae Murray, William S. Hart, Anita Stewart, Antonio Moreno, Justine Johnstone.

78. As Told by Cecil B. DeMille to Adela Rogers St. Johns, "What Does Marriage Mean?" *Photoplay* (Dec. 1920): 28–31; As Told by Cecil B. DeMille to Adela Rogers St. Johns, "More about Marriage," *Photoplay* (May 1921): 24–26, 105. For criticisms of *The Affairs of Anatol* that charged the opposite of what DeMille claimed, see "Great cast. Great director. Great scenery. Absolutely teaches no moral lesson whatsoever," *Exhibitors Herald* (April 1, 1922): 70; *New York Times Film Reviews* (New York: Arno Press, 1970), Feb. 3, 1919.

79. St. Johns, "What Does Marriage Mean?" 28–31; St. Johns, "More about Marriage," 24–26, 105. DeMille claimed he "received more letters concerning the publication" of the first interview "than from any picture he had made."

80. Higashi, "The New Woman," 305–314.

81. St. Johns, "More about Marriage," 24.

82. Of the 12 stories on the topic between 1919 and 1921, DeMille's was the only one with this point of view.

83. Joan Jordan, "Old Lives for New," *Photoplay* (April 1921): 44–46. See also Florence Vidor, "Does Marriage Help or Hurt a Movie Star?" *Chicago Herald and Examiner,* Oct. 2, 1921, pt. V, p. 8.

84. As Told by Marjorie Rambeau to Ada Patterson, "How Can a Stage or Screen Marriage Be Made Happy," *Photoplay* (Feb. 1921): 32–33, 105.

85. The term is D'Emilio and Freedman's, in *Intimate Matters,* 239–274.

86. Ben Lindsey and Wainwright Evans, *The Companionate Marriage* (New York: Boni & Liveright, 1927). My understanding of "companionate marriage" follows that of Paula Fass, *The Damned and the Beautiful: American Youth in the 1920s* (New York: Oxford University Press, 1977), 39–40, 50, 79, 80–83; D'Emilio and Freedman, *Intimate Matters,* 241, 244, 265–70, 273; Christina Simmons, "Modern Sexuality and the Myth of Victorian Repression," in Barbara Melosh, ed., *Gender and History since 1890* (London: Routledge, 1993), 29–33.

87. This was the determination of the Payne Fund Studies, a University of Chicago investigation into films' influence on youth conducted between 1928 and 1932. The research was published in eight volumes between 1933 and 1935. For the popularized, best-selling version, and on the politics behind this anti-industry project, see chapter 1, note 144.

88. "What They Think about Marriage!" 22; Elinor Glyn, *The Philosophy of Love* (London: George Newnes, 1920).

89. Joan Jordan, "Confessions of a Modern Don Juan," *Photoplay* (May 1921): 46. For more on the Latin lover type, see Studlar, *This Mad Masquerade,* 178, 184, 191–193.

90. Clara Kimball Young, "The Technique of Lovers," *Photoplay* (March 1920): 39–41.

91. On Valentino's early life and transgressive masculinity, see Emily W. Leider, *Dark Lover: The Life and Death of Rudolph Valentino* (New York: Farrar, Straus & Giroux, 2003), 4–43; Studlar, "Optic Intoxication: Rudolph Valentino and Dance Madness," ch. 3, in *This Mad Masquerade.*

92. Griffith quoted in Gish, *Dorothy and Lillian Gish,* 81. On Valentino's typecasting, see Leider, *Dark Lover,* 77–97. *Eyes of Youth* (Clara Kimball Young Film Corp., 1919), Library of Congress.

93. June Mathis, "Pursuing a Motion Picture Plot," *Photoplay Journal* (Oct. 1917): 24–25. *Moving Picture World,* June 18, 1921, p. 719, Mathis File, SW-EYD Collection, New York Public Library for the Performing Arts, Theater Collection (hereinafter NYPL-TC). AFI credits Mathis with 113 films in her twelve-year career. See also Mathis Goldwyn Producing Corp., Mathis Biographical File, MHL; Casella, "Feminism and the Female Author," 217–235.

94. Mathis, "Pursuing a Motion Picture Plot"; Katherine Lipke, "Most Responsible Job Ever Held by a Woman," *Los Angeles Times,* June 3, 1923, p. 6; Ivan St. Johns, "Fifty-Fifty," *Photoplay* (Oct. 1926): 46. On sales of the book *Four Horsemen,* see Mott, *Golden Multitudes,* 241, 325, 328. *The Four Horsemen of the Apocalypse* (Metro, 1921).

95. Adela Rogers St. Johns, *Love, Laughter and Tears* (Garden City, NY: Doubleday, 1978), 167.

96. "A Latin Lover," *Photoplay* (Sept. 1921): 21. Robert Sherwood, untitled article in *Life*, March 11, 1921, n.p., Valentino Core Clipping File, MHL.

97. On its box office success and rave reviews, see "'The Four Horsemen' Ride on the Screen," *Literary Digest* (Mar. 26, 1921): 28–29; Lindsay, *The Art of the Moving Picture*, 5; Lasky, *I Blow My Own Horn*, 146–147.

98. Lasky, *I Blow My Own Horn*, 148. Glyn, *Romantic Adventure*, 299–300; "he knew everything": Glyn quoted in Leider, *Dark Lover*, 195; Hardwick, *Addicted to Romance*, 242.

99. *The Sheik* advertisement, *Exhibitors Herald* (Nov. 5, 1921): 12–13; "Letters to the Times," *Los Angeles Times*, Nov. 10, 1921, p. 11. *The Sheik* (Famous Players–Lasky/Paramount 1921), Kino.

100. Although the exotic does not play a role in her argument, this reading illustrates the dynamic described by Janice A. Radway in *Reading the Romance: Women, Patriarchy, and Popular Literature* (Chapel Hill: University of North Carolina Press, 1991). See also Studlar, *This Mad Masquerade*, 150–198.

101. Jackson Lears, *Rebirth of a Nation: The Making of Modern America* (New York: Harper, 2009), 250.

102. "The Motion Picture Autobiographies," Case 9; "The Sheik," *Variety*, Nov. 11, 1921, p. 37; "What the Picture Did for Me," *Exhibitors Herald* (April 8, 1922): 89.

103. *Exhibitors Herald* (April 22, 1922): 76; unsourced clipping, Valentino Scrapbooks, RLC.

104. Dick Dorgan, "A Song of Hate," *Photoplay* (July 1921): 27.

105. Lambert, *Nazimova*, 247. Born Adelaida Leventon to middle-class secular Jews in 1879, she took the generic Russian name Nazimova to hide her ethnic background when she entered Moscow's prejudiced theatrical scene. On her upbringing, see ibid., 3–67.

106. "Nazimova Last of Great Stage Artistes to Heed the Call of the Screen," *Selznick Pictures Magazine*, n.d., p. 4, Alla Nazimova files, SWEYD Collection, NYPL-TC; St. Johns, *Honeycomb*, 117. The Alla Nazimova files in the SWEYD Collection contain a mountain of material dating back to the actress's first U.S. performances in Russian.

107. Herbert Howe, "A Misunderstood Woman," *Photoplay* (April 1922), 24. Alla Nazimova Files, SWEYD Collection, NYPL-TC, contains publicity shots for both causes. "Eccentric": Helen Raferty, "Elsie or Allah?" *Photoplay* (July 1918): 23. "Russian superwoman": "Alla Nazimova," *Motion Picture Classic* (Aug. 1918): n.p, Nazimova Clippings, Film appearances, 1919–1920, SWEYD Collection, NYPL-TC. "Made": "Made," "Open Letter to Nazimova," *Photoplay* (Aug. 1921): 31 (italics in the original). The letter was written by a woman who said she had been a fan since Nazimova's Ibsen days.

108. See Anna McClure Sholl, "Madame Nazimova—A Comparison," *Lippincott's Monthly Magazine* (Nov. 1907) (APS). In 1908, another summary of reviews showed her artistic status; "Maude Adams in a New Incarnation of Peter Pan," *Current Literature* (March 1908) (APS).

109. See Lambert, *Nazimova,* 78–91; DeWitt Bodeen, "Nazimova," *Film in Review* 23.10 (1972): 578–579. "Hedda Gabler," *Current Literature* (Jan. 1907): 60, 152. On Nazimova taking over the play's direction, see Lambert, *Nazimova,* 135–136. See also Gerald Bordman, *Oxford Companion to American Theatre* (New York: Oxford University Press, 1984), 501.

110. Sholl, "Madame Nazimova—A Comparison," 684.

111. "Maude Adams in a New Incarnation of Peter Pan," 319; "What Is Wrong with Our Theaters?" *Current Literature* (Nov. 1907) (APS); "The Transformation of Nazimova," *Current Literature* (Dec. 1907) (APS); "Hedda Gabler."

112. "As a slav," unnamed critic quoted in "The Transformation of Nazimova," 672; "Our actresses," "Hedda Gabler" 60.

113. Frohman quoted in "Hedda Gabler," 152. Frohman was a member of the Theatrical Syndicate, which controlled many of the nation's most important theaters. On Hichens, see Mott, *Golden Multitudes,* 251–252, 325.

114. *Vanity Fair* quoted in Lambert, *Nazimova,* 150, 158–165; Howe, "A Misunderstood Woman," 128; "Nazimova Last of Great Stage Artistes." *War Brides* (Lewis J. Selznick, 1916).

115. *New York Times* quoted in Bodeen, "Nazimova," 585. On replacing Bara with Nazimova, see Lambert, *Nazimova,* 190. On Bara's decline, see Genini, *Theda Bara,* 79–87.

116. On her terms with Metro, see Bodeen, "Nazimova," 587; Lambert, *Nazimova,* 190. "Revolutionary": see Howe, "A Misunderstood Woman," 24–25, 120. "Aristocrat" and "rebel": see Edwin Fredericks, "The Real Nazimova," *Photoplay* (Feb. 1921): 128.

117. "Superlative": "Leading Photoplays," *Current Opinion* (April 1918): 260. "Feminine sex," *Motion Picture Magazine,* quoted in Lambert, *Nazimova,* 210.

118. Most of Nazimova's films have been lost or exist in fragments. I viewed *Camille* (Metro, 1921) on Warner Home Video; *Salome* (Nazimova Productions, 1923) on Video Yesteryear; and *The Red Lantern* (Nazimova Productions, 1919) at Women's Film History Screening, MOMA, 2011. Other descriptions are taken from Bodeen's filmography in "Nazimova," 601–700; "Red Lantern," Alla Nazimova Files, NYPL-TC.

119. "The Red Lantern," *Photoplay* (June 1919): 38–41, 113. On the film's acclaim, see "Red Lantern," Nazimova Files, NYPL-TC.

120. "Chinese boy": Howe, "A Misunderstood Woman," 128; "friends are young girls": *Photoplay* (May 1919), quoted in Lambert, *Nazimova,* 210; protégés: "Plays and Players," *Photoplay* (Sept. 1919): 104.

121. On the open secret of her lesbianism, see Lambert, *Nazimova,* 199, 249; Leider, *Dark Lover,* 137–147.

122. Lawrence Hutton, *Plays and Players* (New York: Hurd & Houghton, 1875), 158. On *Camille*'s popularity, see Stanton, *Camille and Other Plays,* xxvi; Hamilton, "The Career of Camille."

123. Advertisement, *Exhibitors Herald* (Nov. 19, 1921): 23

124. On Germany's dominance of the art film scene in the 1920s, see Baxter, *Hollywood Exiles,* ch. 2. By "art film" I mean pictures allied with contemporary

movements in other arts, rather than with a film genre. Art films place visual, aesthetic qualities first rather than focusing on story elements and genre associations, as was the case with most American films. The stepdaughter of a tycoon, Rambova spent her adolescence in Paris with her godmother, Elsie deWolfe, studying before entering costume and set design at the Imperial Russian Ballet Company in New York and then traveling with the company to Los Angles, where she went to work for Nazimova. See Michael Morris, *Madame Valentino* (New York: Abbeville Press, 1991).

125. Pearl Gaddis, "He, She or It," *Motion Picture Magazine* 13.4 (May 1917): 27. See also Anthony Slide, "The Silent Closet," *Film Quarterly* 52.4 (1999): 30.

126. Mathis quoted in Lambert, *Nazimova*, 201. St. Johns, "Sight-Seeing the Movies."

127. St. Johns, *Honeycomb*, 90–91, 101, 111. Frances Marion describes the parties in *Off with Their Heads!* 6, 101. Moore dedicated her autobiography, *Silent Star,* to Adela Rogers St. Johns, "my friend and mentor since my first days in Hollywood."

128. St. Johns, *Honeycomb*, 118; Zukor, *The Public Is Never Wrong,* 200–202.

129. St. Johns, *Honeycomb*, 114.

130. See the sources cited in note 11 of the part I introduction.

131. Starr, *Material Dreams*, 69, 98. See the statistics cited in note 10 of the part I introduction.

132. "Girls Crave Stardom," *Atlanta Constitution,* June 26, 1921; Booth, "Breaking into the Movies," 76. This monthly serial ran from January to June 1917.

133. Thompson, *Growth and Changes in California's Population*, 48–51, 88–93. In 1920 the city's sex ratio was 97.8 to 100. On the industry's size, see Starr, *Material Dreams*, 98.

134. Gertrude Atherton, "The Lot," *Photoplay* (June 1921): 92–93; Campbell, "Understanding Traditional and Modern Practices of Consumption," 49–51.

135. "Clannish": Mary Winship, "Oh, Hollywood! A Ramble in Bohemia," *Photoplay* (May 1921): 111; "on the edge": "The Jazzy, Money-Mad Spot Where Movies Are Made," 71. Edward Soja, *Thirdspace* (Malden: Blackwell, 1996), 3, 77, 97–98. "Chameleon City" etc.: from *The Strand Magazine. Washington Post,* June 20, 1915.

136. Valeria Belletti to Irma Prina, quoted in Cari Beauchamp, ed., *Adventures of a Hollywood Secretary: Her Private Letters from Inside the Studios of the 1920s* (Berkeley: University of California Press, 2006), 34, 19, 52.

137. Winship, "Oh, Hollywood!" 110; Willard Huntington Wright, "Los Angeles—The Chemically Pure," in Burton Rascoe and Groff Conklin, eds., *The Smart Set Anthology* (New York: Reynal & Hitchcock, 1934 [1913]), 90–102.

138. Allen Cambell, "Bohemia in Los Angeles," unpublished pamphlet, n.d., n.p., Huntington Library, San Marino, CA

139. Winship, "Oh, Hollywood!" 110 (italics in the original).

140. Belletti quoted in Beauchamp, *Adventures of a Hollywood Secretary,* 119, 19, 69–70.

141. St. Johns, *The Honeycomb,* 90–91; Emerson and Loos, *Breaking into the Movies,* 26.

142. On this point, see Sklar, *Movie-Made America,* ch. 8; Hilary-Anne Hallett, "In Motion-Picture Land" (Ph.D. dissertation, CUNY Graduate Center, 2005), ch. 5.

143. On Bohemia's relationship to consumption, see Jerrold Seigel, *Bohemian Paris: Culture, Politics, and the Boundaries of Bourgeois Life, 1830–1930* (Baltimore: Johns Hopkins University Press, 1999 [1986]); Richard Lloyd, *Neo-Bohemia: Art and Commerce in the Postindustrial City* (New York: Routledge, 2006); Campbell, "Understanding Traditional and Modern Practices of Consumption," 40–57. On Murger, see Seigel, *Bohemian Paris,* ch. 2.

144. Henry Murger, *The Bohemians of the Latin Quarter,* trans. Ellen Marriage and John Selwyn (Philadelphia: University of Pennsylvania Press, 2004), xxxiii; Seigel, *Bohemian Paris,* 11.

145. Stansell, *American Moderns,* 225–308; Seigel, *Bohemian Paris,* 40–42; Lloyd, *Neo-Bohemia,* 60–64. Harvey Warren Zorbaugh, *The Gold Coast and the Slum* (Chicago: University of Chicago Press, 1929), 91.

146. Ross, *Stars and Strikes,* 70–75, 85–86; Anita Loos, *A Girl Like I* (New York: Viking Press, 1966), 68. For a more indirect discussion of Bohemian Hollywood, see Emerson and Loos, *Breaking into the Movies,* 26.

147. Marion, *Off with Their Heads!* 85; Coffee, *Storyline,* 57.

148. "Hollywood Studio Club Building Campaign," 1925, file 8, box 1, Young Women's Christian Association of Los Angeles Collection, Hollywood Studio Club, Urban Archives Center, University Library, California State University, Northridge (hereafter Studio Club). On publicity, see "A Studio Club Revue, 1916–1932," file 26, box 1, Studio Club. On motion picture money, see files 6, 13, and 48 in ibid.; Myrtle Gebhart, "The Studio Club Grows Up," *Photoplay,* n.d.; Elizabeth McGaffey, "The Studio Club," n.d., both in ibid., file 22, box 1, Studio Club; "Notice of Completion," April 20, 1926, file 36, in ibid.; "House Information, Hollywood Studio Club," file 8, in ibid.; "Report of the Hollywood Studio Club, Year Ending 1923," file 4, in ibid. Heidi Kenega, "Making the Studio Girl," *Film History* 18 (2006): 134.

149. See, for instance, Ralph Strong, "One Extra Girl," *Picture Play Magazine* 4.2 (April 1916): 54; Rhea Irene Kimball, "The Extra Girls of Essanay Company— Girls, Girls, Girls!" *Motion Picture Magazine* 10.8 (Sept. 1915): 97; Kitty Kelly, "Hearkening to the Call of the Screen," *Chicago Daily Tribune,* January 7, 1916, p. 16. The column by Grace Kingsley, "Ella the Extra Girl," ran in the *Los Angeles Times* throughout 1919. Contrast this reading with Stamp, "It's a Long Way to Filmland."

150. Winship, "Oh Hollywood!" 20–22, 112.

151. Fredrickson, "Defends Manners of Hollywood." See also the editorial "The Real Bohemia"; Hampton, "Cattar Lattan, USA."

152. "Evil Influence of Motion Pictures," Petition 2524, Sept. 6, 1921, in "Motion Picture File 2035, to be known as 2723," and "File 2524," Los Angeles City Clerk's Office, Records and Management Division, City Archives.

153. "A Visit to Movieland"; "The Jazzy, Money-Mad Spot Where Movies Are Made" (italics in the original).

154. "Gullible Girls Who Come to Grief Seeking Film Fame," *Literary Digest* (July 3, 1920): 63–66. See also "For Those Who Look like Mary Pickford," *Literary Digest* (March 6, 1920): 84.

155. "Movie Myths and Facts As Seen by an Insider," *Literary Digest* (May 7, 1921): 38. The article was a condensed version of Benjamin Hampton, "Do You Want to Get into the Movies? Do's and Don'ts by a Manager for the Girl at Home," *Pictorial Review* (April 1921): 5, 49–51 (all italics in the original).

156. Margaret Sangster, "The Girl Problem and the Pictures," *Photoplay* (Sept. 1921): 103–104. See also Margaret Sangster, "Why Girls Don't Leave Home," *Photoplay* (Oct. 1920): 67, 129.

CHAPTER 4. THE MOVIE MENACE

1. "Sex War On in Films," *Los Angeles Times* (hereinafter *LAT*), Jan. 30, 1921, pt. 3, p. 1. On the furor the article prompted, see "Overdoing the Sex Motive in Moving Pictures," *Current Opinion* (March 1921): 362; "Where the Blame Lies for Movie 'Sex-Stuff,'" *Literary Digest*, Feb. 12, 1921, pp. 28–29.

2. "Movie Myths and Facts As Seen by an Insider," 38.

3. Benjamin Hampton, "Too Much Sex Stuff in the Movies? Whose Fault Is It?" *Pictorial Review* (Feb. 1921): 11, 113–116. Typical articles in *Pictorial Review* in this period include "What's the Matter with Marriage: Results of the Contest Announced Last June" (Jan. 1921): 25, 48; Genevieve Pankhurst, "'For Better or Worse'; The Advanced Thought of the Entire World Seems to Favor More Liberal Marriage and Divorce Laws" (Feb. 1921): 68–72; Marion Harland, "What Shall We Do with These Young Girls?" (Nov. 1920): 17; Cornelia Stratton Parker, "It's a New World We Live In: The Woman Who Works; The Third Article in the Series," *Pictorial Review* (April 1921): 23, 60–61.

4. Hampton, *A History of the Movies*, 290–293. See also "Should American Pictures Be Censored?" *Current Opinion* (May 1921): 652–655. Hampton here blamed the controversy on his "sensational article." MacKinnon's "editor's note" preceding "Too Much Sex Stuff" supports this claim. Hampton, "Do You Want to Get into the Movies?" This article of Hampton's was billed as the "second in the series." Next came Jessie Lasky, "Is There Any Sense in Censorship?" *Pictorial Review* (May 1921): 11, 40; and Norma Talmadge, "What Do You Mean by 'Sex Plays'?" *Pictorial Review* (June 1921): 2, 91. Suggesting that he took his cue from the *Eagle* crusade discussed later in this chapter, the editor's note billed Talmadge's article as the "Fourth Article in the Campaign for Cleaner Movies."

5. For coverage that displays the emphasis on Hampton's status and his role in bringing concerns about movie morality to a boil, see "Sex War On in Films"; "Where the Blame Lies for Movie 'Sex-Stuff'"; "Overdoing the Sex Motive in Moving Pictures"; "Should Moving Pictures Be Censored?"

6. Hampton, *A History of the Movies*, 150–169. Hampton served as vice president of the American Tobacco Company and attempted to convince his boss to finance a merger between the distribution company Paramount and the

film producers Famous Players–Lasky and VLSE. On his career, see Ramsaye, *A Million and One Nights*, 744–747; *AFI Catalog of Silent Films*, http://www.afi .com/members/catalogue. "Common Sense and the Film Menace," *Ladies' Home Journal* 38 (April 1921): 24.

7. On the industry's role in the war effort, see DeBauche, *Reel Patriotism*, 104–136. Creel, *How We Advertised America*.

8. Walter Lippmann, *Public Opinion* (New York: Macmillan, 1922); Walter Lippmann, *Liberty and the News* (New York: Macmillan, 1922). On public opinion in the 1920s, see Hanno Hardt, *Critical Communications Studies* (London: Routledge, 1992).

9. Raymond Dodge, "The Psychology of Propaganda," in Robert E. Park and Ernest Burgess, eds., *Introduction to the Science of Sociology* (Chicago: University of Chicago Press, 1969 [1921]), 837. On the survey conducted by University of Chicago sociologist Ernest Burgess, see Grieveson, *Policing Cinema*, 211–212. On the proliferation of these studies, see Jowett, Jarvie, and Fuller-Seeley, *Children and the Movies*.

10. See Painter, *Standing at Armageddon*, ch. 12; *Wid's Year Book 1920* (New York: Wid's Films; Hollywood: Film Folks, Inc., 1920), 333–335. Between 1910 and 1929, more articles were published on "moving pictures and morals" in 1920 and 1921 than in any other two years before or after; see *The Readers' Guide to Periodical Literature* (Minneapolis: H.W. Wilson Co.). Of the 14 articles in the category for 1921, 13 were published before September.

11. Fredrick Boyd Stevenson, "Who Reviewed Photoplay 'The Penalty'?" *Brooklyn Daily Eagle* (hereinafter *BDE*), Feb. 6, 1921, "Music, Art, Theaters, and Women" sec., 1. Many social historians tie the development of middle-class consciousness in the mid-nineteenth century to notions of domesticity, gentility, and conceptions of feminine moral guardianship, suggesting how the deeply gendered complex of ideals associated with "respectability" distinguished the middle class. See Mary Ryan, *Cradle of the Middle Class* (Cambridge: Cambridge University Press, 1981); John Kasson, *Rudeness and Civility* (New York: Hill & Wang, 1990); Scanlon, *Inarticulate Longings*; Robyn Muncy, *Creating a Female Dominion of Reform* (Oxford: Oxford University Press, 1991). Film scholars who have focused on the strategies employed by the industry during the 1910s to achieve respectability include May, in *Screening Out the Past*; Tom Gunning, in *D. W. Griffith and the Origins of American Narrative Film* (Urbana: University of Illinois Press, 1991); William Uricchio and Roberta Pearson, in "Constructing the Mass Audience," *Iris* 17.3 (1994); and Douglas Gomery, in *Shared Pleasures* (Madison: University of Wisconsin Press, 1992).

12. This was the title of the first film history, Ramsaye, *A Million and One Nights*. Ramsaye considered anti-Semitism partially responsible for the industry's postwar troubles, even as he set the mold for viewing producers as good-hearted, Orientalist internationalists spinning tales in a "new Baghdad"; ibid., 482, 833–834. On anti-Semitism's impact on the industry in the 1930s and 1940s, see Steven Carr, *Hollywood and Anti-Semitism* (Cambridge: Cambridge University Press, 2001). See also Gabler, *An Empire of Their Own*. Gabler considers anti-Semitism an underlying cause for all the major producers' behavior and the particular vision of America they created. This popular history is very

suggestive, but relies mostly on psychoanalytic assumptions. Most strangely, by making Jewish producers seem to control every nuance on screens, his discussion supports the paranoid perception of the time.

13. *LAT*, Jan. 6, 1921, pt. 1, p. 3; *BDE*, Feb. 1, 1921, p. 4.

14. Higham, *Strangers in the Land*, 195, 222 (italics in the original); see also chs. 6 and 9.

15. "Alien Propaganda Defeating Efforts at Americanization," *BDE*, Feb. 20, 1921, p. 1.

16. "Flood": quoting Senate Immigration Committee chairman Colt, *BDE*, Feb. 9, 1921, p. 1; "toboggan slide": quoting Colorado representative Valle, a member of the House Committee on Immigration, *LAT*, Jan. 16, 1921, p. 1. On the constructions of racial categories in this era, see Jacobson, *Whiteness of a Different Color*.

17. Frank Crane, "The Jew," *Current Opinion* (May 1921): 596.

18. Quoted in Higham, *Strangers in the Land*, 309. For more on the report, see Robert Fink, "Visas, Immigration and Official Anti-Semitism," *The Nation* (May 4, 1921): 870–873.

19. Fink, "Visas, Immigration and Official Anti-Semitism," 872.

20. Senator Dillingham's report by the Senate Immigration Committee quoted in "New Immigration Measure," *BDE*, Feb. 15, 1921, p. 1. For details on the Dillingham Bill, see *BDE*, "Senate Adopts Bill to Stem Tide of Aliens," Feb. 20, 1921, p. 1. The bill easily passed both houses, only to meet a pocket veto from the lame-duck Wilson; reported in *BDE*, "Immigration Bill and Army Budget Get 'Pocket Veto,'" March 3, 1921, p. 1. The bill became law in May 1921.

21. Higham, *Strangers in the Land*, 310.

22. "Trailing the New Anti-Semitism to Its Russian Lair," *Current Opinion* (April 1921): 501.

23. "Jewry at the End of the War," *The Nation* (May 4, 1921): 677.

24. On the social separation but shared business and political terrain of German Jews and Protestant elites, see Irving Howe, *World of Our Fathers* (New York: Harcourt, 1976), 80; Thomas Kessner, *The Golden Door* (New York: Oxford University Press, 1977), 37, 61–63, 168; William Issel and Robert W. Cherny, *San Francisco* (Berkeley: University of California Press, 1986), 16–17, 204–208.

25. On these stereotypes and the postwar rise in anti-Semitism, see Albert S. Lindemann, *Anti-Semitism before the Holocaust* (Edinburgh Gate, UK: Pearson Education, 2000), ch. 4.

26. *The International Jew, the World's Foremost Problem, being a reprint of a series of articles appearing in the* Dearborn Independent *from May 22 to October 1920* (Dearborn: Dearborn Publishing Co., 1920), 1:6, 48. The *Independent* ran 92 successive articles on "the international Jew." "Selections" were reprinted in a four-volume set titled *The International Jew*. See also *Jewish Activities in the United States*, vol. 2; *Jewish Influence in American Life*, vol. 3; and *Aspects of Jewish Power in the United States*, vol. 4 of *The International Jew* (Dearborn: Dearborn Publishing Co., 1921–1922). Estimates of sales from 1920 to 1922 vary between 250,000 and 500,000. All Ford dealerships were

forced to sell the paper, even after boycotts began to hurt the businesses of many. The articles were more widely distributed in the volumes, with an estimated ten million copies sold and distributed in the United States through the 1920s. Ford was not interested in making a profit in the venture. He accepted no advertising and paid for the reprints and translations into other languages. See Albert Lee, *Henry Ford and the Jews* (New York: Stein & Day, 1980), 14; Baldwin, *Henry Ford and the Jews*, 146.

27. On the response to the "Peace Ship," see "The Ford Peace Party," in *Revolutionary Radicalism: Being the Report of the Joint Legislative Committee Investigating Seditious Activities,* Vol. 1 (Albany: J.B. Lyon Co., 1920), 988–999.

28. Ford quoted in Neil Baldwin, *Henry Ford and the Jews: The Mass Production of Hate* (New York: PublicAffairs, 2001), 77. On Ford's attempt to win public office, see *Revolutionary Radicalism*, 68–70.

29. Joseph Jefferson O'Neill, quoted in Baldwin, *Henry Ford and the Jews*, 91.

30. Madison Grant, *Passing of the Great Race* (New York: Charles Scribner's Sons, 1916), 15–16, 80–81. On Grant's influence and the book's sales, see Carey McWilliams, *A Mask for Privilege* (Boston: Little, Brown & Co., 1948), 56–60; Higham, *Strangers in the Land*, 271–272.

31. "The Jew in Character and Business" (originally published May 22, 1920), in *The International Jew, the World's Foremost Problem*, 10 (hereinafter, *International Jew*).

32. "The Jewish Question—Fact or Fancy?" (June 12, 1920), in *International Jew,* 53, 46–47.

33. "The Jew in Character and Business," in *International Jew,* 12. See also "The Jewish Question—Fact or Fancy?" in ibid., 52–53.

34. Discussions of Ford's attack have ignored its focus on the cultural power of Jews. Articles in later volumes circled back to these particular "regions," examining baseball, jazz music, and publishing. "Preface," *Jewish Activities in the United States,* vol. 2 of *International Jew,* 6.

35. "'Jewish' Plan to Split Society by 'Ideas'" (Aug. 14, 1920), *International Jew,* 2:143.

36. "Jewish Supremacy in Motion Picture World" (Feb. 19, 1921), in *International Jew,* 2:134.

37. "Rise of the First Theatrical Trust" (Jan. 8, 1921) *International Jew,* 2:102.

38. Henry Ford, *Edison: As I Know Him* (New York: Cosmopolitan Book Corp., 1930), 102. On Ford and Edison, see Lee, *Henry Ford and the Jews,* 7, 13, 42, 67–68; Baldwin, *Henry Ford and the Jews,* 11–12, 43, 53–54, 89–90, 322–324.

39. The MPPC pooled sixteen patents and included Edison, Biograph, Vitagraph, Essanay, Kalem, Selig, Lubin, Pathé Frères and Méliès, and the importer George Kleine. An excellent discussion of Edison's strategy is found in Sklar, *Movie-Made America,* ch. 3. By 1912 the patents share of film production and importation had fallen from 100 percent to slightly more than half. Sklar estimates the patents served only half to two-thirds of U.S. theaters. For the pat-

ents' focus on the middle class, see Nancy Rosenbloom, "Progressive Reform, Censorship, and the Motion Picture Industry, 1909–1917," in Ronald Edsforth and Larry Bennett, eds., *Popular Culture and Political Change* (New York: Basic Books, 1991), 45–47.

40. "Jewish Supremacy in Motion Picture World," 2:128–130.

41. "Jewish Control of the American Theater," in *International Jew*, 2:89, 92.

42. "The Jewish Aspect of the Movie Problem," in ibid., 2:117.

43. "Jewish Supremacy in Motion Picture World," 2:125.

44. "The Jewish Aspect of the Movie Problem," 2:117, 94, 126.

45. "Rise of the First Theatrical Trust," 2:104.

46. "Aryan": "The Jewish Aspect of the Movie Problem," 2:119. "Gullibles": "How Jews Capitalized a Protest Against Jews" (Jan. 22, 1921), in *International Jew*, 2:109.

47. Andreas Huyssen, "Modernism's Other: Mass Culture as Woman," in *After the Great Divide* (Bloomington: Indiana University Press, 1986), ch. 4. The author describes transatlantic elites' views of mass culture as the rise of a feminized, degraded commercial mass society.

48. "Jewish Supremacy in Motion Picture World," 2:128.

49. "The Jewish Aspect of the Movie Problem," 131–133.

50. "Jewish Control of the American Theater," 89.

51. "Trailing the New Anti-Semitism to Its Russian Lair," *Current Opinion* (April 1921): 501. After addressing Ford's investigation, the article attempted to establish the *Protocols* as forgeries.

52. Crane, "The Jew."

53. "A Protest against Anti-Semitism," *New York Times* (hereinafter *NYT*), Jan. 16, 1921, pp. 30–31.

54. Baldwin, *Henry Ford and the Jews,* 192–217.

55. For two examples of this view, see Louis Weitzenkorn, "A Jew among the Fords," *The Nation* (May 4, 1921): 652–653; Ralph Philip Boas, "Jew-Baiting in America," *Atlantic Monthly* (May 1921): 658–665.

56. La Guardia quoted in Thomas Kessner, *Fiorello H. La Guardia* (New York: McGraw-Hill, 1989), 125–126. For an indication of how little the campaign affected Ford's stature, see "The Formidability of Ford," *Literary Digest,* June 16, 1923, pp. 8–9. On the central place that "Fordism" occupied in the postwar international reform imagination, see Daniel T. Rodgers, *Atlantic Crossings* (Cambridge: Harvard University Press, 1998), 371–381.

57. James R Quirk, "Oh, Henry!" *Photoplay* (June 1921): 44. One editorial suggested that some industry insiders shared Ford's views. "Family quarrels should be fought in public—a principle which obviously is not being subscribed to by certain persons in the industry who are supplying information for Henry Ford's attack upon the business. These persons may think they are operating secretly, but they are wrong." See *Exhibitors Herald* (Dec. 1921): 30.

58. My view of the Klan owes the most to Nancy MacLean, *Behind the Mask of Chivalry: The Making of the Second Ku Klux Klan* (New York: Oxford University Press, 1994). MacLean characterizes the organization as part of the broader reactionary populist movements that erupted after World War I and

used nationalism, racism, and calls to restore traditional gender roles to heal society's ills. Most current work on the Klan focuses on its role as "a popular social movement, not an extremist organization," addressing "real social problems"; see Leonard J. Moore, "Historical Interpretations of the 1920s Klan," *Journal of Social History* 24.2 (1990): 352, 348.

59. Quotes are from MacLean, *Behind the Mask of Chivalry*, 90, 136, 113. MacLean calls Ford a Klansman but offers no evidence for the charge. On the persistent rumors of Ford's involvement, see also Kenneth T. Jackson, *The Ku Klux Klan and the City* (New York: Oxford University Press, 1967), 274n21. Because the Klan destroyed most of its records, it is impossible to say how many joined. Here, I follow estimates in MacLean, *Behind the Mask of Chivalry*, 5; and Jackson, *Klan and the City*, 4–8. After 1923, women were organized in the Women's KKK. On the original Ku Klux Klan, see Eric Foner, *Reconstruction: America's Unfinished Revolution* (New York: Harper & Row, 1988), 454–459.

60. Klan advertising quoted in MacLean, *Behind the Mask of Chivalry*, 98. See also ibid., 5–7, 104, 98–124. On Klan publicists' use of *Birth* in recruitment drives, see Jackson, *Klan and the City*, 70, 81, 118, 131, 200.

61. MacLean, *Behind the Mask of Chivalry*, 35–38, 144, 138.

62. John Sumner, "Are American Morals Disintegrating?" *Current Opinion* (May 1921): 608–611.

63. New York governor Miller quoted in "Are Women a Menace?" *The Nation* (Feb. 9, 1921): 198. Fredrick Boyd Stevenson, "Marriage and Divorce Equally Easy under the New Law in Red Russia," *BDE*, March 27, 1921, "Women" sec., 1; "Absolute Equality for Women," *BDE*, Feb. 17, 1921, p. 6.

64. "Will the Next World War Be Woman against Men?" *San Francisco Chronicle*, May 9, 1920, Magazine sec., 1.

65. Sumner, "Are American Morals Disintegrating?" 608.

66. Lee Grieveson, "Not Harmless Entertainment," in Charles Keil and Shelley Stamp, eds., *American Cinema's Transitional Era* (Berkeley: University of California Press, 2004), 272.

67. Four states had censorship laws at the start of 1921: Pennsylvania, Ohio, Kansas, and Maryland. Pennsylvania was the first state to pass a state censorship law, in 1911, but problems with the act and lack of funds prevented its enforcement until 1915. William Sheafe Chase, "Catechism on Motion Pictures in Inter-state Commerce," pamphlet published by the New York Civic League, Oct. 1922, 3rd ed., 38–39; Ruth Inglis, *Freedom of the Movies* (Chicago: University of Chicago Press, 1947), 70–71.

68. All four state boards required women members; see Oberholtzer, *The Morals of the Movie*, 70–71.

69. Donald Ramsaye Young, "Motion Pictures: A Study in Social Legislation" (Ph.D. thesis, University of Pennsylvania, 1922), 16–18, 65. A copy of the "Standards of the Pennsylvania Board of Censors" is included in appendix C, 94–99, 212–215.

70. Oberholtzer, quoted in Raymond J. Haberski Jr., *It's Only a Movie! Films and Critics in American Culture* (Lexington: University of Kentucky Press, 2001), 42.

71. Oberholtzer, *The Morals of the Movie*, 6. Ellis Paxson Oberholtzer, *A History of the United States since the Civil War*, Vol. 3 (New York: Macmillan, 1917).

72. "Women Join Fight for Clean Movies," *BDE*, March 3, 1921, p. 7. On the response to *Old Wives for New*, see Sumiko Higashi, "The New Woman and Consumer Culture," in Jennifer M. Bean and Diane Negra, eds., *A Feminist Reader in Early Cinema* (Durham, NC: Duke University Press, 2002), 316.

73. Haberski, *It's Only A Movie!* 43.

74. See Ellis Oberholtzer, "Censor and the 'Movie Menace,'" *North American Review* 212 (Nov. 1920): 641–647; Ellis Oberholtzer, "What Are the Movies Making of Our Children?" *World's Work* 41 (Jan. 1921): 249–253. On these journals' importance, see Rodgers, *Atlantic Crossings*, 66–67. On press reaction to Oberholtzer, see Chase, "Catechism of Motion Pictures in Inter-state Commerce," 14, 63.

75. Oberholtzer, *The Morals of the Movie*, 31, 6–7, 15, 18, 29, 59.

76. Ibid., 27, 28–29, 173, 41, 55, 98–99. On clubwomen, see particularly chs. 4 and 5.

77. Addams quoted in William Chafe, *The American Woman* (New York: Oxford University Press, 1972), 257n16.

78. Works that treat the centrality of motherhood as an important organizing principle in Progressive-era policy include Molly Ladd-Taylor, *Mother-Work: Women, Child Welfare, and the State, 1890–1930* (Chicago: University of Chicago Press, 1994); Linda Gordon, *Pitied but Not Entitled* (New York: Free Press, 1994).

79. GFWC president Alice Ames Winter quoted in Karen Blair, *The Clubwoman as Feminist: True Womanhood Redefined, 1868–1914* (New York: Holmes & Meier, 1980), 98–99. After a controversy over admitting black women, the GFWC decided in 1902 that each state or territorial federation could decide, but then adopted a provision that made this impossible. Blair also notes the club's class snobbery and nativism. On the cresting of its influence after the war, see Rothman, *Women's Proper Place*, 65–66.

80. Young, "Motion Pictures," 19.

81. "Twenty States Have Censorship Bills," *Moving Picture World* (Feb. 10, 1917): 861. On the importance of the GFWC to the NBR, see Charles Matthew Feldman, *The National Board of Censorship (Review) of Motion Pictures, 1909–1922* (Windsor, UK: Arno Press Cinema Program, 1977), 132–154.

82. Between 1907 and 1908, the People's Institute and the Women's Municipal League conducted an investigation of movie theaters and their content that judged films to be basically wholesome entertainment. After New York City's mayor closed the city's movie theaters in 1908, local exhibitors asked the two organizations to evaluate films before release, leading to the creation of the National Board of Censorship. When producers agreed to voluntarily submit films and follow the committee's recommendations, the board's work became national in scope. To emphasize its free speech stance, the organization changed its name in 1916. See Inglis, *Freedom of the Movies*, 73–82; Rosenbloom, "Progressive Reform, Censorship, and the Motion Picture Industry"; Feldman, *The National Board of Censorship (Review) of Motion Pictures*, 4–26.

83. Peck quoted in Betty Shannon, "Club Women Discuss Pictures," *Moving Picture World* (June 10, 1916): 1855.

84. Feldman, *The National Board of Censorship (Review) of Motion Pictures*, 139.

85. The survey by the Chicago Political Equality League found that only 20 percent of 1,765 films were "good," while 21 percent were "bad" and 49 percent "not worth while"; reprinted in Young, "Motion Pictures," 22–24.

86. See Florence Butler Blanchard, *Censorship of Motion Pictures* (Chicago: Englewood Print Shop, 1919), 4–6, 12, 15. State branches of the GFWC that conducted studies included South Dakota, Arkansas, New York, Michigan, Rhode Island, Virginia, and the four with existing boards.

87. "One Standard Favored by Women," *San Francisco Bulletin*, June 9, 1920, p. 9.

88. Of the 67 films rejected in Ohio between July 1919 and June 1921, 35 fell within the category of sex pictures. This number was nearly three times the number of comedies rejected, which was the next largest category. See *Wid's Year Book 1921*, 217. Cuts made by New York's board between Aug. 1 and Dec. 31, 1921, also mostly involved sexual vice. There were 146 cuts made on such grounds; 54 on the grounds of criminality; 40 on others. Cuts to the films were made on the following grounds: a: 85, "Immoral"; 35, "Inhuman"; 54, Tending to Incite Crime"; 61, "Immoral or Tending to Corrupt Morals"; 5, "Sacrilegious." From the Report of Education Department, State of New York, Motion Picture Division, James Wingate, Director, reprinted in William H. Short, *A Generation of Motion Pictures* (New York: National Committee for the Study of Social Values in Motion Pictures, 1978 [1928]), 13, Censorship Collection, MHL. A report by the Chicago Motion Picture Commission revealed that most excisions between Nov. 1917 and Dec. 1920 were for sexual immorality; see Young, "Motion Pictures," 21. For the Pennsylvania board's focus on sexual immorality, see *Report of Pennsylvania State Board of Censors* (Philadelphia: J. L. L. Kuhn, 1917), 8.

89. J. J. Phelan, *Motion Pictures as a Phase of Commercialized Amusement in Toledo, Ohio* (Toledo: Little Book Press, 1919), 9, Censorship Collection, MHL.

90. Quoted in Kunzel, *Fallen Women, Problem Girls*, 55. Kunzel offers a rich exploration of the gendered nature of sex delinquency.

91. Fredrick Boyd Stevenson, "How Brooklyn Is Getting into Action for a Campaign against Unclean Movies," *BDE*, Feb. 13, 1921, "Women" sec., p. 1. "Womanhood": Brooklyn assemblyman W.F. Clayton, who introduced what would become the Clayton-Lusk censorship bill to the legislature on Feb. 16, 1921, quoted in "Censor Bill Passes New York Assembly: Governor Is Expected to Sign It Soon," *Moving Picture World* (April 30, 1921): 936. See also "Censorship Bill Is at Last Introduced in the New York Legislature," *Moving Picture World* (Feb. 26, 1921): 1025.

92. Stevenson, "How Brooklyn Is Getting into Action," 1.

93. Miller quoted in "The Nation-Wide Battle over Movie Purification," *Literary Digest*, May 14, 1921, p. 32; "Miller Joins Fight to Bar Exhibition of Indecent Movies," *BDE*, March 3, 1921, p. 18. On the mayor, see Fredrick

Boyd Stevenson, "Hylan to Take Action on the Movies That Are Depicting Crime and Vice," *BDE,* Jan. 16, 1921, "Women" sec., p. 3.

94. "Miller Joins Fight to Bar Exhibition of Indecent Movies."

95. NBR called a "farce" in Fredrick Boyd Stevenson, "Who Reviewed Photoplay 'The Penalty'?" *BDE,* Feb. 6, 1921, "Women" sec., p. 1; "Dirty and Vicious Films," editorial, *BDE,* Feb. 8, 1921, p. 6.

96. "Await Answer to Immoral Films," April 14, 1919; "Mrs. O'Grady's Attack Illogical, Says Goldwyn," April 15, 1919, both unsourced clippings, Parsons Scrapbook no. 3, MHL. "Mrs. O'Grady Raps Indecent Movies," *BDE,* March 3, 1921, p. 9. "Uncensored Movies Lead Young Astray, Says Mrs. O'Grady," *BDE,* Feb. 8, 1921, p. 9.

97. Stevenson, "Who Reviewed Photoplay 'The Penalty'?"

98. *The Penalty* (Eminent Authors Pictures, 1920). Quotes are from the film.

99. "Clean Movie Fight Gets New Support," *BDE,* March 18, 1921, p. 11.

100. "Catholic Society Backs Clayton Bill," *BDE,* March 21, 1921, p. 5.

101. "Flatbush Meeting Approves Law for Clean 'Movies,'" *BDE,* March 8, 1921, p. 9.

102. Fredrick Boyd Stevenson quoted in *BDE,* Jan. 1, 1921, "Women" sec., p. 1.

103. "Clean Movie Fight Gets New Support"; Stevenson, "Who Reviewed Photoplay 'The Penalty'?"

104. "G.Y. Janes" quoted in Fredrick Boyd Stevenson, "Forty Four State Legislatures Ready to Act on 'Movie' Censorship Bills," *BDE,* Feb. 27, 1921, p. 1.

105. Fredrick Boyd Stevenson, "Members of the Motion Picture Board Will Demand Thorough Investigation," *BDE,* Feb. 20, 1921, p. 1.

106. "Brooklyn Club Women Disapprove 'Woman Pays Club' Doctrine," *BDE,* Feb. 3, 1921, p. 18.

107. "The Woman Pays Party," Jan. 8, 1921, Parsons Scrapbook no. 6, MHL. See also "Earning Her Rights," May 20, 1920, Parsons Scrapbook no. 4, MHL; "The Woman Pays Club," April 18, 1920, Parsons Scrapbook no. 6, MHL.

108. "Brooklyn Club Women Disapprove 'Woman Pays Club' Doctrine."

109. "A 'Home Woman' Victory," *BDE,* Feb. 5, 1921, p. 6; "Absolute Equality for Women," *BDE,* Feb. 17, 1921, p. 6; "Good Advice to Women," *BDE,* Feb. 18, 1921, p. 6; "Out of the Suffrage Camp," *BDE,* Feb. 21, 1921, p. 6.

110. "Should Moving Pictures Be Censored?" 652.

111. *NYT,* March 6, 1921, p. 7.

112. The Thirteen Points, reprinted in "Should Moving Pictures Be Censored?" 652.

113. "Producers Agree to Reform Films," *NYT,* March 15, 1921, 11. See also "Should Motion Pictures Be Censored?" 652. On Waterman's role, see "Miller Joins Fight to Bar Exhibition of Indecent Movies."

114. "Proposed Federal Censorship," *NYT,* March 18, 1921, 2.

115. "Sex War On in Films." The article likened Crafts to a "red rag to a bull so far as the picture people are concerned."

116. Wilbur F. Crafts, Ph. D., *National Perils and Hopes* (Cleveland: F.M. Barton Co., 1910), iii.

117. Rev. Wilbur F. Crafts, Ph.D., ed., *Patriotic Studies of a Quarter Century of Moral Legislation in Congress* (Washington, DC: International Reform Bureau, 1911), 2, 15, 23, 7–8, 10–11, 24.

118. "Quarter Century of Manifold Reforming," *20th Century Quarterly* 18.3 (1919): 5, 126, 128.

119. Seaborn Rodenberry, quoted in Grieveson, *Policing Cinema*, 130. For more on prizefight films, see ibid., ch. 4.

120. "Extracts from Hearings before the Committee on Education, House of Representatives, on Bills to Establish a Federal Motion Picture Commission," 63rd Congress, 2nd sess. (Washington, DC: Government Printing Office, 1914), 1, 6–8.

121. U.S. House of Representatives, Committee on Education, *Motion Pictures Hearings, 1916* (New York: Arno Press, 1978), 8.

122. "International Reform Bureau Plans, 1919–1922," *20th Century Quarterly* 18.3 (1919): 6.

123. On Chase and Crafts's consistent teamwork, see "Extracts from Hearings before the Committee on Education"; U.S. House of Representatives, *Motion Pictures Hearings, 1916*. On Chase's role in New York's 1907 closings, see Staiger, *Bad Women*, 95–96, 98, 102, 107–108.

124. "90 percent": "Producers Agree to Reform Films." For the other quotes in this paragraph, see "Brady Wants Trade to Reform Movies," *NYT*, March 21, 1921, p. 11; Chase, "Catechism of Motion Pictures in Inter-state Commerce," 57–58, 61.

125. "The Nation-Wide Battle over Movie Purification." This article surveys newspapers that had publicized Chase's arguments. See also "In the Name of Liberty," *Moving Picture World* (Dec. 25, 1920): 979.

126. Chase, "Catechism on Motion Pictures in Inter-state Commerce," 57; see also 13, 14, 21, 24, 57–58, 61, 66, 68–71, 76, 121–122.

127. On his possible Klan membership, see Kevin Brownlow, *Behind the Mask of Innocence* (New York: Knopf, 1990), 56. Chase earned praise from *The Searchlight*; see "Canon Chase: Episcopalian Defends the Klan," *The Searchlight*, quoted in Carr, *Hollywood and Anti-Semitism*, 70.

128. Chase, "Catechism on Motion Pictures in Inter-state Commerce," 60, 116, 66, 115–119, 67, 22, 107.

129. Chase quoted in Leigh Ann Wheeler, "Rescuing Sex from Prudery and Prurience: American Women's Use of Sex Education as an Antidote to Obscenity," *Journal of Women's History* 12.3 (2000): 175.

130. "Should Moving Pictures Be Censored?" 652. See also "Overdoing the Sex Motive in Moving Pictures"; "Revamping the Vampire," *The Nation* (Aug. 10, 1921): 140; Gertrude Atherton, "Is There a Moral Decline," *The Forum* (March 1921): 312.

131. Sumner, "Are American Morals Disintegrating?" 610–611.

132. "Movie Abuses a National Calamity," *Literary Digest*, March 12, 1921, pp. 32.

133. "The Nation-Wide Battle over Movie Purification."

134. Sydney Cohen, quoted in *Literary Digest*, Feb. 19, 1921.

135. "Twisting the Political Tale Brings a Roar," *Moving Picture World* (Sept. 10, 1921): 148–149.

136. On the resolution, see *Congressional Record*, 61:5621–5622 (Aug. 24, 1921). On the FTC, see "Final Sections of Federal Trade Bill," *Wid's Daily*, Sept. 10, 1921, p. 2; "'Have Violated No Law' Says Executives of Famous Players," *Exhibitors Herald* (Sept. 17, 1921): 33–36.

137. The law allowed the governor to appoint three censors at $7,500 a year to determine if a movie was "obscene, indecent, immoral, inhuman, sacrilegious" or "would tend to corrupt morals or incite to crime." See Young, "Motion Pictures," 41–46.

CHAPTER 5. A STAR IS BORN

1. "Chicago Best City for Girls," *Chicago Evening American,* Jan. 3, 1913, p. 3.

2. Ibid.

3. Displaying the period's typically careless approach to spelling, the article used "Rappe" throughout, but listed her name as Virginia Rapp under the picture. See also "Tragedy Marked Virginia Here," *Chicago Herald and Examiner,* Sept. 16, 1921, p. 3.

4. *A Foolish Virgin* (Clara Kimball Young Film Corporation, 1916); *Paradise Garden* (Metro, 1917). Harold Lockwood was a popular romantic lead before he died in 1918 during the influenza pandemic. On Julian Eltinge, see Daniel Hurewitz, *Bohemian Los Angeles and the Making of Modern Politics* (Berkeley: University of California Press, 2007), 27–38.

5. *An Adventuress* (Republic, 1920). The film was reissued again as *Isle of Love* in 1922, after Valentino became a star. On the drop in the production of war films by 1920, see DeBauche, *Reel Patriotism,* 166.

6. Jan. 2, 1919, Parsons Scrapbook no. 3, MHL. *His Musical Sneeze* (Sunshine Comedies, 1919); *A Twilight Baby* (Sunshine Comedies, 1920).

7. "A Star at Last," editorial, *Variety,* Sept. 23, 1921, p. 9.

8. "Time to Clean Up the Movies," *Literary Digest* (Oct. 15, 1921): 28–29.

9. Alice Kessler-Harris, "Independence and Virtue in the Lives of Wage-Earning Women in the United States," in Judith Friedlander, Blanche Wiesen Cook, and Alice Kessler-Harris, eds., *Women in Culture and Politics* (Bloomington: Indiana University Press, 1986), 3–17.

10. "S.F. Booze Party Kills Young Actress," *San Francisco Examiner,* Sept. 10, 1921, p. 1. I looked on microfilm at the coverage in eight daily newspapers. Hearst owned three: the *New York American* (hereafter *NYA*); *Chicago Herald and Examiner* (hereafter *CHE*); and *San Francisco Examiner* (hereafter *SFX*). I also looked at the *St. Louis Post-Dispatch* (hereafter *STL*), *Brooklyn Daily Eagle, Los Angeles Times, New York Times,* and *San Francisco Chronicle* (hereafter *SFC*).

11. On the coroner's inquest, see "History of the Case," Rappe Death Report.

12. Assessing the popularity of comedic stars is more difficult than with other types. While the genre of slapstick encountered little opposition from

reformers, most comedians were treated as a separate, slightly vulgarized class. See Koszarski, *An Evening's Entertainment*, 262. For a claim that Arbuckle was rated "second only to Chaplin," see Sklar, *Movie-Made America,* 107. A 1921 poll ranked Arbuckle ahead of Chaplin; see *Moving Picture World* (March 19, 1921): 12.

13. Al Semnacher, "The People of the State of California vs. Roscoe Arbuckle for Murder, in the Police Court of the City and County of San Francisco, Department No. 2, Honorable Sylvain J. Lazarus, Judge," 158, Special Collections, San Francisco Public Library (hereafter Court Transcript).

14. "Arbuckle and Lawyer Leave for Bay City," *LAT,* Sept. 10, 1921, pt. 2, pp. 1, 8.

15. "S.F. Booze Party Kills Young Actress," 1–2. See also "Arbuckle's Death Party Told in Court," *CHE,* Sept. 13, 1921, 1; "Fatty Arbuckle to Face Charge of Murder Today: Death of Actress in Hotel Suite Laid to Comedian," *BDE,* Sept. 12, 1921, p. 1; "Arbuckle Is Jailed on Murder Charge in Woman's Death," *NYT,* Sept. 12, 1921, p. 1.

16. "Arbuckle Is Charged with Murder of Girl: Actress' Dying Words Cause Star's Arrest," *SFX,* Sept.11, 1921, p. 1; "Nurse Relates Last Words of Dying Actress," *NYA,* Sept. 12, 1921, p. 1.

17. "Torn Silk Garments of Dead Girl Found in Los Angles," *SFX,* Sept 12, 1921, p. 2; "Dead Actress in Character," *NYA,* Sept. 13, 1921, p. 3.

18. "Arbuckle Is Charged with Murder of Girl," 1–2. "Bosom friend": "Woman Makes Formal Charge: Dead Girl's Bosom Friend Gives Police More Details," *NYA,* Sept. 13, 1921, p. 1; "protectorix": "'Fatty' in Court and Principal Accusers," *CHE,* Sept. 17, 1921, p. 3; "chaperon": "'Wild Night' in Arbuckle's Rooms Told by Mrs. Delmont, Chaperon of Ill-Fated Virginia Rappe," *NYA,* Sept. 18, 1921, p. 3.

19. See also "Arbuckle Returns to San Francisco and Denies Anything Improper—Men in Party Back Him Up—WOMEN CONTRADICT THIS," *NYT,* Sept. 11, 1921, p. 1. "Actor Denies He's Fugitive: Holds 'Fatty' Blameless; Leaves for New York," *CHE,* Sept. 21, 1921, p. 3.

20. "Miss Rappe Was Designer, Film Actress," *SFX,* Sept. 11, 1921, p. 3; "Dead Actress Rich and Noted for Her Gowns," *NYA,* Sept. 12, 1921, p. 3; "Miss Virginia Rappe Dies following a Party in Movie Actor's Rooms," *NYT,* Sept. 11, 1921, p. 2.

21. The two films were *The Punch of the Irish* (First National, 1921) and *A Twilight Baby* (Sunshine Comedies, 1920). "Many Bruises Are Found by the Coroner on Girl's Body," *SFX,* Sept., 11, 1921, p. 3.

22. "Physician Tells Detail [*sic*] of Physical Examination," *SFX,* Sept. 11, 1921, p. 3; "Facing Charge of Perjury, 2 Girls Testify," *SFX,* Sept. 14, 1921, p. 2.

23. See "Arbuckle Indicted for Murder," *NYT,* Sept. 14, 1921, p. 3.

24. Rumwell quoted in "Remains of Miss Rappe at Morgue," *SFX,* Sept. 11, 1921, p. 3. "Post Mortem by Rumwell Held Illegil [*sic*]," *SFX,* Sept. 12, 1921, p. 3. Brady quoted in "Remains of Miss Rappe at Morgue." Beardslee quoted in Court Transcript, 198–199, 202–203.

25. "Brady Asks Arbuckle Indictment Today: Witnesses Guarded, Intimidation Feared," *SFX,* Sept. 12, 1921, p. 1. See also "Arbuckle Is Jailed on Murder

Charge in Woman's Death"; "Film Comedian Is Locked Up without Bail: Will Not Talk," *NYA*, Sept. 12, 1921, p. 1; "Witness against Arbuckle Recants; Another Missing," *BDE*, Sept. 13, 1921, p. 1; "Arbuckle's Death Party Told in Court."

26. Henry Lehrman quoted in Louis Fehr, "Dead Girl's Fiancé Calls Prisoner Beast: 'Can't Face Arbuckle: I'd Kill Him,' He Says," *SFX*, Sept. 12, 1921, p. 1. Lehrman's first interview was carried in "Fiance of Dead Film Actress Vows Vengeance: 'Must Reckon with Me If He Is Freed,' Says Henry Lehrman," *NYA*, Sept. 12, 1921, p. 1; "'I'd Kill Him,' Says Fiancé of Virginia," *CHE*, Sept. 12, 1921, p. 1; "'Arbuckle Beast from the Gutter; I Would Kill Him,' Declares Virginia's Fiancé," *LAT*, Sept. 12, 1921, p. 1; "Miss Rappe's Fiancé Threatens Vengeance," *NYT*, Sept. 13, 1921, p. 2; "'Fatty' Arbuckle to Face Charge of Murder Today." See also "Won Honors as Girl," *CHE*, Sept. 13, 1921, p. 3; "Girl of High Ideals, Says Her Companion," *NYA*, Sept. 13, 1921, p. 1; "L.A. Realtor Pays Tribute to Virginia Rappe," *SFX*, Sept. 15, 1921, p. 2; "Virginia Rappe, Gifted as Dancer, Shrank from Stage," *CHE*, Sept. 21, 1921, p. 3; "Rappe's Beauty Too Fine for Film Stardom," *CHE*, Sept. 25, 1921, p. 3.

27. "Roscoe Arbuckle Faces an Inquiry on Woman's Death," *NYT*, Sept. 11, 1921, p. 1; "Arbuckle Jailed for Murder: Bail Is Denied," *LAT*, Sept. 11, 1921, p. 1; "Arbuckle Faces Probe in Death of Actress," *NYA*, Sept. 11, 1921, p. 1; "'Fatty' Arbuckle Detained by Police after Actress Dies," *BDE*, Sept. 11, 1921, p. 1; "Hold 'Fatty' Arbuckle in Girl's Death: Virginia Rappe, Former Chicago Girl Dies after Gay Party," *CHE*, Sept. 11, 1921, p. 1; "'Fatty' Arbuckle Detained after Actress' Death," *STL*, Sept. 11, 1921, p. 1.

28. "Arbuckle Dragged Rappe Girl to Room, Woman Testifies," *NYT*, Sept. 12, 1921, p. 1. West Coast newspapers particularly dominated their markets; see Nasaw, *The Chief*, 313–314, 322–323, 386.

29. William Randolph Hearst to Adolph Zukor, Sept. 21, 1921, Zukor Correspondence, file 4, MHL.

30. See Sennett, *King of Comedy*, 64–67; Ramsaye, *A Million and One Nights*, 542–543. See also Ephraim Katz, *The Film Encyclopedia* (New York: Perigee, 1979), 708–709.

31. See note 26, this chapter. Other interviews with Lehrman include "Lehrman Asks Law's Justice on Arbuckle," *SFX*, Sept. 13, 1921, p. 3; "'Convict Him,' Brady Urged by Telegram," *SFX*, Sept. 14, 1921, p. 2; "Lehrman Sends Money to Pay Witness's Bill," *NYA*, Sept. 15, 1921, p. 2; "Brady Again Commended by Lehrman," *SFX*, Sept. 16, 1921, p. 2; "Dead Ears Will Hear Love Words, Fiance Is Sure," *CHE*, Sept. 17, 1921, p. 3; "Virginia Rappe's Beauty Was Too Fine for Film Stardom"; "8,000 at L.A. View Body of Virginia Rappe," *SFX*, Sept. 19, 1921, p. 1.

32. Fehr, "Dead Girl's Fiance Calls Prisoner Beast"; "Chum of Dead Girl Makes New Charges," *CHE*, Sept. 13, 1921, 3; "Mrs. Spreckles Only Deathbed Caller," *NYA*, Sept. 13, 1921, 3.

33. "Falstaff of the Movies and Victim of the 'Party,'" *CHE*, Sept. 14, 1921, p. 2. The event moved from a "gay party" to an orgy immediately after Lehrman's interview; see "Three Striking Poses of Virginia Rappe, Victim in Arbuckle Orgy,"

LAT, Sept. 14, 1921, p. 1; "'Lead the Quiet Life,' Was the Last Advice of Virginia Rappe to Girls; Victim of Orgy," *NYA*, Sept. 14, 1921, p. 3; "Zey Prevost Tells of Wild Orgy," *SFX*, Sept. 15, 1921, p. 2; "Persons Supplying Booze at Orgy Are to Be Prosecuted," *SFX*, Sept. 15, 1921, p. 3; "Tampering with 'Orgy' Witnesses Suspected by the Police," *SFX*, Sept. 16, 1921, p. 2; "Lay Death of Virginia to Third Man at Orgy," *CHE*, Sept. 18, 1921, pp. 1, 3; "'Wild Night' in Arbuckle's Rooms Told at Inquest"; "Third Person with Girl and Actor in 'Orgy,' Is Hint," *NYA*, Sept. 19, 1921, pp. 1, 3; "Brady Wires to Stop 'Orgy' Guest," *SFX*, Sept. 21, 1921, p. 1.

34. Mollie Merrick, "Yesterday's Jester," *SFX*, Sept. 14, 1921, p. 2; "thorough Bohemian": *Dallas Morning News*, Sept. 12, 1921, p. 1.

35. "Stepmother Says Money Ruined 'Fatty,'" *CHE*, Sept. 12, 1921, p. 5; "Fatty Began Life as a $3-a-Day Super," *NYA*, Sept. 12, 1921, p. 3; "Arbuckle Once a Plumber," *LAT*, Sept. 12, 1921, p. 2; "Fatty Arbuckle Had 'Thin' Time in Early Days: Never Good Actor in Stage Roles," *BDE*, Sept. 13, 1921, p. 2; "'Fatty' Former Show Barker," *LAT*, Sept. 13, 1921, p. 2; "Story of Farm Boy's Rise to Film Star," *NYA*, Sept. 13, 1921, p. 2.

36. "Death Party Told in Court," *CHE*, Sept. 13, 1921, p. 1. See also "Girl Witness in Arbuckle Case Accused," *SFX*, Sept. 13, 1921, p. 2; "Witness against Arbuckle Recants"; "Woman Makes Formal Charge: Bitter Legal Battle Is On," *NYA*, Sept. 13, 1921, 1, 3; "Arbuckle Dragged Rappe Girl to Room, Woman Testifies."

37. "'Lead the Quiet Life,' Was the Last Advice of Virginia Rappe to Girls"; "Hope for Fame Lured Actress to Her Death," *NYA*, Sept. 14, 1921, p. 3. See also "Another Girl Was Attacked at Fatal Arbuckle Party," *BDE*, Sept. 13, 1921, p. 1; "Falstaff of the Movies and Victim of the 'Party.'"

38. "Life of Virginia: Miss Rappe's Ambition Led Her to Play with Fire," *CHE*, Sept. 26, 1921, p. 3; "'Wild Night' of in Arbuckle's Rooms Told at Inquest."

39. Robert H. Wilson, "Stories Told Coroner, Jury Conflicting," *SFX*, Sept. 14, 1921, pp. 2–4. See also "Dying Girl Hid Secret, Nurses Say," *CHE*, Sept. 14, 1921, p. 3; "Arbuckle Indicted for Manslaughter," *NYT*, Sept. 14, 1921, p. 2; "Proceedings of the Day," *LAT*, Sept. 14, 1921, p. 2. Alice Blake and Zey Prevost were continually referred to as "show girl witnesses." On blackmail charges, see "Alice Blake Tells of Visit to Arbuckle," *SFX*, Sept. 12, 1921, p. 3; "Alice Blake, One of Death Party Quizzed by Prosecutor," *NYA*, Sept. 14, 1921, pp. 1, 3; "Zey Prevost Tells of Wild Orgy"; "Charge Bribe Offered to Woman Witness in Arbuckle Case," *CHE*, Sept. 15, 1921, pp. 1, 3.

40. "They Walked into His Parlour," *SFX*, Sept. 15, 1921, p. 1; "Entangled in the Web of His Own Weaving," *NYA*, Sept. 25, 1921, p. 4.

41. "Girl Tells Full Story of Death Party," *CHE*, Sept. 15, 1921, p. 3; "Arbuckle Indicted for Manslaughter"; "Dying Girl Hid Secret"; Prevost, Court Transcript, 310.

42. "Tragedy Marked Virginia Here"; "Life of Virginia Rappe One of Work and Hardship," *CHE*, Sept. 19, 1921, p. 3. The latter article was the first installment in an eight-chapter story of Rappe's life run in *CHE*. Other Hearst papers excerpted passages from these articles.

43. "Origins of Miss Rappe: Said to Have Been Daughter of British Noble-man in Chicago Romance," *LAT*, Sept. 20, 1921, p. 1; "New Chapter Shows Heritage of Beauty and Love for Frolics," *CHE*, Sept. 20, 1921, p. 3.

44. "Virginia's 'Nightie Tango' on Liner Startles Passengers," *CHE*, Sept. 23, 1921, p 2. The two women reportedly wore nightgowns over evening gowns for their performance. See also "Miss Rappe Was Designer, Film Actress," *SFX*, Sept. 11, 1921, p. 3; "Dead Actress Rich and Noted for Her Gowns," *NYA*, Sept. 12, 1921, p. 3; "Broken Love Affair Leads Virginia into Movie Career," *CHE*, Sept. 24, 1921, p. 3.

45. Annie Laurie, "What's Gone Wrong with World Today? Old Ideals for Women Is on Way Out," *SFX*, Sept. 13, 1921, p. 3. "Annie Laurie" was a pseud-onym for Winifred Black, notorious for her stunt journalism and emotional style. See Nasaw, *The Chief*, 73, 99–100.

46. Annie Laurie, "Old Rules for Girls Supplanted by New Now: What's a Little Pitch among Friends?" *SFX*, Sept. 14, 1921, p. 2. See also Winifred Black, "Orgy Menace Is Grave, Says Winifred Black," *NYA*, Sept. 15, 1921, p. 2; "Rappe Death Held as Warning to Girls: God Is Speaking through Lips of the Dead Actress, Says Dr. L. Gordon," *SFX*, Sept. 19, 1921, p. 3.

47. "Orgies in City Ready to Stage New Tragedy," *NYA*, Sept. 13, 1921, p. 1. "History of the Case," Death Report, reported on in "Rid San Francisco of De-bauchees, Says Coroner's Verdict," *SFX*, Sept. 15, 1921, p. 2. "Girl Tells Full Story of Death Party"; "Class Arbuckle with Debauchee, Gangster, in Coroner's Jury Verdict," *LAT*, Sept. 15, 1921, p. 1.

48. The Police Court trial would not begin until Sept. 22. "Not guilty" was not included among "Four Possible Verdicts in Trial of Film Actor," *NYA*, Sept. 19, 1921, p. 3.

49. Jack Arnold, "Good Will Win," letter to *LAT*, Sept. 27, pt. 2, p. 4. See also "Will Arbuckle's Plight Clear Moral Atmosphere? Asks Cleric," *SFX*, Sept. 23, 1921, p. 1.

50. "League Hears Discussion of Arbuckle Case," *NYA*, Sept. 20, 1921, p. 1. Arbuckle's films were banned in England; see "English Crusade Starting on Sex and Doubtful Film," *Variety*, Oct. 21, 1921, p. 38.

51. "The Arbuckle Incident," *LAT*, Sept. 13, 1921, pt. 2, p. 4; Madam Q., "These Beauties Reap Same Harvest: 'Wine, Women and Song Killed Virginia,'" *CHE*, Sept. 18, 1921, p. 3; "Education of Girls Needed, Says Doctor, *NYA*, Sept. 14, 1921, p. 3.

52. "Banning the Arbuckle Films," editorial, *BDE*, Sept. 13, 1921, p. 5. Cen-sors could not pull Arbuckle's and Rappe's films out of theaters through "any legal method"; see "Some Officials Issue Orders against Films," *NYA*, Sept. 13, 1921, p. 2; "Laughter Greets Arbuckle Films in One Theater Here: No Action by the State Board," *BDE*, Sept. 13, 1921, p. 1.

53. *Motion Picture World* (Sept. 24, 1921): 324; *NYT*, Sept. 14, 1921, 3; "Society Leaders' Millions to Back Better Pictures: Arbuckle Scandal's Effect," *Variety*, Sept. 16, 1921, p. 1. It would be impossible to list all the stories of out-rage. On the same day that *Variety* made this report, the *NYT* ran two with a similar tone; see "Says Films Poison Youth," and "Would Close All Movies," *NYT*, Sept. 14, 1921, p. 2.

54. Louis Mayer to King Vidor, quoted in Berg, *Goldwyn,* 106.

55. "Evil Influence of Bad Motion Picture Resorts," Proximo Club to City Council, n.d., file 2524, "Motion Picture File to be known as 2723," Los Angeles City Archive.

56. "Democracy": Henry Weeks to *LAT,* Sept. 20, 1921, pt. 2, p. 2; "liberty": L.J. Bergere to *LAT,* Oct. 29, 1921, pt. 2, p. 10. A representative sample of anti-industry letters to *LAT* includes Evelyn Frances, "The Arbuckle Case," and H.W. Coffin, "Intolerable," Sept. 16, 1921, pt. 2, p. 11; Mary Andrews, "The Industry," Sept. 18, 1921, pt. 3, p. 38; Mrs. William Francis, "Says They're Bad"; Alice Scudder, "Favors Censor," Oct. 16, 1921, pt. 2, p. 3.

57. "Christian citizenship": Presbytery of Los Angeles to City Council, Sept. 28, 1921, file 2723, Los Angeles City Archive; "Anglo-Saxon development": Alfred Borden to *LAT,* Oct. 6, 1921, pt. 2, p. 6. On the petition, see "Censor Ordinance Action Deferred," Sept. 8, 1921, *LAT,* pt. 2, p. 11; "Causes Censor," *Wid's Daily,* Sept. 19, 1921, p. 1. LA City Ordinance no. 377778, approved Dec. 24, 1917, provided for the employment of one commissioner of films to pre-pass all films, but it was never enforced. The groups involved in pressing the LA City Council included the Ministerial Union; the Church Federation; the Anti-Saloon League; the Proximo Club; Pastor R.P. Shuler, representing the "over thirteen hundred members" of Trinity Methodist Church; and the Presbytery of Los Angeles, located in Pomona, representing "75,000 adherents." Those most active organizations opposing the measure included the Los Angeles Theaters Association; Los Angeles Chamber of Commerce; American Legion; Merchants and Manufacturers Association of Los Angeles; and Affiliated Pictures Interests, representing all branches of labor involved in making motion pictures. These efforts are documented in "Motion Picture File 2035 to be known as 2723" and "File 2524," 1921, Los Angeles City Archive. The Sept. 14 City Council meeting on the issue was reported in "Was His Worst Enemy,' *LAT,* Sept. 14, 1921, p. 6.

58. "Ministers in Censor Clash," *LAT,* Sept. 27, 1921, pt. 2, pp. 1, 9. On Edmundson, see also "Pastor Opposes Censorship," *LAT,* Oct. 29, 1921, pt. 2, p. 11. For protests against the Ministerial Union's attack on Edmundson and the censorship ordinance, see American Legion to City Council, Sept. 26, 1921; American Legion to City Council, Sept. 28, 1921, both in file 2723, Los Angeles City Archive.

59. Lillian Thomas to *LAT,* Sept. 18, 1921, pt. 2, p. 2. A representative sample of pro-industry letters to the *LAT* includes Edmond Fortune, "Defends Actors," Sept. 19, 1921, pt. 2, p. 2; John Blackwood, "The World Is Jealous," Oct. 6, 1921, pt. 1, p. 6; Mrs. A. Perkins, "Likes the Movies," Oct. 16, 1921, pt. 3, p. 34; T.W. Sheffield, "Censorship UnAmerican," Oct. 17, 1921, pt. 2, p. 2.

60. J.E. Tilley to *LAT,* Oct. 3, 1921, pt. 3, p. 2. Michael Rudolph, Esquire, to the City Council, Sept. 28, 1921, file 2723, Los Angeles City Archive; petition, n.d., ibid.

61. Merchants and Manufacturers Association of Los Angeles to City Council, Sept. 24, 1921, file 2723, Los Angeles City Archive. See also Los Angeles

Chamber of Commerce to City Council, n.d., ibid.; "Disaster Seen in Censorship," *LAT*, Sept. 29, 1921, pt. 2, 2.

62. "Film Studios May Quit City," *LAT*, Sept. 25, 1921, p. 6. For the complete letter, see MPPA to City Council, Sept. 23, 1921, file 2723, Los Angeles City Archive.

63. "Film People Tell Views," *LAT*, Sept. 13, 1921, pp. 1–2; "Film World Is Rended," *LAT*, Sept. 12, 1921, pp. 1–2; "Booze Parties Reported," *LAT*, Sept. 13, 1921, p. 3; "Cinema Colony Stirred," *LAT*, Sept. 15, 1921, p. 1; "May Seize Arbuckle's Booze Here," *LAT*, Sept. 23, 1921, p. 1.

64. "Snap Judgment on Arbuckle Deplored," *LAT*, Sept. 14, 1921, p. 2. See also "Officials Seeking Notoriety Try to Hang Arbuckle, Says Schenck," *LAT*, Sept. 13, 1921, p. 2; "Brady Won't Try to Clean Up Film Life," *LAT*, Sept. 14, 1921, p. 4; "Cinema Colony Stirred," 1–2; "Should Not Blame Motion Pictures," *LAT*, Sept. 23, 1921, p. 2; "Hart Feels Sorry for Film Comedian," *LAT*, Sept. 23, 1921, 2.

65. Dore Oliphant Coe, "Inspector of Films," *LAT*, Sept. 26, 1921, pt. 2, p. 4. See also "The Arbuckle Incident"; Alma Whitaker, "Public Idols," *LAT*, Sept. 14, 1921, pt. 2, p. 4; "Was His Own Worst Enemy," *LAT*, Sept. 15, 1921, p. 2; "The Mire and the Rose," *LAT*, Sept.17, 1921, pt. 1, p. 4; "My Brother's Keeper," *LAT*, Sept. 21, pt. 2, p. 4; editorial from the *Portland Oregonian*, reprinted in *LAT*, Oct 18, 1921, pt. 2, p. 4.

66. "Quiz Arbuckle Companion," *LAT*, Sept. 17, 1921, p. 1; "Here to Trace Arbuckle's Rum," *LAT*, Sept. 16, 1921, p. 2; "Push Arbuckle Liquor Case," *LAT*, Sept. 17, 1921, p. 2; "Fail to Trace Arbuckle Rum," *LAT*, Sept. 18, 1921, p. 2; "Fishback Hasn't Told All," *LAT*, Sept. 20, 1921, p. 2; "Death Case Booze Not from Here," *LAT*, Sept. 22, 1921, p. 2; "Athletic Club Outs Arbuckle," *LAT*, Sept. 13, 1921, p. 1; "Estimate Cash For Arbuckle," *LAT*, Sept. 13, 1921, p. 2; "Comedy and Tragedy," *LAT*, Sept. 13, 1921, p. 3; "Arbuckle's Furniture Attached," *LAT*, Sept. 13, 1921, p. 3; "Tailor and Tire Maker Sue Fatty," *LAT*, Sept. 17, 1921, p. 2.

67. "The Arbuckle Incident"; "Censorship—Cause and Effect," *LAT*, pt. 2, p. 4. See also Dore Oliphant Coe, "Inspector of Films," *LAT*, Sept. 26, 1921, pt. 2, p. 4; "For Whom Do They Speak?" *LAT*, Oct. 6, 1921, pt. 2, p. 4; "Picture Puzzles," *LAT*, Oct. 24, 1921, pt. 2, p. 4.

68. "The Arbuckle Case," *Moving Picture World* (Oct. 1, 1921): 513.

69. Martin Quigley, "A Million Dollar Carousal," *Exhibitors Herald* (Oct. 8, 1921): 39. See also "Scandal Hits Industry," *Variety*, Sept. 16, 1921, p. 35.

70. "Arbuckle Case Seized as Ammunition by Reformers," *Exhibitors Herald* (Oct. 1, 1921): 55; "Investigation of Industry's 'Political Activity Planned,'" *Exhibitors Herald* (Sept. 10, 1921): 39; "'Have Violated No Law' Says Executives of Famous Players," *Exhibitors Herald* (Sept. 17, 1921): 33–36.

71. "The Arbuckle Situation," *Wid's Daily*, Sept. 13, 1921, 1. See also "Arbuckle Film Withdrawn," *LAT*, Sept. 12, 1921, p. 1. "Arbuckle Films Barred by Every Theatre in Chicago," *CHE*, Sept. 13, 1921, p. 3; "Cancel Arbuckle Films: Moving Picture Houses All over the Country Take Action or Are Ordered To," *LAT*, Sept. 13, 1921, p. 3; "600 Theaters Here Exclude Arbuckle," *NYT*, Sept.

14, 1921, p. 2; "Exhibitors Withdraw Arbuckle Comedies," *Moving Picture World* (Sept. 24, 1921): 382.

72. "Ban Rappe Films," *Wid's Daily*, Sept. 16, 1921, pp. 1–2. The MPTOA's accusation that First National reissued Rappe's films seemed to spark the action; see "First National Orders Cancellation of All Films Showing Virginia Rappe as Result of Protest by M.P.T.O.," *Wid's Daily*, Sept. 18, 1921, p. 1; "Bars Virginia Rappe Films," *LAT*, Sept. 22, 1921, p. 2; "Brady Won't Try to Clean Up Film Life." Arbuckle left Sennett to form an independent company, Comique, after which he became a contract player at FPL/Paramount in 1919.

73. Martin J. Quigley, "Let This Be a Lesson," *Exhibitors Herald* (Oct. 1, 1921): 39; "plain, every-day": T.H. Smith letter to *Exhibitors Herald* (Oct. 1, 1921): 80.

74. Martin Quigley, "Keep Out of Politics!" *Exhibitors Herald* (Oct. 22, 1921): 39. "'Herald' to Supply Slides for the Public Rights League," *Exhibitors Herald* (Oct. 15, 1921): 45–48. This weekly campaign ran in the *Herald* throughout 1922.

75. "S.F.-Hollywood 'Booze Railroad' Traced," *SFX*, Sept. 18, 1921, p. 1. For a sample of funereal stories, see "Remains of Virginia Go Tonight," *CHE*, Sept. 16, 1921, p. 2; "Miss Rappe's Body Departs," *SFX*, Sept. 17, 1921, p. 2; "8,000 at L.A. View Body of Virginia Rappe," *SFX*, Sept. 19, 1921, p. 3; "Funeral of Actress Held in Hollywood," *NYA*, Sept. 20, 1921, p. 3. "Secrets of the Ku Klux Klan Are Exposed: Menace of Anti-Jewish, Anti-Catholic and Alien Organization Revealed," *SFX*, Sept. 18, 1921, pp. 1–2. Headlines regarding the two investigations were entwined throughout much of the coverage. See, for instance, "Girl Tells Full Story of Death Party" and "Grand Goblin Risks Death to Expose Ku Klux Secrets," both in *CHE*, Sept. 15, 1921, p. 1.

76. "Police Judge Will Exclude Men at Trial," *SFX*, Sept. 21, 1921, p. 2. "Cowboys Mob Arbuckle Film," *SFX*, Sept. 18, 1921, p. 2; "Cowboys Shoot Up Arbuckle Film Then Burn It," *NYA*, Sept. 18, 1921, p. 2. On the ersatz event, see "Arbuckle Film Not Burned," *NYT*, Sept. 22, 1921, p. 3.

77. "Arbuckle in Fear of Big Throng," *SFX*, Sept. 17, 1921, p. 1. "Police Judge Will Exclude Men at Trial"; "Preliminary in Arbuckle Case Begins Today," *SFC*, Sept. 22, 1921, p. 1.

78. On the Women's Court in California, see Beverly Blair Cook, "Moral Authority and Gender Difference: Georgia Bullock and the Los Angeles Women's Court," 77 *Judicature* 144 (Nov.–Dec. 1993): 30–45. Cook argues that such courts arose to remove women defendants from men's observation and intimidation, to treat morals complaints as women's problems, and to allow women to protect and discipline other women. On women's relationship to jury service, see Linda Kerber, *No Constitutional Right to Be Ladies: Women and the Obligations of Citizenship* (New York: Hill & Wang, 1998), ch. 4.

79. See, for instance, "Women's Court Is Endangered by Amendment," *SFC*, Aug. 20, 1920, p. 2.

80. "Vigilant Leagues Not Formed in Spirit of Vengeance or Retribution," *The Clubwoman* 19.3 (Dec. 1921): 30. The article reprints a speech by Mariana Bertola in which she noted that the group had been "misnamed," as its original

name was the Vigilant Committee. I use the abbreviation WVC because the press called it this, as did the entry in Louis Lyons, ed., *Who's Who among the Women of California* (San Francisco: Security Publishing Co., 1922), 197. Annie Laurie, "Vice Ring Tries to Stop Citizens," *SFX*, Dec. 12, 1920, p. 3.

81. "Women Meet to Pledge Aid in Purging City," *SFX*, Dec. 14, 1920, p. 2. Elinor Richey, *Eminent Women of the West* (Berkeley: Howell-North Books, 1975), 11–12. See also Papers of Dr. Aurelia Reinhardt, Olin Library, Mills College, Oakland, California. *San Francisco: Its Builders Past and Present*, Vol. 2 (San Francisco: S. J. Clarke Publishing Co., 1913), 269–272.

82. For a sampling of stories in this vein, see "Bay City Women Stirred," *LAT*, Sept. 15, 1921, p. 6; "Arbuckle to Be Tried on Murder Charge in Death of Film Actress," *STL*, Sept. 16, 1921, p. 1; "Bail Denied," *CHE*, Sept. 17, 1921, p. 2; "Brady Determined to Push Case against Arbuckle," *LAT*, Sept. 16, 1921, p. 1; "Arbuckle Arraigned for Murder," *NYA*, Sept. 17, 1921, p. 3; "Women Want Only Justice," *LAT*, Sept. 17, 1921, pp. 1–2; "Physician Went on Trip after Hearing Dying Actress' Story," *NYA*, Sept. 18, 1921, p. 1; "Testify to Bruises on Virginia Rappe," *NYT*, Sept. 23, 1921, p. 5.

83. "Women Want Only Justice," 1. Bertola quoted in "Women Vigilants Plan to Watch Law Enforcement," *SFX*, Sept. 21, 1921, p. 2.

84. Bertola quoted in "Vigilant Women Condemn Wild Orgy of Arbuckle," *SFX*, Sept. 15, 1921, p. 2; "Women Vigilants Plan to Watch Law Enforcement." "Women Jam Courtroom to See Comedian," *SFX*, Sept. 23, 1921, p. 2; "Crowds Pack Courtroom and Halls to Hear Arbuckle Testimony," *SFC*, Sept. 23, 1921, p. 5. Reportedly every one of the "155 seats" in the courtroom was filled, and "women lined the aisles, stood on window sills, and even crowded for seats in the prisoners' dock. . . . Outside approximately 500 lined the halls." Mrs. Harold Lawrence Seager, "Club Leader Raps Talkers and Curious," *SFX*, Sept. 23, 1921, p. 3.

85. Myrtle McQuarrie, "More Mature Women, Fewer Girls at Trial," *SFX*, Sept. 21, 1921, p. 2.

86. "'Like Howard St. Gang Case,' Says Leader," *SFX*, Sept. 14, 1921, p. 3.

87. "Girl Victims Spent Night of Torture," *SFX*, Dec. 6, 1920, p. 2. See also "Lawyer Fails to Shake Girl in Grilling: Jesse Montgomery Withstands Cross-Examination and Attack upon Her Past Character," *SFX*, Dec. 18, 1920, p. 2.

88. "Vice Gangsters Slay Three Officers: Lynchers Storm Santa Rosa Jail," *SFX*, Dec. 6, 1920, pp. 1–2; "3 Gangsters Lynched by Santa Rosa Mob," *SFX*, Dec. 10, 1920, pp. 1–2.

89. "Lynching of Gang Flayed by Governor," *SFX*, Dec. 11, 1920, p. 2; "Sonoma Jury Says Sheriff Did Full Duty," *SFC*, Dec. 11, 1920, p. 3.

90. "New Outrage Bared: Police Shake-up On," *SFX*, Dec. 11, 1920, p. 1. This was the headline the day after the lynching. See Hearst's editorial "Free San Francisco of Criminal Elements, Is Plea of Mr. Hearst," *SFX*, Dec. 19, 1920, p. 1.

91. "20 More Gangsters Sought for Howard Street Horrors," *SFX*, Dec. 5, 1920, p. 10; Annie Laurie, "Where Is Justice in California? 100 Girls Ravaged in Six Months," *SFX*, Dec. 6, 1920, p. 3; "Park Assault Laid to Trio by Girl of

17," *SFX*, Dec. 9, 1920, pp. 1–2; "Girl, 20, Sobs Recital of Attack by 19," *SFX*, Dec. 11, 1920, pp. 1–2; "Spud Sullen As New Victim Accuses Him," *SFX*, Dec. 12, 1920, p. 1.

92. "Progressive San Francisco Sweeps Away Traditional Barriers of Complacency amidst Scenes of Wildest Enthusiasm," *SFX*, Feb. 16, 1921, p. 1. "Civic League Launches Vice Investigation," *SFX*, Dec. 10, 1920, p. 2; "Women Form Association to Purge S.F.," *SFX*, Dec. 11, 1920, p. 3; Annie Laurie, "Vice Ring Tries Threats to Stop Citizens, but Clean-up Work Will Not Halt," *SFX*, Dec. 12, 1920, p. 3; "S.F. Citizens Determined to Check Vice," *SFX*, Dec. 13, 1920, p. 2.

93. Lyons, *Who's Who among the Women of California*, 197.

94. "Boxer Will Attack Girl's Reputation," *SFX*, Dec. 16, 1920, pp. 1–2; "Murphy Will Plead Alibi in Face of Charges by Girls," *SFX*, Dec. 17, 1921, pp. 1–2; "Annie Laurie, "The Underworld's Taking Heart Again; Maybe They Forget Women Can Vote Now," *SFX*, Dec. 18, 1920, p. 3; "Vigilant Committee Plans Cleanup of Law Enforcement," *SFX*, Jan. 4, 1921, p. 7.

95. Laurie, "The Underworld's Taking Heart Again"; Annie Laurie, "Keep the Fires Burning—That's Women's Objective," *SFX*, Dec. 24, 1920, p. 2.

96. Gale Gullett, "City Mothers, City Daughters, and the Dance Hall Girls," in Barbara J. Harris and JoAnn K. McNamara, eds., *Women and the Structure of Society* (Durham, NC: Duke University Press, 1984), 150–154.

97. On the campaign, see "Report Urges Judge's Recall, City Cleanup," *SFX*, Dec. 14, 1920, p. 2. On the report of the dismissals, see "Report Asks That Roche Quit Office," *SFX*, Dec.14, 1921, p. 1. "New story teller": Laurie, "The Underworld's Taking Heart Again."

98. Annie Laurie, "Women of City Aroused: Mass Meeting Is Electric with Feeling," *SFX*, Dec. 14, 1920, p. 3; "Club Thrown Open to S.F. Working Girls," *SFX*, Dec. 15, 1920, p. 2; "Abolish Vice, S.F. Women's Clubs Demand," *SFX*, Dec. 15, 1920, p. 2; Annie Laurie, "Indeterminate Sentences—What of Them?" *SFX*, Dec. 15, 1920, p. 2; "Charges against City Dances Aired," *SFX*, Dec. 18, 1920, p. 3; "Clubwomen Aid Zone Plan," *SFX*, Dec. 23, 1920, p. 1; Laurie, "Keep the Fires Burning"; Laurie, "Vileness Bred at Public Dance Halls: Let's Go Back to Our Pre-war Standards," *SFX*, Dec. 31, 1920, p. 1.

99. Dr. Mariana Bertola, "A Cursory Glance over the San Francisco District," *The Clubwoman* 9.5 (Feb. 1921): 12. See also "Vigilant Committee Plans Cleanup by Law Enforcement," *SFX*, Jan. 18, 1921, 4. "Disreputable Crowd Haunts Charge," *SFX*, Dec. 15, 1920, p. 1; "Winter Garden to Be Closed," *SFX*, Dec. 21, 1920, p. 1; "9 'Closed' Dance Hall Licenses Are Renewed," *SFX*, Dec. 28, 1920, p. 1.

100. "Dance Hall Girls Storm Club Women's Meeting," *SFX*, Dec. 31, 1920, pp. 1–2.

101. "Jury Dissents with Police on Dance Halls: Inquisitorial Body Stormed by Girls," *SFX*, Jan. 4, 1921, p. 1; "Women's Clubs Welcome Jury Dance Hall Shift," *SFX*, Jan. 6, 1921, p. 1.

102. "Police Judges Recalled: Lazarus and Jacks Victors by 4000 Votes," *SFX*, March 2, 1921, p. 1.

103. See Kerber, *No Constitutional Right to Be Ladies*, ch. 4. Jury service followed woman suffrage in 1913.

104. "Titan haired Amazon": *NYA*, Dec. 5, 1921, p. 1. See testimony of doctors Shelby Phipps Strange (Court Transcript, 31); William Ophuls (Court Transcript, 39); and Arthur Beardslee (Court Transcript, 209–211).

105. "Arbuckle Evidence: Two Doctors Say Virginia Rappe Was Slain," *CHE*, Sept. 23, 1921, pp. 1, 3; "Medical Experts Detail Bruises on Dead Girl's Body," *SFX*, Sept. 23, 1921, 2.

106. Prevost, Court Transcript, 301, 310, 299; Blake, Court Transcript, 336.

107. "Testimony Is Vulgar," *LAT*, Sept. 25, 1921, p. 1; Prevost, Court Transcript, 300; Blake, Court Transcript, 337.

108. "Fatty's Pal Tells of Ice Bath to Girl," *CHE*, Sept. 25, 1921, p. 1. See also Semnacher, Court Transcript, 167. Other accounts include "Arbuckle's Boast Is Revealed: Admission of Actor Given by Semnacher," *SFX*, Sept. 25, 1921, p. 1; "Arbuckle's Confession: Admitted He Hurt Girl, Pal Swears," *CHE* (final edition) Sept. 25, 1921, p. 1; "Amid Laughter Arbuckle Told of Putting Ice on Girl in Pain," *NYA*, Sept. 25, 1921, p. 1; "Testimony Is Vulgar."

109. "Amid Laughter Arbuckle Told of Putting Ice on Girl in Pain"; "Testimony Is Vulgar." Semnacher, Court Transcript, 168. "Arbuckle's Confession."

110. Before the Police Court trial ended, papers ran dozens of reports built around the "testimony" of Delmont, who never testified. See "Brady Closes People's Case against Star," *SFX*, Sept. 28, 1921, pp. 1–2; "Accuser Fails to Testify," *CHE*, Sept. 28, 1921, pp. 1–2; the Court (Lazarus), Court Transcript, 348–349.

111. Semnacher, Court Transcript, 274.

112. Lazarus, Court Transcript, 350. The testimony was covered in "Arbuckle on Bail for Manslaughter," *NYT*, Sept. 29, 1921, pp. 1–2; "Fatty Will Be Tried for Manslaughter," *CHE*, Sept. 29, 1921, pp. 1, 3; "Actor Escapes Accusation of Capital Crime," *NYA*, Sept. 29, 1921, pp. 1, 3; "Murder Count Is Rejected by Police Judge," *SFX*, Sept. 29, 1921, pp. 1–2; "Arbuckle Out on Bail; Held for Manslaughter," *LAT*, Sept. 29, 1921, pp. 1, 3.

113. "Arbuckle on Bail for Manslaughter," 1; "Murder Count Is Rejected by Police Judge," 1. See also "Women Criticize District Attorney," *SFC*, Sept. 29, 1921, p. 1. Mrs. Hamilton quoted in "Women's Ban on Arbuckle Films Voiced," *SFX*, Oct. 13, 1921, p. 8. On the California Federation of Women's Clubs endorsement, see "L.A. Women's Clubs Oppose Arbuckle," *SFX*, Oct. 5, 1921, p. 3.

114. "Morality Clause for Films," *NYT*, Sept. 22, 1921, p. 8; "Morality Test for Film Folk," *SFX*, Sept. 22, 1921, p. 2.

115. "Raising the Standard," editorial, *LAT*, Sept. 25, 1921, pt. 2, p. 4; "A Million Dollar Carousel," *Exhibitors Herald* (Oct. 8, 1921): 42. On demands for silence, see "Scandal Hits Industry," *Variety* (Sept. 16, 1921): 35.

116. Swanson, *Swanson on Swanson*, 167–168.

117. Moving at typically glacial speed, the FTC ordered divorcement of exhibition from production and distribution in the Paramount Case in 1948; see Maltby and Craven, *Hollywood Cinema*, 71–73.

118. "New Organization of Distributors and Producers Planned—Will Hays Offered Presidency," *Wid's Daily*, Dec. 9, 1921, pp. 1–2; "Says Hays Accepts," *Wid's Daily*, Dec. 21, 1921, p.1; "Hays Accepts Offer to Head Producer-Distributor Alliance," *Exhibitors Herald* (Jan. 28, 1922): 43–45. Accounts vary

as to the development of the idea for the MPPDA and the precise timing of the approach to Hays. See Sklar, *Movie-Made America*, 82–83, 132; Jowett, *Film*, 152–159; May, *Screening Out the Past*, 179, 205; Ramsaye, *A Million and One Nights*, 814–817. All authors agree that the Arbuckle scandal convinced producers to go ahead with hiring Hays and instituting the MPPDA.

119. "Arbuckle Trial Ends in Disagreement: Grand Jury to Probe Tampering Charges," *SFX*, Dec. 5, 1921, pp. 1, 3.

120. On Harding's election, see Hawley, *The Great War and the Search for Modern Order*, 44–49. On Hays as an architect of "advertised politics," see McGerr, *The Decline of Popular Politics*, 169–171; Braeman, "American Politics in the Age of Normalcy," 17–18. On his use of newsreels, see Ramsaye, *A Million and One Nights*, 811–813.

121. "How to Make Virtue Popular," editorial, *CHE*, Jan. 17, 1922, p. 8. See also "Hays to Quit Cabinet for Movie Post," *CHE*, Jan. 15, 1922, p. 6; "Moral House-Cleaning in Hollywood," *Photoplay* (April 1922): 52–53; "Will Hays—A Real Leader: A Close-up of the General Director of the Motion Picture Industry," *Photoplay* (May 1922): 30–31.

122. "Mary Pickford Accused of Perjury," *CHE*, Jan. 4, 1922, p. 1. "Arbuckle Jury 10 to 2; Calls Judge," *NYA*, Feb. 2, 1922, p. 1. The never-solved murder of director William Desmond Taylor wrecked the careers of Mary Miles Minter and Mabel Normand; see "Star Tells of Movie Murder," *CHE*, Feb. 3, 1922, p. 1.

123. On the referendum, see "Industry Directs Guns at Massachusetts Censorship," *Exhibitors Herald* (Oct. 25, 1922): 43.

124. *Beyond the Rocks* (Paramount, 1922). Swanson, *Swanson on Swanson*, 173.

125. Adrienne L. Mclean and David A. Cook, *Headline Hollywood: A Century of Film Scandal* (New Brunswick, NJ: Rutgers University Press, 2001), 1–11. See also note 10, ch. 4.

126. "McNab Pleads for Arbuckle: Poetry Quoted in His Slam against Women," *LAT*, April 12, 1922, p. 2. See Alvin V. Sellers, *Classics of the Bar: Stories of the World's Greatest Legal Trials*, Vol. 8 (Baxley, GA: Classic Publishing Co., 1922).

127. I found no transcript for any of the following three trials. The first biography interested in clearing the comedian's name was David Yallop, *The Day the Laughter Stopped* (New York: St. Martin's Press, 1976). Yallop claims to have obtained copies of the transcripts, but in comparing his use to the one in my possession, I found that he misrepresents the dialogue. Two other popular biographies display similar tendencies: Andy Edmonds, *Frame Up! The Untold Story of Roscoe "Fatty" Arbuckle* (New York: William Morrow, 1991); Stuart Oderman, *Roscoe "Fatty" Arbuckle* (Jefferson, NC: McFarland, 1994). All three basically follow McNab's characterization of Rappe. On Arbuckle's career, see Young, *Roscoe "Fatty" Arbuckle*. Young also presents a similar portrait of Rappe, relying on Yallop, whom he otherwise criticizes, and an oral history by Arbuckle's wife. When I asked Young about the evidence he used for his portrait of Rappe, his reply demonstrated his absorption of such assumptions himself (email in my possession). Although he also treats the apocryphal inci-

dent of the WVC spitting on Arbuckle as fact, a much better analysis of the scandal is Gary Alan Fine, "Fatty Arbuckle and the Creation of Public Attention," in *Difficult Reputations*, ch. 4.

128. Breen quoted in Black, *Hollywood Censored*, 170, 171. See also Thomas Doherty, *Pre-Code Hollywood: Sex, Immorality, and Insurrection in American Cinema, 1930–1934* (New York: Columbia University Press, 1999); Frances Couvares, "Hollywood, Main Street, and the Church: Trying to Censor the Movies before the Production Code," *American Quarterly* 44.4 (Dec. 1992): 584–616.

129. Lea Jacobs, *The Wages of Sin: Censorship and the Fallen Woman Film, 1928–1942* (Madison: University of Wisconsin Press, 1991).

CONCLUSION

1. As Told by Roscoe Arbuckle to Adela Rodgers St. Johns, "Love Confessions of a Fat Man," *Photoplay* (Sept. 1921): 22–23, 102.

2. St. Johns, *The Honeycomb*, 13, 16, 21 (italics in the original). Alice Ames Winters File, MHL. Winters was president between 1920 and 1924. In 1929 she became associate director of the MPPDA's Studio Relations Committee.

3. St. Johns, *The Honeycomb*, 31.

4. Ivan St. Johns, "Fifty-Fifty," *Photoplay* (Oct. 1926): 46.

5. See Cott, *The Grounding of Modern Feminism*, ch. 6.

6. Elaine Tyler May, *Homeward Bound: American Families in the Cold War Era* (New York: Basic Books, 1988), 41–47, 60–67, 143–146.

7. Theodore Dreiser, "Hollywood: Its Manners and Morals; Pt. 1, The Struggle on the Threshold of Motion Pictures" (Nov. 1921), in *Taylorology* 41 (1996), http://www.public.asu.edu/~ialong/Taylor41.txt (*Shadowland*, Nov. 1921) (accessed May 16, 2012). On his time there, see Theodore Dreiser, *American Diaries, 1902–1926*, ed. Thomas Riggio et al. (Philadelphia: University of Pennsylvania Press, 1982), 360–420.

8. Edgar Rice Burroughs, *The Girl from Hollywood* (New York: Ace, 1979 [1923]), 54. The novel was first serialized in *Munsey's Magazine* between June and Dec. of 1922.

9. Hollywood (Famous-Players Lasky, 1923). James Cruze remains understudied, see Karl Brown, "James Cruze," *Films in Review* 37.4 (1986): 234 – 236; R. Starman, "James Cruze: Cinema's Forgotten Director," *Films in Review* 36.10 (1985): 460 – 465.

10. On Hughes, see James Kemm, *Rupert Hughes* (Beverley Hills: Pomegranate Press, 1997). Kemm notes (20–21) that the "easy moral code" of his heroines and his works, many of which offered "an enthusiastic brief for a woman's rights to a career apart from family ties," shocked some.

11. "Famous Writers Who Write in Hollywood," *LAT*, July 23, 1922, p. 30. The article calls Hollywood "what Greenwich Village tried to be before it was invaded by fat grass widows from Keokuk" and Hughes its highest-paid writer

12. Van Doren, "The Revolt from the Village: 1920."

13. "Billy Sunday of the Movies," *Los Angeles Times, LAT*, April 30, 1922, p. 31.

14. Hughes, *Souls for Sale*, 1, 167–168, 163, 168, 220, 186, 403.

15. Susan Faludi, *Stiffed: The Betrayal of the American Man* (New York: William Morrow, 1999); Estelle Freedman, *No Turning Back: The History of Feminism and the Future of Women* (New York: Ballantine Books, 2002).

16. On mass culture's doublespeak, see Susan Douglas, *Where the Girls Are: Growing Up Female with the Mass Media* (New York: Random House, 1994); Joanne Meyerowitz, "Beyond the Feminine Mystique: A Reassessment of Postwar Mass Culture, 1946–1958," *Journal of American History* 79.4 (March 1993): 1455–1482; Meyerowitz, "Women, Cheesecake, and Borderline Material," *Journal of Women's History* 8.3 (Fall 1996): 9–33.

17. On women's declining professional opportunities in film, see Mahar, *Women Filmmakers in Early Hollywood*; Cooper, *Universal Women*.

18. Hugo Münsterberg, *The Photoplay: A Psychological Study* (New York, 1916), 157.

19. My own view is that one continuous wave of feminism has emphasized different elements at different times. See also Jennifer Scanlon, *Bad Girls Go Everywhere: The Life of Helen Gurley Brown* (New York: Oxford University Press, 2009).

Acknowledgments

I went to graduate school because I wanted to write a history book that people might enjoy reading. My greatest debts are to the people who sustained my faith in that enterprise, beginning with my sister, Kaitlin Hallett, who acted as the ideal reader in my mind's eye and whose belief in my abilities is built into who I am. My advisor, David Nasaw, performed a similar feat in graduate school, focusing my inchoate intellectual interests on a topic and offering blasts of his great good humor in moments when gloom loomed. Barbara Welter and the late George Custen provided valuable mentorship in this project's early stages. I also thank the history department at the CUNY Graduate Center for awarding me its E.P. Thompson dissertation fellowship, which provided the financial support needed to lift this project off the ground. The camaraderie and constructive criticism of my fellow graduate students there did the most to keep it aloft, making my debts to Kelly Anderson, Marcella Bencivenni, Marcia Gallo, Carol Giardina, and Carol Quirke both pleasurable and difficult to repay.

The John Randolph Haynes Foundation helped to finance my earliest trip to Los Angeles, where my first discovery was a fascination for a city I expected to dislike. It helped that several of my oldest friends, including Fia Perera, Randy Redroad, and Richard Register, had migrated there from New York to work. Over the years they made sure I got the most from my trips and served as constant reminders of the creativity and smarts of those who make the film industry whir. William Deverell offered early advice about where to look for things, and the staff of the Margaret Herrick Library, headed by Barbara Hall, were unfailingly good-natured about my innumerable requests.

While writing this dissertation and turning it into a book, I have had the good fortune to pass through several places and institutions that supported its completion. Gabrielle Spiegel welcomed me to Johns Hopkins with her inimical warmth, and the history department there provided a model of intellectual engagement that left a deep impression. I was also lucky enough to earn the companionship and advice of Mark Blyth, Jennifer Culbert, Donald Ganns, Diana Keener, and Akim Reinhardt while in Baltimore—and beyond. At Rutgers University I became particularly indebted to Ann Fabian, Alison Isenberg, Jackson Lears, and Karen Parker Lears for their friendship and support. From the start, Eileen Gillooly smoothed my entrance to Columbia University, and she has never stopped. I have also appreciated the mentorship of Alice Kessler-Harris and the comradeship and friendship of Marwa Elsharky, Evan Haefeli, Rebecca Kobrin, Hagar Kotef, Line Lillevik, and Caterina Pizzigoni. The department of history at Columbia gave me a career development award that financed my procurement of the book's illustrations. The field of women's film history is filled with generous and convivial scholars, and among them I particularly thank Shelley Stamp and Jane Gaines for their inspiration and encouragement. Finally, I always knew I wanted this to be a University of California Press book, and I have Niels Hooper to thank for making it one. The press appears to me a model of high-quality professionalism, and I thank particularly Kim Hogeland and Steven Baker for shepherding this project through its final stages.

My thanks also to those who fail to fit into any neat category related to the production of this book, but whose support of its author, and her children, has been irreplaceable, including Robin Aronson, the staff of Basic Trust, Alexander Bowie, Carolyn Brown, Ragunath Dindial, Michele Grodberg, Sylvain Etcheverry, Sterenn Fichant, Ron Genereaux, Regan Hallett, Gregory Metz, Dan Polin, Emma Ramos, Hank Richards, Nancy Riley, David Stone, and Treece Tappan Wright.

In teaching me to, above all, trust my instincts and to settle for nothing less than enjoyable, meaningful work, I thank my mother, Kathryn J. Hallett, for setting me on the path that ended with this book. The arrival of my sons, Miles and Jackson Hallett-Brown, surely slowed the completion of it, but almost entirely in ways their mother appreciates. They will forever remain her favorite production. Finally, it would take a very different genre, a poem perhaps, to express my debts to my husband, my love, my camerado, Christopher Leslie Brown. What I owe him is impossible to capture in words, but now there will be a bit more time to show him.

Index